DISTANCE EDUCATION

DISTANCE EDUCATION

A Systems View

SECOND EDITION

Michael G. Moore
Penn State University

Greg Kearsley
University of Alberta

WADSWORTH
CENGAGE Learning

Australia • Brazil • Japan • Korea • Mexico • Singapore • Spain • United Kingdom • United States

Distance Education: A Systems View, Second Edition

Michael G. Moore, Greg Kearsley

Publisher: Vicki Knight

Education Editor: Dan Alpert

Development Editor: Tangelique Williams

Assistant Editor: Dan Moneypenny

Editorial Assistant: Erin Worley

Technology Project Manager: Barry Connolly

Marketing Manager: Dory Schaeffer

Marketing Assistant: Andrew Keay

Advertising Project Manager: Tami Strang

Project Manager, Editorial Production: Jennifer Klos

Print Buyer: Doreen Suruki

Permissions Editor: Stephanie Lee

Production Service: Sara Dovre Wudali, Buuji, Inc.

Copy Editor: Alan DeNiro, Buuji, Inc.

Cover Designer: Ross Carron

Cover Image: Brenda Beirne/Getty Images

Compositor: Buuji, Inc.

For product information and technology assistance, contact us at **Cengage Learning Customer & Sales Support, 1-800-354-9706**

For permission to use material from this text or product, submit all requests online at **cengage.com/permissions** Further permissions questions can be emailed to **permissionrequest@cengage.com**

Library of Congress Control Number: 2004103063

ISBN-13: 978-0-534-50688-9

ISBN-10: 0-534-50688-7

Wadsworth
10 Davis Drive
Belmont, CA 94002-3098
USA

Cengage Learning is a leading provider of customized learning solutions with office locations around the globe, including Singapore, the United Kingdom, Australia, Mexico, Brazil and Japan. Locate your local office at: **international.cengage.com/region**

Cengage Learning products are represented in Canada by Nelson Education, Ltd.

For your course and learning solutions, visit **academic.cengage.com**

Purchase any of our products at your local college store or at our preferred online store **www.ichapters.com**

Printed in Canada
3 4 5 6 7 11 10 09

Dedicated to the memory of our colleague,
Dan Coldeway

BRIEF CONTENTS

Preface

Chapter 1   Basic Concepts   1

Chapter 2   The Historical Context   24

Chapter 3   The Scope of Distance Education   46

Chapter 4   Technologies and Media   72

Chapter 5   Course Design and Development   100

Chapter 6   Teaching and the Roles of the Instructor   135

Chapter 7   The Distance Education Student   161

Chapter 8   Management, Administration, and Policy   187

Chapter 9   The Theory and Scholarship of Distance Education   219

Chapter 10   Research and Studies of Effectiveness   236

Chapter 11   The Global Span of Distance Education   257

Chapter 12   Distance Education Is about Change   288

Appendix   Sources of Further Information   307

Glossary   323

References   333

Index   351

CONTENTS

Preface   xvii

Chapter 1   Basic Concepts   1

A Definition and Clarification of Some Terminology 2

Levels of Distance Education   4
Single Mode Institutions   4
Dual Mode Institutions   4
Individual Teachers   5
Virtual Universities and Consortia   5
Courses and Programs   6

Distinguishing Technology and Media   6

Why Distance Education?   7

A Systems View and Model   8
The Idea of System   8
How a Systems View Helps Us Understand Distance Education   9

Components of a Working Distance Education System   11
Is Teaching Like Flying?   12
Sources of Knowledge   12
Design of Courses   14
Delivery of Course Material and Interaction via Technologies   15
Interaction: The Role of Instructors   15
Learners in their Learning Environments   17
Management and Administration   18
Interdependence of Subsystems in a Distance Education System   18

Inputs and Outputs   19

Distance Education Is about Change   19

Viewpoint: Sally Johnstone   22

Summary   22

Questions for Discussion or Further Study   23

Chapter 2   The Historical Context   24

First Generation: A Brief History of Correspondence Study   24
Society to Encourage Studies at Home   27
A Story of Distance Education in the High School:
   The Benton Harbor Plan   28
Correspondence Education in the Armed Forces   30

Second Generation: The History of Broadcasting   31
Radio   31
Television   31
Unfulfilled Dreams   32
Instructional Television Fixed Services   32
Cable Television and Telecourses   32

Third Generation: A Systems Approach; AIM and the OU   33
AIM and the Invention of the Systems Approach   33
Birth of the Open University   34
Wedemeyer and the OU   35
Global Spread of the Systems Approach   35
The American Response   36

Fourth Generation: Teleconferencing   38
Satellites and Interactive Video-Conferencing   38
Business TV   40
Interactive Video in the K–12 Schools   40
Two-Way Video-Conferencing   41

Fifth Generation: Computer- and Internet-Based Virtual Classes   42
Computer Networks   42
Arrival of the Internet and Web-Based Education   43
Viewpoint: Von Pittman   44

Summary   45

Questions for Discussion or Further Study   45

Chapter 3   The Scope of Distance Education   46

Correspondence Education and Home Study   46

Independent Study   47

Replacing Print with Electronic Media   49

Telecourses 49

Distance Education in Higher Education: NCES 2001 Survey 50

Open Universities 51
Channel One 52

Interactive Television: Satellite and Cable Networks 56
Business TV and Corporate Training 56
Examples of Business TV 57
Interactive Video in Higher Education 58

Online Learning and Virtual Universities 59
Virtual Schools 62
K–12 Online Learning: The Oregon Network for Education 63
Corporate Training 64
Vendors 65
Certification and Testing Companies 66
Military Education 66
Viewpoint: Chere Campbell Gibson 69
Course Sharing Initiatives 69

Summary 70

Questions for Discussion or Further Study 71

Chapter 4 Technologies and Media   72

Print 73
Study Guides 73
Newspapers and Newsletters 74
Preparation Time and Impact of Electronic Publishing 74
Limitations of Print 75

Audio and Video Media 76
Production 77

Radio and Television 78
Main Strengths and Uses of Broadcasting 78
Instructional Television Fixed Service (ITFS) 79
Hawaii: Instructional Television across the Islands 80
Cable Television (CATV) 81
Direct Broadcast Satellites (DBS) 82
Streaming Video 82

Teleconferencing 82
Audio-Conferencing 82
Audio-Graphics 83
Desktop Video-Conferencing 84
Video-Conferencing 84
Teleconferencing for Medical Education 86

Computer-Based Learning   86
Computer Conferencing   87
Web-Based Learning Systems   88
Knowledge Management Systems   88
Internet2   89
Lucent Technologies' Knowledge Net Project   90

Media and Technology Selection   90
Media and Technology Selection Procedures   92
Media Richness and Social Presence   94

Media and Technology Integration   95
Decisions about Multiple Technologies   95

Media Standards   96
Viewpoint: Zane Berge   97

Summary   98

Questions for Discussion or Further Study   99

Chapter 5   Course Design and Development   100

Instructional System Design   100
Stages in Instructional Design   101
A Planned Approach   102

The Development Team   103
The Author–Editor Model   103
Anatomy of Home Study Courses   104
The Course Team Model   105
Strengths and Weaknesses   106
The "Lean Team"   107

Designing the Study Guide   108
Creating Lessons or Units   109
Writing Style   110
Layout   111

Designing an Audio-Conference   111
1. Design the Study Guide   111
2. Outline Segments and Activities   112
3. Make a Class Roster   112
4. Test, Test, and Test   112

Designing a Satellite Video-Conference   113
Components of a Satellite Teleconference   113

Design and Development of Web-Based Courses   115
Authoring Tools   116
Web Documents   116
Integrated Learning Systems   116
Web Design Principles   116

Designing and Developing the Online Course: A Lean Team in Action   118
Designing for Accessibility: Students with Disabilities on the Web   118

Designing Student Participation   120

Designing Self-Directed Learning   120

Monitoring and Evaluation   121

Copyright   124

General Design Principles   124
Viewpoint: Randy Garrison   126

Summary   126

Questions for Discussion or Further Study   127

**Appendix: Design Schedule for an Online Course
at Penn State University's World Campus   128**

Chapter 6   Teaching and the Roles of the Instructor   135

How Distance Teaching Differs   135

Some Specific Functions of the Instructor   136
Handling Assignments   138
Student Expectations   138
Reflections of a Correspondence Teacher   139

More about Interaction   140
Learner–Content Interaction   140
Learner–Instructor Interaction   140
Learner–Learner Interaction   141
A Hierarchy of Interaction   141
Interaction versus Presentation: Keeping a Balance   145

The Instructor's Role in Teleconferencing   145
The Site Coordinator   146
Instructing by Audio-Graphic Web Conferencing   148

Teaching Online   149
Conducting Asynchronous Discussions   149
Student Voices: The Value of Asynchronicity   150
Tips for Online Instructors   150
Synchronous Online Instruction   152
Questions for Online Teachers in the High School   153
Social Aspects of Online Learning   153

Examination and Test Security   155

Faculty Perspectives: Some Findings from Research   155
Viewpoint: Lani Gunawardena   156

Summary   158

Questions for Discussion or Further Study   160

Chapter 7   The Distance Education Student   161

The Nature of Adult Learning   161
Why Do Adults Enroll in a Distance Education Course?   162
Anxiety about Learning   163

Providing Access   166

Factors Affecting Student Success   166

Kember's and Billings's Models of Student Completion   169
Billings's Model of Course Completion   171
Educational Background   171
Personality Characteristics   171
Extracurricular Concerns   172
The Second Language Student   173
Course Concerns   173
Cross-Cultural Considerations: Distance Education in Alaska   174
Study Skills   175

Student Attitudes   175
Classroom versus Distance Learning   175
Resistance to Distance Education   176

Student Support: Guidance and Counseling Services   179
Orientation   181
Administrative Assistance   181
Social Interaction   182

A Realistic View of the Distance Learner   183
Viewpoint: Sir John Daniel   184

Summary   185

Questions for Discussion or Further Study   186

Chapter 8   Management, Administration, and Policy   187

Strategic Planning   187
Defining the Mission   188
Deciding Whether to Proceed   188
Tracking Technology   190

Administering the Program   191

Staffing   191
Deciding on Full- versus Part-Time Staffing   192
Training and Orientation of Staff   192
Staff Monitoring and Assessment   193

Learner Support Centers, Libraries, and Teleconference Sites 193
Libraries 194
From the Margins to the Mainstream:
  Developing Library Support for Distance Learning 195
Teleconference Learning Sites 195

Budgeting 196
Budgeting at Different Levels 196
Budgeting the Administration 197
Scheduling 197
Scheduling the Student 198

Quality Assessment 198
Some Data about Administration 199
Benchmarks for Success in Internet-Based Distance Education 201

A Realistic Assessment of Quality 202

Regional Accrediting Commissions 204
Accrediting Commission of the Distance Education
and Training Council (DETC) 204

Policy: Institutional, State, and Federal 204

Policy Barriers to Distance Education Are Falling 206
At the Federal Level 206
At the Regional Level 206
At the State Level 206
At the Institutional Level 207

Institutional: Faculty Policy 207
Intellectual Property Policy: The Example of Brigham Young University 208

State Policy on Funding and Administration of K–12 Programs 208

Implementing Institutional Change 209

A National Policy Issue: The Digital Divide 210
Penn State: Developing a Policy for an Institution-Wide System 211

Policy Initiatives to Reduce the Digital Divide 212
Federal Government 212
Private Sector 213
Nonprofit Sector Examples 213
Community Level Examples 214

Case Study in National Policy Making 214
National Planning in South Africa 215
Viewpoint: Michael Beaudoin 216

Summary 217

Questions for Discussion or Further Study 218

Chapter 9   The Theory and Scholarship of Distance Education   219

The Importance of Theory   219

A Very Short History of Scholarship   220

History of a Theory of Distance Education   221
History of the Term *Distance Education*   222
Otto Peters   222
Toward a Pedagogical Theory   222

Theory of Transactional Distance   223
Distance Education as a Transaction   223
Dialogue   224
Guided Didactic Conversation   225
The Growing Importance of Dialogue   225
Course Structure   226
Structure and Dialogue Measure Transactional Distance   227

Learner Autonomy   227

Desmond Keegan   229

Randy Garrison   229
Collaborative Learning and the Social Construction of Knowledge   230

System Dynamics of Saba   231

Other Applications of Theory of Transactional Distance   231

Theory and the Student   232
Viewpoint: Farhad Saba   233

The Theory and the Practitioner   234

Summary   234

Questions for Discussion or Further Study   235

Chapter 10 Research and Studies of Effectiveness   236

The General Situation Regarding Research   237

Effectiveness as Dependent on a Technology   238
Descriptive Case Studies   239

Comparing Learner Achievement   240
Beyond "No Significant Difference"   242
Effective Course Design   243
Course Design Teams   244
Media and Technology Selection   245
Combining Media and Technologies   246

Effective Teaching Strategies   246

Cost Effectiveness   248
Variables to Include in Cost-Effectiveness Analysis   248
Some Examples of Cost-Effectiveness Studies   250
Economies of Scale   250
Faculty Time and Other Hidden Costs   251

Research on Policy   252
Viewpoint: Curtis Bonk   255

Conclusion   255

Summary   256

Questions for Discussion or Further Study   256

Chapter 11 The Global Span of Distance Education   257

A Brief World Tour   258

China: A National System   258
Organizational Structure of China's Distance Education System   259

Korea: A National Policy   261
Korea National Open University (KNOU)   262

Brazil: A National System of Teacher Training   262
Course Design   262
Implementation   263

Finland and Norway   264

Australia and New Zealand   266

The Republic of South Africa   268
University of South Africa (UNISA)   268
Other Systems in RSA   269
A Major Policy Development   270

The United Kingdom: The Open University   271
Courses of Quality   271
Course Design and Learner Support   272
Technology   272

Turkey: The World's Largest Distance Teaching University   272

Some Other National Institutions   273
India   273
Pakistan   273
Thailand   274
Malaysia   274
Germany   274
The Netherlands   274
Portugal   275
Spain   275

    Canada   275
    Venezuela   276
    Costa Rica   276

    Arab States   276

    Consortia and Virtual Systems in Some Other Countries   277

    Africa   279
    The Global Digital Divide   280

    **Distance Education, International Agencies,
      and National Development**   282

    UNESCO   283

    The World Bank   284
    The African Virtual University   285
    Viewpoint: Michael Foley   286

    Summary   286

    Questions for Discussion or Further Study   287

Chapter 12 Distance Education Is about Change   288

    The Changing Supply of Information   288

    Changing Access to Information   289

    Changes in Relation of Knowledge to Economic Development   290

    Changes in Technology   292
    What Technological Changes Lie Ahead?   293
    Does Technology Add Value and If So, What Is It?   293

    Changes in Program Design: Learning Objects   295

    Organizational Change   297
    A New Supply Model of Distance Education Organization   298
    A New, Demand-Driven Model of Distance Education   299

    Globalization and Commercialization   300

    Changes Needed in Use of Terminology   302
    Viewpoint: Neil Postman   304

    Summary   304

    Questions for Discussion or Further Study   305

Appendix   **Sources of Further Information**   307

Glossary   323

References   333

Index of Authors   351

Subject Index   357

PREFACE

When we wrote the first edition of this book, we prefaced it with the statement that distance education appeared to be growing in importance, and that as a consequence we anticipated a growing need for university courses and training in this field. Since then, the field has indeed grown in scale and significance, even more than we anticipated. In particular, the last 10 years have brought a sea change in the extent to which the practice and study of distance education has become accepted, both in academia and in corporate training contexts. Several explanations can be suggested why so many individuals and institutions have abandoned long held prejudices against learning that occurs outside the campus and the classroom, but nobody would deny that the principal stimulus for change has been the emergence of new technology. It is the arrival and expansion of new communications technology that has brought distance education to the attention of millions of potential distance learners in America and around the world. This same technology, a combination of personal computers, the Internet, and World Wide Web, now sitting on the desks of almost every professor, teacher, and trainer in the developed world and beyond, has drawn millions of these educators to experiment with ideas and techniques of distance teaching. In turn, institutions employing these educators have welcomed the opportunity of expanding their student catchment areas far beyond their traditional, geographically restricted, boundaries—and thus increasing the productivity of their faculty. Accompanying these technology-driven changes have been changes in national (and global) economic policies that have compelled educational institutions to accept a reduction in the state's subsidy of education and to adopt a more entrepreneurial and business orientation to providing education as a service in a competitive market. One visible effect of this has been the rise of new for-profit providers; another has been the invention of new forms of collaboration among older institutions aimed at holding off the new competitors. Finally we would note the growth in the past decade in the popularity of so-called constructivist views of learning. This is a point of view about the teacher–learner relationship that is not unfamiliar to older distance educators, weaned on the traditions of "independent study." Constructivism, because it is derived from classroom practice, has helped many more classroom teachers to discover that there is more to teaching and learning than what goes on in the classroom on campus; on the contrary, they find that they can access richer learning environments in students' homes and workplaces, providing structure and dialogue with their students through the media of communications technologies.

From these few observations it should be apparent why we have been motivated to prepare a new edition of *Distance Education: A Systems View.* It is because so much has changed in the technologies used for teaching at a distance, in the ways distance education is organized, in who is learning and how they are taught, and in state and institutional policy. Further, there has been a decade of research and scholarly advance, represented in a significant increase in formally organized knowledge, published in journal articles, books, and dissertations as well as in online sources.

Not all is new, however. In fact one of the biggest threats to good practice as well as good scholarship in distance education is the common failure of newcomers to the field to understand what a depth of knowledge there is. It hardly needs saying that how to design and support learning at a distance was not invented with the arrival of the Internet, but it is surprising how many professors appear to think it was. With so many people coming to distance education with little or no prior training or study of the field, the basic facts presented in the First Edition of this book are, if anything, even more needed than before. We believe for example that every distance teacher or administrator or policy maker who has to make decisions about distance education will find it valuable to know something of the history of the field, since history shows that the decisions facing users of the new technology were also faced by the predecessors who used printed texts, broadcasting and teleconferencing technologies. Similarly the principles of instructional design, learner support, and organizing and administering resources, as well as distance education theory, all have to be applied in changing technological and social contexts. But before they can be intelligently applied, they must first be understood. And so, in this new edition, while describing and analyzing the evolution of distance education over the past ten years, we are very firm in our commitment to presenting this on a foundation of the established theory and the principles of good practice that were reported in the previous work.

Nowadays, as we are all aware, the challenge we face, along with our students, regarding information is not to find enough of it, but discriminating what information, in the near-infinity of what is available, is most important. Thus keeping in mind that our goal is to provide an introductory, user-friendly textbook, we have considered one of our main tasks is to be highly selective in what we include, and to be spare in our presentation. So this book is not exhaustive or all-inclusive; it is neither an encyclopedia nor a compendium of research (for such a book, see Moore and Anderson's *Handbook of Distance Education, 2003*). What we are offering here, as in the First Edition, is an introduction and overview of the field, organized in chapters that deal in turn with each of its main parts, drawing attention to the main principles and illustrated with a selection of cases.

For students in colleges of education and for practicing teachers, this book describes and explains the character of teaching at a distance and what research and experience says about learning at a distance. For educational administrators, we review the tasks and some of the challenges in organizing and managing the resources needed to deliver the distance education program. We review the range of technologies available, including some that have been around a long time but still have strengths that newer technologies do not always have. For people who are interested in developing programs as well as those who may have to use programs developed by others, we think it helpful to review how instructional design principles are applied in the distance education context. Additionally, there are chapters on the current scope, the history and theory, the international experience, and some of the policy issues involved in distance education. And here we should introduce our basic theme, which is that in both its study and its practice, distance education is best understood and best practiced when it is viewed as a total system. When studying distance education, it is not enough to know only the history, or the theory, or the principles of instructional design, or the organizational structures. None of these can be understood in isolation; it is necessary to understand *all* even though at a relatively elementary level, thus providing the theoretical framework within which you can then chose specific areas for in-depth study and research. As practitioners, it is also essential to understand the components of the system, and to be comfortable in working as part of a system, knowing that one's skills have much greater value when integrated with other specializations, resulting in the design and delivery of programs of higher quality and lower cost than could be achieved when acting alone.

When you have finished this book you will know the outlines of the field and be ready to choose one or more areas for in-depth study. To help with this next stage, we have thoroughly revised the Appendix. As before, it includes a substantial set of references, a glossary, details of the principal journals, and contact details for some of the organizations involved in distance education. By contrast to the First Edition, this book provides Web site addresses for a large number of organizations as well as online documents. There is a chapter, as before, on "Research and Studies of Effectiveness" of distance education, in which we introduce some of the main areas of research. However we should also take this opportunity of warning that in using these references you understand that what we have written about each item of research cannot be used as a substitute for reading the original document.

We would like once again to thank those who contributed to the original development of this book and now to its revision. They include colleagues at both our universities and also the reviewers of drafts of the manuscript. Many people have been helpful in preparing this revision and we can mention only the most notable. Kay Shattuck of Carroll Community College, used the First Edition in her own teaching and on that basis made several substantial contributions, particularly to Chapter 10. Joe Savrock undertook the preparation of the index and Haijun Kang was most helpful in preparing the bibliography; Bill Anderson and Linda Black also used the First Edition in their online teaching and made valuable contributions to several chapters. Among graduate students who have been especially helpful are Arlo Bensinger and Creso Sa. Additionally the following are thanked for contributions to the international chapter: Aisha Al-Harthi, Insung Jung, Ari Matti Auvinen, Andrew Higgins, Wayne MacIntosh, Fiona Spence, Alan Tait, and Meltem Albayrak-Karahan. We wish to thank John Daniel, Michael Foley, Michael Beaudoin, Zane Berge, Randy Garrison, Sally Johnstone, Fred Saba, Curtis Bonk, Von Pittman, Lani Gunawardena and Chere Gibson for their responses to our invitation to share insights into the future of distance education. We also wish to acknowledge the valuable insights and suggestions of the following revision plan reviewers: Muhammad K. Betz, Southeastern Oklahoma State University; Temba C. Bassoppo-Moyo, Illinois State University; Simone Conceicao, University of Wisconsin–Milwaukee; Doreen K. Gosmire, University of South Dakota; Lynn Milet, Kutztown University; and Mark Mortensen, University of North Texas. Finally, we also express our thanks to Dan Alpert, our consistently supportive editor at Cengage Learning, our publisher.

Michael G. Moore (Ph.D., University of Wisconsin-Madison)

Michael G. Moore is known in academic circles for leadership in conceptualizing and developing the scholarly study of distance education. In 1972 he published the first statement of theory about distance education in English, and has achieved a number of other notable "firsts" in this field. While teaching the first course in this subject at University of Wisconsin-Madison in the mid-1970s, he was contributory to founding the national annual conference there. Coming to Penn State in 1986, where he now holds the rank of Professor in the College of Education, he established The American Center for Study of Distance Education. He founded the first American journal (*American Journal of Distance Education*), established the first sequence of taught graduate courses, a national research symposium, a popular online community of interest (Distance Education Online Symposium), and a national leadership institute. With approaching a hundred publications (including the 2003 *Handbook of Distance Education)* and a larger number of major presentations in more than 30 countries, Moore also has down-to-earth practical knowledge of teaching and training in all technologies and for most client groups. In recent years he has designed and teaches graduate courses online for Penn State's World Campus. As a consultant he specializes in setting up, evaluating, and training in large distance education systems, as well as program level needs analysis, course design and development, instructor training, and evaluation. Originally trained as an economist and grounded in an early adult education career of seven years in East Africa, Moore maintains a special interest in economic and social development, undertaking numerous research, evaluation and training projects for the World Bank, the IMF, UNESCO, and several national governments.

Greg Kearsley (Ph.D., University of Alberta)

Greg Kearsley is an independent consultant specializing in the design and delivery of online education. He has taught at the University of Maryland, Nova Southeastern University, and the George Washington University, as well as developed online courses for many organizations including NCREL, Walden Institute, and the University of Wisconsin. Dr. Kearsley has written more than 20 books on the subject of technology.

CHAPTER 1

Basic Concepts

In this chapter we will introduce some basic ideas about distance education. We will provide a definition and an explanation of how distance education can be seen at different levels of organizational complexity. We will also indicate the importance of a systems approach as necessary to understanding distance education as well as successful practice.

The basic idea of distance education is simple enough: students and teachers are in different places for all or most of the time that they learn and teach. Being in different places, they depend on some kind of technology to deliver information and give them a way of interacting with each other.

To use these technologies well depends in turn on using the kind of design and communications techniques that are special to those technologies, and different from what teachers normally use in the classroom. Using these technologies and techniques for distance education requires more time, planning, and money. Being a student at a distance is also different; one needs different study skills and different communications skills; the mode of education usually appeals to a different sector of the population from those who go to regular schools. Consequentially, these students need different kinds of support, and need help with different kinds of problems. Furthermore, ways must be found to manage and administer programs provided in this way. As institutions and even states and nations try to do this, they find that it is necessary to develop new policies. Sometimes it is necessary to set up entirely new institutions or departments, or enter into new interinstitutional partnerships.

As you can see, when you start to think about all the implications of the separation of learners from teachers, an idea that at first seems very simple in fact becomes quite complicated.

A Definition and Clarification of Some Terminology

To capture the multidimensional nature of this field we will use the following definition:

> Distance education is planned learning that normally occurs in a different place from teaching, requiring special course design and instruction techniques, communication through various technologies, and special organizational and administrative arrangements.

The main things to emphasize regarding this definition is that our study of distance education is a study of:

- learning *and* teaching
- learning that is *planned* and not accidental
- learning that is *normally* in a different place from teaching
- communication through *various* technologies

If you reflect on these four characteristics, you will find that the definition encompasses a host of other terms that you have probably already encountered in your reading.

For example, many people use the term "distance learning" when they do not really mean to focus *only* on learning but to include teaching, too. However, learning *and* teaching is not the same thing as learning! When you want to study learning *and* teaching you need to use the term "education," the term that correctly describes a two-sided relationship.

Learning in education is also, by definition, *intentional*. What you learn by accident when looking out of the classroom window is not education, nor is what you learn randomly when surfing the Web distance education. The kind of learning we study in education is learning that is planned and where one person—the student—sets out, deliberately, to learn and is assisted by another—the teacher—who deliberately designs ways of helping that person to learn. This is a good place to dispose of another common cause of misunderstanding—the distinction between education and training. In this book, training is regarded as a domain within the general universe of education, usually aimed at planned learning of practical skills. Everything said about education applies to training, but if we find it necessary to address training specifically we will say so. Similarly we use the term "teaching" synonymously with instruction, and use "teacher" and "instructor" interchangeably. The term "faculty" refers to teachers in higher education.

Classroom teachers increasingly use technology to provide individual learning programs for out-of-class study in support of face-to-face group methods. The term that has recently come into use to describe this is "blended learning." However, teaching in the classroom complemented by technology is not the same thing as teaching that is *dependent* on technology. This is why the definition of distance education uses the word *normally*. It is perfectly reasonable for a classroom teacher to use technology, but the *normal* place of learning is the same as the *normal* place of teaching. In distance education, it is equally reasonable for students to occasionally meet together and perhaps with the teacher, but the normal place of learning is not in the presence of the teacher, but at a distance. In distance education, technology is the *sole* or *principal* means of communication, which of course is not the case in a classroom.

Another way of discriminating between distance education and other forms of education that use technology is to ask: where are the principal educational decisions made? In other words, who decides what is to be learned, when and how it is to be learned, and when learning has been satisfactorily completed? If such decisions are made in a classroom, this is not distance education. If they are made elsewhere, and communicated from the instructor to the learner by means of a technology, the program is distance education.

Other confusion occurs when people define education by the technology used. The oldest of these terms is "correspondence education," meaning education where the means of distributing teaching materials and interaction between teachers and learners is through the postal system. More recent popular terms include "e-learning" and "asynchronous learning." The prefix "e" stands for "electronic"—but those who use it usually do not mean all forms of electronic communication, including radio, videorecorders, and so on. Usually e-learning refers to distance education delivered on the Internet. Similarly, "asynchronous learning" usually refers to those forms of distance education in which communication is through Internet technologies that support asynchronous (not-at-the-same-time) communications such as e-mail, Web sites, and online bulletin boards. And of course people who talk about e-learning and asynchronous learning nearly always mean to include teaching.

Another term commonly associated with distance education is "open education" or "open learning." This term is used in European and other countries with a tradition of very elitist higher education, where it is often connected to "distance learning" in the acronym "ODL," meaning "open and distance learning." The idea is that distance education can open access to learning and give greater autonomy to the student. Historically, advocates of distance education in the United States have considered the attainment of both of these goals to be important attributes of their approach, which is why correspondence education at the university level has been referred to as "independent learning." However, there are programs of distance education that are not "open," just as there are programs of face-to-face education that are.

Another term sometimes considered synonymous with distance education is "distributed learning," characterizing its availability at any place and any time. The focus on the place of learning led many for-profit schools to use the term "home study" to describe their programs.

When you come across these terms in articles and other venues, you have to figure out what the particular author means, since they are usually very loosely used. You will also need to remember them when doing an online document search, because not all the useful articles and Web sites about distance education have correct labels. The fact is that all of these terms fall within the domain of distance education, and are covered by the definition of distance education given previously.

Levels of Distance Education

Turning from basic terminology to look at the organization of distance education, the first thing to note is that in terms of organizational structure, distance education exists at a number of different levels.

Single Mode Institutions

Distance education is the sole activity of the single mode institution. All the faculty and staff of the institution are exclusively devoted to distance education; their duties are different from those at a traditional college, university, school system, or training department. This model has not found much favor in the United States in the public sector, though there have always been a lot of small (and a few large) for-profit dedicated institutions. The most notable examples of dedicated institutions are overseas, the "open universities" that you will read about later.

Example:
Athabasca University (http://www.athabascau.ca) is Canada's leading single mode distance-education university. It serves about 25,000 students a year, following a period of rapid growth which has seen student enrollment double in the late 1990s. Some 150,000 students have benefited from AU's programs since the government of Alberta created the university in 1970. Athabasca University's programs are predominantly available through individualized study, in which all materials and a collect-call link with a tutor are included in the fees. Seminar and teleconference delivery modes are also provided and a growing number of programs and courses are offered online or with online enhancements.

Dual Mode Institutions

A dual mode institution is one that adds distance education to its previously established campus and class-based teaching. By the year 1998, over a third of the 5,010 higher educational institutions in the United States offered electronically delivered distance education courses. By now, the proportion could be as large as 80 percent. To manage the special design and teaching activities needed for sustained quality distance education programs, the dual mode institution sets up a special unit alongside the resources dedicated to conventional teaching. This unit normally has an administrative staff, instructional designers, and technical specialists whose sole responsibilities are distance education. It seldom has its own faculty; most such units call on the faculty of the parent body to provide subject expertise. The regular on-campus faculty usually does the teaching, often with support from part-time faculty. They are all managed by the distance education unit.

Example:
Like many other public agencies, voluntary organizations and businesses that are not primarily educational institutions, the U.S. National Park Service (NPS) (http://www.telnps.net/) delivers a large distance education program. It provides training to its 20,000 employees with a lot of videoconferences delivered to

some 60 downlink sites across the nation as well as Guam and Puerto Rico.

Pennsylvania State University is a dual mode university, with a special unit called the World Campus (http://www.worldcampus.psu.edu) to deliver degrees and continuing professional education "anytime, anywhere." "Regular" faculty teach the courses, and the World Campus provides a full range of learner support services—including library access, registration and records, advising, technical support, assessment, career services, and informal learning and social opportunities.

Individual Teachers

Some of the conventional institutions distributing their teaching by distance education methods do so without a special unit; instead, they simply let individual teachers design and deliver their own courses. Without having a specialist unit as in a dual mode institution, the design, teaching, and administration of these programs rests with the on-campus teachers and administrators. The difference from the dual mode institution can be pictured if you think of how a dedicated unit would be able to systematically organize an arrangement with the campus library to support the distance learners, compared with what an individual professor or even department could negotiate. Similarly, think of making arrangements to supply books through the bookstore; or obtaining a grant from a donor to support program development; or—most difficult—getting a number of teachers to work together as a course team. Individual teachers working in the framework of resources that were set up for—and are good at—providing the on-campus forms of teaching and learning can rarely achieve high-quality distance education or sustain it for very long.

Virtual Universities and Consortia

The term "virtual" is used very loosely and is applied at times to all three types of organization. Generally intended to emphasize the high-tech character of Internet-based communication, marketers in both dual and single mode institutions use "virtuality" to sell distance education as a more exciting high-tech enterprise than older textbook-based methods. One of the more meaningful uses of the term is to describe the consortium—an organizational arrangement of two or more institutions that work together in designing or delivering courses, or both. The National Technological University (NTU) (http://www.ntu.edu) is a consortium of about 50 universities providing more than 500 graduate and continuing education courses in engineering fields, primarily using satellite telecommunications, delivered to more than 1,000 receiving sites worldwide. Another example is Army University Access Online (e-ArmyU) (http://www.earmyu.com). Founded in January 2001, more than 20 colleges and universities provide courses to nearly 31,000 soldiers at more than 20 Army bases worldwide, with plans for up to 80,000 students to be enrolled by 2005. Other consortia include: Western Governors University, California Virtual University, and the Automotive Virtual University. Overseas examples include: the British Aerospace Virtual University and the University for Industry (UK), Global Virtual University (New Zealand), and the Virtual University of the Asia Pacific.

Courses and Programs

In a dual mode institution or the individual teacher's class as described previously, the course is usually a sequence of study of a body of subject matter that is structured according to the norms of the parent institution. In both cases, it is an adaptation for the distance learner of the classroom course. Since a conventional American university graduate course is likely to be about 150 hours of study, the distance education course, nowadays usually taught online, will be of the same duration. In other institutions the course could be much shorter, and in single mode distance education institutions overseas is likely to be longer, as much as 450 hours.

Courses are taught by a wide variety of technologies. In other words, a distance education course is *not* necessarily an online course—though it could be. What makes a distance education course is not its technology or its length. What is common to every course is that it has both learners and a teacher, content organized around a set of learning objectives, some designed learning experiences, and some form of evaluation. A course is more than content. An informative Web site, like an encyclopedia, is not in itself a course.

The word "program" is another term with different meanings. Sometimes "program" refers to a radio or television presentation, or a selection of other media that make up part of a course. Frequently a teaching institution will refer to its "program" to describe the total offering of its courses. Usually the meaning will be clear from the context but we need to alert you not to take these terms for granted when you meet them in reading. Instead, make sure you know what a particular author means when using the term.

Distinguishing Technology and Media

It is common to use the terms "technology" and "media" as synonyms but strictly speaking this is not right. It is the technology that is the vehicle for communicating messages, and the messages are represented in a medium. There are four kinds of media:

- text
- images (still and moving)
- sounds
- artifacts

Text is distributed in books and study guides, and electronically online. Sound is distributed on compact discs (CDs), in audiotapes, by telephone, and also online. Visual images are distributed in books and other forms of paper technologies, on CDs, in videotapes, broadcast, and also online. Thus, each technology supports at least one medium—and some can support more than one.

The power and attraction of online technology is that it has the potential to carry *all* forms of media. However, as we all know, most learners do not yet have technology that enables delivery of video and many can not receive audio in this way.

In distance education, the issue of Internet access is not the most important issue regarding technology and media. If such an advanced technology is not available it is usually possible to receive the teaching-learning messages by a simpler technology. A far bigger problem is the *quality of the media* produced for distribution via the technology. In the United States in particular we often have a preoccupation with setting up advanced technologies at the expense of investing in high-quality media for distribution on those technologies.

One of the most common mistakes regarding technology is to overinvest in a particular technology, and to attempt to load more of the media on that technology than it can optimally carry. This "technology-led" approach has in the past overextended various technologies in turn; that is printed text, broadcasting, and teleconferencing. The infamous "talking head" TV lecture was an example of a technology (television) superb at communicating certain kinds of visual images, which was nevertheless misused to communicate a heavy load of dense information that would have been better distributed on a different technology (almost certainly print). Today we see the same phenomenon in the overuse of online communications. To illustrate our point, think of the poor technical quality of video clips transmitted on the Internet compared to the video disc you rent from the video store.

Although each medium has its distinguishing characteristics, there is also variability in each medium determined by the technology that distributes it. Text, for example, comes in different forms and these can be mixed—and mixed with different kinds of images—to deliver messages that have different degrees of abstractness and concreteness. Sounds can be delivered with or without images to effect different degrees of social presence and intimacy. Each medium can be used in a more or less highly structured way; think of the difference between a radio news show and a call-in chat program delivered by the same medium by the same technology. Similarly, each medium has a greater or lesser facility for carrying different styles and types of interaction. In a high-quality distance education system, considerable expertise and time is devoted to analyzing the educational messages in order to determine the optimum combination of media and technologies necessary to deliver the teaching program for the best effect. This is a theme we will return to in later chapters.

Why Distance Education?

Policy makers at institutional and governmental levels have introduced distance education to meet what they perceive as certain needs, which include:

- increasing *access* to learning and training opportunities
- providing opportunities for *updating skills*
- improving the *cost effectiveness* of educational resources

- supporting the *quality* of existing educational structures
- enhancing the *capacity* of the educational system
- *balancing inequalities* between age groups
- delivering educational campaigns to specific *target audiences*
- providing emergency training for *key target groups*
- expanding the capacity for education in *new subject* areas
- offering combination of education with *work and family life*
- *adding an international dimension* to the educational experience

This is not an exhaustive list, and some of the needs overlap, but it should give some idea of the many reasons why distance education has received greater interest from planners in recent years, and suggests some of the reasons there is likely to be further development.

A Systems View and Model

Throughout this book we will often refer to distance education systems. We believe a systems view is very helpful to an understanding of distance education as a field of study, and that adopting a systems approach is the secret of successful practice.

The Idea of System

We could be very complicated in our discussion of what is meant by a system, but in keeping with the approach in this book, we will keep it simple. Let us take an example of a system. An example is our body, because each of us human beings is a system. The main characteristic of the human system is that every part of the body has a role to play in making the whole body work effectively. There are some parts that could be cut off and the body would still function, but there are many parts that are so indispensable that without them all the others, no matter how healthy in themselves, will cease to operate. And take away or damage even the less important parts and the whole organism will deteriorate. On the other hand, building up one part without any attention to the others is also likely to result in damage to the whole body. The healthy body is one in which *all* the parts are healthy and all the parts play their roles in harmony with each other. That is the principal characteristic of a system. In order to understand a system, or to correct a malfunction in a system, it is necessary on the one hand to understand each of the parts and to be able to diagnose which of them may not be working properly. However, it is also necessary to understand the effect of each part on all the others, and the effect of those others on the individual part under scrutiny.

Let us go one step further and point out that systems exist at different levels of complexity. Although the human body is itself a very complex system, it is only *part* of bigger systems. For example if we were to decide to study a football team or a symphony orchestra, we have to look at how the different human systems are integrated and functioning as a larger system. In other words, we could think of the individual body as one subsystem within the larger system.

A distance education system consists of all the component processes that operate when teaching and learning at a distance occurs. It includes learning, teaching, communication, design, and management. Just think what is actually meant when we use a term like "learning": consider how complex is the subsystem composed of ten adult learners, each of whom interacts with each other, an instructor, and with the content of a course. Consider also how, as these processes occur, they are impacted by, and have an impact on, certain forces in the environment where they operate—the physical, the political, economic, and social environments in particular. So even these frameworks within which the educational system operates can be seen as part of a larger super-system. You can't fully understand, for example, a Brazilian footballer unless you understand the place that football occupies in the culture and national self-concept of that nation. Similarly you cannot fully understand the problem of developing distance education in the American university without considering the history of the Land Grant movement and the culture of independence in the faculty of the American university. Although we may choose to study each of these subsystems separately, we must try also to understand their interrelationships. Keep in mind the wider contexts as we focus on any single part of the system, and remember that anything that happens in one part of the system has an effect on other parts of the system.

How a Systems View Helps Us Understand Distance Education

In Figure 1.1 we illustrate (within the limitation of a two-dimensional diagram) some of the macrofactors (the "big" forces) that impact and interact with each of the more immediate parts of the system that we will study.

To understand this, imagine what appears to be a relatively straightforward decision that a group of faculty and others will take in the subsystem that we will call the course design system. They are considering how many hours a unit of instruction should be and what the students can be expected to learn. The very wording of the issue, as we have stated it, carries hints that prior decisions have been taken (or perhaps assumed). They include philosophical positions on the nature of knowledge and how people learn; and on decisions already taken about the structure of the course, its content, and its selection against other possibilities—decisions that have been influenced if not determined by the kind of educational organization in which they develop the course. The culture and mission of the organization, its structure, its funding, and the views and experience of its faculty will all, among many other organizational variables, come into play as the immediate design question is addressed.

Some of these influences have been determined by institutional policy, which is itself influenced by state and national policies. In the minds of people discussing the issue will be the considerations of its implementation by

Figure 1.1   A Conceptual Model of Distance Education

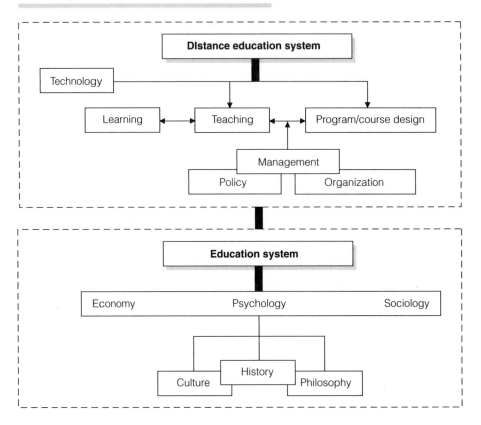

the people who have to teach the course once the design decisions have been undertaken. And all of these factors are determined by more fundamental constraints imposed by the overall educational system within which the distance education institution or unit has to operate. (The institution is likely to want accreditation, for example, and therefore the learning objectives will be influenced directly or indirectly by the standards set by its accrediting agency.)

Furthermore, all of these interactions occur within broader institutional and national contexts. The institution has its own culture based on the shared views about the place of education in society, the faculty and staff's views about learning and other aspects of psychology, and other shared (and at the same time diverse) philosophies. All these are contained within a wider frame, which includes the history of the nation, state, institution, the culture that has emerged from that history, and the general philosophical assumptions of the society in which the distance education system is set. Look inside the box we have labeled "education system" and you would be able to see educational history, educational psychology, educational sociology, economics of education, and so on. So you see how there are systems within systems, within systems . . . all of which act on and interact with each other, and which interact on any process that we may select for special study.

Obviously in this introductory book we will not be able to go far in discussing the wider contexts mentioned here. It is sufficient that you are aware of this broader interpretation of the systems view. Our study in this book will be limited to the main *subsystems* in the distance education system itself. Thus we will devote chapters to teaching, course design, management and policy, and learners. We will give a chapter to the history of distance education and one on distance education in other countries—when it will probably be quite easy to see the impact of wider socioeconomic and political forces. Oh yes, there is a chapter on technology! Are you surprised (because we think it is something that distinguishes this book from most others) that we do not begin with a discussion of technology, but that we place technology clearly in its place—albeit an important one—in the context of a total system?

Components of a Working Distance Education System

Let us turn now from thinking about the systems view of distance education as a field of study to see what a distance education system should look like in practice.

In Figure 1.2 (see p. 14) we present a general model that describes the main component processes and elements of a distance education system. Whether in the most sophisticated distance education institution with hundreds of thousands of students, or in a simple one-teacher class, there has to be a system that accommodates all or most of the elements listed in Figure 1.2. There must be:

- a source of knowledge that is to be taught and learned
- a subsystem to structure this into materials and activities for students that we will call courses
- another subsystem that delivers the courses to learners
- teachers who interact with learners as they use these materials in making their knowledge
- learners in their different environments
- a subsystem that monitors and evaluates outcomes so that interventions are possible where failures occur
- an organization with a policy and a management structure to link these different pieces

We will examine each part of this system briefly, and throughout this book we will focus on each of these components in turn.

Is Teaching Like Flying?

An idea of what a service looks like before the adoption of a systems approach can be found in most industries. We could take the airline industry—or perhaps you prefer to think about health care (or chose your own example and compare with what follows). In the early days of commercial aviation, passengers would be met by the pilot and an assistant on the runway. The crew would receive payment for tickets, accompany the passengers and their luggage to the airplane, and then fly them to their destination. It was not only the airplane (the technology) that was primitive; equally primitive was the *organization* of the process of passenger transportation. Today the airline is organized as a system. This means, first, that there is specialization of labor—work previously done by one person is broken down into many tasks with each done by a specialist. There is a sophisticated, computer-supported management of the workflow, which ensures everyone's work fits with everyone else's. There is close monitoring of the performance and output of each member of the team, with various feedback loops built in so that a manager can spot a potential breakdown before it interrupts the flow of productivity in the system. A lot of thought goes into planning, especially in determining which markets to work in. No one airline attempts to fly everywhere and the most profitable are usually those with a relatively narrow "niche" market. Productivity depends on major up-front investments in new technology and training. No single individual, not even the pilot, is able to move the passenger without the contribution of hundreds of other workers, including technicians, communications specialists, and administrators of all kinds. The result of this organizational feat is the provision of a service on a vast scale at a per-passenger cost that could not have been imagined at the beginnings of the airline industry. When we compare the airline with a school, university, or training department, we see the direction that a systems approach can offer us. As with the airline, a

Sources of Knowledge

The sources of the content to be taught and the responsibility for deciding what will be taught in an educational program is that of the organization providing the program. This may be a single or dual mode institution like a university, college, or school; the training unit of a business corporation, government department, or voluntary agency; a single professor, teacher, or trainer in the class; or a consortium. At any of these organizational levels there must be content specialists who—through academic study—know the field and its literature, theory, contemporary practice, and problems; and—in the training field—are people with highly developed skills that they can transmit. Bearing in mind that distance education requires the use of technology and that planning and producing media programs for delivery by technology is expensive, choices have to be made by the managers of the organization about what par-

distance education system only becomes cost-effective *with quality* when it can take advantage of economies of scale. This means that the larger the number of users of the system, the lower the cost for each person. This concept, so familiar in other walks of life, comes about as a result of the "division of labor" and integration of the work of the different specialists. Strangely, education is one of the few areas of modern life where division of labor, or specialization, is still not practiced to any great extent. In traditional classrooms, individual teachers develop and deliver their own courses. They try to be effective communicators, curriculum designers, evaluators, motivators, group discussion facilitators, as well as content experts. This is an extremely wasteful use of human resources, when the content and objectives of so many courses are identical—not to mention the wide variation in quality it produces. Simply adding a new technology to this "craft" approach to teaching does not give good distance education, and because the capital costs of the equipment needed are so high and the resources and time required to develop good courses are considerable, it is not financially viable either. Instead, courses need to be developed by teams of specialists and taken by many students across a large number of educational institutions. Just as it is not simply the skill of a pilot even when added to new technology that makes an airline work, so neither the teacher alone nor the technology will make distance education work, though of course these are both critical components of any system.

The biggest challenge facing education today is for legislatures to develop policies that help educational organizations move from a craft approach to a systems approach, for administrators to redistribute the human and capital resources in their charge into a total system, and for teachers to be trained to work as specialists within such a system.

SOURCE: Based on an editorial by Michael G. Moore in the *American Journal of Distance Education*, 7:1, 1–10, 1993. Reprinted by permission of the author.

ticular content will be taught. Ideally there will be a subsystem for scanning the social environment (some people would call it a market), and for making the determination of what to teach on the basis of data about needs and demand. This includes finding out what knowledge students themselves feel they need.

Although the principal source of knowledge is usually the faculty or staff of the organization, other sources include external consultants. Sometimes a noneducational entity will enter into an agreement with an educational organization to have a program designed specifically to meet its corporate needs. Students are also considered a source of knowledge according to contemporary constructivist philosophy, which leads to the inclusion of project work and other self-directed learning activities in the design of courses.

Figure 1.2   A Systems Model for Distance Education

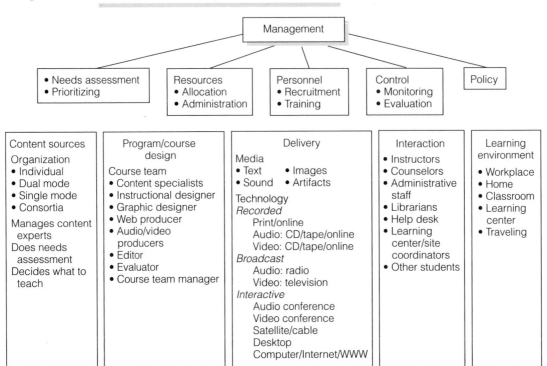

Design of Courses

Content, or subject matter, does not make a course. In a course, the content is organized into a carefully designed structure that is intended to make it as easy as possible (that is not the same thing as "easy"!) for the student to learn. It is not impossible, for example, to learn the geography of a country by studying an atlas, but an atlas is not a course. A course on the geography of that country consists of carefully selected parts of the whole picture, each one set in a context, introduced and explained, with certain features highlighted and with connections made (between rainfall and crop production, for example), which the unguided study of an atlas would not provide. Therefore, preparing a distance education course requires not only the content expert but also instructional designers who can organize the content according to what is known about the theory and practice of information management and the theory of learning.

Since the courses and the teaching will be delivered by technology, the course materials need to be designed by specialists who know how to make the best use of each available technology. Although there are some content experts who also have instructional design skills and others who have knowledge of technology, very few are equally expert in all three areas. It is better if these responsibilities are carried by different specialists. The instructional designers should work with the content experts to help them decide on such matters as: the objectives of the course, the exercises and activities the learners will undertake, the layout of text and graphics (whether in hard copy or on Web site materials), the content of recorded audio or video segments, and the questions for interactive sessions by online chat sessions or by audio or video conference. Graphic designers, Web producers, and other media specialists should be brought in to turn the ideas of the content experts and instructional designers into good quality course materials and programs. Decisions must be taken about which part of the instruction can most effectively be delivered by each particular medium. Finally, evaluation and research experts must plan how to evaluate individual student learning, as well as the effectiveness of all aspects of the distance education course, in order to ensure that it works; in other words, to meet the needs of students and the teaching organization and provide cost-effective instruction.

Because so many skills are needed to design a distance education course, the best courses are designed by course teams in which many specialists work together, their work coordinated by a team manager.

Delivery of Course Material and Interaction via Technologies

In all education there has to be communication between a teaching organization and a learner. In distance education this communication takes place through some form of technology. The technology most talked about today is the computer with its browser linked into the Internet. Other technology includes printed media (usually books or study guides), CD-ROMs, audio and videotapes/discs, radio and television, computer software, and audio- and video-conferencing. These technologies can be classified in a number of ways, but one that we find particularly useful is the differentiation between recorded and interactive technologies. CD-ROMs are of the former type, while the audio-conference is the latter. There are several basic principles in using technology, one of which is to recognize that no single technology is optimal for delivery of every kind of message to all learners in all locations. Following that, another principle is that it is always desirable to have at least one recorded technology primarily suited to the delivery of content and another that is suitable for interaction between learner(s) and instructor(s).

Interaction: The Role of Instructors

Besides receiving course materials distributed by technology, distant learners need to communicate with people at the teaching institution, particularly the people appointed as instructors. Where the teaching materials distributed by technology are produced for a mass audience, the communication that goes on between learners and instructors aims to assist every individual to convert that common information into personally relevant knowledge. Compared to what may be called the presentation phase of distance teaching, when course materials are designed and then distributed, this interactive phase of distance teaching is equally significant. The nature and extent of the interaction that is deemed appropriate varies according to the organizational and designers' teaching philosophy, the nature of the subject matter, the maturity of the students, their location, and the technology used in the course. The interactions between instructors and students will be based on issues and questions determined by the course designers. Until the arrival of the Internet these interactions were often conducted between an instructor and a group of students by means of teleconference technologies. The group teleconference is still quite widely used and it is still quite common for interaction to be by means of written communications through the mail, especially in less technologically advanced countries.

A common difference between distance education and conventional education—and one that many people consider necessary for high-quality distance education—is that in a distance education course it is common for the interaction to be conducted by specialist instructors who have played little or no part in the processes of designing and delivering the course. As mentioned earlier, in a systems approach, courses are usually designed by teams of instructional designers, media and technology experts, as well as content experts. The cost of such teams and the cost of designing media of good quality is high, so the numbers of students that must take the course for it to pay for itself is greater than in classroom education. Because of the large numbers, it is not possible for the designers to be the instructors also. Neither, from a pedagogical point of view, is it desirable they should be, since instruction requires a special set of skills, different from those of designers and subject experts, and is better done when it is the work of persons who devote themselves to the study and development and practice of those skills. Thus the normal procedure in a systems approach to distance education is that once the courses have been designed and distributed through technology, students are allocated by the teaching organization to instructors, often referred to as tutors, who interact with them to provide individualized instruction on the basis of the designed materials.

In the systems approach, quality control by continuous assessment of every part of the system is very important. A key component of this is the production at regular intervals of a product by each student, usually referred to as the assignment. It is the course design team that sets assignments based on the content of each unit of a course, and the assignments are undertaken by each student, who send them to their instructor either electronically or by post. Instructors review, comment on, evaluate, and return the assignments, forwarding the evaluation report to the administration of the institution, which uses it as part of its monitoring process.

In many programs, educators feel it is also desirable that learners interact with each other. With teleconferencing technology, designers can set up cooperative learner groups, and instructors are in a position to facilitate peer support and student knowledge construction. With the arrival of Internet technology this can be done asynchronously, and students can participate in "virtual" groups without having to physically attend a receiving site, as with audio- or video-teleconferencing.

As well as interacting with instructors, whose main job is to help students learn the content of the course, students may also interact with specialists in various forms of student support. Student support personnel may deal with problems arising from poor study techniques, or help to solve time management problems or even personal problems that interrupt a student's progress. Students will also interact with administrative staff when registering for courses or checking their progress. In some systems the distance education agency organizes special face-to-face meetings; for example, when it is necessary to have a laboratory experience that can not be simulated or in any other way delivered by technology.

Learners in Their Learning Environments

The student's learning environment is also part of the distance education system, having considerable impact on the effectiveness of those parts of the system controlled by the educational agency. This environment in which people interact with their course materials and interact with their instructors may be their workplaces or homes, in a classroom or at a learning center, in hotels, or on airplanes. The most popular place for listening to audio discs and tapes is when commuting to work in a car. Many stories are told about distant learners in demanding locations—on battlefields, in submarines, in lighthouses, and in prisons. One of our students, a nurse, reported a discussion she had about distance learning theory when "scrubbing up" in preparation for work in an open heart operation! Learning in the workplace or at home is challenging because there are many distractions. To overcome these and other work-, social-, and family-related distractions, students must consciously train themselves in disciplined study habits. They must, for example, find their own times and places where they can study comfortably by scheduling a "training period" at work or a "quiet time" at home, with the cooperation of coworkers or family. The proper design of distance education course materials can also contribute to the success of learning in the workplace or home. Most designers believe that courses should be organized into short, self-contained segments, with frequent summaries and overviews. Some emphasize the need to link academic content to real-life work, community, and home issues aimed at helping students integrate their study with everyday interests, so that instead of being distractions, they become resources for their learning. Student support personnel can take on the task of helping students make the personal and social adjustments that help make a good learning environment.

The environment of students whose courses are delivered by teleconferencing is usually that of a small group in a classroom or conference room. To take advantage of such a setting, instructional designers should create activities that involve interaction among the members of each group, and perhaps also interaction with groups at other sites. It is also desirable to have a site coordinator who ensures that the teleconferencing equipment is operating properly and the room facilities are satisfactory.

Some agencies—especially the big institutions you will read about later—can set up local learning centers where students may take part in face-to-face sessions. They may hold supplies of instructional materials and equipment, perhaps a small library. They may provide carrels for individual study, or they may provide rooms for group meetings or private meetings with tutors or counselors. Learning centers need to be run by a knowledgeable administrator who may need a support staff, depending upon the center's size.

Management and Administration

As you can imagine from what has been said already, making all the pieces work in a distance education system requires a considerable degree of management sophistication, almost certainly more than in any other educational field. Managers are responsible for all the subsystems that lead to the design, delivery, and implementation of the program, beginning with the difficult process of assessing the needs of learners who are not easily accessible. This is important not only because they reside in distant locations, but because distance education courses have to be designed a considerable time in advance of the actual teaching of the course. Managing resources is critical. Because a large part of the teaching is in the form of programs that have to be prepared long in advance of the enrollment of the students, considerable up-front investment of money and other resources is needed, long before it may be recouped by payment of tuition fees. Using technology, and competing with other institutions, means that substantial sums must be spent to ensure good quality media programs. Under these circumstances, management can neither afford to teach every possible course nor can it afford to make wrong judgments about which course to offer.

Administrators must ensure that money, personnel, and time are managed so that courses are produced on time and numerous work tasks fit together. Suitable faculty and staff must be recruited and trained. Since instructors as well as students may be at a distance from the teaching institution, special procedures must be developed and maintained for recruiting, monitoring, and supervising them. Feedback and evaluation mechanisms are vital because if any part of the system breaks down, the whole system is in jeopardy; potential problems have to be identified before the breakdown occurs. Management also must participate in the political process, helping policy makers to understand the potential of distance education, obtaining funding, and bringing about the organizational culture change that is needed to accommodate unfamiliar ways of teaching. To obtain economies of scale, it is often necessary to link up with other institutions and share the market, a process requiring unusual foresight and diplomacy on the part of senior managers.

Interdependence of Subsystems in a Distance Education System

The elements that we have just introduced—content (or knowledge), design, communications technologies, interaction, learning environment, and management—are essential subsystems in every distance education organization. Even with this preliminary view, it should be clear why we said previously that there is a great deal of interdependence among these elements. For example, the exact nature of the design, the communications technology used for delivery, and the nature of the interaction all depend upon the sources of knowledge, upon student needs, and upon the learning environment for a particular course. Selection of a particular delivery technology or combination of technologies should be determined by the content to be taught, who is to be taught, and where the learning will take place. Design of the instructional media depends upon the content, the delivery technology, the kind of interaction desired, and the learning environment. All these will be influenced by policy and management. Furthermore, changes in one component of a distance education system have immediate effects on all of the other components.

Unfortunately, most educational organizations have been very nervous about introducing new organizational and pedagogical subsystems for the purpose of distance education. The tendency is to add new communications technology to the existing system and then leave the other subsystems little changed. Investing in technology without regard to the other subsystems is a recipe for mediocrity at best, for disaster at worst. This is what is happening quite widely. Our concern with this explains why we consider the individual teacher as compared to the dual and single mode institutions, to be the least valuable form of distance education organization.

Inputs and Outputs

Another way of looking at the interrelationships among the components in a distance education system is to use a common technique in systems modeling, viewing the system in terms of inputs and outputs. Figure 1.3 lists some of the inputs and outputs of a distance education system. We suggest you try to think of others.

All the factors listed in the input column effect in some way the output variables. Few of the relationships are direct, but—as you would expect given the inter-related nature of the subsystems in every system—they are multiple in nature. For example, student characteristics affect many of the output variables and student completion rates are a function of many of the input factors. Indeed, with enough understanding of distance education, it is possible to identify a relationship between every input and output variable listed previously.

Distance Education Is about Change

As you read this book you will recognize, if you don't already, that distance education is both a cause and a result of significant changes in our understanding of the very meaning of education itself as well as more obvious changes in understanding about how it should be organized. At the most obvious level, distance education means that more people are obtaining access more easily to more and better learning resources than they could in the past,

Figure 1.3   Inputs and Outputs of Distance Education

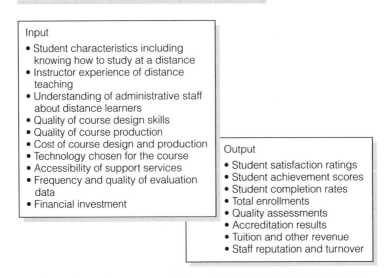

Input
- Student characteristics including knowing how to study at a distance
- Instructor experience of distance teaching
- Understanding of administrative staff about distance learners
- Quality of course design skills
- Quality of course production
- Cost of course design and production
- Technology chosen for the course
- Accessibility of support services
- Frequency and quality of evaluation data
- Financial investment

Output
- Student satisfaction ratings
- Student achievement scores
- Student completion rates
- Total enrollments
- Quality assessments
- Accreditation results
- Tuition and other revenue
- Staff reputation and turnover

when they had to accept only what was locally provided. As the use of distance education spreads, previously disadvantaged populations, such as rural and inner city students, can take courses from the same institutions and same faculty that were previously only available to students in privileged, mainly suburban areas. Handicapped and disabled students can also have access to the same courses as everyone else—even if they are homebound or institutionalized. Adults who need specialized training for career enhancement or basic skills can take courses without having to be away from home or their current jobs. Students in one country can learn from teachers and fellow students in others. Courses can be accessed whenever the student wants at his or her preferred pace, from almost any location. Overall, distance education opens up many new learning opportunities for many people. Beyond access, distance education gives a greater degree of control to the learner in relation to the teaching institution, with effects on what the institution offers to teach and the way it teaches. We are in the middle of a Copernican revolution as it becomes ever more apparent that the learner constitutes the center of the universe, and that teaching no longer drives learning; instead, teaching responds to and supports learning. Such freedom and opportunity, however, mean that students must accept the consequence of assuming more responsibility for managing their own learning, in terms of when they will study, how much they want to learn, and seeking out information and resources. Some students will need help in making the necessary adjustments in their expectations of the teaching institution and in their competencies as students (see Figure 1.4).

As more institutions set up distance education systems, the roles of instructors will be different. In moving to a distance education system, some instructors will have the job of preparing materials without being involved in interaction with students; or if they do, they will have to use the communica-

Figure 1.4   The Student at the Center of the System: A Copernican Revolution!

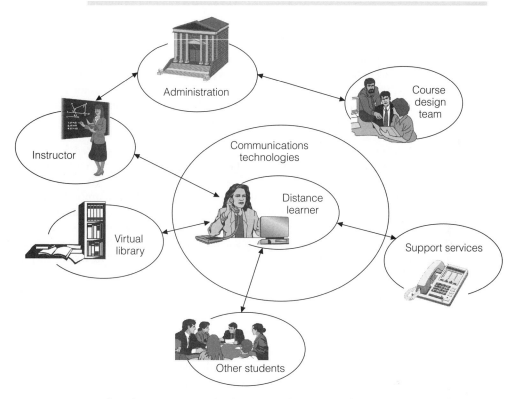

Based on Chute, 2003. Reprinted with permission from Lawrence Erlbaum Associates, Inc. and the author.

tions technologies, and so learn to teach quite differently. Good managers will find appropriate positions for those teachers who want to be content specialists, those who prefer to provide interactive support to students, and those who are good at designing and producing mediated communications.

Administrators too will perform different and new duties. Instead of worrying about classroom availability and class scheduling, they will be concerned with ensuring that the various resources are available—and often in distant locations—for the design and delivery of courses as well as student support. They have to develop new admissions procedures, and find alternatives to "residency" as criteria of excellence.

Thus the growth of distance education implies major changes of the culture as well as the structure of those schools and training organizations that decide to become involved. There are rewards but also there are costs of making these changes. The cost is in the stress on existing employees of making the changes. The reward includes the potential of being able to reach students anywhere in the country or the world. An unavoidable cost is that every school or training group offering similar instruction will find itself in competition with every other and that means making difficult decisions about what to offer and what not to offer. A key idea in distance education is the

Viewpoint: Sally Johnstone

The emergence of open educational resources (i.e., MIT's OpenCourseWare initiative) is enabling distance learning as well as campus-based students to gauge the quality of their courses against what is being taught at other institutions. I think this will give students worldwide more convenient benchmarks for quality as well as greater opportunities to push their distance learning faculty and institutions to improve.

The fiscal restraints on U.S. public higher education caused by tight state budgets are pushing state policymakers to examine intra-state collaborations on academic materials and programs. Several states have already mandated non-competitive funding policies for electronic distance learning among public institutions. There are also several projects developing multistate collaborations for distance learning programs. In addition to consolidating some distance learning programs, it could result in stronger academic and nonacademic services to distance learning students as single campuses move away from trying to provide everything to everyone.

SOURCE: Sally Johnstone, Director WCET (the Western Cooperative for Educational Telecommunications)

principle of comparative advantage. This means that each school, university, or training group should decide what subjects it has an advantage in, compared to competing organizations; it should then specialize in providing instruction in that subject. The future educational system will have no geographic boundary, but each organization will be more focused and specialized in the range of subjects it offers. This will also mean that all educational providers will need to rethink their marketing strategies.

As a result of these changes, the quality of distance education will continue to rise. The higher quality will be recognizable. Distance education courses are open to public scrutiny since they are delivered by mediated programs that can be accessed easily. This leads to a new emphasis on quality and accountability for educational offerings in general, with distance education proving increasingly competitive with conventional education.

Summary

This chapter has introduced some basic ideas about distance education and proposed that a systems model is essential to both the understanding and the practice of distance education. The main points are:

- Distance education organizations should be studied and evaluated as systems. A system includes the subsystems of: knowledge sources, design, delivery, interaction, learning, and management. In practice the better these are integrated, the greater will be the effectiveness of the distance education organization.

- When organizations adopt a systems approach to distance education, there will be an impact on teachers, learners, administrators, and policy makers; and significant changes in the way that education is conceptualized, funded, designed, and delivered. Not least will be the opening of access and improvements in quality.

For further discussion about a systems approach to education, see Banathy (1993), Reigeluth and Garfinkle (1994), and Kerzner (2001).

Questions for Discussion or Further Study

1. Identify examples of the four different types of distance education organization. Can you list some advantages of each of the different types?
2. Look at the list "Why distance education?" and suggest examples of organizations motivated in the ways listed.
3. Is teaching like flying? Discuss.
4. Look at Figure 1.3. Can you connect each input to every output?
5. Discuss Sally Johnstone's comments on future directions of distance education.

CHAPTER 2

The Historical Context

Although some people think distance education only began with the invention of the Internet, this is wrong. You can only understand the methods and issues in distance education today if you know their historical background. This is what we will summarize in this chapter.

As illustrated in Figure 2.1, distance education has evolved through several historical generations. The first generation was when the medium of communication was text and instruction was by postal correspondence. The second generation was teaching by means of broadcast radio and television. The third generation was not so much characterized by communications technology but rather the invention of a new way of organizing education, most notably in the "open universities." Next, in the 1980s, we had our first experience of real-time group interaction at a distance, in audio and video teleconference courses delivered by telephone, satellite, cable, and computer networks. Finally, the most recent generation of distance education involves teaching and learning online, in "virtual" classes and universities, based on Internet technologies.

First Generation: A Brief History of Correspondence Study

The history of distance education begins with courses of instruction that were delivered by mail. Usually called correspondence study, it was also called "home study" by the early for-profit schools, and "independent study" by the universities.

Beginning in the early 1880s, people who wanted to study at home or at work could, for the first time, obtain instruction from a distant teacher. This was because of the invention of a new technology—cheap and reliable postal services, resulting largely from the spread of the railway networks. In 1878,

Figure 2.1   Five Generations of Distance Education

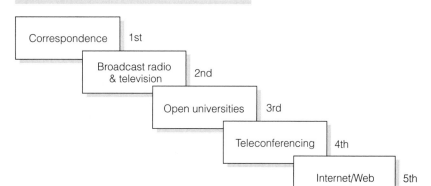

Bishop John H. Vincent, cofounder of the Chautauqua Movement, created the Chautauqua Literary and Scientific Circle. This organization offered a 4-year correspondence course of readings to supplement the summer schools held at Lake Chautauqua (Scott, 1999). Corresponding through the mail was first used for higher education courses by The Chautauqua Correspondence College. Founded in 1881, it was renamed the Chautauqua College of Liberal Arts in 1883 and authorized by the State of New York to award diplomas and degrees by correspondence (Bittner and Mallory, 1933). About the same time and not far from Chautauqua, in Scranton, Pennsylvania, a private vocational school called the Colliery Engineer School of Mines began to offer a correspondence course on mine safety. Such was the success of this course that the school soon began to offer other courses, and in 1891, it renamed itself the International Correspondence Schools (ICS). It is now part of the Thomson publishing empire. It is known as Education Direct (see http://www.educationdirect.com).

It should be noted that similar experiments in using the mail to deliver teaching occurred in other countries. In Great Britain, Isaac Pitman used the national postal system in the 1840s to teach his shorthand system. In Europe, in the mid 1850s Charles Toussaint, a Frenchman, and Gustav Langenscheidt, a German, began to exchange language instruction, leading to the establishment of a correspondence language school. Similar initiatives were taken around the world as one country after another developed their postal systems. Courses were usually in vocational subjects, or as we would say today, were "noncredit" courses. In England a group of professors at the elite University of Cambridge went so far as to try to establish an academic degree by correspondence as a way of opening up access to higher education for working people. The idea was firmly rejected by the administration, with the beneficial effect—for the United States—that one of its leading advocates, a Methodist minister called Richard Moulton, emigrated there. He became acquainted with another theologian, William Rainey Harper, and jumped on the opportunity to work with Harper in setting up exactly the kind of university courses that Cambridge had rejected.

William Rainey Harper had acquired an interest in teaching by correspondence as a professor at the Baptist Union Theological Seminary in Morgan Park, Illinois where he used the method to teach courses in Hebrew. In his summers he was a volunteer at the Chautauqua Institutes and it was he who introduced the method of correspondence there, extending the Institute's educational programs across the country and throughout the year. In 1892, Harper was appointed to be the first president of the new University of Chicago. Inspired by his experiences at Chautauqua and by Richard Moulton's egalitarian vision of using the technology of the mail system to open opportunities for learning to the adult population, he began his tenure as president by setting up a correspondence study program, thus initiating the world's first formal program of university distance education.

The principal motive for the early correspondence educators was the vision of using technology to reach out to those who were otherwise unprovided for. At the time, this included women, and perhaps for this reason, women played an important part in the history of distance education. A notable leader was Anna Eliot Ticknor, who as early as 1873 established one of the first home study schools, the Society to Encourage Studies at Home. The purpose of this "school" was to help women, who were denied for the most part access to formal educational institutions, with the opportunity to study through materials delivered to their homes (Nasseh, 1997).

Other examples of the use of correspondence for the education of women are found in the histories of the Land Grant universities. For example, in 1900, Cornell University appointed Martha Van Rensselaer to its faculty to develop a program for women in rural up-state New York; within three years there were three credit courses offered by correspondence. In 5 years, the program enrolled more than 20,000 women (Cornell University, 2001).

Correspondence instruction at the Land Grant universities was developed on the policy foundation of the 1862 Morril Act. The Morril Act's democratic ideals directed that educational opportunity would be open for people from all backgrounds. The universities were also meant to play a greater part in the daily life of their communities than any university ever had before. Moving away from Old World values, they introduced instruction in the practical arts of agriculture, engineering, business, and home economics. These new ideas were encapsulated by the "Wisconsin idea," which claimed that the boundaries of the university campus would be the boundaries of the state (Altbach, 2001). In fulfilling this mission, correspondence instruction was a powerful tool, which explains why the Land Grant universities led the world in developing the correspondence method. According to one of the first histories of correspondence teaching (Bittner and Mallory, 1933), by the year 1930, 39 American universities offered correspondence teaching; quoting Dorothy Canfield Fisher, they report that there were: "about two million students enrolled every year in correspondence schools . . . four times the number of

Society to Encourage Studies at Home

"Miss Ticknor bethought herself of those whose homes were far away from the centers of learning and universities, and yet who craved educational advantages for themselves and their families. . . . It may be truly said that from her desk in Boston, Miss Ticknor laid out and directed courses of study over the country. By a well organized system of distribution, she sent books, engravings, photographs, maps, all that makes the outfit of thorough instruction, to the doors of families living far from libraries, museums or colleges."

SOURCE: Elizabeth Carey Agassiz. *Society to Encourage Studies at Home* (Cambridge, MA: Riverside Press, 1897). Quoted in Mackenzie and Christensen (1971).

all the students enrolled in all the colleges, universities and professional schools in the United States" (Bittner and Mallory, p. 31).

There was rapid growth in the for-profit sector also, though here the sales practices of some of the private schools brought the method into some disrepute. As a consequence, the for-profit schools organized The National Home Study Council (NHSC) in 1926 to regulate schools and promote ethical practices and professionalism. In 1994 the NHSC changed its name to the Distance Education and Training Council (DETC). Two years before the formation of NHSC, the university correspondence educators also formally codified their standards of practice under the umbrella of the National University Extension Association (NUEA).

In 1968 one of the most thorough studies of correspondence education was sponsored by both the NHSC and the NUEA. Called the Correspondence Education Research Project (CERP), it reported that approximately 3 million Americans were studying through this method nationwide (MacKenzie et al., 1968). Of those, nearly 10 percent were in college programs, more than 20 percent in private schools, and about 9 percent in other categories; more than 50 percent were studying in the armed services.

In 1969, in an attempt to distinguish themselves from the home study schools, university correspondence educators decided to call their method "independent study." Previously known as the Correspondence Study Division, they became the Independent Study Division of the National University Extension Association (NUEA), later the National University Continuing Education Association (NUCEA), and since 1996, the University Continuing Education Association (UCEA). The Independent Study Division was abolished along with other UCEA divisions in 1998. In 1992 a new organization, the American Association for Collegiate Independent Study (AACIS) was formed to advance the interests of independent study professionals, especially in providing professional continuing education.

A Story of Distance Education in the High School: The Benton Harbor Plan

In the fall of 1922 in Benton Harbor, Michigan, Mr. S. C. Mitchell was appointed principal of the local high school. Benton Harbor High School, situated in a working class community, had about a thousand students. Mitchell felt that the curriculum was too heavily biased towards college preparatory subjects, and decided that there should be more vocational subjects. This was not a popular notion in the educational culture of those days and there was no hope of obtaining faculty to teach such subjects. Therefore, Mitchell approached one of the nation's most respected for-profit distance education schools, The American School in Chicago. He enrolled a group of nine students in their correspondence courses and undertook to supervise the students in his classroom. Success led to expansion, so that by 1937 Mitchell had 304 pupils enrolled in 38 different courses.

The practice became known as "supervised correspondence study" and spread around the country, so that by 1930 similar projects had been attempted in more than a hundred public high schools. In 1938 it was the subject of a report presented by J. S. Noffsinger to the First International Conference on Correspondence Education (Noffsinger, 1938). According to Noffsinger, "it was soon demonstrated that supervised correspondence study was not only a valuable method for enriching the curriculum with vocational subjects, as Mitchell had proven at Benton Harbor, but that it was also most valuable in offering a solution to at least three other problems in the secondary field, namely: (1) the isolated student, (2) the enriching of the curriculum in the small one-, two-, and three-teacher high schools which numerically constitute one-half of all public high schools in the United States, and (3) vocational guidance" (p. 85).

A significant contribution to the spread of the idea of supervised correspondence study occurred in 1928 when the University of Nebraska adopted it as the basis of an experimental high school under the direction of K. O. Broady. Like Noffsinger, Broady was a giant pioneer of distance education. Two years later Broady received a $5,000 grant from the Carnegie Foundation for the development of this activity. In the following year, 1933, the U.S. Department of Education issued a special bulletin on the subject called "High School Instruction by Mail," and the next year the first conference on Supervised Correspondence Study was held in Cleveland, Ohio.

Several aspects of this story are of contemporary interest:

1. *The method itself.* Insert the on-line technology of communication, and what Noffsinger wrote over a half-century ago sounds very similar to what many teachers are trying today: "two class periods are spent by each pupil per day under supervision in study and preparation of the lesson assignments, which, when completed are turned over to the supervisor in charge of forwarding to the correspondence center for review, correction, and additional instruction if necessary" (p. 84).

2. *Faculty.* It doesn't look as if they had much more or less formal training than they do today, though at least one training program was established.

According to Noffsinger, beginning in 1934 "and during each subsequent summer term thereafter Teachers' College Columbia University has been offering a course on the technique of supervised correspondence study. The enrollment in these classes during the past five years has been generous in number and undoubtedly has done much to promote the idea of the value in this type of instruction as well as to familiarize a large number of school executives with the techniques employed" (p. 88).

3. *Cost effectiveness:* Even then the cost effectiveness was recognized, for "during the period of the recent depression, when all costs were being carefully scrutinized . . . correspondence courses were costing $7.01 per pupil per year, as compared by the classroom method, to a cost of $23.95 for agriculture, $17.31 for home economics, $14.60 for physical science, and $10.05 for commercial subjects" (p. 84).

4. *Completion rates.* According to L.D. Smith of the Senior High School in Beaver Falls, Pennsylvania, "about sixty eight percent of our students finish the courses they start. It is only rarely that a student changes courses many times and then only under the sanction of his supervising instructor. Nevertheless the student is conscious of the fact that such changes can be made and will be made until a field is found in which there is success. . . . " (p. 86).

5. *Public–private partnerships.* According to Noffsinger: "this story would not be complete without mentioning the cooperation of the American School, Chicago, Illinois and the International Correspondence Schools, Scranton, Pennsylvania, two private correspondence schools that contributed through their officials most generously from their successful experience in the correspondence field which extended over more than forty years and whose enrollments have exceeded the five-million mark. Their great variety of vocational courses which literally have cost millions of dollars to develop and produce, and which are universally recognized for their high quality and pedagogical soundness have always been available to this movement on a cost basis" (p. 88).

6. *How the establishment responded to innovation.* A letter written by one Director of Secondary Education described what happened when it was proposed to introduce the supervised correspondence study method in his state. Apparently the accrediting body (the Southern Association), set up a committee to check out the plan and particularly to vet the potential private partner. Members of this committee became convinced that a quality program was possible "in spite of the fact that previously the majority of the committee had been thoroughly skeptical of such a plan" (p. 87). The plan was never realized, however. "Before the Committee had a chance to present its report, very decided objections were made by institutions interested in developing their own extension courses. The plan was killed, not by high school men but by representatives of higher institutions. It was not given fair consideration" (p. 87).

Modern supervised correspondence study at high school and elementary levels has turned to the application of Internet communications, opening new opportunities

(continued)

continued

for the curriculum as well as exciting interactions among students around the world. In this the University of Nebraska remains the leader, a testimony to the foundations laid by Broady and his colleagues, as well as to the pedagogical soundness of the Benton Harbor concept.

According to S. C. Mitchell: "What we sought at Benton Harbor was to find a method of training that could be given under the supervision of our regular teaching staff without breaking the social contacts of the school group, that would be flexible enough to meet every need, not too expensive for our resources, and of a grade we could accept toward graduation" (p. 84).

Written nearly three-quarters of a century ago, that still sounds like a good model for a high school distance education program or indeed many other distance education programs. Don't you agree?

SOURCE: Noffsinger (1938).

Correspondence Education in the Armed Forces

Founded in 1941, the United States Army Institute was transformed in 1943 into the United States Armed Forces Institute (USAFI), headed by William Young (who was director of correspondence education at the Pennsylvania State University) and located in Madison, Wisconsin. By 1966, USAFI offered over two hundred correspondence courses in elementary, high school, college, technical and vocational subjects, catering for some half million students (Brothers, 1971). More than 7,000,000 members of the armed services took high school courses and approximately 261,222 enrolled in college courses before USAFI closed in 1974 (Watkins, 1991, p. 30). USAFI pioneered computerized marking of assignments, a 24-hour phone-in counseling service, and the use of tutorial groups linked to the correspondence curriculum. These and other ideas were taken up by the director of correspondence instruction at the University of Wisconsin, an ex-naval officer, Charles Wedemeyer. He had taken a strong interest in correspondence as a means of training naval personnel during his wartime service and this interest continued as a result of his association with USAFI on behalf of the university. We will meet Wedemeyer again soon in this history.

In 1974 the U.S. Department of Defense replaced USAFI with a program called the Defense Activity for Non-Traditional Education Support (DANTES), a program of correspondence education that in effect outsourced the delivery of correspondence courses to the universities and private schools. In organizing this, DANTES cooperated with the Independent Study Division (ISD) of the National University Continuing Education Association (NUCEA) in promoting and delivering independent study programs and courses (Wright, 1991, p. 54).

Second Generation: The History of Broadcasting

Radio

When radio appeared as a new technology in the early part of the twentieth century, many educators in university extension departments reacted with optimism and enthusiasm. The first educational radio license was issued by the federal government to the Latter Day Saints' University of Salt Lake City, in 1921 (Saettler, 1990). In February 1925, the State University of Iowa offered its first five for-credit radio courses. Of the 80 students who enrolled that first semester, 64 would go on to finish their coursework at the university (Pittman, 1986).

Radio as a delivery technology for education, however, did not live up to expectations. The lukewarm interest shown by the university faculty and administrators, and the amateurism of those few professors who were interested, proved a poor match for the fierce commitment to the broadcast medium exhibited by commercial broadcasters who wanted it as a medium for advertising.

Television

Educational television was in development as early as 1934. In that year, the State University of Iowa presented television broadcasts in such subjects as oral hygiene and astronomy; by 1939 the university's station had broadcast almost 400 educational programs (Unwin and McAleese, 1988). In that same year, a high school in Los Angeles experimented with television in the classroom (Levenson, 1945). After World War II, when television frequencies were allocated, 242 of the 2,053 channels were given to non-commercial use. In addition to programs broadcast on these channels, some of the best educational television was pioneered by commercial stations. The NBC aired Johns Hopkins University's *Continental Classroom,* which some higher education institutions used for credit instruction, and CBS broadcast their *Sunrise Semester.* Although commercial broadcasters gave up on these public service offerings, educational television fared better than educational radio because of the contributions of the Ford Foundation. From 1950 onwards, Ford gave many hundreds of millions of dollars in grants for educational broadcasting. In 1962 the federal Educational Television Facilities Act funded the construction of educational television stations. In 1965 the Carnegie Commission on Educational Television issued a report that led to Congress passing the Public Broadcasting Act of 1967, setting up the Corporation for Public Broadcasting (CPB).

In 1956 the public schools of Washington County, Maryland were linked in a closed circuit television service, and about the same time the Chicago TV College pioneered the involvement of community colleges in teaching by television. In 1961 the Midwest Program on Airborne Television Instruction involved six states in designing and producing programs broadcast from transmitters transported on DC-6 airplanes. According to Unwin and McAleese

Unfulfilled Dreams

" . . . it is no imaginary dream to picture the school of tomorrow as an entirely different institution from that of today, because of the use of radio in teaching."

SOURCE: Statement to the Federal Radio Commission from the State University of Iowa, 1927 cited by Pittman (1986).

(1988), this project, which lasted 6 years, helped break down state barriers to the exchange of educational programming, as well as set the way for future educational broadcasting by satellite.

Instructional Television Fixed Services

Instructional Television Fixed Service (ITFS) came on the scene in 1961 when the FCC issued an experimental license to the Plainedge School System on Long Island, New York (Curtis and Biedenback, 1979). ITFS is a low-cost, low-power, over-the-air distribution system that delivers up to four channels of television pictures in any geographic area but only to a radius of about 25 miles. Schools and other educational institutions could receive transmissions using special antenna costing about $500. Public school districts used ITFS for sharing specialist teachers and providing teacher continuing education courses. A pioneering effort in this was the Stanford Instructional Television Network (SITN) which in 1969 began broadcasting 120 engineering courses to 900 engineers at 16 member companies (DiPaolo, 1992). Beginning in 1984, California State University, Chico used ITFS to deliver computer science courses to Hewlett-Packard employees to all their locations in five states.

Cable Television and Telecourses

The first cable television (CATV) began operation in 1952. In 1972 the Federal Communications Commission (FCC) required all cable operators to provide an educational channel. Educational programs delivered by broadcast or cable television were referred to as "telecourses." Among the early leaders in this provision were the Appalachian Community Service Network based at the University of Kentucky, The Pennsylvania State University's Pennarama Network, the privately funded Mind Extension University, The Electronic University Network, and the International University Consortium (Wright, 1991, pp. 55–63). By the mid-1980s, there were around 200 college level telecourses produced by universities, community colleges, private producers, and public and commercial broadcasting stations, distributed either by the producers themselves or by the Corporation for Public Broadcasting (CPB).

More than 1,000 institutions of postsecondary education signed on each year for courses distributed by the Adult Learning Service of the CPB, enrolling more than 600,000 adult students. Starting in 1981, The Annenberg Foundation supported the CPB on a project that provided funds typically in the 2–3 million dollar range for university-level telecourses. The courses integrated television programs with textbooks, study guides, and faculty and administrator guides. They were marketed to colleges and universities throughout the whole country and used by colleges and universities as part of their regular course offerings and by university correspondence programs. The Southern California Consortium, for example, consisted of community colleges, led by Coastline Community College. It successfully bid for and was awarded $5 million to produce one of the outstanding telecourses, *The Mechanical Universe.*

Third Generation: A Systems Approach; AIM and the OU

The late 1960s and early 1970s was a time of critical change in distance education, resulting from several experiments with new ways of organizing technology and human resources, leading to new instructional techniques and new educational theorizing. The two most important experiments were the University of Wisconsin's AIM Project and Great Britain's Open University.

AIM and the Invention of the Systems Approach

The purpose of the Articulated Instructional Media Project (AIM)—funded by the Carnegie Corporation from 1964 to 1968, and directed by Charles Wedemeyer at the University of Wisconsin in Madison—was to test the idea of joining (i.e., "articulating") various communication technologies, with the aim of delivering high-quality and low-cost teaching to off-campus students. The technologies included printed study guides and correspondence tutoring, programs broadcast by radio and television, recorded audiotapes, telephone conferences, kits for home experiments, and local library resources. Also "articulated" into the program was student support and counseling, discussions in local study groups, and use of university laboratories during vacation periods.

Wedemeyer's idea regarding students was that using a variety of media meant that not only could content be better presented than through any one medium alone, but also meant that people with differing learning styles could choose the particular combination that was most suited to their needs. To bring together the expertise needed to produce such integrated multimedia programs, AIM invented the idea of the course design team, formed of instructional designers, technology specialists, and content experts (Wedemeyer and Najem, 1969).

AIM represented a historic milestone and turning point in the history of distance education. This was the first test of the idea of distance education as a total system. AIM tested the viability of the theory that the functions of the teacher could be divided, and teaching could be improved when those functions were assembled by a team of specialists and delivered through various media. It tested the idea that a learner could benefit from both the presentation strengths of the broadcast media, as well as the interaction that correspondence and telephone made possible. It expected learners to be self-directed as they worked with the mediated instructional materials, but provide human helpers to facilitate interaction and to give help when needed (Wedemeyer and Najem, 1969).

In 1965 Wedemeyer gave a lecture about AIM in Wiesbaden, Germany, after which he was approached by administrators from England's Oxford University who told him about an idea then circulating in Britain for a "University of the Air" that would teach primarily by television. Wedemeyer was invited to Britain to explain AIM at several universities and also to government officials. His accounts included an emphasis on what he considered the failures in the AIM experiment. "AIM," wrote Wedemeyer, "was an experimental prototype with three fatal flaws: it had no control over its faculty, and hence its curriculum: it lacked control over its funds: and it had no control over academic rewards (credits, degrees) for its students. The implications were clear: a large-scale, non-experimental institution of the AIM type would have to start with complete autonomy and control" (Wedemeyer, 1982, p. 23). It is this statement—reflecting the experience that Wedemeyer shared with his British friends and with British politicians that as much as any other provides the reference for the genesis of the single mode distance teaching institutions, particularly the open universities. (Moore, 2004)

Birth of the Open University

In 1967 the British Government set up a committee to plan a revolutionary new educational institution. At first the idea was simply to use television and radio to open access to higher education for the adult population. In November 1967, officials from the planning committee visited Wisconsin to study the methods and achievements of the AIM project. Soon after, Wedemeyer was invited to meet with them in London. Two years later, as the "Open University" (OU[1]) began to take shape, he moved to the site of its new headquarters to spend several months in the home of Walter Perry, the first vice-chancellor (the head of the university) assisting in developing the new institution. What emerged was the premier national distance education university. It would enjoy economies of scale by having more students than any other university, having a strong level of funding, and employing the fullest range of communications technologies to teach a full university curriculum to any adult who wanted such education. As Wedemeyer was able to claim later: "Almost the entire educational geography of an open educational system was identified in the AIM experiment"

[1]The Open University is known in the United Kingdom as "the OU." However since there are open universities in other countries we will often refer to the first open university as UKOU (i.e., United Kingdom Open University). The term BOU (i.e., British Open University) is sometimes seen but is technically incorrect, since the OU's mandate extends to all the United Kingdom (i.e. Great Britain and Northern Ireland).

Wedemeyer and the OU

You bear some responsibility for the emergence of the Open University in this country. It was your talk on Articulated Instructional Media (AIM) that stimulated us to produce at Nottingham the first university course in this country in which television broadcasts and correspondence instruction were integrated; and it was this experience which produced interest in the University of the Air idea.

Walter James, founding Director of Studies at the UKOU, addressing Charles Wedemeyer on the occasion of his being awarded the OU's Honorary Doctorate.

SOURCE: Cited in Wedemeyer, 1982, p. 24.

(Wedemeyer, 1982, p. 24). In particular, with AIM's three fatal flaws in mind, British policy makers stood firm against the objections and pressure from the higher education establishment that they should receive funding to undertake distance education by setting up units inside conventional universities. Instead, policy makers made the courageous decision to establish a fully autonomous institution, empowered to give its own degrees, with control of its own funds and its own faculty. The UK Open University has justified the decision, emerging as a world class university by any criterion, as well as a model of a total systems approach to distance education.

Domestically and internationally, with an annual enrollment of more than 200,000 adult students and around 20,000 graduates each year, the UKOU demonstrates not only the potential of distance education to provide opportunity regardless of geographic location, but even with an open "first come, first served" enrollment policy, it demonstrates that distance is no barrier to the delivery of education that is of very high quality. In official evaluations, the OU is ranked near the top of UK universities in both research and teaching, and it achieves these results with a superior cost-effectiveness, with a full-time equivalent student being 40 percent of the average cost in the traditional universities. It enrolls more than a third of all part-time students in the UK and graduates about 1 in 12 of all university graduates. And this is all distance education!

Global Spread of the Systems Approach

In part due to those achievements, the UKOU has been widely emulated in other countries. Because of the large scale needed to obtain both quality and cost effectiveness, many of these open universities are large, or as described by a previous vice-chancellor of the UKOU, they are "mega-universities"; that is to say, distance teaching institutions having more than 100,000 students (Daniel, 1996). See Table 2.1 for a list of mega-universities.

Table 2.1   **Mega-Universities**

Country	Name of Institution	Established	Enrollment
China	China TV University System	1979	530,000
India	Indira Gandhi National Open University	1985	242,000
Indonesia	Universitas Terbuka	1984	353,000
Iran	Payame Noor University	1987	117,000
Korea	Korean National Open University	1982	210,578
Spain	Universidad Nacional de Educación a Distancia	1972	110,000
Thailand	Sukhothai Thammathirat OU	1978	216,800
Turkey	Anadolu University	1982	577,804
UK	The Open University	1969	157,450

SOURCE: Adapted from Daniel (1996).

In addition to the mega-universities listed in Table 2.1, there are many other open universities, including: the Al Quds Open University in Jordan, the Andra Pradesh Open University in India, Athabasca University in Canada, the Open Universiteit Heerlen in the Netherlands, the FernUniversität in Germany, the National Open University in Taiwan, the Open Polytechnic of New Zealand, the Open University of Israel, the Universidad Estatal a Distancia in Costa Rica, the Universidad Nacional Abierta in Venezuela, the Universidade Aberta in Portugal, and the University of the Air in Japan.

Although there are differences, these institutions share important similarities: they are single-mode distance teaching institutions, dedicated solely to this approach to teaching and learning, employing teams of specialists to design courses, and enjoying economies of scale through large enrollments (see Chapters 3 and 11 for more on the UK Open University).

The American Response

Among the few countries that did not set up a national open university, the most notable is the United States, the nation that gave birth to almost all the main methods on which the success of the OUs depend. Numerous explanations for this have been given. One is that there did not exist in the United States the same political motive—that is the removal of barriers to higher education—that brought the British policy makers to invest in a very big way in distance education. The United States already had an open educational system, and the state universities had plenty of distance education. Furthermore, where open universities were successfully established, the scale of provision was nearly always national. This required national political commitment and leadership, particularly in facing up to the higher education lobbies. The distributed political control of higher education in the United

States, with each state having to deal with its own higher education establishments, made it impossible to obtain a national policy or set up a national delivery system.

However, some institutions were set up in the United States in the late 1960s and 1970s that, though smaller, borrowed some ideas from the open universities. Among the first of these was Nova University of Advanced Technology, a nonprofit institution inaugurated in 1964. It offered degree programs both in the classroom and at a distance through regional centers in the state of Florida. Ten years later, it changed its name to Nova University and in 1994 merged with the Southeastern University of the Health Sciences to become Nova Southeastern University (Nova Southeastern University, 2003). In 1971, the Empire State College was created within the State University of New York to deliver bachelor and associate programs exclusively at a distance. This is a campus-less institution, with no permanent faculty. Its enrollment reaches 6,000 per year. Goddard College and Syracuse University started special adult degree programs, and Regents College started external degree programs in 1970; Thomas Edison College of New Jersey did the same in 1972.

One of the first consortia forms of organized distance education was the University of Mid-America (UMA). UMA was established by nine Midwestern universities, based at the University of Nebraska with Dr. D. McNeil, a friend of Wedemeyer's and enthusiastic follower of the UKOU developments as first president. The idea was that some of the advantages of the UKOU could be achieved as each of the universities produced courses that would be available to students throughout the consortium (McNeil, 1980). UMA was discontinued in 1982, due to low enrollments, high video production costs, and loss of funding support; this in turn was a reflection of insufficient political support in the member states.

The OU's emphasis on learner support in its regional tutorial and counseling services also led to an increased attention to this in the United States, and to an increased sophistication in student service units (Wright, 1991, pp. 55–63). The 1980s also saw improvement in the quality of course study guides, resulting not only from the OU's example but also helped by the introduction of computerized desktop publishing systems.

Although this discussion has focused on higher education, it should be noted that neither today or in the past has the majority of American distance learners been in higher education. By 1984 there were approximately 400 "single mode," private home study schools. They offered courses in about 600 areas of study, primarily continuing education courses aimed at the professions and vocations. Although colleges and universities listed in the National University Continuing Education Association accounted for 300,000 students, schools associated with the National Home Study Council (NHSC) enrolled 4,000,000 students, with the armed services accounting for 700,000. Electronics, business, and computing had become the most popular fields of study (Zigerell, 1984, p. 3).

Fourth Generation: Teleconferencing

Distance education that emerged in the United States in the 1980s was based on the technologies of teleconferencing, and therefore was normally designed for group use. This appealed to a wider number of educators and policy makers being a closer fit to the traditional view of education as something that occurs in "classes," unlike the correspondence or the open university models, which were directed at individuals learning alone, usually in "home study."

The first technology to be used in teleconferencing on a fairly wide scale during the 1970s and into the 1980s was audio-conferencing. Unlike previous forms of distance education, which were primarily one-to-one exchanges between a learner and the teacher by correspondence, or were receive-only transmissions of broadcast lessons by radio or television, audio-conferencing allowed a student to answer back, and for instructors to interact with students, in real time and in different locations. An audio teleconference could be conducted with individual students at their homes or offices using regular handsets, but normally it meant using special equipment consisting of a speaker and microphones, and one or more different groups of learners. Almost any number of sites could be joined together, either by an operator or by means of a bridge—a device that automatically links a large number of callers simultaneously. The first major educational audio-conference systems was at the University of Wisconsin and was a direct outcome of the Articulated Instructional Media project. Known as the Educational Telephone Network (ETN), it was set up in 1965 by Dr. Lorne Parker, one of Wedemeyer's students, with the immediate purpose of providing continuing education for physicians. Starting with 18 locations and a single weekly program, the system expanded to 200 locations in university campuses, county courthouses, libraries, hospitals, and schools with over 35,000 users and more than 100 programs every week. Approximately 95 percent of the network time was used for continuing or non-credit education, with considerable emphasis on the professionals, mainly doctors, lawyers, pharmacists, nurses, engineers, ministers of religion, librarians, and social workers.

Satellites and Interactive Video-Conferencing

The age of satellite communications began on April 6th, 1965 with the launching of the Early Bird satellite. It delivered 240 telephone circuits or one channel of television over the North Atlantic and was considered a technological miracle. By the end of 1967, four International Telecommunications Satellite Organization (INTELSAT) satellites were in orbit. Very early in the evolution of this technology, American universities began to experiment with transmitting educational programs. One of the first of these was the University of Alaska, which offered continuing education courses for teachers. Another was the University of Hawaii's Pan-Pacific Education and Communications Experiments by Satellite (PEACESAT), created in 1971 to provide satellite programs over some 20 Pacific Islands. These early satellite services operated at low power and the equipment required to transmit and receive signals was expensive. Programs were usually transmitted to receiving stations and then distributed locally by ITFS or cable networks (which we will discuss soon). Newer technology for Direct Broadcast Satellite (DBS) that developed in the 1990s allowed individuals to receive programs directly in their homes or for individual schools to receive directly at the school.

Although it was the UK Open University that led to an explosion of interest in distance teaching in the rest of the world, what caused a similar interest in the United States was the availability of satellite technology. The American organizational device for using this new technology—whether for broadcasting educational television, or for interactive teleconferencing—was the consortium, a voluntary association of independent institutions that shared the costs, the work, and the results of designing, delivering, and teaching educational courses.

One of the first such consortia, the National University Teleconferencing Network (NUTN), was conceived at a NUCEA meeting in Washington, DC in February 1982. J.O. Grantham, Director of University Extension at Oklahoma State University, took the lead in convening a planning conference the following month in Kansas City. Of the 70 member institutions of NUCEA, 40 participated, agreeing to work together to plan and deliver educational programs by satellite. The Network was established with 66 universities and the Smithsonian Institution as members, and with its base at Oklahoma State University. Over the next 10 years, the network grew to more than 250 organizations either providing or receiving a range of over 100 programs in such areas as: aging, agriculture, AIDS, child abuse, tax planning, reading instruction, engineering, interpersonal relationships, international affairs, marketing, medicine, and social and political affairs. NUTN provided programs to as many as 6,000 people at a time, located at some 200 receive sites. It moved its headquarters to Old Dominion University in 1994.

The National Technological University, based in Fort Collins, Colorado, was established in 1984. It is an accredited university offering graduate and continuing education courses in engineering, and awards its own degrees. NTU is a virtual university with no faculty or campus of its own; it delivers courses taught by faculty at major universities around the country. Initially, courses were provided from a pool of 24 universities, and this grew to some 50 participating institutions. Courses are uplinked to NTU by satellite from the originating university and then redistributed by satellite by NTU. Downlinks are located in some 500 locations, including universities, private sector companies, and government agencies. Interaction in such systems is nearly always by audio, such as by telephone.

Both NUTN and NTU illustrate some of the key elements of teleconference consortia and a new form of market-driven distance education that emerged in the 1980s. Because they represent a pool of large universities, they could offer a broader selection of courses to prospective clients (either individuals or organizations) than any single member. Secondly, members of the consortium could compete against each other to offer the best quality and most timely courses—introducing a competitive element at all levels (including individual professors and the courses they teach) that had been largely absent from the U.S. educational system. As a result, the needs of the customers (students, employees, and companies) began to dictate which courses were marketable, and thus worth teaching, not the often esoteric interest of academics.

Business TV

The latter half of the 1980s and the 1990s saw the emergence of a large distance education industry outside higher education, with training for corporations and continuing education for the professions delivered through "Business TV"; that is, interactive video and audio delivered by satellite. By 1987, a study of Fortune 500 companies showed half using this delivery system. IBM had its Interactive Satellite Education Network (ISEN) with originating studios in four cities, and receive sites in thirteen. Federal Express had daily programs to 800 downlinks nationwide. Kodak Corporation sent twice weekly, 2-hour long training programs nationwide. Tandem Computers broadcasted to eleven European countries as well as to 72 sites in North America. Finally, Domino's Pizza sent a mobile uplink to any store in the country where an employee had something to teach the rest.

For organizations not having their own satellite networks, time could be bought on one of several business satellite networks. An example was AREN, The American Rehabilitation Educational Network, which provided professional continuing education for health care professionals at nearly 100 sites nationwide. One of AREN's programs, Management Vision, was broadcast to 240 sites in 1986–1987 and 650 sites in 1987–1988. Corporations made up 60 percent of Management Vision subscribers, hospitals 30 percent, and colleges most of the remainder.

The Public Service Satellite Consortium (PSSC) was a collaborative group representing a broad spectrum of business TV users, such as The American Hospital Association, The American Law Institute, American Bar Association, The National Education Association, the AFL–CIO, and the U.S. Chamber of Commerce. All of these organizations used satellites on a regular basis in their continuing education programs. For example, The Health Education Network was a subscription driven network with over 300 hospital members, focusing on in-service training of medical personnel and patient education with approximately 40 programs monthly.

Interactive Video in the K–12 Schools

In 1987, the federal Star Schools Program Assistance Act was passed by Congress. The Act authorized a 5-year budget of $100 million to promote the use of telecommunications for instruction in math, science, and foreign languages at the K–12 level. The program stipulated that funds be allocated to state-level partnerships, and required matching funds from the participating states. The Office of Educational Research and Improvement in the Federal

Department of Education administered the Star Schools program. The first award under this project was for $19 million a year, for 2 years, to four regional partnerships. The Midlands Consortium consisted of five universities in four states; the TI-In network based in Texas included three state agencies, four universities, and a private corporation, Ti-in Inc. Additionally, $5.6 million was awarded to a third consortium of state education agencies and state television authorities, SERC, to provide high school courses in 19 states. These consortia covered 45 states and reached almost 3,000 schools. They provided over 8,000 students with high school credit courses; 32,037 participated in science programs. In 1990, four new grants, totaling $14,813,000, were awarded to consortia located in the northeastern and northwestern United States.

The Star Schools program had tremendous impact on distance education in K–12 classrooms, particularly in getting equipment installed and programs developed, and providing teachers with training (Martin, 1993; Worley, 1993). One of the most important effects of the project was to stimulate collaboration among provider agencies located in different states to deliver across state boundaries.

In addition to the Star School consortia, many states established their own satellite interactive television efforts for school instruction. The National Governors' Association Report for 1989 reported that ten states operated a statewide or regional teleconference education network, and fourteen were planning one. The most famous of these were:

> Oklahoma's Arts and Sciences Teleconferencing Service (ASTS) was a partnership of the Oklahoma State University and the state Department of Education. One of the most popular offerings of ASTS was a German language course, which was distributed to hundreds of high schools around the country.

> Kentucky established the Kentucky Educational Television (KET) system and installed satellite downlinks at every school in the state at a cost of $11.5 million. During the 1991/1992 school year, over 2,300 students were enrolled in KET math, foreign language, and science courses.

> Other states that established educational satellite networks included: Alaska—where the LearnAlaska network served 250 communities—Georgia, Indiana, Nebraska, Missouri, Virginia, and Utah.

Two-Way Video-Conferencing

The Star Schools, university, and business TV systems described previously used one-way video/two-way audio communications. Participants at all sites could see and hear the presenters from the originating site, but could only respond by audio. Participants could not see other participants, only hear them. As the 1990s wore on, two-way video-conferencing became more widely available.

There are several ways of providing two-way video-conferencing. The older and more expensive method provided signals from one studio to another using technology that transmitted data at "T1" (1.5 megabits per second). The video signals were compressed by a device called a codec. The earliest codecs were as large as a refrigerator, but by the mid-1990s they could be fitted inside a personal computer so that video-conferencing became possible at transmission rates as low as 56 kbps (kilobits per second). Using a T1 network, Michael G. Moore at Penn State University initiated the first full graduate courses delivered by two-way compressed video teleconference in January 1986 linking students in a studio on the campus at University Park with groups in Erie, Pennsylvania.

Two-way or multi-point video-conferencing became easier and less costly with the development of fiber-optic telephone lines that permitted transmission of higher data rates, which allowed video-conferencing between small groups of learners or individual learners and their instructors, with the video displayed on personal computers.

Fifth Generation: Computer- and Internet-Based Virtual Classes

Computer Networks

The early computer systems developed in the 1960s and 1970s were large mainframes that involved rooms full of equipment. They were connected to terminals with keyboards either by coaxial cables within buildings, or remotely by using telephone connections. A precursor of computer networking was the project developed during the 1970s at the University of Illinois called the PLATO (Programmed Logic for Automatic Teaching) project, which allowed a number of sites to communicate via either dial-up lines or dedicated connections. PLATO introduced the idea of an electronic network form of instruction, as well as originating a number of well-known commercial products, such as Lotus Notes (Inglis et al., 1999).

After Intel invented the microprocessor in 1971, and the first personal computer, the Altair 8800, came onto the market in 1975, the use of computer-based instruction increased significantly. By 1989, according to the U.S. Bureau of the Census, 15 percent of all households in the United States had a personal computer and nearly half of all children had access to computers at home or in school. In addition, graphics, color, and sound became possible, and authoring languages made computer-based instruction easier to develop. But most importantly, the cost barriers to availability of computers came down. Educational software (also called courseware) became a major business enterprise and thousands of programs were published at all levels and in all subject domains. In 1969, the U.S. Department of Defense, through its Advanced Research Projects Agency (ARPA), set up a network to link the computers of the armed forces, universities, and defense contractors. In the mid-1980s, the National Sciences Foundation (NSF) developed NFSNet, a network of five supercomputer centers connected to universities and research organizations. NFSNet was upgraded in 1987 and again in 1992. It could be used for exchanging e-mail and data files, and accessing bulletin boards and library facilities (Inglis, Ling, and Joosten, 1999).

The earliest way of linking computers for instruction of groups rather than individuals was referred to as audio-graphics. The graphics were transmitted to a computer on one telephone line to enhance the audio presentation on another line. Peripherals attached to the computers included tablets and light pens, cameras to transmit slow-scan pictures, and scanners for transmitting documents. When linked through a bridge, the computers at a number of sites allowed students and teachers to interact in real time with the graphic and visual images as well as the audio messages. As early as 1989, Moore at The Pennsylvania State University began experimenting in using audio-graphics as a way of internationalizing teaching about distance education, teaching full graduate courses to cohorts of students in Mexico, Finland, and Estonia, as well as in the United States. Another major experiment in distance education by computer conferencing was the Electronic University Network. This was an undergraduate degree program earned by taking courses from 19 universities with accreditation awarded by Thomas Edison College in New Jersey. Courses were delivered on computer disk and in print; interaction with instructors occurred through computer, telephone, and mail. The New York Institute of Technology developed a similar program.

Arrival of the Internet and Web-Based Education

The use of computer networking for distance education got a big boost with the arrival of the World Wide Web, a seemingly magical system that allowed a document to be accessed by different computers separated by any distance, running different software, operational systems, and different screen resolutions. The first Web browser, called Mosaic, appeared in 1993, and it was this software that gave educators a powerful new way of opening access to learning at a distance. It has been estimated that in 1992 the Web contained only fifty pages, but by 2000, the number of pages had risen to at least one billion (Maddux, 2001). In 1995, only 9 percent of American adults accessed the Internet, totaling 17.5 million users. By 2002, 66 percent of American adults were going online, a total of 137 million users. Accessing the Web from home or workplace, on average, they spent 8 hours per week online (Greenspan, 2002).

In the 1990s, a number of universities started running Web-based programs. Examples of providers of entire degree programs offered through the Web included the Online Campus of the New York Institute of Technology, Connect Ed in partnership with the New School for Social Research in New York, and the International School of Information Management. Penn State University offered the first graduate degree in Adult Education through its online program, the World Campus. By the end of the decade, 84.1 percent of the public universities, and 83.3 percent of the 4-year public colleges offered Web-based courses. Seventy four percent of community colleges also offered

Viewpoint: Von Pittman

The Empire Strikes Back

Distance education's future within the American higher education establishment will become more, not less, controversial. During the second two decades of the twentieth century, collegiate-level correspondence study grew rapidly, in terms of numbers of schools offering courses and student enrollments. With the onset of the Great Depression in 1929, there came a large and noisy reaction. Once a novelty, correspondence study became a threat in the minds of many academics. Critics wrote sensational attacks upon correspondence study—one of which effectively ended the programs at Columbia and the University of Chicago—and various professional organizations began to stipulate limits on the use of correspondence courses in degree programs.

Once again, some academics are defining distance education as a threat to the traditional university. Today's attacks, with titles such as Digital Diploma Mills, and unburdened with empirical evidence, posit the inferiority of distance education. While many professors take distance education as a matter of course, others—including some in faculty unions—are still trying to impose limits on its utility in earning a degree. As public funding for higher education shrinks and the expense of maintaining traditional institutions soars, we can expect faculty and administrative opposition to become more bitter and divisive. Distance education will become increasingly more controversial.

SOURCE: Von Pittman, University of Missouri-Columbia

online courses. The rates were lower for private universities and private 4-year colleges, 53.8 and 35.5 percent respectively (Green, 2001).

Just as each previous generation of technology—that is, correspondence, broadcast radio and television, and interactive video and audio conferencing—produced its particular form of distance learning organization—the spread of Internet technology stimulated new thinking about how to organize distance teaching. This has been the case in established single mode open universities and correspondence schools, but also especially in dual mode institutions and those single–mode, face-to-face teaching institutions that never before considered distance education but are now converting to dual mode status. New technology has also led to the emergence of new forms of single mode, purely electronic universities and to new combinations and collaborations among institutions of all types. For more on this, see Chapter 3. Finally, for in-depth research reviews of the history of distance education, see Pittman (2003), Feasley (2003), and Bunker (2003).

Summary

Distance education has evolved through five generations, identifiable by the principal communications technology employed.

1. The first generation of correspondence/home/independent study provided the foundation for individualized instruction at a distance.

2. The second generation of broadcast radio and television had little or no interaction between teachers and learners except when linked to a correspondence course, but added the oral and visual dimensions to the presentation of information to distance learners.

3. The third generation—the open universities—emerged from American experiments that integrated audio/video and correspondence together with face-to-face tutorials, using course teams and an industrial approach to the design and delivery of instruction in a systems approach.

4. The fourth generation used interactive teleconferencing by audio, video, and computer, giving the first real-time interaction between learners and learners, as well as learners and instructors at a distance. This was especially favored in corporate training.

5. The fifth generation of online Internet-based virtual classes has led to a worldwide explosion of interest and activity in distance education, with new organizational structures, collaborative constructivist learning methods, and the convergence of text, audio and video on a single communications platform.

Questions for Discussion or Further Study

1. What similarities and differences can you see in the methods used for designing and delivering instruction in each of the five generations in the history of distance education?

2. What similarities and differences do you see in the learner populations in each of these generations?

3. Why couldn't the United States develop a national open university? Was this a good thing?

4. Do you detect any differences or changes in the motivation of the institutions that provide distance education in the latest generation, compared to the others?

5. Discuss Von Pittman's viewpoint.

CHAPTER 3

The Scope of Distance Education

Moving from concept and history as described in previous chapters, we now turn to examine the current extent of distance education by reviewing the main types of institutions and their programs. Almost every university, college, large corporation, or school district in the United States is now involved in providing some type of distance education. This chapter provides short descriptions of provision in private correspondence institutions, public universities and colleges, corporations, the armed forces, consortia of different institutions, and virtual universities.

Correspondence Education and Home Study

Today as in the past, millions of people in the United States and even more in less developed countries study in distance education programs in which the main medium of communication is text sent through the post (i.e. by correspondence). Of these, the largest number in the United States takes courses from private home study schools accredited by The Distance Education and Training Council (http://www.detc.org). The DETC estimates that more than 4 million people enroll in their courses every year. The Council accredits more than 60 schools offering more than 1,000 different subjects, such as training of beauticians, truck drivers, jewellers, gun repairers, cooks, hotel managers, and travel agents. Almost all these courses are presented in print and distributed by mail, with interaction between instructors and students also by mail. CD-ROMs and the Internet are also increasingly used.

Two of the most famous home study schools are The American School, founded in 1897 in Chicago, and The International Correspondence Schools (ICS), founded in 1891 in Scranton, Pennsylvania. Since its founding, ICS has provided courses to over 12 million students; it is now owned by Thomson

Publishing and has been renamed Education Direct (http://www.education
direct.com). It offers more than 40 diploma programs in technical skills, such
as electronics and auto mechanics, computers (PC repair, programming), and
business (accounting, marketing), as well as associate degrees in business and
engineering. Another historically important home study school is the Hadley
School for the Blind, founded in 1920, which provides high school and continuing education for the blind and their families using braille, large print, and
audiocassettes (http://www.hadley-school.org).

The U.S. military and other government agencies make extensive use of
correspondence study in their training programs. For example, the Air Force
Institute for Advanced Distributed Learning (AFIADL) offers approximately 350
courses in every aspect of Air Force training, from specialized military subjects
to career development skills (see http://www.maxwell.af.mil/au/afiadl).

Home study courses generally involve a relatively low degree of interaction between student and the instructor and no interaction with other students. Assignments are submitted and graded at regular intervals and usually
the student decides when to take a final examination; this is usually done
under the supervision of a proctor. This is generally an individual, self-directed
form of study.

Independent Study

The term "independent study" was chosen in the mid-1960s by university
administrators to describe their correspondence courses and to distinguish
them from the private, for-profit schools. There are more than 150 universities providing such courses in the United States (see http://www.ucea.edu/
Distance02.htm). Compared with courses offered by DETC institutions, the
content tends to be more academic than vocational, and it is likely there will
be more interaction between instructors and students. In addition to the
printed study guides and texts, university independent study courses are
more likely to include other technologies, such as videotapes, television
broadcasts, CD-ROMs, and use of the Internet. Access to independent study
courses for credit is not as open as access to home study courses, since students must satisfy the entrance requirements of the university offering the
courses.

As in private schools, there is a tremendous variety in the independent
study courses available. Offerings include degree programs at the associate,
bachelor, or masters' levels, as well as certificate programs, and noncredit
courses. Table 3.1 lists some examples. Many universities allow their on-
campus students to take their correspondence courses as a way of solving
class scheduling problems. Usually no distinction is made in transcripts
between the grades awarded for courses taken in class and courses taken
by independent study. Although most home study schools have an open
enrollment policy (i.e., students can register and begin a course at any time),

Table 3.1   Examples of Independent Study Courses

Arizona State University, Extended Campus (http://www.dlt.asu.edu)
Nearly 100 credit courses are offered by the Colleges of Business, Education, Fine Arts, Liberal Arts, and Public Programs.

Example: Language and Literature Department offers courses in French, German, Italian, and Spanish. Students have 1 year to complete each course.

Penn State University (http://www.worldcampus.psu.edu)
Associate, bachelor, and master degree programs are offered as well as many certificate programs (credit and noncredit).

Example: Small Business Management Certificate. Requires completion of 8 courses, with 8 months allowed for completion of each course. Course content and activities are available in printed formats, communications for most of the courses, including lesson submissions and access to additional resources, are handled via the Web or e-mail.

Syracuse University (http://www.suce.syr.edu)
Offers 11 degree programs through the Independent Study Program (ISP) including AA, BA, MS, MBA, MLA, and MSc programs. All programs require some degree of campus residence. A number of online courses are offered in conjunction with ISP.

Example: The School of Information Management has been offering master's degree programs since 1993. Programs require a 7-day summer residence plus the possibility of 2-day on-campus sessions.

UCLA Extension (http://www.uclaextension.edu)
The program provides 4,500 courses a year serving over 65,000 students annually.

Example: The Writing program offers 16 courses ranging from "Writing Humour for Fun and Profit" to "Introduction to Screen Writing." All courses are now offered online.

University of Wisconsin, Extension (http://www1.uwex.edu/ce/)
In conjunction with the 26 UW campuses, Extension provides courses to more than 200,000 learners each year from across Wisconsin, the United States, and worldwide.

Example: Collaborative Nursing Program is a joint effort of the nursing programs at 5 UW campuses. Students can earn a bachelor's degree and study at home, at work, or at distance learning sites throughout the state.

universities may require students to wait until the beginning of a semester to begin a course.

Some universities provide high school courses through independent study. As we noted in Chapter 2, the University of Nebraska-Lincoln has been the leading institution in this, offering such courses since 1929. It currently offers 160 courses in 15 subject areas (see http://nebraskahs.unl.edu). Other universities that operate high school programs include: Alaska, Brigham Young (Utah), Kansas, Indiana, Iowa, Michigan, Minnesota, Missouri, North Dakota, Ohio, South Carolina, Texas, and Wisconsin.

Replacing Print with Electronic Media

The American Association of Collegiate Independent Study (AACIS) is a professional association of administrators and academics in independent study. In 2001, AACIS conducted a survey of its members. The members were asked, When would you anticipate your program's enrollments in online courses to exceed those in print-based courses? Respondents indicated: 0–5 years: 7 (29 percent), 6–10 years: 10 (42 percent), 11–20 years: 2 (8 percent), 20 + years: 1 (4 percent), Never: 0, and Already has: 3 (13 percent). Table 3.2 presents further details of the study.

Telecourses

The term *telecourse* covers those courses in which the principal communication technology is recorded and broadcast (i.e., not live) video. Course materials may be as simple as videotaped classroom sessions, or may be produced with sophisticated instructional design and to very high production standards. Telecourses can be distributed in a variety of ways: through videotapes, broadcast on cable or satellite, by ITFS (Instructional Television Fixed Service) networks, or as streaming video over the Internet.

As noted in Chapter 2, one of the first significant efforts in the telecourse area was the work of the Chicago community colleges, which started to offer an Associate of Arts degree by television in 1956. Today, hundreds of community colleges as well as universities across the country offer telecourses for credit in their degree programs or for noncredit learning. Table 3.3 lists some of the major producers. PBS serves as a national coordinating center for college telecourses; its "PBS Campus" (http://www.pbs.org/campus) provides access to 120 credit courses at more than 400 colleges.

In 1981 the publisher Walter Annenberg made a grant of $150 million to the Corporation for Public Broadcasting (CPB) to be used for the improvement

Table 3.2 Independent Study in Print and Online

	Print	Print and Media	Online with Textbook	Entirely Online
Number of courses currently offered	2193	401	593	127
Number of new courses developed during the year	28	4	122	22
Number of course revised during the year	295	40	161	1

SOURCE: AACIS (2001)

Table 3.3   **Major Sources of Telecourses**

Annenberg/CPB (http://www.learner.org)

Coast Learning Systems (http://www.coastlearning.org)

Dallas Telelearning (http://telelearning.dcccd.edu)

Great Plains National (http://gpn.unl.edu)

INTELECOM (http://www.intelecom.org)

PBS/Adult Learning Service (http://www.pbs.org/asl)

of higher education through telecommunications. One of the Annenberg/CPB Project's main contributions has been the provision of funds, typically in the $2–3 million range, for the production of exemplary telecourses. More than 170 college-level credit courses have been produced. The Annenberg/CPB Project does not produce programs itself, but enters into agreements with producers who compete for the Project's funding. For example, the Southern California Consortium, led by Coastline Community College, was awarded $5 million to produce *The Mechanical Universe.* Such a course includes not only television programs, but textbooks, study guides, and faculty and administrator guides. Teams of television and other media specialists, instructional designers, and content experts drawn from the contracting institution or consortium design the courses, and usually including experts from universities and colleges nationwide. Once produced, telecourses are bought by colleges and universities that provide their own instruction and student support either on campus or through their independent study divisions, and also give their own testing and credit (see http://www.learner.org).

Many telecourses are delivered by the Adult Learning Services (ALS), part of PBS in cooperation with 190 public television stations and over 2,000 colleges around the country. In any one year, about 60 percent of American colleges and universities have licensed telecourses through the PBS and nearly 96 percent of the nation's public television stations have broadcast college telecourses. Since its creation in 1981, more than 5 million students have earned college credit via PBS/ALS telecourses (http://www.pbs.org/als/about_als/index.html). In addition, some states have set up their own telecourse organizations. For example, the Consortium of Distance Education (CODE) is a consortium of approximately 30 community colleges in New Jersey, New York, and Pennsylvania set up to manage sharing of telecourses (http://www.codenetwork.org).

Distance Education in Higher Education: NCES 2001 Survey

In 2001, The National Center for Educational Statistics (NCES) published results of a survey of distance education in postsecondary institutions. Here are some facts from this survey:

- During the 12-month 2000–2001 academic year, 56 percent (2,320) of all degree-granting institutions offered distance education courses. A further 12 percent reported plans to offer courses in the next 3 years.
- 90 percent of public 2-year and 89 percent of public 4-year institutions offered distance education courses, compared with 16 percent of private 2-year and 40 percent of private 4-year institutions.
- Credit granting courses were offered at the undergraduate level by 48 percent of all institutions, and at the graduate level by 22 percent of all institutions.
- In the 12-month 2000–2001 academic year, there were an estimated 3,077,000 enrollments in all distance education courses offered by 2-year and 4-year institutions. (Note that the survey asked only about electronically delivered programs and thus excluded some print-based programs.)
- An estimated 127,400 different distance education courses were offered in the 2000–2001 academic year.
- About one-quarter (27 percent) of the institutions offered 10 or fewer courses, and 15 percent offered more than 100 courses.
- The majority of institutions used the Internet, with 90 percent reporting that they used asynchronous communication and 43 percent used synchronous communication.
- Fifty one percent used two-way video with two-way audio, and 41 percent used one-way prerecorded video (telecourses). 29 percent used the CD-ROM as a principal delivery technology and 19 percent used multimedia packages.
- Sixty percent participated in some type of distance education consortium. Of those institutions, 75 percent participated in a state consortium, 50 percent in a consortium within a single university system or community college district, 27 percent in a regional consortium, 14 percent in a national consortium, and 4 percent in an international consortium.

For details, see http://nces.ed.gov/surveys/peqis/publications/2003017.

Open Universities

When the United Kingdom Open University (UKOU) was established in 1969, it was not the first major university dedicated solely to distance learning. The right to such a title probably belongs to The University of South Africa, which began its nationwide distance education system soon after the end of World War II. In fact the British studied the South African experience as well as that of Australia, the Soviet Union, Japan, and the United States as they prepared plans for their Open University in the late 1960s. Within a few years the UKOU had proven itself to be so excellent and so successful that it transformed distance education (many would say higher education in general and became a

Channel One

Channel One is a commercial television news program offered free of charge to schools by Primedia, Inc (http://www.channelone.com). The 12-minute program airs daily in approximately 12,000 middle and high schools around the country; which Aiken (2000) estimates is viewed by 8 million students each day. Primedia provides a Ku-band satellite dish, color television monitors, and a VCR to each school which agrees to show the program. The program is normally shown before or after classes and during lunch periods, so that it doesn't reduce classroom time. Each program provides highlights of national and world news from the perspective of teenagers as well as "lifestyle" items. In addition to this perspective on the news, a coverage that lasts 10 minutes, the programs also include 2 minutes of public service announcements of direct interest to teenage viewers and commercial advertising targeted at this population. The inclusion of commercials has made Channel One very controversial—many teachers, administrators, and parents feel this is a particularly corrupting influence in classrooms. Indeed, many school boards and districts have tried through legal means (unsuccessfully) to prevent Channel One from being aired in their schools and a U.S. Senate hearing was conducted in 1999 (see http://www.obligation.org/ussenatehearing.html).

A study by Johnston and Brzezinski (1992) that evaluated Channel One in 11 schools around the country found:

- 60 percent of the teachers would recommend it to other teachers without any reservations.
- Students in all the schools watched the program at least 3 days a week and in many schools students watched every program.
- Students reported that the "lifestyle" segments of the program more interesting to them than the news segments.
- About half of the students felt that they learned something important from the programs most of the time.
- Overall, students who watched the programs did not score better on tests of current events.
- Few teachers discussed the content of programs in their classes or integrated programs into their teaching activities.

Gormly (1999) found that most educators interviewed about Channel One believed that the benefits outweighed the disadvantages. Aiken (2000) measured the effectiveness of Channel One news on 78 randomly selected 8th graders' knowledge of current events and found significant statistical differences in knowledge when compared with nonviewing students. Although Channel One programs have won many honors, including a Peabody award, the educational value of its programs is still open to question after more than a decade.

For further discussion, see Tiene (1993).

model for similar institutions around the world. With over 2 million graduates since 1972 and more than 200,000 students taking courses every year, a full-time staff of 2,800 and a part-time staff of over 5,000 tutors and counselors, with 13 regional and 330 local learning centers across Britain and overseas, the UKOU is one of the most successful examples of a total systems approach to distance education.

As mentioned in Chapter 1, it is necessary to be clear about the use of the term "open." In the United Kingdom at the time of the establishment of the OU, admission to higher education was very restricted; it was particularly difficult for children of working class homes to obtain admission. Introducing distance education was a political decision taken by a Labour government as a means of breaking down barriers and opening up opportunity. Thus the term "open," which is often attached to "distance education" in Europe, very specifically reflects that political ambition of the founders of the UKOU. In the United States, where higher education has never been as "closed" as in Europe, it is important that we do not confuse the *method* (i.e., distance education) with the political *policy* (i.e., "openness"). In particular, it is necessary to understand that although there is a substantial body of theory about the method of teaching and learning at a distance there is little theory of "open" education.

Combining the vision of openness with the methods of distance education, most open universities adhere to the following principles of the UK Open University:

- Any person can enroll, regardless of previous education.
- Study is done at home, work, or anywhere the student chooses.
- Course materials are developed by teams of experts.
- Tutoring is provided by other specialists.
- The enterprise is large scale, usually national, in scope.
- It enrolls large numbers and enjoys economies of scale.
- There are large investments, mostly from public funds.
- A wide variety of technologies are used.
- A highly integrated system combined with heavy investment result in high quality.

There are exceptions or modifications to some of these principles. For example, although the UKOU admits anyone on a "first come, first served" basis, it imposes a lower age limit, and enrollment in a particular course may require prerequisites; UKOU courses have fixed start dates and schedules that all students must meet; some courses may insist on participation in local study groups or residential weeks; purchased as well as university produced materials (such as texts or tapes) may be used; and tutoring may not be provided to all students or for all courses.

Since they are distance education institutions, a distinguishing characteristic of all open universities is their commitment to the use of audio, video, and computer based technologies, integrated with print in a very systematic way. The UKOU produces its courses in association with BBC television (initially it was to be called "The University of the Air") in Europe's largest educational broadcasting studios. CD-ROMs, audio, and videotapes are components of most courses, and online learning is being integrated into existing as well as new courses. However, as with independent study courses in the United States, print materials provide the backbone of most open university courses. Open universities have now established a tradition of investing money, time, and human resources to ensure their printed materials are extremely well designed and well produced, very attractive to study from, and pedagogically sound. However, to correct any impression that an institution that values printed text is not also capable of innovation with new technology, Table 3.4 summarizes some data about online learning at the UKOU.

For more information on the UK Open University, see Chapter 11 and also visit: http://www.open.ac.uk. Some information about other open universities around the world is also given in Chapter 11.

Although the United States does not have an open university (partly because the "always open" Extension departments of the state and other universities provide the kinds of opportunities the British looked for when they set up the UKOU), there are a number of other innovative institutions that share some special characteristics with the open universities. We have already mentioned some of these in Chapter 2 and would like to introduce another here.

Western Governors University was formed following a 1995 meeting of the Association of Western Governors (http://www.wgu.edu). A joint project of 19 states and Guam (Krieger, 2001), WGU is a nonprofit institution designed to offer courses developed by its members. Bates (2000) suggests that the main motive of the Western states in setting up WGU was the frustration regarding university responses to business and industry's needs in training the workforce. Its programs are in the fields of business, information technology, and education. Therefore, the WGU does not design courses itself. Rather, it is an administrative body, which endorses, presents to the public, and coordinates the provision of distance education courses from participating traditional universities. However, it does provide its own degree programs and certification.

WGU is innovative in that it "opens" the educational process by focusing less on how much time a student puts in to obtain credits, and more on evaluating outputs; that is to say, the knowledge the student acquires, regardless of where, how, and when it is acquired. This allows students to make progress toward a degree based upon work and life experience as well as traditional study. All WGU courses are online; it doesn't spend money on maintaining traditional tenured teaching faculty, but instead assigns mentors to help students design and complete their individualized academic plans.

In spite of the highly publicized launching of this initiative, WGU was slow to take off. Student enrollment was just 208 in the 1999–2000 academic year. In September 2000 the state of Utah released a report with severe criticism of the organization for its low enrollments. Later that year, the Inter-Regional Accrediting Committee (IRAC) granted WGU the status of "Candidate

Table 3.4   Online Learning at the United Kingdom Open University

- £30 million (about $50 million) invested in learning online
- About 160,000 OU students and tutors online
- 80,000 assignments—one in ten of all assignments—submitted electronically
- Online access is required in 178 courses and optional in a further 97
- 773,000 CD-ROMs, 30,000 floppy disks and 3,000 DVDs produced in 2001
- 32 million pages on the Courses and Qualifications Web site accessed in 2001
- 3.5 million "page hits" on the Learner's Guide in 2001
- 172 course-related websites have links to 3,825 external resources
- Synchronous conferencing includes online audio and audio-graphics

for Accreditation" (Krieger, 2001). By mid-2001, the Accrediting Commission of the Distance Education and Training Council (DETC), granted accreditation to WGU. In early 2002, the university claimed its enrollments rose to 2,500 students. Of those, 450 took WGU's degree or certificate programs and the other 2,050 students took courses "to supplement other educational goals." Some observers think the WGU lacks sufficient funding to develop its full potential. Certainly, the experience of many open universities has shown that costs are often underestimated in the beginning. Also, the organizational structure that makes WGU a broker of both individual courses and full programs, and the dependence on the state institutions for course development, seems to be not yet completely refined (Bates, 2000).

Empire State College, which is part of the State University of New York (http://www.esc.edu) and Thomas A. Edison State College in New Jersey (http://www.tesc.edu) are other notable examples of American universities that emphasize "open" policies in making admission convenient and flexible and provide study opportunities that are equally convenient and flexible through distance education methods.

Nova Southeastern University (http://www.nova.edu), founded in 1964 and based in Fort Lauderdale, Florida, offers graduate degrees (master's and doctoral) through a system of regional learning centers. It achieves cost-effectiveness, like the UKOU, by relying on adjunct faculty. Students are assigned to groups called "clusters" that meet together for weekend face-to-face seminars. A professional educator (usually a professor located at a university in the area) is hired to coordinate the academic and administrative affairs for each cluster and serve as liaison between the students, faculty, and the university. Students stay in their cluster until they complete their program.

Walden University, based in Minneapolis, Minnesota, offers graduate programs in administration/management, health services, human services, and education (http://www.walden.edu). Walden uses procedures similar to Nova, organizing weekend sessions regionally, with adjunct faculty and three-week summer sessions held at the University of Indiana, Bloomington.

Perhaps the most important point to bear in mind about the open universities, from the American point of view, is the pressure and the stimulus that their success in demonstrating the principles of a systems approach have had on institutions in this country, including new "virtual institutions" that have emerged with the availability of online technologies. It is not a coincidence that the quality of course design and delivery in the United States improved—and distance education became much more accepted—following the establishment of the UKOU than had been the case for nearly 100 years before that.

For further details about open universities worldwide, see Daniel (1999).

Interactive Television: Satellite and Cable Networks

The use of satellite to deliver courses was the most talked about form of distance education and training in the last two decades of the twentieth century, just as delivery by Internet is uppermost in people's minds at the beginning of the twenty-first century. It is estimated that there were over 60,000 receive sites in the United States by the middle of the 1990s. Unlike the other forms of distance education discussed so far in this chapter, satellite-based courses are usually delivered to students in groups according to a schedule determined by the teaching institution. What makes them different from telecourses is that they are interactive, with feedback, questions, and discussion transmitted—usually by telephone links—from the audience to the content experts in a distant studio.

Business TV and Corporate Training

As we saw in Chapter 2, distance education became a training approach of significant interest to American corporations with the evolution of interactive television delivered by satellite, which became known as Business TV. Companies found they could provide training that was very specific to their particular products at their branch offices and plants around the country and world, used their own private television network, and was received by means of a satellite dish located outside local offices or plants. In recent years there has been a tendency to outsource programming and delivery to specialist vendors.

Business Television (BTV) Link is a corporate satellite user group that includes satellite television pioneers such as Ford Motor Co., American Express, General Electric, Anheuser Bush, and RE/MAX.

Business TV proved to be a cost-effective way to provide employee training. For example, when there is a new product, the capability of training the entire sales force at one time means more standardized training, more immediate sales, and hence extra revenue. One authority (http://juntunen.com/ BrainStorm/whitepapers/btv.asp#eleven) reports, on behalf of a vendor of satellite programs, that Business TV results in a:

Examples of Business TV

"CompUSA's Business Television network, CompTV, delivers employee training and business update broadcasts from its top executives to employees at more than 200 stores nationwide. In addition to live, interactive programs, CompUSA will use DISH Network's PVR (Personal Video Recorder) technology for viewing broadcasts. CompUSA will use this technology to easily capture content without re-broadcasting to adjust for employees in different time zones and schedules . . . " (http://www.cvssystems.com/Press/0602031.cfm).

"The RE/MAX Satellite Network (RSN) offers cutting edge training by bringing the best minds in the business right into your office and even in your home through DishTV. More than 100 different shows air during a 3-month programming cycle and include Accredited/Designation Courses, Business, Management, Sales, Technology and more" (http://www.remax-cahi.com/eSource/training/rsn.asp).

For over a decade, Automotive Satellite Television Network (ASTN) has delivered effective training to automotive dealerships nationwide via satellite. ASTN's award winning training content meets the needs of today's dealership professionals in a cost efficient manner, claiming that "[o]ur content focuses on the areas that directly impact your bottom line such as: Sales, Management, F & I, Reception, Motivation Mixed Operations e-commerce and more" (http://www.pwpl.com/auto/).

After analyzing the training needs of their organization at field level, managers and training professionals of Ford Credit Inc. identified a need for 80 courses to provide the full range of knowledge their employees need. Much of the training was self-paced and delivered by way of in-office learning centers. Instruction in lease termination and renewal is offered to dealers through FORDSTAR, the company's satellite communication network (Keister, 1997).

- 64 percent decrease in costs for new product introductions
- 81 percent reduction in product cycle time
- 50 percent reduction in time-out-of-field

Business TV programming accomplishes other functions important to companies besides delivering formal training courses. One of these is the development and maintenance of company morale and employees' motivation. These broadcasts provide details about current operations or problems as well as focusing on examples of outstanding employee performance. It is common for the senior executives of companies to make regular appearances to explain policies and answer questions.

At one point there were over 80 private business TV networks in the United States, some of which reached thousands of sites and millions of employees. Today many of these have given way to online communications systems.

Interactive Video in Higher Education

The National University Telecommunications Network (NUTN) has a membership of approximately 50 universities, community and junior colleges, and vocational and technical institutes with nearly every state represented. NUTN courses consist of one or more broadcasts, with video delivered by satellite, and with interactions conducted among receiving sites by telephone (see http://www.odu.edu/dl/nutn). Most courses offered by NUTN are continuing education courses produced by the member institutions. A member institution develops the video-conference on a topic of current interest, using expert presenters, and offers the programs to other institutions throughout the country. Other members provide reception facilities. The typical program consists of a live video presentation transmitted by satellite and an audio discussion and question period. Each receiving site pays a registration fee to the originating institution; these fees typically range from $200–500 per site. The NUTN administration helps members market the courses, but does not get involved in their production or transmission, which is the responsibility of the originating site. NUTN also conducts some training activities.

The National Technological University (http://www.ntu.edu), when it was established in 1984, was also based on the idea of delivering satellite video courses. It offers its own master's degrees in a variety of engineering fields, as well as continuing education courses, mainly in engineering also. NTU has no faculty of its own or campus, and uses satellite, compressed digital video (CDV), and computer technology to deliver more than 1,000 courses taught by faculty from 50 major universities to more than 1,000 work locations internationally. NTU clients are not individual students, but organizations. Over 200 major corporations and government agencies subscribe to NTU and pay fees for each course they receive. Corporations cooperating in NTU included Boeing, Kodak, General Electric, IBM, Motorola, and Xerox. The organizations decide which employees will participate and arrange on-site facilities for taking part in the programs. NTU has granted more than 1,600 master's degrees to individuals who have completed one of their programs of study. In any one year, more than 30,000 technical professionals participate in NTU's noncredit Professional Development short courses.

Besides NUTN and NTU, several other consortia were created in the 1980s to provide interactive video-conferencing programs in specific content areas or for certain audiences. Some of the most important are:

- AG*SAT (Agricultural Satellite Network) is a consortium established to provide courses on agricultural topics. With 32 institutional members, it evolved into the American Distance Education Consortium (http://www.adec.edu).

- The SCOLA (Satellite Communications for Learning) consortium distributes foreign language news broadcasts from 35 countries to be used as the basis of educational programs by its member schools and cable systems (http://www.scola.org).

- The Community College Satellite Network (CCSN) was set up in 1989 by the American Association of Community and Junior Colleges.

- The Black College Satellite Network (BCSN), broadcasting primarily from Howard University, has programs aimed at 105 colleges located in 23 states and the District of Columbia.

- Various state level consortia, such as the Indiana Higher Education Telecommunications System (IHETS) and OneNet, the Oklahoma Telecommunications Network. Mississippi State University began to deliver interactive video courses in 1993 and provides more than one hundred courses to 200 sites throughout its state and to locations as far away as Hawaii, the Philippines, and Japan.

- An interactive video distance learning project called Project Jump Start was carried out in 1995 at Buffalo State College in New York State, with courses taught to college and high school students in 14 undergraduate subjects and funded through a cooperative arrangement between Bell Atlantic and the Center for Applied Research in Interactive Technologies (CARIT) (Fusco and Ketcham, 2002).

In recent years, all these systems have had to accommodate their programming to the emergence of online technologies, in some cases by closing programs and in others by merging what can be offered by the two technologies. The satellite delivered program can be more suitable for presentations of live lectures, demonstrations, or films; while the online program provides opportunity for small group interactivity, communication from individual participants to instructors, and in-depth follow-up search activities.

In the 2000s, the Star Schools program evolved away from satellite teleconferencing programs towards programming for delivery on the Internet. Although some of the original Star Schools consortia have disbanded, among those that have survived are the Satellite Education Resources Consortium (SERC) (http://www.serc.org), and the Telecommunication Education for Advances in Math and Science (TEAMS) (http://teams.lacoe.edu). Information about these and other current projects can be found at http://www.ed.gov/prog_info/StarSchools.

Online Learning and Virtual Universities

The biggest technological development in distance education in the past decade has been the rapid emergence of the Internet and World Wide Web. Almost all distance education programs, including correspondence and independent study, now have some online presence. In some institutions online learning has replaced telecourses and interactive video courses. Some institutions have been created specifically to offer online learning—usually calling themselves "virtual universities" (see Table 3.5).

Jones International University (JIU) was originally established in 1987 by entrepreneur Glenn Jones—when it was called Mind Extension University. Mind Extension University provided courses through cable television, but it turned to the Web in 1995, changed its name, and claimed to be "the first fully online, accredited university." Like many other online universities, JIU aims to capture an adult audience, mainly working professionals. Its courses have a professional development character with emphasis at undergraduate, master's, and certificate levels in the fields of business, education, communications, and information technology (http://www.jonesinternational.edu/). About half of its students have tuition paid by their employers, and most are enrolled in nondegree or certificate programs. In 1999, the North Central Association of Colleges and Schools accredited JIU, a decision that rendered the university more credibility. Some in the academic community contested this accreditation, which was defended by the Association (Crow, 1999).

The University of Phoenix (http://www.universityofphoenixonline.com/) is one of the largest and most successful online universities. It is a for-profit, proprietary higher education institution, founded in 1976 by CEO John G. Sperling. The North Central Association of Colleges and Schools granted it accreditation in 1978. The University of Phoenix is a dual-mode institution; it delivers courses both in classrooms (through 55 campuses and 98 learning centers in 18 states) and through distance.

Most (90 percent) of Phoenix Online's faculty is part time. Its full-time faculty designs the courses, and instructors facilitate the online lessons. There is an emphasis on standardizing courses, and instructors work in a highly structured environment. The university claims that it prefers "practitioner faculty," who have full-time employment in the discipline they teach. Methods emphasize teamwork, problem-solving activities, and practical application of knowledge (Krieger, 2001). Since it began offering online courses in 1979, it has grown tremendously; in 2003, it had over 70,000 students and 4,000 online instructors. The focus of Phoenix is on working adults, and its courses have a vocational orientation. Degrees are offered online in business, management, technology, education, and nursing. The degrees range from an Associate of Arts in General Studies to a Doctor of Management in Organizational Leadership. The majority of students (43 percent) are enrolled in the College of Undergraduate Business, followed by the College of Graduate Business (20 percent).

Capella University (http://www.capella.edu) is another private, for-profit, Web-based virtual university. Its CEO Steve Shank founded it in 1993, aiming at an adult professional audience. Capella has institutional procedures that resemble those of the traditional universities: the individual professor teaches his or her own courses, for no more than 12 students. However, most of its 170 faculty members are part-time, as with Phoenix Online and Jones International. CU was granted accreditation in 2000 by the North Central Association. It offers degree programs in business, education, psychology, human services and technology, at the certificate, bachelor's, master's, and doctoral levels (Krieger, 2001).

Table 3.5   **Virtual Universities**

Barnes & Noble University—free courses taught by authors

Canadian Virtual University—13 universities and 250 programs

Cardean University—5 major business schools offering an MBA

Colorado Community Colleges Online—13 colleges offering Associate degrees

Georgia Virtual Technical College—34 technical colleges, 750 courses

Illinois Virtual Campus—69 colleges and universities

Jones International University—Undergraduate and graduate programs

Michigan Virtual University—700 professional development courses

Kentucky Virtual University—10 colleges and universities

SUNY Learning Network—56 universities and colleges in New York State

University of Phoenix—Undergraduate and graduate programs

The Fielding Graduate Institute (http://www.fielding.edu) was founded in 1974 as a distance learning institution specifically for mid-career adults—one that would create a national learning community in the behavioral sciences. It was an early adopter of computer conferencing (see Rudestam and Schoenholtz-Read, 2002) and now makes extensive use of online learning.

Some virtual universities have been created by conventional universities for the delivery of their own programs; examples are Penn State's World Campus, University of Illinois Online, and the University of Texas Telecampus. Temple University established Virtual Temple, New York University created NYU Online, and the University of Maryland University College set up its for-profit unit. Cornell University had to redesign its eCornell initiative into a non-degree, continuing education effort.

States have created virtual universities to serve as portals for the postsecondary institutions in that state, and do not offer courses or programs of their own. Examples include: Arizona, Florida, California, Illinois, Iowa, Kentucky, Maryland, Minnesota, and Texas.

However, some of the most talked about virtual universities quickly passed away. California Virtual University was abandoned in 1999 (Blumenstyk, 1999). Fathom, an ambitious consortium of megastars in education and the arts, closed in 2003.

Some institutions described as virtual universities have been created as a means of marketing a product. For example, Barnes & Noble University (http://www.barnesandnobleuniversity.com) offers free courses to the public taught by authors and experts as a way to increase book sales. Macromedia University (http://macromedia.elementk.com) provides online courses to teach people how to use the multimedia design programs sold by Macromedia. Other information technology companies, including Microsoft, IBM, Cisco, Sun, and Novell provide extensive online education programs relevant to their products.

For listings and descriptions of virtual universities, see the Distance Education Clearinghouse site at http://www.uwex.edu/disted/virtual.html.

Virtual Schools

Although K–12 schools have been interested in the use of technology for a long time, they have been slow to set up virtual schools. Reasons for this include lack of network access, a face-to-face teaching culture that includes some political resistance, and lack of teacher training. However, in recent years at least 12 states have established some form of virtual schools intended to offer K–12 classes to students anywhere in those states. In addition, there are virtual high schools offered by some universities, as well as local school districts and private/charter schools. Some examples are the secondary curriculum via distance education offered by University of Idaho, and the program of University of Nebraska. All these programs started out with a correspondence course model, and have been adding Internet-based courses. Clark (2003) surveyed virtual schools and reported that at the time of his report, an estimated 40–50,000 students were enrolled in online classes and most of these students were taking Advanced Placement courses.

One of the first and most established virtual high school is called Virtual High School, Inc. (http://www.govhs.org). Established in 1996 as a partnership between the Hudson, Massachusetts school district and the Concord Consortium, VHS offers over 100 courses in arts, business, foreign languages, language arts, life skills/health, math, science, social studies, and technology education. These courses are developed and taught by teachers at the VHS schools (162 in 2003) located in 21 states and overseas. Each participating school pays an annual membership fee to belong to VHS and this entitles its students to course access. For a detailed evaluation of VHS, see Zucker et al. (2003) based upon studies conducted by the Center for Technology in Learning at SRI (http://ctl.sri.com).

Another example is Keystone National High School (http://www.keystonehighschool.com), which was founded and licensed by the state of Pennsylvania in 1994 and accredited in 1998. It provides both correspondence courses and Internet based courses and offers year-round enrollment, with a full-credit high school curriculum that aims to meet the needs of home-schooled students as well as those enrolled in public and private schools.

Major information technology companies also offer educational and training programs to K–12 schools. IBM (http://www.ibm.com/education/) has formed partnerships with 15 school districts and 6 states in a project that declares as its aim the reinvention of American schools (and selling a lot of products and services as a result). Microsoft also provides programs to K–12, including an online magazine (http://www.microsoft.com/education/).

For a review of research related to distance education in the schools, see Clark (2003).

K–12 Online Learning: The Oregon Network for Education

Like many states, Oregon has a number of sources for K–12 online classes. Here are some of the providers:

Bridges for Learning

Bridges for Learning offers courses delivered using the Internet and built around skills and objectives outlined in state and national performance standards. Instruction is learner-centered and real-world oriented. Courses require extensive field and project work. Students are expected to participate regularly online through synchronous and asynchronous forums.

Corvallis Online

Corvallis Online seeks to provide students with opportunities to learn online and to earn Corvallis School District credit. Courses are taught by Corvallis School District teachers, and are available free to students within the Corvallis School District who are enrolled in Corvallis schools, or who are home schooled. Each Corvallis online course is limited to 10 students and is aimed at students who have scheduling conflicts, need acceleration or remediation, have medical needs, have a preference for a self-directed style of learning, or are home schooled.

COOLSchool

Eugene School District 4J field-tested its Internet-based COOLSchool during the 1995–1996 school year and now offers 42 COOLSchool classes to high school students throughout Oregon and around the world.

NW WebSchool

Serving over 104,000 students within its 20 districts, the Northwest Regional ESD has created NW WebSchool, a distance learning program utilizing dynamic text and rich multimedia, including pictures, sounds, and video clips—all integrated into comprehensive, standardized, and self-paced courses.

OSU K–12 Online

Oregon State University's K–12 Online program opened September 2003 with 23 high school courses. Courses are offered in both an 18-week (standard semester) and 9-week (fast track) format. OSU also offers College for High School Students, which enables academically ready high school students to take Oregon State University courses for college credit.

Portland State University

The High School Independent Study program at Portland State University has 40 fully accredited high school courses taught by certified Oregon high school teachers. The university is in the process of converting all its independent study

(continued)

continued

courses to the Web, although most courses are still correspondence-based, with materials delivered by regular mail.

SK Online

SK Online is a program of the Salem-Keizer School District 24-J that provides a Web-based curriculum to students living in and around the Salem-Keizer Public School District. The program is targeted to any school-aged student who has a need for acceleration or remediation; is credit deficient, has scheduling conflicts in a traditional school; has limited English proficiency; or is home schooled, medically fragile, pregnant and parenting, expelled, or "in diversion."

Southern Oregon Online School

The Southern Oregon Online School (SOOS) is a consortium of 10 high schools in southern Oregon. It offers core curriculum courses built around skills and objectives outlined in Oregon's performance standards and delivered using a combination of Internet and video technologies.

For more details about Oregon Network, see http://oregon.org/K12participants.htm.

Corporate Training

Marchese (1998) states that private business spends $58 billion annually on employee training and about 85 percent of the Fortune 500 companies are subsidizing distance education for their employees. A survey conducted by SRI in 2003 (Barron, 2003) reported that 41 percent of responding organizations were using online learning. Most large corporations develop their own online training to meet the specific needs of their business and employees, and many have set up their own corporate universities. According to one estimate by the Corporate University Xchange, there are over 1,000 such entities. Some of these corporate universities, like Motorola University, have built physical campuses, while others such as Dell University only exist virtually. Companies like Microsoft, Oracle, Novell, and Cisco are all in the direct-provision business. According to Adelman (1997) Sun Microsystems' Educational Services division offers over 200 courses in classroom, Web-based, and CD modes. Hardware and software manufacturers have provided a plethora of training products as a means to support their customers. For example, Cisco's "Seminars, Events, and Training" page (http://cisco.com/public/Events_root.shtml) includes a worldwide events calendar and information on Cisco's certification programs. Sun Microsystems' page (http://sun.com/service/) wraps support, education, consulting, integration, and channel services, as well as direct access to Sun's online support tools, under one umbrella; further indicating the integration of training into the design, manufacturing, and distribution of information technologies (Saba, 1998). Some businesses have teamed up with universities to provide training for their employees. For example, MetLife has teamed with Drexel University to offer a distance master's degree in information systems; the Saturn Corporation and Bechtel National Inc. formed a partnership with the University of Tennessee; Western Governors University is supported by 14 business partners including Sun, IBM, and AT&T. For research reviews of distance education for corporate training, see Oblinger and Rush (2003) and Berge (2003).

Vendors

There are vendors (see Table 3.6 for examples) who offer off-the-shelf online distance education courses as well as tailor-made courses for specific companies. For example, eCollege is a company comprised of educators and technologists that partners with University of Colorado and another five universities to deliver courses online; it contracted with Microsoft to deliver Microsoft 2000 productivity courses to university faculty. The "100 Degrees Online Grant Program" is eCollege's effort to sell a range of online degree and certificate programs.

SmartForce, another "e-learning" company (with sales of $168 million in 2000), claims to be the world's largest e-learning company, serving over 2,500 corporate customers and having over 30,000 e-learning objects in its library. It provides online mentors, a library of laboratory simulations, threaded discussion forums, and the chance to interact with guest speakers on a pay-per-view basis.

VCampus Corporation (http://www.vcampus.com) distributes a library of more than 5,200 Web-based courses, and has delivered more than 2.5 million courses to over 700,000 adult learners. Another example is NETg, which has provided 700 online modules for the National Institutes of Health's (NIH), including over 100 codeveloped with Oracle Education, with the majority devoted to database administration, and an "Internet Masters Series" developed with Netscape.

One form of online learning that is particularly popular in corporations is Web conferencing. This involves the simultaneous use of voice and shared whiteboards (the latter usually used for showing PowerPoint slides), and may also involve video or sharing of application programs. This form of distance education is readily adopted by trainers who had their first exposure to distance education in the video teleconferencing and audio-graphics boom of the 1980s. Delivering a Web conference is very similar, except that the numbers of trainees at each screen are generally smaller and the audience is distributed more widely. There are a number of vendors that sell Web conferencing services, Centra (http://www.centra.com), WebEx (http://www.webex.com), and Placeware (http://www.placeware.com); these vendors provide training and technical support to customers and participants. All the company has to provide is the subject matter experts who deliver the presentations.

Table 3.6   **Online Training Vendors**

Digital Think—IT, Business skills, Financial Services (http://www.digitalthink.com)

ElementK—IT and Management courses (http://www.elementk.com)

ExecuTrain—IT and Management courses (http://www.executrain.com)

Netg—IT, Professional Development, MBA (http://www.netg.com)

Global Knowledge—IT courses (http://www.gobalknowledge.com)

SkillSoft—IT and Business skills courses (http://www.skillsoft.com)

Ninthhouse—Business skills (http://www.ninthhouse.com)

SmartPlanet—IT courses (http://www.smartplanet.com)

MindLeaders—IT and Business skills courses (http://www.mindleaders.com)

New Horizons—IT, Business skills, Office Productivity (http://www.newhorizons
.com)

Certification and Testing Companies

There are three testing companies that dominate this market. They are: Prometric (acquired from Sylvan Learning Systems by Thomson Corp. of Canada for $775 million cash), CatGlobal (a division of Houghton-Mifflin), and Virtual University Enterprises (VUE, a division of National Computer Systems). Prometric operates about 2,500 testing centers in 140 countries. VUE has nearly 1,500 locations, including 20 in Mexico, 28 in Russia, 23 in Brazil, 19 in South Africa, and 50 in China. CatGlobal offers wholly online computer-based testing from servers in 16 countries. Some vendors have developed their own certification. Learning Tree International (http://www.learningtree.com), for example, will qualify you as a "certified professional" in Cisco Router or Oracle7 Database Administrator on completion of course work (minimum of 22 days and $4,500 for Cisco; 19–24 days and $4500 for Oracle) and passing examinations.

Military Education

As you saw in Chapter 2, the U.S. military has always been a major user of distance education, and it should come as no surprise that it has actively embraced online learning. There have been numerous distance education programs involving interactive satellite television in military settings. The Army Logistics Management College has offered one-way video/two-way audio programs on its Satellite Education Network (SEN) for a number of years to thousands of learners within the armed forces and government agencies. The Air Technology Network (http://atn.afit.edu) is operated by the Air Force Institute of Technology; the program reached over 18,000 students at 69 sites across the United States. The navy operated the CNET Electronic Schoolhouse Network which downlinks classes to major naval training centers around the country. The Government Education and Training Network (http://getn.govdl.org)

provides programs of interest to DOD agencies. The army's TNET system can send and receive training from over 110 other TNET locations and over 300 sites in other military and state networks, including all SEN sites. TNET provides the full transfer of video, audio, and data between all sites and allows tactical communications equipment to be included as part of the video-conferencing infrastructure. The navy's video teletraining (VTT) system used digital video compression to network 11 sites and 16 classrooms; it was available 24 hours a day, and in use for 10 hours a day.

Over \$2 billion have been allocated for distance education in the 1997–2007 period (United States General Accounting Office, National Security and International Affairs Division 1997). Distance education programs in the Department of Defence (DOD) are supported by a vertically and horizontally massive technological infrastructure. For example, the National Guard's Distributive Training Project (DTTP) is comprised of 250 learning centers, with another 150 under development, supporting programs in all 50 states and all U.S. territories. These centers are outfitted with two-way audio and video-conferencing and Internet and Web capabilities (Bond, Poker, and Pugh, 1998, 1999; Bond and Pugh, 2000; Book, 2001). This network was conceived from the beginning as the basis for supporting distance education in the civilian communities, and so the centers are open for adult education and college programs, professional teleconference meetings, and telemedicine in rural and small communities (Donovan, 2000).

In 1997 the army had only 100 military-owned television network sites (United States General Accounting Office, National Security and International Affairs Division, 1997) but plans to have established over 800 high-technology, high-bandwidth distance learning centers linked by a land-based, commercial telecommunications network by 2005. The goal is to have a digital training facility within 50 miles of every soldier's work location (Freeman, 2002). Unique perhaps to the armed services, mobile systems are required to meet the needs of the most geographically isolated military learners. The U.S. Marines and navy have been working on setting up deployable Learning Resource Centers that will deliver courses to sailors in hard-to-reach locations such as on ships in the middle of the ocean (Jones et al., 2003).

One of the most ambitious efforts is the army's virtual university. A \$600 million budget will be spent on a target of having 80,000 soldiers studying via the Army University Access Online, better known by the name of its Internet portal, EArmyU (http://www.earmyu.com) (Kenyon, 2002; Kutner, 2000). Launched in 2001, it provides soldiers with access to over 168 certificate and degree programs offered by 32 institutions, with the most enrollments going to Central Texas College, Troy State University, Thomas Edison State College, Saint Leo University, Rio Salado College, and Embry-Riddle Aeronautical University. The levels of these programs range from certificate, associate, bachelor, and master's degree. All soldiers taking EArmyU courses are eligible for tuition assistance and all course credits earned are transferable across participating institutions. The Army Continuing Education System (ACES) includes a network of learning centers at army bases worldwide. In addition, soldiers receive computer equipment, technology support, Internet accounts, and service through the GALILEO online library at the University System of Georgia. In 2003, nearly 31,000 men and women at more than 20 army bases in the United States and abroad were enrolled in the program. In the beginning, the consortium of institutions that provided courses was managed by a noneducational corporation, the Price-Waterhouse Coopers consulting firm, on a $359 million multiyear contract. Online tutoring was provided through Smarthinking, a specialist company hired by Price-Waterhouse Coopers.

In November 2000, the U.S. Navy entered into an agreement with 16 institutions to provide a variety of associate and bachelor's degree programs. Because of the mobile lifestyle of sailors, the navy wanted institutions to provide courses through various technologies and not only online. The same types of degrees are offered by several of the cooperating institutions, thereby providing sailors with a choice of both program and institution. Guidance in the selection process is given by navy advisers and the institutions' representatives. Institutions selected at the first stage of the navy program included: Dallas County Community College District, George Washington University, University of Maryland University College, City University (Renton, Washington), Coastline Community College, Embry-Riddle Aeronautical University, Empire State University, Florida Community College, Florida State University, Fort Hays State University (Kansas), Old Dominion University, Rogers State University (Oklahoma), Thomas Edison State College, Troy State University, and Vincennes University (Indiana) (Carr, 2000).

The Air Force Institute for Advanced Distributed Learning (AFIADL), a merger of the Air Force Distance Learning Office with the Extension Course Institute, provides training and general educational programs for the Air Force, Air National Guard, and Air Force Reserve. The Institute also provides career development courses to personnel throughout the Department of Defense and to civil service employees in other federal agencies. AFIADL offers a resident and a nonresident curriculum. The nonresident curriculum covers over 400 courses in three categories: professional military education courses, specialized courses and career development courses. Specialized and career development courses are available on CD-ROM or computer-based instruction, in such subjects as: weather, aircrew operations, medical, nursing, command control systems operations, communications-electronics systems, and information management (http://www.au.af.mil/au/schools/afiadl.html).

Other military schools that are developing their own distance education programs include the Army National Guard (http://www.arng.army.mil), the Defense Acquisitions University (http://www.dau.mil), and the Air University (http://www.au.af.mil/au). For further information, see Westfall (2003) in regard to the air force; Freeman (2003) in regard to the army; and Jones, Blevins, Mally, and Munroe (2003) in regard to the U.S. Marines. You can find out more about the army's distance learning program at http://www.tadlp.monroe.army.mil, the U.S. Marines' at http://www.tecom.usmc.mil/dlc, the navy's at http://www.navylearning.navy.mil, and air force's at https://afvec.langley.af.mil.

Viewpoint: Chere Campbell Gibson

Technology has brought us access to information to a degree unheard of in the past. As I reflect on the future of teaching and learning with technology and distance education, I see a decrease in the presentation of content and an increase emphasis on the learning process. Learning through authentic problem solving, inquiry-based learning and context-based problem posing will be accentuated at all levels of education. Learners will be challenged to work on increasingly more complex problems as well as to engage in problem identification itself. Working with others, both within disciplines and across disciplines in interdisciplinary problem solving teams, will be encouraged to help learners broaden their repertoire of skills to critically assess information and create knowledge, as well as apply it. I truly believe the future will focus on the use of the available tools and information for personal, organizational and community growth. Teaching content becomes less relevant—tool mastery, mastery of the processes of learning, both alone and with others, working within and across disciplines for problem solution, as well as problem identification and critical assessment of resources, will come to the fore. (I hope!)

SOURCE: Chere Campbell Gibson, University of Wisconsin-Madison

Course Sharing Initiatives

There have been a number of initiatives aimed at sharing in the distribution of Web-based materials. One of the earliest was the World Lecture Hall created by the University of Texas, Austin, in 1993 (http://www.utexas.edu/world/lecture), which has a database listing thousands of courses in over 70 subjects. In 1997, MERLOT (Multimedia Educational Resource for Learning and Online Teaching) (http://www.merlot.org) was established by the California State University system and now comprises 15 other partner institutions. The MERLOT database includes thousands of courses in seven subject areas. All courses are peer reviewed and reviewer's ratings and comments can be viewed with the course description. The Maricopa Learning Exchange (http://www.mcli.dist.maricopa.edu/mlx/index.php) is another database of Web-based courses aimed at the needs of community college students.

One of the most talked about efforts at course sharing has been the Massachusetts Institute of Technology (MIT) open courseware project—an effort to make MIT course materials available free to the public (http://ocw.mit.edu). At the time of its official launch in September 2003, materials related to more than 100 courses from 27 departments were available. The goal is to have almost all of the thousands of courses offered by MIT online by 2007. For each course, the syllabus, readings, lecture notes, schedule, assignments, exams, and study materials are provided. The considerable discussion that the project has provoked within the higher education world highlights the issue of product versus *process* in higher education, (i.e., although it appears that MIT has given away valuable "intellectual property," it really has not since the educational process requires a resource more valuable than readings and lecture notes. This is the value added by the instructor and involvement in interaction with peers).

Summary

As this chapter illustrates, there are many forms of distance education in the United States. Table 3.7 summarizes the main characteristics of the four major approaches discussed in terms of degree of interaction (contact between faculty and students), quality of production (a result of time and money invested in program design, use of multimedia, etc.), degree of flexibility (i.e., enrollment and completion of courses), and level of target population.

- The two types of correspondence courses (home study and independent study) differ in all attributes. Home study schools primarily offer print-based courses in vocational subjects with low to moderate production quality, maximum scheduling flexibility, and minimum interaction with instructors and other students. Independent study programs provide university courses with a moderate degree of production quality, interaction with instructors, and moderate flexibility (enrollment and completion dates may be scheduled).

Table 3.7   Comparison of Distance Education Approaches

	Degree of interaction/ Quality of production	Degree of flexibility	Target population
Home study	Minimal Low–Moderate	High	Vocational and technical; associate degree
Independent study	Moderate Moderate	Moderate	University: undergraduate, some graduate and continuing education also noncredit
Open universities	High High	Moderate	University: undergraduate, some graduate and continuing education also noncredit
Interactive	Low–Moderate	Low	K–12, university, corporate and military
Television	Low		
Internet/online learning	High Low–moderate	High	K–12, university, corporate, military

- Open university programs typically offer university courses with a very high level of production quality and interaction, and a moderate degree of flexibility.

- Interactive television consortia provide a range of "talking head" programs with a low level of flexibility (due to scheduling) and with levels of interaction that can range from low (large numbers in many sites) to moderate (small numbers in few sites).

- Internet/online learning is used extensively for higher education and for corporate training, and to a lesser extent at the K–12 level. It offers a high level of interaction and high degree of flexibility but low to moderate quality in production, particularly regarding the quality of video and audio components.

Questions for Discussion or Further Study

1. Select a specific school, college, company, or other organization that you are interested in and research what they are doing in distance education or training. How does it compare to similar institutions described in this chapter?

2. Look at Table 3.2 and discuss the data about delivery by print compared to online delivery. Does this surprise you, and if so, why?

3. "Some of the most talked about virtual universities quickly passed away." Discuss this. Check out some of the institutions mentioned in this chapter. How are they doing?

4. Look at Table 3.7 and discuss what would be needed to raise each of the characteristics there to the "High" level. What would be the effects for the institution of making such changes?

5. Discuss Chere Campbell Gibson's view of future developments.

CHAPTER **4**

Technologies and Media

In previous chapters we have already mentioned most of the communications technologies and the media used in distance education. In this chapter we will discuss them a bit more, and give some special attention to their pedagogical characteristics. This is a subject that is also relevant in the chapter that follows, too, where we discuss course design and development. In a total systems approach, designers try to use a rich combination of all the media, delivered by the most convenient technologies, so that the learners benefit from the pedagogical strengths of each of them.

Because communication is so central to distance education, every student and practitioner needs to know a little about each of the technologies, and also the media they deliver. It is definitely not necessary to have an expert's knowledge about how the technologies work, or be able to fix them if they go wrong. As distance educators, we depend on expert computer programmers, camera persons, engineers, and producers to see that the technologies that will carry our teaching work the way they are supposed to work. We need to know enough about them to be able to ask intelligent questions, make suggestions, know when something isn't working as it should, and above all, know the limits and the potential of each of the technologies. Some of the questions we need to have in mind when we think about technology and media are:

1. What are the characteristics of different communication technologies and media, and how can they be used in distance education?

2. Which communications' media and technologies are the best for a given subject or student group?

3. How can media and technologies be combined for maximum effectiveness?

You should keep these questions in mind as we now review each of the main technologies; that is, print, recorded audio and video, interactive audio and video, and Internet technologies.

Print

Text is undoubtedly the most common medium used in distance education, and in spite of the growth of online communication that uses text, most text is still delivered in print. Print takes various forms, including textbooks, books that reproduce articles or chapters, manuals, course notes, and study guides. Print materials include highly expensive art books or encyclopedias but also very inexpensive materials. They can be distributed easily via the public mail or private delivery services. The creative skills of writing and illustration, as well as the production capabilities of printing or duplication, are widely available. On the consumer side, students and teachers are very familiar with printed materials, and are likely to have a good understanding of how to manipulate them and make the most of them. Furthermore, print materials are highly portable, and they do not easily deteriorate or break, which makes them dependable and convenient to use.

In distance education, instruction that is based mainly on printed text is called correspondence study (or as we saw in Chapter 2, home study or independent study). The most basic characteristic of correspondence study is that it is not only the presentation of information by the teacher that is done in print. The interaction is by the medium of text as well, though it is likely to be typed or even handwritten rather than printed. This interaction is always individual and private. It can allow students to study at their own pace and in their own time. The interaction by mail is, of course, slow, but in fact this appeals to more reflective learners, and it makes print the technology of choice for many adult students. Besides correspondence instruction, almost all distance education courses use print in some form, regardless of what other technology they employ. The most common and most important form of print used in such courses is the study guide.

Study Guides

Study guides can present the organization and structure for the course, even when it is delivered primarily by another technology. Courses that use video or other electronic technologies substantially are usually built around a printed students' guide and a printed instructors' guide. Course designers pay a great deal of attention to the printed study guides since they form the anchor for the other technologies. Although the study guide is likely to present subject matter, it should do more than this. It should also contain directions and guidance for the students in their study of the subject matter, and provide a structure for interaction between learners and instructors, whether by correspondence or some other technology. There is no technology better, for example, than the study guide for communicating the instructors' goals and objectives and their general approach and philosophy about the subject. Why? Because these are matters that the learners need to review quite frequently, and when they do so they need to be able to reflect, to analyze, and to apply to their own circumstances what is being communicated there. Other technologies present information in a more fleeting and impressionistic way, which is not suited to these processes. The study guide may give the instructor's opinions and advice concerning pathways through the subject; for example, by suggesting how much time to spend on a particular topic or exercise. As every teacher knows, the logical order or structure in the content of any field is not necessarily the appropriate psychological order for its study. Textbooks are invariably designed to comply with the logic and structure of the discipline. The author of the study guide, however, can break free from the structure of the content and the structure of the textbook and make a structure that in their (the designers') view will best help the student to master the content. The style in which the author writes the study guide should reflect the author's relationship to his or her students. It is inevitably more impersonal than a small face-to-face tutorial, or the interaction in writing between correspondence instructors and individual students, but it should come across as friendly, encouraging, and supportive. This is not an academic paper, nor a learned text, but a form of *teaching*. It should be apparent that some of these characteristics of teaching by text in print should also apply in teaching by text online. More will be said about the design of study guides in Chapter 5.

Newspapers and Newsletters

One way of using print for training in the workplace is through the publication of newsletters. These can carry a sequence of articles on employment-related issues such as good health and safety practices. There have been occasional experiments in creating a structured course around newsletters, newspapers, or magazines. For example, the School of Education at the University of Connecticut teamed up with *Technology & Learning* magazine to offer a professional development course for teachers about technology in schools. Participants established their own local learning groups consisting of at least three people with a designated leader. Course activities were based upon articles in each issue of the magazine and each group met monthly to discuss its members' work. The use of e-mail as a means of distributing newsletters has made this form of disseminating information more popular (perhaps to the annoyance of some).

Preparation Time and Impact of Electronic Publishing

The quality of print materials can vary considerably, and there is usually a relationship between quality and the time taken in designing the materials. The kinds of study guides used in large-scale distance education courses offered by open universities and telecourse producers, which involve the work of large design teams, may take many months or even years to develop. Materials must be collected from subject matter experts and written and edited through several drafts, graphics must be created, copyright releases must be obtained, designs must be tested out, and so on.

Electronic publishing technology has had a tremendous impact on the speed of producing print materials. Before the advent of personal computers, an author's manuscript was typeset, meaning that a master copy of the page was created, and printing plates were made. This process required the work of typesetters, illustrators, and design and layout artists. Publishing in this way usually took several months, and printing took several weeks, if not months, from the time of handing over the manuscript. When the process is done electronically, text, illustrations, diagrams, and pictures can all be created and revised much faster and, then, either sent to a printer, or printed on a laser printer. Such "desktop publishing" using word processing and page-layout software makes it possible for anyone with a personal computer to produce reasonably good print materials. Documents can be transmitted online and file-sharing technologies make it easy for authors and editors to interact with each other. It is now technically very simple to deliver the text materials directly to the student in online form, eliminating the need for print entirely. However, to date, most people prefer to read large amounts of information in printed format rather than on a computer display. Desktop publishing also makes it possible to produce small quantities of documents for courses with limited enrollments or in which the subject changes a lot. Previously this was uneconomical.

The emergence of the Web and Web page creation software has made electronic production and distribution of documents even easier. Once a document has been created in a suitable Web format (i.e., HTML or XML), it can be uploaded to a file server and becomes immediately available for viewing by anyone in the world who has an Internet connection and a Web browser. Furthermore, it is relatively easy and inexpensive to include photographs and other graphics in documents. However, Web documents are designed primarily for viewing on the screen and often produce poor quality printed documents. So, although the Web has facilitated print materials in some ways, in others it has been a hindrance.

Limitations of Print

Print media may have some limitations, as do other media, but most can be overcome through good design decisions. On the side of the learner, it would seem that the ability to read and write would be an essential prerequisite for using print. However, there have even been successful correspondence courses for illiterate farmers in third world countries, in which communication has not been primarily through text but through drawings, assisted by literate village leaders who have been supplied with study guides written at a very basic level.

The main point about print is that if it is designed at the correct level, most people, if they have the motivation, can learn from it. Motivation is a more critical variable than the medium, and its absence may pose a serious limitation on the effectiveness of the medium, since print probably requires more self-motivated attention than, for example, moving pictures on television. A more serious problem with text than learners' low levels of intrinsic motivation is the effect of the low quality of many textual materials that cause many students to become demotivated. Many study guides and other printed materials are prepared too cheaply and too carelessly as add-ons to an electronically transmitted program, with the result that they are unattractive and uninteresting. These shortcomings are not limitations of the printed technologies *per se,* but rather the way educators use them.

Audio and Video Media

With the widespread availability of audio and video cassette players (VCRs) in the 1970s and 1980s, both technologies became very convenient and cost-effective ways to disseminate instructional materials. Audiocassette players were highly portable and allowed people to study where they wish. The number of people having VCRs in their homes grew during the 1980s, making home study with videotape materials quite feasible. Furthermore, audio and video-cassettes were easy and inexpensive to distribute via mail or delivery services.

At the UK Open University, the introduction of audiocassettes was found, to the surprise of researchers, to be the most important technological innovation in its first 20 years, in terms of the numbers of students and courses affected and the impact on learning. The Open University mailed more than 750,000 hours of audiocassette teaching material, making audio delivered on cassette the most widely used medium after printed text (Bates, 1990, p. 101).

By the late 1990s, players of compact discs (CDs) and digital video discs (DVDs) became the dominant technologies for distributing recorded audio and video programs and proved to be more durable and cost-effective than cassettes. Similarly "CD-Read Only Mode" (CD-ROM) discs allowed the distribution of computer-based learning programs incorporating audiovisual components. Because these are digital recordings, it is possible to randomly access material anywhere on the disc, which is much more user friendly than having to rewind a tape.

The main problem with the use of audio and video media in distance education is that it requires creativity and professional expertise to make good quality programs, and creativity costs more time and money than most institutions are willing to spend. Sadly, the result is that these media are badly underused, quite often being limited to carrying a lecture, which is a very poor use of such potentially rich resources. In a good delivery system, such direct transmission of information would be done with print technology. Some of the ways that recorded audio can be used include:

- talking students through parts of the textual material; for example, analyzing the argument in an article, or explaining formulae and equations

- talking about real objects that the student holds for observation; for example, rock samples, reproductions of paintings, materials used in a home experiment
- talking students through manipulating procedures such as a computer operation, so that their hands are free for the practical work
- listening to human interactions; for example, decision making in a business course or conduct of meetings, with the text explaining what is happening on the tape
- collecting the views and experiences of specialists, experts, or personal experiences of famous people
- providing examples of sounds that are integral to the learning objectives, such as music in a music course, a Shakespeare soliloquy, or examples of conversation in a foreign language course
- providing access to sounds of natural phenomena such as a volcanic eruption or a space shot, or special events such as the inauguration of a president
- dramatization of historical events

Video would also be suitable for most of these purposes. Video is a powerful medium for capturing and holding attention and for conveying impressions. Because of its capability to show people interacting, video is a good medium for teaching interpersonal skills. It is also a good medium for teaching any kind of procedure since it can show the sequence of actions involved; it can show close-ups, slow or accelerated motion, multiple perspectives, and so on. Both audio and video can be used to present the views of experts, which increase the credibility and interest of the materials. Audio and video are also especially effective at conveying attitudinal or emotional aspects of a subject. Spitzer, Bauwens, and Quast (1989); McMahill (1993); and Stone (1988) discuss the effects of using video in college-level distance learning.

Many organizations have created distance learning programs based primarily on recorded videotapes with a wide variety of "production values" (i.e., production quality). For example, the Association for Media-Based Continuing Education for Engineers (http://www.amcee.org) offers hundreds of engineering courses, each course consisting of a set of low-production value videotaped lectures. Most of the PBS/CPB "telecourses" are available in videotape format (Levine, 1992) and are usually of high production value. Many large corporations provide much of their employee and customer training in the form of videotape materials.

Production

Producing audio or video materials is generally more expensive than creating printed materials because it involves specialized skills not only of production but also engineering. There are very few subjects for which either a script or at least a story-board outline of what is to be recorded would not be needed. Even with modern digital tape recorders and camcorders, experienced technicians are needed to obtain dependably good quality audio or video reproduction. Professional talent such as an announcer or actors may be needed. One of the most critical parts of every production is the selection of what content to include and what to exclude, which means using expert editors and editing facilities and equipment. Although these considerations are not obstacles to the production of audio/visual materials, they do indicate why it is important and necessary to plan the use of the time and money required to create such materials.

The current generation of digital audio and video editing software for personal computers has proven to be both a blessing and to some extent a bane for distance education. On the one hand it has made it possible for almost anyone to produce audiovisual materials (analogous to the impact of desktop publishing on print production). These programs make it possible to do special effects and sequences that previously required very expensive equipment. Furthermore they make it relatively easy to put audio and video directly onto CD-ROMs or upload it to the Web and hence distribute it inexpensively. The drawback to this technical freedom is a plethora of extremely amateurish home movie level of production. There are very few subject specialists who have the time and knowledge to be excellent producers as well, so in general it is best to leave those technical aspects of making audio and video materials to people who have invested their careers in acquiring and maintaining professional skills.

Radio and Television

As we saw in Chapter 2, broadcasting audio and video by radio and television has been used for educational purposes for many years. With the emergence of satellite networks, teaching by television became very popular at all levels of education.

We need to keep in mind the distinction between general broadcast television; that is to say, what is available to any member of the public who has a television receiver, and what is sometimes referred to as "narrowcast" television, which are programs transmitted by private channels such as the National University Teleconference Network, or business TV channels. These programs can only be received by sites that have paid a license fee, or are otherwise authorized to receive them. Among other differences, programs for general broadcasting are usually of much higher production value, with more scripting and studio production, location shots, drama, music, and editing.

Main Strengths and Uses of Broadcasting

Both broadcast and narrowcast radio and television have the attraction of "immediacy." They can be used to give up-to-the-minute reports about the subject matter of a course. They can be used for talks, phone-ins, and panel discussions. When programs are transmitted in association with a study guide and written assignments, they help keep students on track and give a comforting sense of the wholeness of the course. They may be designed to give distant learners a perception that they are part of a community of people involved in the same issues. Since broadcast programs can be seen and heard by the general public, they are a powerful recruiting instrument, since potential students can see or hear the kind of subjects that are discussed in the courses. Broadcasting, especially television, has a certain prestige that helps create a positive image of the distance teaching institution in the minds of the general public.

Radio has the advantages of being a very flexible medium, allowing for a report from anywhere in the world and allowing swift updating of material at low technical costs. By comparison, television is much more expensive and it is usually better to reserve this technology to deliver content that has a long "shelf-life."

Four key principles to guide the decision to use broadcast television have been described by a senior producer at the BBC/Open University Production Centre in the United Kingdom. They are:

1. *Integration.* The material has to be closely tied to the rest of the course. Radcliff (1990) writes: "Unless it is actually serving very specific teaching needs, however attractive and well made it is, it will not be worth spending money on it, so it has to be closely integrated with the rest of the course material, including the assessment system" (p. 116).

2. *Specialization.* It is important to use television *only* for what it can do best and not what can be done just as well—and therefore more cheaply—in print or other technology.

3. *Quality.* Broadcast programs should be produced with the highest quality production standards, and then have a good shelf life to recover the costs. This means they should last for several years and can be used many times over. Obviously this means making careful decisions about the content of a program, and putting into print, or audio content that which will not last long.

4. *Cost effectiveness.* Programs should only be made where they are pedagogically justified, and can be used often enough with sufficient numbers of students to make them cost efficient (Radcliff, 1990).

Instructional Television Fixed Service (ITFS)

ITFS (http://www.itfs.org) uses microwave transmission (having a range of about 25 miles) and special antennas to receive the signal. Because ITFS is a relatively inexpensive technology, it became a popular form of transmission of teaching over small areas. An ITFS studio is similar to a general broadcasting studio, though perhaps smaller and less complex. A network of receive-sites at schools, training centers, or off-campus classrooms is established where students meet to take rather conventionally taught classes. Usually, a telephone bridge is used so that students can have audio contact with the instructor during the program to ask or answer questions. In some cases, the ITFS transmission feeds into a cable system which redistributes the programs to people at

Hawaii: Instructional Television across the Islands

Hawaii presents a good case study of broadcast and narrowcast distance education as technology links the five major islands that comprise the state. This is
accomplished by the Hawaii Interactive Television System (HITS), a partnership
of the Hawaii Department of Education, the University of Hawaii, and the Hawaii
Public Broadcasting Authority (KHET). It was approved and funded by the state
legislature in 1984 ($2.5 million) and began full-scale operation in 1990. HITS is
an interactive closed-circuit television network that consists of four outgoing
channels from Oahu to each of the other islands and a single channel from each
island back to Oahu. The system uses point-to-point microwave, ITFS, cable, and
satellite links to connect classrooms on each of the university's campuses; and
the KHET complex at the main campus on Oahu (see Figure 4.1).

University classes are broadcast live to the campuses on other islands and
directly to homes when cable is used. The University has responsibility for programming, the Hawaii Public Broadcasting authority for assuring reliable television transmission, and the State for installing and maintaining all transmission

Figure 4.1   HITS State Network

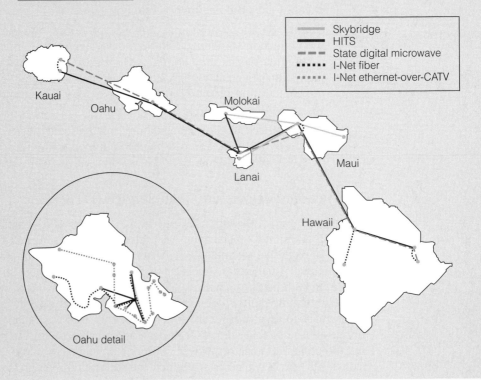

equipment. Besides producing its own programs, the University also supports the production of classes for the Department of Education, including in-service training for teachers. In addition, HITS is connected to Skybridge, a two-way video network operated by the Maui Community College for educational broadcasting to residents of Maui. The UH-Manoa campus has a Ku-band satellite uplink that allows it to deliver live video programs to the continental United States. Although each UH campus manages local programming, the Office of Information Technology (OIT) provides coordination for all system-wide programs and liaison with the Hawaii Public Broadcasting Authority and the Department of Education. Each semester, OIT prepares a master ITV schedule which is based upon user demand, state needs, the willingness and capability of university departments to deliver courses, and the ability of campuses to support ITV courses.

The successful use of ITV has provided access for students to a wide curriculum and allowed for intercampus collaborations. Specialized courses are no longer cancelled due to low enrollments (e.g., students across the UH system enroll in Chinese 201 and 202, Hawaiian 301 and 401). Faculty can collaborate on teaching (i.e., one professor teaches the lecture portion of chemistry by television while faculty on other campuses facilitate laboratory sections). Other resources are being shared across the UH system (e.g., an Employment Training Center provides skills training programs by television supported locally by Learning Assistance Centers).

SOURCE: *Ed* Vol. 6. (December 1992 issue)
For more information, visit: http://www.hawaii.edu/its/.

home or in their offices. Being an over-the-air transmission technology, ITFS suffers the same problems of frequency crowding and interference as other over-the-air systems. ITFS can communicate programs recorded from, or fed from, a satellite downlink. ITFS services can be purchased from a number of providers.

Cable Television (CATV)

Cable television (CATV) involves the distribution of television signals through a coaxial or fiber optic cable connected directly to the viewer's television set. Distance education programming is usually provided by local schools and colleges; it is possible to deliver national programs via cable television. For example, in the 1980s Mind Extension University offered undergraduate and graduate programs on over 200 cable affiliates across the United States. Students watched the programs at home and used the telephone to call in questions or comments. CATV is no longer just coaxial cable, since most systems have been converted to fiber-optic cable, allowing the transmission of data as well as video. Many schools, companies, and colleges have closed-circuit systems in their facilities which are used to distribute internally produced programs or outside broadcasts (Holmes and Branch, 1994).

Direct Broadcast Satellites (DBS)

Direct Broadcast Satellites (DBS) use a small and inexpensive satellite dish (about 1–2 foot in diameter) that makes it feasible for students to directly receive programs at their home or office. DBS technology is widely used in the United States for television reception (e.g., DIRECTV and DISH Network). Because of its cost-effectiveness, it has been suggested that this technology could replace other methods of video broadcast and narrowcasting. To illustrate, at the time of writing, the installment of a DISH Network satellite dish and receiver costs about $200 to $300. Some receiver models that automatically program the video cassette recorder (VCR) cost around $400. The DISH Network basic service subscription fee for the educational package starts at $22.99 per month. After subscription to EchoStar through a DISH network, students can receive class broadcasts on their televisions at home (see http:// distance.nau.edu/Services/methods.aspx and http://www.universityhouse .nau.edu).

Streaming Video

With the emergence of the World Wide Web (WWW), a new form of video distribution called streaming video became possible. This involves putting video into digital format and then allowing people to download it in compressed form from a Web server. Depending upon the connection speed of the user and the capabilities of their personal computer, it may be possible to play video clips at near real-time speed (i.e., 30 frames/second).

A number of institutions now use streaming video to provide video-based instruction. The Stanford Center for Professional Development uses streaming video to deliver its online courses—which were previously distributed in videotape and broadcast form. The Illinois Institute of Technology uses streaming video in its School of Law for distance learning classes. Most providers of on-line courses add at least an introductory clip that is accessible by students having access to Internet by cable or a relatively fast modem. For some examples of streaming media in university courses, see http://pocahontus.doit .wisc.edu/index.html

Teleconferencing

Teleconferencing for distance education describes instruction by means of some form of interactive telecommunications technology. There are four different types of such technology, each giving a different form of teleconferencing: audio, audio-graphics, video, and computer (Web based).

Audio-Conferencing

Participants in an audio-conference are connected by telephone lines. Individual participants can use their regular telephones, while groups can use a speakerphone or specially designed kits of speakers and table-top microphones. For a significant number of participants to interact with each other, it is desirable to use a "bridge" that connects lines automatically. The bridge may be provided by a telephone company, or the organization conducting the teleconference might purchase its own. The University of Wisconsin-Madison Extension has made the most extensive use of audio-conferencing. In 1966, it created the Education Telephone Network (ETN) which, at its peak in the 1980s, served 32,000 students and connected over 200 sites in 100 towns and cities across Wisconsin. Parker (1984) described some of the technical and educational issues associated with audio-conferencing. Garrison (1990) examined its benefits and effectiveness. Schaffer (1990) discussed faculty training and course design based on experiences at the University of Wyoming. Sponder (1990) discussed the use of audio-conferencing in rural Alaska with particular focus on its use by Native American students. Cookson, Quigley, and Borland (1994) surveyed the policies and practices associated with the use of audio-conferencing for graduate instruction at seven major universities. The technology remains available but neglected by educators who are locked into a concept of distance education that is entirely dependent on computer-based technology. It should be noted that a limited form of audio-conferencing is possible through that technology also. Educators who study the substantial literature about audio-conferencing will become aware of many possibilities for on-line audio-conferencing as well as the traditional form.

Audio-Graphics

Audio-graphics technology adds visual images to audio, also transmitted over telephone lines. There are several computer-based systems that allow the transmission of graphics and data. Electronic blackboards can be used also; they transmit anything written or drawn at one site to television monitors or visual display units at the others. Each site sees anything drawn on the computer screen (using a graphics tablet) as well as hearing the audio. Some of these systems include a digitizing camera that produces an image of anything placed in front of it, including drawings, objects, and people's faces. Audio-graphics systems are well-suited to courses that require still images or notational information (e.g., formula, equations). For this reason, they have been especially popular in the teaching of science and engineering classes. McGreal (1993) describes an interesting application of a computer-based audio-graphics system in Ontario secondary schools. Representatives of museums and galleries take students on "electronic tours" of their institutions by showing photographic slides that have been digitized as computer graphics. In addition to asking questions at any time, students can point to things on the screen that they want to know more about. Gilcher and Johnstone (1989) conducted a critical analysis of the use of audio-graphic systems at nine different educational institutions and provide guidelines for successful projects. Different aspects of audio-graphics are discussed by Gardner, Rudolph, and Della-Piana (1987); Gunawardena (1992); Idrus (1992); Knapczyk (1990); and Smith (1992).

As noted with regard to audio-conferencing, many audio-graphic applications now use Web conferencing systems (as discussed later in this chapter).

Desktop Video-Conferencing

The use of desktop video-conferencing and Internet Video Collaboration is becoming increasingly important. Desktop video systems offer video teleconferencing capabilities as well as multipoint-shared software tele-collaboration. Students at multiple sites can not only see and hear each other, but they can simultaneously collaborate on the same software application. The International Telecommunications Union (ITU) standards for data tele-collaboration and interoperability among switched digital networks H.320, LAN/WAN environments H.323, and analog voice networks H.324 have dramatically accelerated the deployment of innovative distance learning solutions.

As networks migrate to even higher bandwidth capacity, educators will experience superior audio and video quality and multimedia capabilities that are desirable for many distance learning solutions. Fiber-optic backbone networks are often designed in private networks for increased throughput, reliability and overall quality. With the deployment of public Asynchronous Transfer Mode (ATM) networks and Education Service Provider (ESP) networks, many of today's distance learning systems will migrate to broadband ATM networks.

With desktop video conferencing and Internet Video Collaboration the instructor's desktop computer and the participants' desktop computers become learning tools. As with group video conferencing, there are some specific guidelines for the workspace which will enhance the effectiveness of the technology to facilitate learning programs. We learned to provide enough workspace around the computer and display, avoid strong back lighting such as facing the camera

Video-Conferencing

As we discussed in Chapter 3, video-conferencing—sometimes called Interactive Television (ITV)—can be an excellent technology for delivering distance education programs. Video-conferencing permits two-way transmission of televised images via satellite or cable. One version, slow-scan video transmits a fresh picture every 20–30 seconds using standard telephone lines, making it as cost-effective as audio or audio-graphics conferencing. Compressed video is a technology that provides full-motion (30 frames per second) pictures, though with a low resolution. It requires use of a device called a codec (compression decoder) by both transmitting site and receivers. The codec is a technology that takes analog signals, compresses and digitizes them, and transmits them over digital phone lines. Other types of equipment, such as television monitors, video cassette recorders/players, microphones, cameras, and computers are also used.

These technologies result in three main types of video-conferencing:

1. Small room conferences are designed primarily for groups of no more than about 12 participants at any site.

towards a window or other strong light source, avoid aiming the camera at ceiling lights, and if possible, use only cool white (3200 degree Kelvin) fluorescent or white incandescent lights. Clear incandescent or older fluorescent lights tend to cause yellowish video images.

The number of participants sharing a desktop video PC should be no more than two or three at each location. Beyond that number, it is too hard for individuals to see or be seen on the computer monitor. A larger monitor can be attached to the computers, but generally that reduces the quality of the live video image. One of the most important items of internet video collaboration is the "Share Application." The Share Application enables the instructor and the participants to share a software program and work in the same documents. What is critical is the shared application can create real-time interactive learning activities from brainstorming to software programming applications. The learners can participate together to design reports, graphs or charts, or collaborate on research projects all at a distance. If used effectively, Internet video collaboration shared applications can dramatically enhance collaborative learning goals in a distance learning environment.

The physical learning environment and the pedagogical skills employed by the instructor are both critically important in the planning of distance learning programs. Having the right video teleconferencing technology in place is only half the story; skillfully presenting a relevant learning experience that is well organized, appropriate to the learning context, and very interactive is essential to enable the learners to achieve their goals and expected outcomes.

SOURCE: Chute, 2003. Reprinted with permission from Lawrence Erlbaum Associates, Inc. and the author.

2. Classroom conferences using compressed video enable large groups to see and be seen on classroom monitors.

3. Desktop conferences use personal computers linked by computer video-conferencing software and are best for one-to-one interaction. Telephone companies also sell "videophones" that can also be used for one-to-one interaction.

The experience for the student and the performance of the instructor are significantly different in each of these structures, even though they are all referred to as video-conferencing.

The initial cost of classroom video teleconferencing equipment and leasing the lines to transmit conferences may be prohibitive for some organizations, compatibility of different methods of compression technology might cause some problems, and the skills needed to perform on ITV for large audiences might challenge instructors. Nevertheless, students and instructors generally like distance education courses delivered by video-conferencing (see Rifkind, 1992).

Teleconferencing for Medical Education

Although teleconferencing has been employed in all disciplines and subject domains, it has been particularly popular in the health care field as a means of providing continuing medical education. Almost all health care professionals are required to take courses regularly to stay up-to-date with new developments in medicine, and medical personnel are widely scattered around any state so that it is difficult to organize face-to-face classes for most of them. Furthermore, expertise on certain diseases or treatments is very scarce; teleconferencing can be used to disseminate such expertise to a wide audience in a timely manner. The use of video-conferencing is especially valuable because it allows new medical procedures and equipment to be demonstrated. Anderson (1987) provides the historical background to the use of video teleconferencing in the health care industry. Hartigan and St. John (1989) discuss the use of video teleconferencing to provide AIDS training in third world countries. Kuramoto (1984) and Major and Shane (1992) describe the use of video teleconferencing for nursing education.

Emerging multimedia and network technologies have increased the role of distance education in the health-care domain. An example is The Georgia Statewide Academic and Medical System (http://www.gcsu.edu/OIIT /GSAMS)—a video-conferencing system that connects approximately 59 different health-care sites in the state for medical education and telemedicine as well as another 300 participating sites. For more details about distance education in the health care domain, see Moore and Savrock (2001). For research oriented discussions of video-conferencing technology, see Chute (2003) and Wisher and Curnow (2003).

Computer-Based Learning

Traditionally, computer-based learning refers to self-managed study programs that the student uses alone when working on a personal computer, the instructional program provided on a disk, and nowadays on a CD-ROM (see Cannings and Finkel, 1993; Kearsley, Hunter, and Furlong, 1992). This contrasts with computer conferencing or Web-based learning in which the student interacts with the instructor and other students via a network. The main strength of computer-based instruction is that it can provide a high quality opportunity for the student to interact with subject matter under his or her complete control. Older programs relied heavily on simple question and answer formats and these materials were not very stimulating. Newer designs embody more sophisticated teaching strategies involving inquiry methods, simulations, and games. (see Dodge, 1995; Palloff and Pratt, 1999; Schank, 1997). In addition, new methods for organizing information using hypertext and hypermedia provide more powerful learning options.

Computer Conferencing

Computer conferencing allows students and instructors to interact, either asynchronously or in real time using personal computers to deliver a variety of text, voice, visuals, shared applications, and video. The simplest and oldest forms of synchronous computer conferencing are so-called "chat" systems, which allow people to interact by typing messages to each other. Since everyone in the class sees all the messages, a chat session is like a multiperson conversation, but in text form. Although chat systems are not a particularly powerful tool for online classes, they do allow "Question and Answer" sessions and a chance for participants to complement the more useful asynchronous communications on forums and bulletin boards with the experience of exchanging ideas spontaneously. The primary role of the instructor in a chat session is to act as a "host" (also referred to as a moderator or facilitator) to keep the discussion focused on a particular topic or learning activity. We will discuss strategies for effective chat sessions in Chapter 6.

Voice interaction in a computer conference that is designed for students in groups has usually been accomplished using a telephone bridge—as we described it for the audio-conference. This requires two separate phone lines—one for the voice connection and one for the computer as we described for audio-graphics systems. However, some systems use IP (Internet Protocol) voice technology, which means the audio capabilities of the computer are used—and only one phone line is used for both voice and data. The quality and reliability of Voice IP is often not as good as using telephone transmission and although it might work for small numbers of individual students, it is currently (in 2004) not very satisfactory for groups of students. One golden rule for teaching by any technology is that the technology *must* be reliable and the sound quality must be good enough not to interfere with the message. Instructors should *not* use a technology unless these characteristics are assured.

In computer conferencing, visuals are often in the form of PowerPoint slides that have been prepared offline and loaded into the conferencing computer system, although some software allows graphics to be created within the system. Shared whiteboards allow participants to enter information on the current screen and see the results in real time. This is very useful for an instructor who wants to ask a question and see the responses from all participants immediately. The shared application capability allows a participant to let all other participants see whatever application is running on his or her system. For example, a person could present a spreadsheet or data analysis program while providing an oral explanation. Video transmission is another option with some systems—anyone with a machine equipped with a digital camera can transmit (but just one image at a time and of very limited quality).

Computer conferencing has become popular for corporate training since it does not require a significant change in teaching methodology or investment in special technology. Training sessions are scheduled and the instructor makes a presentation. The only new factor is that the presentation is delivered electronically and all participants are located remotely. However, to be effective, the instructor has to know how to make the session interactive (a subject discussed further in Chapter 6).

For more about the use of computer conferencing to provide synchronous training, see Barron (2000) or Hofmann (2000).

Web-Based Learning Systems

With the emergence of the Web in the late 1990s, a new form of computer-based learning became possible. As explained in Chapter 3, Web-based instruction became very popular in higher education, especially for graduate programs. Mainly this is because it accommodates the "lone instructor" type of distance teaching, but its adoption has also been driven by the marketing of integrated learning systems such as Blackboard, WebCT, FirstClass, eClassroom, Web-4M, and Groupware. All of these provide capabilities not only for asynchronous and synchronous communications but also include student management resources and testing functions. Business providers sometimes refer to these tools as "e-learning solutions." Integrated learning systems provide the benefits of both synchronous and asynchronous communications on one platform, as well as access to the huge reservoir of Web resource materials. Most instructors have found the most valuable feature to be the asynchronous threaded discussion forum in text (called bulletin boards in older systems). A discussion forum allows students and instructors to interact by posting and reading messages, while each has flexibility regarding when they do it. Usually a Web-based course involves a number of assignments or activities; students post their responses to the discussion forums and the instructors post comments there also. More about instruction on the Web will be found in Chapter 6.

For more on Web-based learning, see: Bonk, 2002, Beer, 2000; Kearsley, 2000; Khan, 1997, 2001; McCormick and Jones, 1997; and Porter, 1997.

Comparisons of the different Integrated Learning Systems can be found at:

http://www.edutools.info/course/compare/all.jsp

http://www.marshall.edu/it/cit/webct/compare/index.htm

http://www.knowledgeability.biz/weblearning/softwaretools.htm

Knowledge Management Systems

A form of online learning that has emerged in the training world is knowledge management (see: Rosenberg, 2000; Tiwana, 2000). "A knowledge management system (KMS) is a distributed hypermedia system for managing knowledge in organizations" (from FOLDOC, the Free Online Dictionary of Computing, http://wombat.doc.ic.ac.uk/foldoc/foldoc.cgi?Knowledge + Management + System). Knowledge management conceptualizes various ways to capture and distribute the collective and cumulative learning that lies in an entire organization. This knowledge is found in the form of guidelines, case studies (so-called "best practices"), databases, newsletters, and seminar series. An important element of knowledge management is the use of technology to collect and distribute this information. Some proprietary technologies for this are: Knowledge Portal, Lotus Knowledge Discovery System, Text Analysis, and Knowledge Mining. An account of one knowledge management system is shown in the accompanying panel on Lucent Technologies' Knowledge Net Project (see pp. 90–91).

One of the simplest ways to implement knowledge management in an organization is through the development of checklists or job aids. These procedural guides summarize knowledge about specific tasks and reduce the time needed by new employees when learning how to do their jobs. The technology used to improve performance in this fashion is called an electronic performance support system (see Gery, 1991; Stevens and Stevens, 1995).

One of the guiding principles of knowledge management is that information should be available when needed or "on demand" in an immediately useable form. According to the knowledge management philosophy, if a person only needs to learn about one concept or specific skill, the learning system should make it easy to access information and training about just that topic. This approach contrasts with traditional courses, which attempt to provide a collection of competencies and knowledge in preparation for its use and requires a different instructional design approach.

Part of the knowledge management system of the World Bank is a distance education network called the Global Distance Education Network. This system links a core site with nodes in different parts of the world, with the aim of organizing the most relevant knowledge for people involved in distance education for developing countries (see http://www1.worldbank.org/disted/). For more information about knowledge management, see: http://www.research.ibm.com/journal/sj40-4.html.

Internet2

Internet2 (http://www.internet2.edu) is the name of a consortium consisting of 205 universities working in partnership with industry and government to develop a more advanced Internet. It is widely regarded as a major evolution in networking and in time will have major impact on distance education. Starting in 1999, the consortium began to deliver its Abilene Network service. This network can provide connectivity of 10 gigabits-per-second between each Abilene connected desktop. Internet2 also offers next generation Internet Protocol (IPv6) service. The effect is to allow Internet users to experience vastly improved quality network services, enabling applications such as high definition television (HDTV). When this next generation technology is generally available, it should be able to deliver real time audio and video services of a technical quality that at present can only be obtained on recorded technologies such as CD-ROMs.

Lucent Technologies' Knowledge Net Project

In 1998, Lucent Technologies expanded its KM with additional initiatives and was ranked among the top two-dozen companies practicing KM. One of these projects, the Knowledge Net, was implemented in 1999 by the Professional Services Organization, an externally focused consultancy in the call-center market. The Knowledge Net project tested assumptions about the use of communities of practice and communities of interest as a means for focusing consultants on the use of core knowledge that they needed to do their jobs, smarter, better, and faster. The Knowledge Net project was built upon some underlying principles of Knowledge Management. The communities had specific roles and responsibilities like: mentor, Subject Matter Expert (SME), and community leader. Researchers tested the value of those roles and found them useful in dividing the labor of a knowledge community. They also found that to fully exploit the capabilities of KM they needed certain types of infrastructure enhancements to the technology systems that needed to be funded and supported at the Chief Information Officer (CIO) and Chief Executive Officer (CEO) organization levels. Without that executive support, KM would only have a "ripple" effect at a departmental level and not realize a "tsunami" impact that is possible with an enterprise-wide commitment to knowledge management and knowledge sharing.

CRM Portal

In 1999, based on promise in the potential of Knowledge Net and other KM initiatives, senior management created the CRM Portal to address the KM needs of a strategic solution group for Lucent's CRM (Customer Relationship Management) business. This was a unit responsible for changing the focus of the call-center business from one of hardware, software, and services to one

Media and Technology Selection

From the preceding sections, it should be clear that there are a large number of technological and media options available for the delivery of distance learning courses. A consistent problem throughout the history of distance education has been the tendency of educators to become fixated on a particular technology and to try to deliver all the different components of their courses on that technology. The latest technology to capture attention is, of course, the Internet and World Wide Web. Our challenge as educators is to be creative in deciding what is the best medium or mixture of media for a specific course or program, and what is the most appropriate technology for delivering it. In setting up programs and designing courses, a basic principle of a systems approach is to recognize that each medium has its special strengths and weaknesses and that these must be considered when deciding how to deliver each part of the program or course to its particular target population. At present, for

that focuses on the impact on our customer's customers. The technology support system developed in house was a vertical portal rich in contextual metadata, associating knowledge assets with different job groups each with unique job tasks. Anyone could nominate a knowledge asset to the CRM Portal. The CRM Portal was able to track usage by user, by asset and by nominator. This capability gave Lucent Technologies the potential of identifying key contributors to the company's body of knowledge, key users of that knowledge and the ability to learn about the use of knowledge within the company. In addition, it gave the company a basis for drawing peer attention to those who contributed to the body of knowledge and to those who most used it. This made possible the ability to contact users to get at other measures of quality of assets. For example, the company could determine whether the use of the asset had a positive impact on business results. If a positive result was achieved, they could then determine to what extent, and in what area of the business it impacted (i.e., growing or protecting revenue, reducing expenses, improving customer and/or employee satisfaction. This tracking enabled the company to reward such behavior accordingly, further driving the cultural transformation toward awareness of knowledge as capital.

A managing-editor function was assigned to a single person in each strategic solution group who ensured consistency in the application of the metadata and added some as well. Finally an indexing tool was used to make some of the last metadata decisions. Key reinforcement practices were undertaken to maintain the visibility of the CRM Portal and its assets to the user community. This was accomplished through monthly calls with key audience groups and specific familiarization sessions done with those responsible for making content decisions for their solution. These were called "First Friday's" conferences.

SOURCE: Reprinted with permission from Lawrence Erlbaum Associates, Inc. and the author.

example, the Internet is very poor at delivering recorded video programs, but that is not in itself a reason for *not* choosing to use video. It means that if video is appropriate for the teaching objectives, then it should be provided through some other technology.

Table 4.1 summarizes some of the strengths and weaknesses of the main technologies. Here we concentrate on their characteristics as *delivery* channels; we are not including the very important aspects of designing and making programs, a topic we will consider in Chapter 5. As summarized in Table 4.1:

- *Print* of high quality is quite expensive to produce and distribute, though this technology does lend itself to low-cost production, too. A book or study guide does not break down, and therefore is very reliable. Print carries large volumes of information very efficiently, and the student can read the material whenever and as often as desired. For students having little formal education, text in print can seem a passive medium.

Table 4.1   **Strengths and Weaknesses of Different Technologies**

	Strengths	Weaknesses
Print	Can be inexpensive Reliable Carries dense information Learner-controlled	May seem passive May need longer production time and significant cost
Audio/video recordings	Dynamic Give vicarious experience Learner controlled	High development time/costs
Radio/television	Dynamic Immediacy Mass distribution	Very high development time/costs for quality Scheduling
Teleconferencing	Interactive Immediacy Participatory	Complexity Unreliability Scheduling
Computer and Web-based learning	Interactive Learner controlled Participatory	High development time/costs Equipment required Some unreliability

- *Audio/video recordings* can present information in an entertaining and stimulating manner. They have the great merit of being controllable by the user, so a student can play and replay each item on a tape or disc as often as desired. Manufacturing the discs and tapes is not expensive, but program creation and production usually is.
- *Radio and television* can give immediate, up-to-the-minute information, and allow any subject to be illustrated with exciting and colorful dramatizations. Because these technologies require a huge investment in program development, production, and distribution, they are best suited to programs that have a large student population.
- *Teleconferencing*—including Web-based conferencing—provides the advantages of quick and easy interactivity, with a high degree of human interest, but involves the use of complex and sometimes unreliable equipment (although audio-conferencing is usually quite simple, cheap, and dependable).
- *Computer-based* programs can provide a high volume of text in dynamic formats that may be more attractive to those students who are not motivated by printed materials. Their use requires the appropriate program software, which may be expensive to create.

Media and Technology Selection Procedures

The summary of the general strengths and weaknesses of different technologies in Table 4.1 indicates some further selection considerations. For example, if development time and budgets are very limited, a combination of fairly simple printed materials and a series of audio teleconferences would appear to be better choices than attempting to make audio/video recordings or using radio and television or computer-based instruction. On the other hand, if motivation of the students is a serious concern, introducing the use of the more dynamic and interactive technologies would be a primary consideration. In some settings, the reliability and simplicity of the delivery system might be a major factor, in which case print would be favored and teleconferencing or computers would not, but a series of audio tapes might be very suitable. If teleconferencing is desired, it is usually unwise to select the video technologies until full consideration has been given to the audio, computer, and audiographic, since the former are more expensive, need more preparation, *much more* technical support, and greater sophistication on the part of the instructor. Of course, these generalizations about different categories of technologies have to be reviewed for a particular learning situation in a specific distance education system.

There are numerous long-established models to guide the process for selecting media and technology, including: Heinich, Molenda, and Russell, 1985; Lane, 1989; Reiser and Gagne, 1983; and Romiszowski, 1974. The main steps in all these models are as follows:

1. Identify the media attributes required by the instructional objectives or learning activities.

2. Identify the student characteristics that suggest or preclude certain media.

3. Identify characteristics of the learning environment that favor or preclude certain media.

4. Identify economic or organizational factors that may affect the feasibility of certain media.

   (Caution: not all authors are as careful as we are in differentiating media and technology, so sometimes you need to look to see if the terms are being used interchangeably.)

In this four-step model, the first step specifies that the nature of the learning involved, as specified in the instructional objectives or learning activities, should be the starting place for choosing the media to be used. For example, if the learning requires an auditory stimulus or response (such as is likely in foreign language instruction), then a sound medium is necessary. The second step involves the identification of any student characteristics that might be relevant. For example, if the students are known to be poor readers, emphasis on audio/visual media would seem appropriate, whereas it might be silly to send information on a tape to graduate students who are perfectly capable of reading such information in text. The third step is to examine the learning environment in terms of media suitability. Some media are better for learning at home, others for learning with other students at learning centers, others may be more suitable for learning at work; the learning environment in rural areas in most developing countries favors distribution of materials by mail and broadcast television. The last step is to assess economic or organizational factors such as the budget and expertise available and past or existing experience in the use of particular media.

Bates (1990) provides the ACTIONS model for making decisions about the use of technology, suggesting that the factors to be considered can be summarized as follows:

A ccess: where will students learn; at home, or work or local centre?

C osts: what are capital and recurrent; fixed and variable?

T eaching functions: what are presentational requirements of the subject? Required teaching and learning approaches?

I nteraction: what kind of teacher and student interaction will be possible?

O rganization: what changes in organization will be required to facilitate the use of a particular technology?

N ovelty: will the "trendiness" of this technology stimulate funding and innovation?

S peed: how quickly and easily can material be up-dated and changed? How quickly can new courses be produced using this technology? (p. 5)

Media Richness and Social Presence

Media richness and social presence are two characteristics that should be taken into account in deciding which media to use. Media richness refers to the capability to convey a broad spectrum of information, including immediacy of feedback, multiple cues, language variety, and personal focus (Daft and Lengel, 1986). Richer media, such as face-to-face and real-time video conferences are more appropriate for tasks involving differences in interpretation, whereas leaner media, such as e-mail and written documents, are more appropriate for analyzable tasks (Rice, 1992). According to social presence theory, media can also be distinguished by the extent to which they permit communicators to experience others as being physically or psychologically present (Short et al., 1976). Media differ, for example, in their capacity to transmit information about facial expression, direction of looking, posture, dress, nonverbal and paraverbal cues. Tasks that involve interpersonal skills, such as negotiation or resolving conflicts, demand media that provide high social presence, such as face-to-face meetings or teleconferences; whereas the exchange of routine information has few social presence requirements and is adequately served by computer-mediated communication or written documents.

The considerations just described, when applied in conjunction with understanding of the strengths and weaknesses of the different technologies, provide some ideas that can be used to make decisions about the most appropriate ways of delivering a given distance education program or course. However, what matters eventually is not so much what technologies are employed, but *how well* they are used. The effectiveness of any technology does not depend entirely on the characteristics of the technology but upon the quality of the course design, each lesson design, and the quality of the interaction that the instructor is capable of. Effective use of a technology depends upon having adequate experience with it in distance learning applications. Even familiar technologies, such as print or television, require special adaptations in distance learning settings. This is why it is so important to have media and technological expertise as part of the distance learning development team.

Media and Technology Integration

So far in this chapter, we have discussed each type of technology separately. However, in most distance education programs and courses, a combination of media is used and also a combination of technologies. No single technology is likely to address all the teaching and learning requirements across a full course or program, satisfy the needs of different learners, or address the variations in their learning environments. Using a mixture of media allows for differences in student learning styles or capabilities. Some students prefer the reflective thinking style associated with print while others thrive on the impulsive live dialog in a teleconference. Consequently, the more media alternatives that are provided, the more effective the distance education course is likely to be for a wider range of students. Another reason to have multiple media and multiple technologies is to provide redundancy and flexibility. Should there be a problem with the distribution of one technology, the other can compensate. For example, a program that uses video distributed by broadcast television in conjunction with text in computer conferencing can rely on either medium to deliver information if one fails. Similarly, videotapes are a good backup for students who miss a television program. Faxes can substitute for certain aspects of teleconferencing if necessary. Captioning a videotape or television broadcast is a good idea, not only to make the information accessible to the hearing impaired, but also to provide a safety factor if the sound is poor or lost.

Decisions about Multiple Technologies

Unfortunately, each technology added to a course or program is likely to increase the development time and its cost, as well as the cost of administration. Thus, some degree of parsimony must be practiced in selecting the number and type of media and technologies to be used. One obvious step is not to introduce a new technology until full consideration has been given to those that are already available. It is surprising how many organizations have invested in expensive technologies like satellite channels or setting up their own videoconferencing studio without finding out if they can rent the necessary channels, or trying to achieve their goals by means of the telephones already on their desks, or by means of printed materials that could be produced by a competent designer on the office computers using a word processing program. The quality of their programs would have been much better if they had invested their money in hiring people able to *make good media rather than buying new technology.* The extent of use is another consideration; is the technology likely to be used a number of times in a course or across different courses? On the other hand, the requirements of a particular learning segment or a group of learners may be so compelling that something new is justified, even though it has not been used before or is only needed for one aspect of a course or program.

When integrating different media into a single course, one of the most important design considerations is to ensure that the media work together. There is always the possibility that learners will get "lost" when they go from one component to another. For this reason, it is highly desirable to provide the learner with a course "map" (usually part of the study guide) that depicts the different media used and how they relate to each other. In addition, it is a good idea to have each medium include directions on where to go next. For example, the study guide might recommend that the learner listen to an audio segment before reading a chapter in the textbook; at the end of the audio segment, instructions would be provided to return to reading a particular page in the chapter. Links in a Web site can be a wonderful tool, but designers have to be very careful to ensure students don't get lost in cyberspace!

Media Standards

One of the ongoing dilemmas with technology is the emergence of different proprietary formats and the incompatibility among them. The classic battle was between the VHS and Betamax formats for videotape in the 1970s. There have been many different file formats and operating systems associated with personal computers over the years, much to the annoyance and frustration of computer users. In fact it seems that every major new software application raises a battle over standards as each company tries to establish its format as the dominant one in the market. The latest version of this debacle concerns standards for online courses.

Since the Internet and Web makes it quite easy to share course materials, there has been a great deal of interest in establishing standards for online courses that would facilitate such sharing and thus minimize duplication of effort. The main issues are:

- documentation and cataloging of lessons
- the design of exchangeable components of instruction
- ensuring that different course providers can exchange data such as that on student registration and records

The first problem has been addressed by the creation of a set of uniform categories for describing a course and building these categories into authoring tools and learning management systems called metadata. Categories include:

Viewpoint: Zane Berge

In the next 10 years, our PDAs, tablets, cell phones, wireless technology, satellites, and voice recognition will transform into unimagined technology. All this will drastically increase the ease of use and access to information and communication. In the decades to come, learning technology will be powerful, ubiquitous, and seamless to the learner—any time and any place. While this technologically rich environment will be extremely convenient and comfortable to the learner, my caution is that, in and of itself, the technology will not improve learning any more than a new schoolhouse will improve learning in our brick-and-mortar classrooms today.

SOURCE: Zane Berge, University of Maryland

subject matter, intended audience, grade levels, developer, authoring system used, and date of creation.

The second problem has been addressed through the development of "learning objects." This is a method that seeks to define self-contained, portable learning units. The idea underlying learning objects is that they are small units of instruction on single topics or skills and do not depend upon external materials; that is to say, they stand alone and can be shared across different systems without complications. In essence, this is no different than the usual instructional design practice of organizing content into "chunks" or modules; however, being context-independent is a more stringent criterion. Furthermore, there are many questions about the "grain size" of a learning object—whether it is equivalent to a section, lesson, screen, page, or chapter. For discussion of learning objects, see the overview provided by Hodgins and Conner (2000), Longmire (2000), or Downes at http://www.atl.ualberta.ca/downes/naweb/Learning_Objects.htm.

The third problem requires that all system developers use common data formats—probably the most difficult aspect of implementing standards. This problem has been addressed by the use of the XML language and a set of standards based upon it. The most widely adopted standard is SCORM (Sharable Content Object Reference Model), which the Department of Defense developed. SCORM builds upon efforts from the IMS Global Learning consortium, the IEEE standards committee, the Aviation Industry CBT committee, and ARIADNE (Alliance of Remote Instructional Authoring and Distribution Networks for Europe). SCORM specifications have been adopted by all major vendors of authoring tools and learning management systems, ensuring that any online learning materials developed using these systems will adhere to the standard and hence be interoperable across systems. More information about SCORM and its implementation can be obtained from the ADL Web site at http://www.adlnet.org.

In the final analysis, it's not clear if all the effort to develop standards for online learning will succeed or not. Even if materials are well documented, designed as learning objects, and developed in a common format that makes them work across all systems, administrators and managers of educational programs may not use them. Although the time and cost savings of using them could be tremendous, there are strong local jealousies and local pride of ownership when it comes to teaching that work against the kind of sharing that is implied in this new approach. On the other hand, the Internet and Web may make it so easy that people actually will begin to do it.

Summary

In this chapter, we have discussed the various delivery technologies available for carrying the text, audio, and video media that are the life-blood of distance education:

- Almost all distance education courses use print technology in the form of study guides and textbooks. Audio and video programs are delivered on tapes and discs. Television technologies include: broadcast, ITFS, CATV, DBS, and streaming video. Teleconferencing (audio, audio-graphics, video, and computer) is widely used. Computer-based learning is extensively used in corporate training. All technologies have been impacted by the rapid rise and popularity of Internet and World Wide Web technology.

- There is no "right" or "wrong" technology for distance education. Each medium and each technology for delivering it has its own strengths and weaknesses. One of the worst mistakes an organization or an instructor can make is to become dogmatically committed to delivery by a single medium.

- The technology selection process should be undertaken for each course and media selection for each learning objective, since they all have different requirements, depending upon the objectives, learners, and learning environment.

- Furthermore, a combination of media should be selected to meet the diversity of the subject matter and learners' needs, as well as to provide redundancy and flexibility.

- Current efforts to develop standards and employ learning objects methodology may result in sharing of online course materials. This would give vast economies and efficiencies with improvements in quality arising from saving duplications.

- How a medium is used is more important than what particular technologies are selected. This indicates the significance of the design and implementation considerations discussed in subsequent chapters.

Further discussion about the use of technology in distance education can be found in Moore and Anderson (2003), Bates (2000, 2003), and Kruse and Keil (2000).

Questions for Discussion or Further Study

1. What do you see as the strengths and weaknesses of learning from text on the computer compared to a printed study guide or manual?

2. Pick a teaching or training application to be developed for distance learning and discuss what parts of that course you would recommend be delivered on audio and what on video, what in real time and what asynchronously.

3. In what ways do you think the experience for the student and the performance of the instructor are different in each of the video-conferencing formats described in this chapter?

4. Do the commercial forces associated with selling communications technologies hinder or help the development of distance education?

5. Discuss Zane Berge's view of the future.

CHAPTER 5

Course Design
and Development

Any institution that provides distance education must organize the work of different specialists, who generate content and teaching strategies and arrange them into courses. The content must be structured in a form suitable for distance learning, and prepared for distribution through one or more of the technologies reviewed in Chapter 4. Interaction between learners and instructors, whether asynchronously or in real time, must be planned.

There are many questions that must be addressed in the design and development of a distance education course or program. They include:

- What content should be included or left out?
- How will the material be sequenced and structured?
- What media will be used to present the different "chunks" of material?
- What teaching strategies will be used?
- How much interaction will there be between students and instructor, students and students?
- How will learning be evaluated and what form will feedback to students take?
- What production methods will be used to create the materials?

Instructional Systems Design

In addressing these questions, most organizations follow certain steps commonly referred to as ISD, or Instructional Systems Design. ISD emerged after World War II, with its origins in the pressure for designing training more efficiently during the war. It is a product of several theoretical perspectives on learning and teaching; these include systems theory, behavioral psychology, and communications and information theory (see Dick and Carey, 1985; Richey, 1986).

Stages in Instructional Design

Figure 5.1 illustrates the decision model that underlies the ISD approach. The central idea is that the development of instruction can be divided into a number of stages, each of which requires certain critical design decisions.

In the *Analysis* stage, the designers must conduct some form of task or job analysis—or in an academic area must analyze content—to identify the specific skills that are involved in the task or job or to identify performance that would demonstrate mastery of subject matter. Another step in the analysis stage is to identify the characteristics of the learners and the learning environment, and to find out what these students need to know if they are to be able to perform the desired behavior at the desired level.

In the *Design* stage, the required performance of the students as a result of the course and each of its components are articulated as learning objectives in very specific terms. Learning objectives have been classified by educational psychologists such as Bloom (1956) and Gagne et al. (1992). Bloom's hierarchy lists six levels of objectives in the cognitive domain: knowledge, comprehension, application, analysis, synthesis, and evaluation. Gagne describes five types: intellectual skills, cognitive strategies, verbal information, motor skills, and attitudes. A learning objective consists of a behavior, the conditions under which it should be evaluated and a criterion for its measurement. Thus, test items matching the objectives can be created in the design stage. Since each objective defines a specific behavior, the media are selected to communicate the information the students need and to provide opportunity for them to practice that particular behavior. If, for example, a college wishes its students to "know Hamlet," this goal will have to be broken into many specific objectives; for each it will have to be decided what can be achieved by reading, by listening, by viewing, and by practicing (e.g., speeches). Testing and feedback will have to be designed to ensure the student eventually can perform, in writing or orally, what is specified in each objective.

Course designers must invest in an exhaustive effort to articulate what they believe their students should learn and how that learning will be demonstrated, as a result of their study in every module (typically the most gross

Figure 5.1   Model of the Instructional Systems Design (ISD) Process

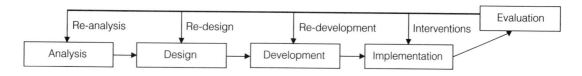

division of a course), every unit, every lesson, and every part of each lesson. This does not (as some people think) limit distance teaching to merely low level, easily measured cognitive objectives at the expense of learner creativity, learner involvement, or even learner self-direction; nor does it deny the development of problem-solving skills or knowledge and sensitivities in the affective domain. All these and similar high-level learning—provided it can be defined by subject specialists—can be articulated to the students and their instructors in terms of what the learners will be able to do and what learners will be able to present as evidence of their accomplishment, by the end of the module, unit, lesson, or part of the lesson. If—as is sometimes suggested—the behavior of a successful student in a given subject truly cannot be described, then indeed it would be difficult to specify a learning objective, but then it is equally impossible to construct a teaching program when it is not known what it is that one is trying to teach! Fortunately there are very few such cases; more often than not, the inability to define learning in terms of student behavior is a result of lack of knowledge about the procedure by the instructor(s). When helped to achieve such specificity regarding their goals, most instructors appreciate the better quality that such clear vision brings to their teaching.

During the *Development* stage, designers and producers create the instructional materials that communicate what is needed for achieving the learning objectives. They include Web pages, films, study guides, books, audio tapes and teleconference outlines. Teachers and staff may also need training at this stage.

The *Implementation* phase is a bit like the performance of a play that has been written and rehearsed; the audience (i.e., the students) arrives. They register; their instructional materials are delivered, and they interact with their instructors and perhaps other students, based on the materials and teaching plans so carefully designed in advance.

Evaluation activities include ongoing ("formative") testing and grading, unit by unit, module by module, at the Implementation stage, as students work through the course, as well as occasional investigations to assess the effectiveness of particular course materials and procedures. The results of this formative evaluation can lead to intervention to change the analysis, design, or development procedures; but mainly it leads to changes in implementation, when results of student tests show the need for intervention with particular instructors. Summative evaluation at the end of the course may lead to improvements in any of the phases of the model when the course is offered in the future.

A Planned Approach

The ISD approach emphasizes planning. As little should be left to chance or *ad hoc* decision making in the implementation stage as possible. Each stage of the ISD cycle results in a *product* that must be delivered in order that later steps in the ISD process can move forward. For example, in the design phase, it is the statement of learning objectives that enables the development of an evaluation plan that outlines how the course will be assessed and how learning will be measured. Planning the teaching strategies, such as how information will be presented and what activities learners will be expected to do, cannot begin until the objectives and evaluation plan have been prepared. Each of the different stages of course design is a subsystem, linked together into a system. In Figure 5.1, the five stages are shown as a cycle, since this is an ongoing process. For example, even though the activities of analysis are conducted at the beginning of a development effort, they could be revisited at any time if there is a question or problem about the validity of the instructional needs, the learners, or the learning environment. Evaluation of one course or part of the course is very closely related to the analysis of need for a subsequent course.

The extent to which some or all of the procedures are followed in each stage of the ISD cycle depends upon several factors. One is the understanding of the educators involved; another is the commitment of the teaching institution to the ISD approach and the extent to which the institution is actually organized to support it. It is a time-consuming process and can be expensive. It is difficult for an individual teacher to follow the model except superficially because of the time needed. Open universities, large corporations, and the Department of Defense tend to employ ISD approaches more extensively and more intensively than do traditional universities or home study schools. This is partly a result of the training that is given to employees of those institutions; partly the greater funding they often have; and partly the way that such organizations are organized to support a total systems approach to education and training.

Many academics resist the discipline and the supervision implied in working in a systems way. However there is very little doubt that there is a direct relationship between the time and effort put into the Instructional Systems Design and the ultimate quality of the distance education program.

For further discussion of ISD and instructional design principles, see Briggs, Gustafson, and Tillman (1991); or Leshin, Pollock, and Reigeluth (1992).

The Development Team

On several previous occasions, we have suggested that designing and teaching a distance education course should be a team effort. The size of the team may be small, with as few as two individuals (the "author–editor" model) or may be a large group of twenty or more people (the "course team" model). The size and nature of the team depends mainly on how the providing institution has organized its distance education program, which in turn reflects its mission and the policies of its management. Developing a course by using only one or two people is far less intrusive on the mainstream activity of a dual mode institution than developing a course with a course team.

The Author–Editor Model

The author–editor model was the usual method of course development in correspondence instruction, when a subject matter expert wrote the draft of a correspondence study guide and an editor polished it up in readiness for

Anatomy of Home Study Courses

In 1998, the Distance Education Training Council (DETC) surveyed its 61 institutional members to collect data about their courses. Here are some of the results:

Course Development

43 percent—created by both in-house and outside authors
41 percent—use published textbooks with study guides produced in-house
26 percent—use published textbooks with study guides and outside authors
16 percent—created entirely by in-house staff
12 percent—created entirely by outside authors

Completion Time

The "most popular course" of each institution, on average, contains 31 lessons and each lesson takes 7 hours to complete. The course has 15 examinations with an average of 39 questions per exam. The average completion time is 9 months. The average nonstart rate is 16 percent, the average completion rate is 57 percent, and the average graduation rate is 38 percent.

Course Components

The typical course includes: 31 percent—online communication, 21 percent—audio tapes, 17 percent—hardware or kits in the course, 14 percent—video tapes, 11 percent—Internet time, 10 percent—CD-ROM disks, 12 percent—using job-related tools or devices, 7 percent—multimedia disks, and 6 percent—mandatory resident training.

Course Delivery

The predominant technologies used to deliver course content are: 55 percent—text in loose-leaf binders with study guides, 43 percent—soft cover texts, 8 percent—hard bound "published" texts, 11 percent—audio/visual, 4 percent—CD-ROM or disk, 4 percent—interactive, and 3 percent—Internet/Web-based delivery.

Support Services

Methods used to provide support services to students are: 72 percent—e-mail, 68 percent—toll-free telephone, 48 percent—computer-generated personalized responses, 27 percent—Internet download capability, and 26 percent—faxed materials.

Student Contact

Other services provided: 91 percent—instructors' write comments on assignments, 71 percent—personalized letters from instructors, 48 percent—proctored examinations, 41 percent—instructors' comments online, 17 percent—online library services, and 12 percent—instructors use cassette tapes for comments.

Evaluation

Ways of measuring program quality: 83 percent—course completion statistics, 82 percent—student evaluations, 24 percent—professional organization recognition, 20 percent—employer evaluations, 15 percent—passage of licensing/certification examinations, and 3 percent—employment/placement.

production. The course development process is a matter of getting reviews from other experts and perhaps potential students, obtaining copyright clearances, designing page layout, proofreading, making corrections, and printing or duplicating the text.

Although the author–editor approach developed as the favored way of producing printed correspondence courses, an analogous practice occurs with some Web-based instruction, where an academic or other content expert provides the subject matter, which a Web designer then authors for placing on a server.

What is usually missing in these arrangements is an instructional designer and the investment of time that the ISD approach requires. At best, the editor or Web designer must try to influence the author to produce learning objectives, evaluation criteria, and teaching strategies, which some content specialists are willing and able to do, and others are not.

The familiar pattern is for a content expert to think of learning objectives as content to be presented, rather than what learners will be required to know. Such experts invariably present a volume of material in excess of what a student can learn in the time available. A competent instructional designer always ascertains the study time available, and then tailors the content accordingly! Sometimes a Web designer can achieve these ends, but in real life, editors and Web designers are outranked by authors, and the author's will usually prevails.

The Course Team Model

The single mode open universities use the team approach to course design, and the UK Open University (UKOU) provides the best known examples of this model. Each course is designed and produced by a team that might consist of as many as 20 or more people, in which every member is a specialist. At the design stage of the ISD process, a group of academics who are specialists in different aspects of a subject writes outlines of what should be taught in their particular specialties, and engages in extensive negotiations regarding the allocation of the student's time budget for study in the course. They produce drafts of learning objectives and content of each unit and module into which the course time budget is structured. As well as taking responsibility for content in the study guide, the academics assemble books of readings, make audio and video recordings, plan Web pages and Web based activities, and design tests and exercises, all with the assistance of specialists in these tasks. These technical experts include: Web producers, text editors, graphics designers, radio and television producers, instructional designers, librarians, and even a specialist photolibrarian. On every team are one or more specialists in the adult distance learning process, people with close contact with the ultimate users of the course materials.

As draft course outlines and objectives are debated, decisions are taken about teaching strategies, such as, for example, what proportion of time is to be spent on readings versus audio or video materials. From the first exploratory meetings of experts and practitioners in the field to define the objectives and content, the process depends on many formal and informal meetings, a lot of telephone and e-mail consultation, and a great deal of argument. In the team's regular meetings to review each component of the course as it is designed, arguments may be fierce regarding what content to include, and especially on what is to be left out, with subject experts defending their own territory against their rivals. Criticism of the draft material is also intense. The course team, as well as external readers, comment on each draft. The materials are written and rewritten, to take into account the various criticisms, and must be approved by the whole team before finally being approved for production.

Eventually after several separate drafts have been presented (in the case of UKOU practice there are three), a prototype for the study guide on that subject emerges. Then photographs or artwork can be commissioned, audio and video components can be scripted, and the production process can begin; with audio and video programs being carefully integrated with the printed study guide and even the discussion questions for tutorials at study centers or online being planned to fit well with the audio, video and text materials. Copyright clearance must be obtained for material from secondary sources, for which purpose the single mode institution is likely to maintain a specialist copyright office. Manuals for instructors who will implement the course include guidelines about what is required in each assignment—the vital student product that forms the basis of formative assessment. Finally, meetings are held in the field with representatives of students, tutors, and employers to test the course materials and ensure that they are effective.

Managing the course development process in a course team is a very complex business, with many tasks to be accomplished by different people. It is usually desirable to have a senior academic to head up the team and steer the process, and an administrator to be responsible for ensuring that each task in the development schedule (which often lasts 1–2 years) is completed on time.

Strengths and Weaknesses

Both the author–editor and course team approaches to the development and delivery of distance education have their strengths and weaknesses. The author–editor model is a great deal cheaper than a course team, and results in relatively quick development and modification of courses. In American universities where faculty have other responsibilities at least as great as those of preparing courses for distance teaching, it has proven, so far, impossible to find an organizational structure that can successfully demand more of their time than that required by the author–editor model. There are disadvantages with this, however. Neither the content specialist nor the editor/Web designer is an instructional designer, but even if one of them has instructional design skills, the content and teaching strategies are derived from the knowledge and experience of only one or two people. The greater wealth of knowledge and experience in the course team almost inevitably means the course materials will be superior. Furthermore, the course team, since it has representatives of different technologies and media, encourages the use of multiple media;

whereas the author–editor model typically results in teaching being delivered by a single medium—the medium that the editor is expert in. The course team approach, however, is very labor intensive and therefore expensive, and it involves a lengthy development period. It can be justified for courses with large enrollments having long-term use, whereas it would not make economic sense for a course with very small enrollments or short life expectancy. To obtain the benefits of the team approach at a cost-effective level, it is necessary for administrators to organize the presentation of courses to larger populations, and thus to obtain economies of scale that make the team approach viable. This takes us back, yet again, to the underlying problem of weak organizational structures arising from weak institutional and national policies that often prevent the application of the best practice. In the United States, *virtual* course teams of specialists from different institutions have been assembled by some of the consortia described in Chapter 3. A particularly good example of a virtual national course team being assembled to achieve all the benefits of the single mode university team is the Brazilian case described in Chapter 11.

The "Lean Team"

In dual mode institutions where courses have not only been delivered by correspondence, but also by television, video-conferencing, or the Internet, the author–editor partnership has sometimes expanded to include a number of other specialists, though not on a scale comparable to the course teams of the single mode institutions. Table 5.1 gives an example of such a "lean team." Later we will show the members of a Web-based instruction "lean team."

Table 5.1 lists some of the activities and personnel involved in producing a distance education program in which television is the primary delivery technology. (Of course in a single mode institution where courses are designed by a course team in the fashion we have described, subgroups like the one shown in Table 5.1 also exist.)

Some special skills and attitudes are needed to be a successful member of a design team, and these are not the skills and attitudes normally associated with university academics. First, it has to be recognized that *no individual is*

Table 5.1   Teamwork in Producing Instructional Television Program

Creation of script	Subject specialist(s), scriptwriter, researcher, archivist
Preparation of graphics	Instructor(s), graphics designer
Preparation of set	Producer, lighting director, technicians
Video preproduction	Producer, editor, production assistant
Location filming	Instructor, producer, camera crew
Broadcast	Instructor(s), director, engineers, camera crew
Site support	Administrative assistant, site coordinators

a teacher in this system, but that indeed it is the system that teaches. Even the content is not "owned" by a professor, but is the product of group consensus. Team members have to be willing to bury their egos and relinquish decision making control to the team, to be willing to compromise and to adhere to decisions taken by consensus. Adhering to procedures and policies established by the group is essential if the work is to flow smoothly. For example, if a standard format is established for a study guide or for a Web site, course writers and designers can not prepare their material in any other format, or there could be an over-run in the time allocated for editing and layout of the guide.

Holmberg and Bakshi (1992) describe how a course team worked at Athabasca University. More information about the course team experience can be found in the UKOU journal *Teaching at a Distance* and its successor *Open Learning.*

Designing the Study Guide

Almost all distance education courses are based on a study guide, which provides a map of the course and the framework for the other materials to rest on. Much of the presentation of information, and analysis, explanation, and discussion that an instructor might make in a face-to-face setting can be put into the study guide. Traditionally the study guide is distributed in printed form, but it may be placed on an Internet server.

A typical study guide contains the following:

1. An introduction to the course and a statement of its goals and objectives
2. A calendar and schedule of when specific lessons or activities are to be completed
3. A map that makes the structure of the course clear
4. Guidance about how to use the time allotted for study
5. A substantial presentation of information relevant to each objective, with the instructor's commentary and discussion
6. Explanation of relationships between contents of reading and other media
7. Directions for activities and exercises
8. A set of self-testing questions to be answered or issues to be discussed for purpose of self-evaluation
9. An explanation of the grading scheme and other course requirements
10. Directions and advice regarding the preparation and submission of written and other assignments
11. An annotated bibliography and other references
12. Suggestions for application work or other activity outside the course
13. Suggestions regarding good study techniques
14. Information about how and when to contact an instructor or counselor

The study guide is quite different from a textbook or book of readings. These are intended primarily to communicate information; the study guide is intended to communicate teaching. It has sometimes been referred to as "a tutorial in text." Even an online course can be considered "a tutorial in text."

Here are some of the elements to be considered when designing the study guide (see Rowntree, 1986 or Duchastel, 1988 for further details); see also Table 5.2.

Creating Lessons or Units

The information and activities that are communicated in distance learning materials should be organized into self-contained lessons or units. One of the reasons a person enrolls in a distance learning program, rather than simply research the subject alone, is that a course of study provides a structure of the content and the learning process.

Table 5.2   **Some Principles for Text Design**

Principles for Writing Sentences

Use the active voice
Use personal pronouns
Use action verbs
Write short sentences
Do not put excessive information in a sentence
List conditions separately
Keep equivalent items parallel
Avoid unnecessary and difficult words
Unstring noun strings
Avoid multiple negatives

Principles for Organizing Text

Put sentences and paragraphs in logical order
Give an overview of the main ideas in the text
Use informative headings
Provide a table of contents

Typographic Principles

Use highlighting techniques, but don't overuse them
Use 8–10 point type for text
Avoid lines of text that are too long or too short
Use white space in margins and between sections
Use ragged right margins
Avoid using all upper case

Graphic Principles

Use illustrations, tables, and graphs to supplement text
Use rules (lines) to separate sections or columns

SOURCE: Based on Felker et al. (1981).

The place to start is to lay out how the team will use the number of hours the student is to devote to the subject. If, for example, the course is 150 hours in length and there are 15 weeks for its completion, the course can be constructed in 15 units of 10 hours each. Then the amount of reading, writing, viewing, listening, practicing, and testing can be designed within this time budget.

Each unit might correspond to a single instructional objective, and include some form of evaluation activity that allows the students to check the extent to which they have learned the material. Some teams might want to break each unit into 15–20 minute segments of study. In this way, a unit could correspond to what would be done in a 90-minute classroom session, but consist of six separate activities. For one period the students may read the study guide; then be told to make some notes, then to listen to an audio tape or online audio-clip, next to do a self-test, and finally to read the study guide again. In distance education courses that involve teleconferences, each unit of the study guide could correspond to a separate teleconference. In an online course, the designers might budget a period of time for searching the Web in an individual or group project and some time may be given to participation in a discussion forum.

Although some academic purists may express the view that breaking the course material into many small units makes it "choppy" or disconnected, there are several reasons why it is a good idea to break the course down into a series of units and short lesson segments. For one thing, it makes it easier for the student to fit study into the normal, active adult life style; covering three segments of a unit might use up exactly the time of a daily railroad commute, or the time that is available when the child is in day care. Short segments also help the students to concentrate, and makes information easier to assimilate and to integrate. Segmenting the content and activities allows students to stop when they want to, providing a sense of closure and progress. It is also easier to identify student problems when the material is divided in this way, since they can be localized to a specific objective or learning activity.

Instructional designers should aim to bring integration to the pieces by discussing the relationships among content in the introduction to each unit and also in summaries; as well as by designing evaluation activities that require the students to make their own comparisons and linkages.

Writing Style

Although all authors can be encouraged to develop some personal writing styles, it is important that study materials be written in a conversational rather than a literary or scholarly tone. This means using the first person rather than the third, and using as simple a vocabulary as the subject and level of student allows. The study guide is meant to substitute for the normal explanations given by an instructor in a classroom or instructor's office, and the language should reflect this. The way in which difficult concepts are recognized as such, the use of personal anecdotes or examples, comments reflecting different opinions or disagreement with the text or readings, and the raising of questions for students to think about, all help to establish a more conversational atmosphere in the study guide. Ideally, the design team can project an instructor's personality into the study guide, so the students have a sense of being "taught" by a specific individual. Although this may appear to be inconsistent with the point made earlier about a distance education course being taught by a team, it is not. The course *is* designed and delivered by a team, but at the point of interface of the learner with the system, the designers provide a named and knowable human face, which humanizes the experience from the student's point of view.

Layout

Just as the experienced classroom teacher has a repertoire of oral and visual techniques for drawing attention to certain points, ways of planting questions or ideas in the students' minds, and techniques for provoking responses and for helping students bring synthesis and closure, so all these must be accomplished by designers of teaching at a distance. One of the techniques for doing this is the creative positioning of text and graphics on the printed page or the online screen. Probably the most important factor in organizing printed text is allowing ample "white space" in the document so it is visually attractive and avoids overloading the learner with too much information at one time. White space in text literally gives the student "space to think." Online, the same principle applies, with care taken not to put too much information in one screen. In the same way, choice of typefaces, indentation, graphics, and headings all play pedagogical roles in the study guide, whether in print or online. Use of color can be helpful both in structuring the content as well as in producing an attractive and interesting document or Web site, but successful application depends on professional understanding and judicious selection from among alternatives.

Designing an Audio-Conference

Audio-conferencing is an excellent technology for delivering small scale distance education, since it can be used with a minimum of technical assistance and is cheaper than other forms of teleconference. It can also be a valuable part of a multimedia delivery system. Unfortunately it is now overshadowed by enthusiasm for text-based online conferencing, which is a pity because an audio-conference can be a very nice complement to the text. In Chapter 6, we will discuss some aspects of conducting a successful audio-conference. Here we will suggest a few steps to take in designing such an event.

1. Design the Study Guide

The first step in designing a course based on audio-conferences is the creation and distribution of a study guide, readings and other recorded materials. The series of audio-conferences will provide the opportunity for elaboration, explanation and exchange of ideas, and bring a lot of life and color to the learning experience, but they have to be designed to complement the density and depth of information that can best be communicated by a textbook or other reading. Therefore it will still be necessary to provide a study guide that gives the background information necessary to understand the content and to participate in the discussions. As mentioned before, an online study guide can be an excellent complement to the audio-conference technique.

2. Outline Segments and Activities

Every audio-conference must have a structure. The structure is more open than that of a radio program, and probably more open than a video-conference. However, although from the point of view of the students in the conference there may appear to be no tight structure and there may appear to be considerable freedom to be spontaneous in participating, the instructor should have a very firm understanding at all times of where the students are in the sequence of planned events, and where they are going next. For this reason, one of the most important design steps is to prepare an outline of the planned audio-conference that identifies the segments and student activities against a schedule. In most programs a typical segment is likely to be about 10–15 minutes in length and correspond to a specific learning objective. Such segments should ideally correspond to the segments in study guides, as discussed previously, except that the material in the audio segment consists of comments, questions, or ideas intended to promote interaction. It could involve an interview (live or taped), panel, debate, role playing, brainstorming . . . or simply a short introduction by the instructor. It should never consist of simple reading from notes or a text. A very valuable technique is to organize students to make brief presentations of assignments or their own projects.

3. Make a Class Roster

A third preparatory step is for the instructor to prepare a class roster with background information about each student that can be referred to easily during an audio-conference. This allows the instructor to ask specific students questions related to their interests or experience, and enables the instructor to control both excess and inadequacy of inputs by different individuals. This class roster can be distributed to all students as well to facilitate interaction.

4. Test, Test, and Test

As we have stated before, the reliability of the communications technology is an absolute essential prerequisite for a successful teleconference. Students should never have difficulty hearing—even in a video-conference that is more important than seeing. The technology should be made as transparent as humanly possible. The simplest way of ensuring this is to test the connections and sound quality before the students arrive. But not only once. An hour before the class may be too late to fix a serious problem. Our practice is to test a month before the beginning of the sequence of teleconferences, then a week prior to the first event, then the day before, and finally the hour before. After the course is underway and things are operating smoothly, we test the day before and the hour before the class. In this way we have been able to avoid the embarrassments and disillusion we have witnessed where instructors have simply plugged in the audio equipment, experienced noise or other problems, and had a disastrous session, usually blaming the hardware when in fact the basis of the problem was their failure to set it up and test it adequately.

Designing a Satellite Video-Conference

Satellite video-conferences are frequently "one-off" events, but they can also be organized in a sequence similar to the audio-conference discussed previously. Similar design considerations to those listed for the audio-conference apply, but there is likely to be more supporting personnel involved in the video-conference. This brings its benefits, but also adds to the responsibilities of the instructor. A typical satellite video-teleconference is 1–3 hours in duration, originates from one site, and is broadcast to many locations nationally or internationally. Usually the video image is transmitted to the distant sites and communication from the sites to the transmitting station is by audio (i.e., telephone). Most successful video-conferences involve a local component (e.g., panel of local experts or small group discussion sessions), which helps participants apply the content of the program to their own setting. A satellite video-teleconference is a more structured event—with less interaction—than an audio, audio-graphic, or two-way video-conference or an online discussion forum, because of the larger number of sites and larger number of people involved. The balance between presentation and interaction in a satellite video-teleconference leans more towards the presentation than the interaction.

Components of a Satellite Teleconference

Here are the major components and activities that have to be designed for the satellite video-teleconference:

1. *Locating and preparing site coordinators.* Good site coordinators can make or break a teleconference. In some organizations this is an official job responsibility (though probably not full time) but in most cases someone will be designated or will volunteer for the role. Since it must be assumed that the site coordinator may not have much experience, it is important to provide detailed guidelines (checklists are ideal) for tasks that they should perform; their progress in following these guidelines should be checked by telephone. The site coordinator identifies local experts who are willing to participate; and also arranges for technical support, equipment needed facilities, and catering.

2. *Selecting the teleconference presenter and moderator.* Popular presenters are usually experts in their field but also have the kind of dynamic personality that projects well on television. Once the presenters have been selected, they must provide material for graphics, videotaped segments and the participants' package. The moderator should have content expertise as well as television and teleconferencing experience. The moderator must manage the presenters, deal with participants' questions and any discussion that occurs, as well as follow the instructions of the director or producer. If interaction is considered important in a particular program, then it is the moderator's job to ask the questions and stimulate the discussion.

3. *Preparing the satellite teleconference announcement and participant materials.* The teleconference announcement plays a critical role in attracting participants and establishing their expectations about the content. Announcements provide details on the originator, date and time of transmission, satellite bands, rationale, objectives, intended audience, content outline, credentials of presenters and their topics, registration fees, restrictions on taping or reuse, and cancellation policy. Site coordinators should be provided with posters, a press release and a promotional videotape to help them market the teleconference locally. Participant materials (presenter biographies, readings, bibliography, resource lists) ensure that participants have all the necessary reference materials to prepare themselves for the teleconference. In order to distribute them to the sites in a timely fashion, it is necessary to prepare them well in advance. This means finalizing all details of the teleconference quite early (typically 6–9 months before the teleconference date).

4. *Preregistration/registration.* Participants must usually pre-register for the teleconference and be provided with details about the location, agenda, background on the experts, and relevant readings. Typically, participants receive packages of materials when they register. On-site registration should begin well before the teleconference starts (e.g., 1–2 hours).

5. *Preconference activity: rehearsal.* A well-executed video-teleconference is a complicated undertaking and it must be rehearsed if everything is to go smoothly. The moderator should go through the complete script with the producer/director and practice each segment. Presenters should run through their segments a number of times so they are comfortable with the timing, camera angles, and use of graphics and videotapes. Panel discussions and call-in questions can also be practiced with the site coordinators—they will not be exactly the same during the teleconference but the general nature will be the same. Before the teleconference begins, participants should have an opportunity to meet each other as well as the local experts. This meeting may take the form of an informal "coffee hour" or formal presentations by the local experts in a panel format.

6. *Test period.* In the hour before the teleconference, technicians check out the satellite signal as well as the television monitors, speakers, and microphones (or fax) to be used for questions.

7. *The teleconference.* A schedule should be prepared according to the principles illustrated in the previous section regarding audio-conferencing. This will be particularly important at the transmitting site where camera work is needed to cover a variety of events and the technical personnel need to know what to expect. With some systems that force the instructor to manage cameras and other equipment, having a well-prepared schedule is even more critical.

8. *Interaction.* During the teleconference, there should be opportunities for participants at each site to ask questions and make inputs. This has to be managed by the local site coordinator in conjunction with the originating site. Participants may ask their questions directly or give them in written form to the site coordinator to ask or even to fax. Back-up arrangements have to be planned to deal with transmission problems during the conference (a satellite link is more likely to be interrupted than an audio link).

9. *Postconference activity.* After the teleconference, the local experts may be asked to comment or answer questions. Participants might break into working groups or discuss specific issues. Alternatively, the teleconference may be followed by a social event that allows informal discussions.

10. *Wrap-up and evaluation.* The moderator should summarize the main points of the teleconference and any themes that emerged in the postconference discussions. An evaluation questionnaire should be completed by participants to assess the effectiveness and value of the teleconference.

For more on video-conferencing, see Payne (1999).

Design and Development of Web-Based Courses

Web-based instruction can be a valuable component of a multimedia course, or a course can be delivered on the Web alone. It is an increasingly common practice in conventional teaching institutions to require the faculty to take on a small number of students at a distance, teaching a course designed entirely by the classroom instructor. Among the drawbacks to this is the weak quality of most do-it-yourself instructional design and especially the inability of the Internet to deliver good quality video and sound, even if the instructor is able to design audio and video programs.

Whether the Web materials are designed by the classroom instructor or by a Web designer on behalf of a course team, there are at least three approaches to the process of design and development. They are: (1) by use of authoring tools, (2) by designing materials as Web documents, and (3) by using Integrated Learning Systems.

Authoring Tools

Some of the best known authoring tools for designing instruction to be delivered on computers are Authorware, Toolbook, Director, and Flash. These tools allow a designer to create interactive sequences, animations, tests, and multimedia presentations. Although powerful, these tools are not easy to learn. They were designed prior to the emergence of the Web and although they all can be used to produce Web programs, this is a relatively complicated process.

Web Documents

The simplest way to produce Web-based learning materials is create them as Web documents (in HTML format) using a Web editing program such as Microsoft FrontPage or Macromedia Dreamweaver. Also, the latest versions of Microsoft Word and PowerPoint can save documents directly in Web format. They can then be uploaded to a server and the URL provided to students to allow access. Links can be placed in the documents to allow movement throughout the documents or to access external documents. However, it is not possible to develop interactive exercises or tests without using a Web programming language such as Javascript or Java. Most do-it-yourself instructors use this approach to put syllabi, study guides, readings, handouts, and other course materials online for their students.

Integrated Learning Systems

If an online course is being delivered via an integrated learning system, such as Blackboard or WebCT, the content can be designed using the editing capabilities of this system. The system provides a structure for the creation of the course materials, and the instructors decide which of the options provided they want to use. Content can be typed in directly or cut and paste from other documents. Editing devices are also provided for the creation of exams and surveys. Although it takes a little time to get used to creating courses via an Integrated Learning System, most instructors are comfortable using them within a few weeks. Also, although use of an Integrated Learning System makes it relatively easy and quick to develop an online course, it does not allow for the creation of interactive activities or multimedia. For that, authoring tools must be used.

Web Design Principles

Regardless of how content is created for online courses, the same kind of creativity must be put into the layout and design of Web pages as we discussed earlier with regard to print. Although Web design principles are similar in some respects to those for print design, there are additional factors to be considered, due to the nature of screen displays and user controls. The most important considerations are readability, usability, and information complexity. Like print documents, screens must be made as easy to read as possible. This depends upon typography, layout, writing style, and organization. Web sites must also be easy to use (i.e., to navigate) because if they become too complex, most users will get frustrated and stop using them. A style guide for Web design is provided by Lynch and Horton (2002), and Nielsen (1999) also discusses Web usability. A very fine Web site maintained by the National Cancer Institute (http://www.usability.gov/) has a wealth of information about web design that includes the following checklist for writing content:

- *Use blank space well.* If you have no blank space, users won't find the different pieces of information. They won't see your "chunks."
- *Cut out words.* Write a draft. Leave it for a day or so. Go back to it and try to make your point even more succinctly.
- *Keep paragraphs short.* A one sentence paragraph may be fine.
- *Keep sentences short.* You can often put secondary information in another sentence, in a table, in fragments, or leave it out entirely.
- *Use fragments.* In frequently asked questions (FAQs) for example, don't repeat words from the question in the answer.
- *Use the users' words.* In moving to the Web if your audience is expanding, you should change words for your broader Web audience.
- *Use bulleted lists.* Lists are an excellent way to break up text.
- *Use numbered lists for steps in a procedure.* If you are telling people how to do something, it is a procedure and has steps. Set them out in a numbered list.
- *Use tables.* A table is a visual way of representing a series of "if, then" sentences.
- *Give examples.* Users love examples. They often go right to the examples instead of reading the text.
- *Meet users' expectations for the way information is displayed.* For example, if you are giving an address, write it on separate lines like an address.
- *Use icons or small pictures to enhance the words.* Without being overly cute, you can add a touch of humor and help users at the same time.
- *Include pictures and other graphics, when appropriate.* Use pictures, line art, charts, and other graphics functionally.

Other guidelines for the design of Web-based courses are provided by Driscoll and Alexander (1998), Hall (1997), Horton (2000), and Lee and Owens (2000).

Many university Web sites provide guidelines to faculty about online course design; for example, see:

http://www.fgcu.edu/onlinedesign

http://www.edtech.vt.edu/edtech/id

http://online.fsu.edu/onlinesupport/instructor/templatetoolkit

Other online resources regarding the design of online learning materials are:

> http://www.cast.org, http://www.rit.edu/ ~ easi
> http://ncam.wgbh.org, http://trace.wisc.edu
> http://www.dlrn.org/educ/course/

Research reviews on Web based instruction are provided by Davis (2003), A. G. Chute (2003), Bonk and Dennen, (2003), Naidu (2003), and Hall et al. (2003).

Designing and Developing the Online Course: A Lean Team in Action

We have attached as an Appendix to this chapter a checklist used at the Penn State University WorldCampus to guide personnel involved in the design and development of online distance education courses. We think it will give you an insight into the working of a small team and also illustrates the systems approach, where the work of each individual, at each step, depends on the arrival of a product from a preceding step. It also shows how the designers have to work against a strict time-line in order to have the course ready for distribution when scheduled. Table 5.3 shows the specialists who make up the design team.

Designing for Accessibility: Students with Disabilities on the Web

U.S. Census data indicate that 20 percent of the Americans—about 27 million people—has some kind of disability. Online courses are both a boon and a bane to disabled individuals. On one hand, they provide learning opportunities free from the complications of attending classes. On the other hand, many Web-based courses present new problems; for example, screens that are difficult to view, sites that are difficult to navigate, color that cannot be distinguished, and audio that cannot be heard. The promises and pitfalls of online

Table 5.3   The Web-Based Instruction Development Team

Lead designer
Lead faculty (the main author for the course)
Instructional materials designer (IMD)
Technical typist
Instructional technologist (listed as "IT rep")
Graphic artist
Production specialist

learning for disabled individuals are discussed by Cantor (2001); Kim-Rupnow, Dowrick, and Burke (2001); and Robertson (2002). Designing online courses so they are accessible to disabled learners is more than merely the right thing to do. Section 508 of the U.S. Rehabilitation Act mandates that all government funded information technology (which includes Web-based courses designed by any federal or DOD agency) must be fully accessible to persons with disabilities. To see what the regulations mean in terms of Web document and site design, see: http://www.access-board.gov/508.htm.

Table 5.4 lists some recommendations to Web designers to accommodate individuals with disabilities.

For more on distance education and students with disabilities, see Kim-Rupnow, Dowrick, and Burke (2001); and Perdue and Valentine (2000).

Table 5.4   Recommendations for the Design of Web Pages for the Disabled

- Provide text descriptions as alternatives for all graphics and images (using the Alt = text field).
- Provide text transcripts for audio and video sequences.
- Provide text-based versions of screens that involve extensive use of frames and image maps.
- Make links descriptive enough so they can be understood independent of the text.
- Make backgrounds simple and uncluttered.
- Select colors for text and backgrounds that provides high contrast.
- Don't use flashing or audio alerts (unless they can be disabled).
- Summarize the information in tables in case it can't be deciphered.
- Be as consistent as possible in the layout of pages.
- Provide alternate content for any multimedia component that requires plug-ins (or don't use that content).
- Ensure that keys can be used instead of the mouse to navigate and select options.
- Allow the user to select control options and configure screen layouts.
- Have your pages tested by disabled individuals.

The following suggestions have been made for responding to specific disabilities:

- Visual disabilities: People who are blind do not have use of the monitor, nor their mouse. Instead of reading Web pages or viewing the images, they need to listen to the Web through a software program that acts as a screen reader. People who are not blind but have low vision can benefit from enlarged, high-contrast visual displays. When working on a computer, they often use screen enlargement software.
- Hearing disabilities: Either closed or open captioning for Web-based multimedia can be provided in the same way that it is used in watching television shows or movies.
- Physical disabilities: If a mouse is required to access a certain link or function, that Web page is inaccessible to these individuals and so access via the keyboard is critical.
- Cognitive or neurological disabilities: Individuals with cognitive impairments benefit from graphics or icons that supplement the text.

SOURCE: See Web Accessibility in Mind (WebAIM), available at http://www.webaim.org/

Designing Student Participation

Regardless of what form of distance education is being designed, one element that must be uppermost in the designers' minds is the extent of student participation that is needed, and how to engineer it. In an audio, video, computer-based or Web-based course, this is usually achieved by setting up discussion groups, or making students contribute their own presentations. More structured activities such as quizzes, role play, or simulations can also be arranged. Students need to be given a chance to ask (or answer) questions and in most subjects need an opportunity to express opinions. Participation in this kind of activity can be integrated with a print-based course or video-telecourse by the addition of a teleconference, or by setting up student discussion groups at local sites. People are naturally more cautious at a distance, especially when they are not able to see the other participants, and more so in asynchronous rather than synchronous communication. For this reason, whatever the form of communications technology used, participation is not likely to happen unless it is well planned and instructors have training to facilitate it.

If it is not possible to provide an interactive technology, and study is limited to recorded materials such as the printed study guide or audio/videotapes, getting the student to interact with the subject is even more challenging. One way course designers can achieve some degree of student participation is to present questions or problems that require a response; for example, at the end of each unit. Such items can be multiple choice or open-ended questions, with the answers discussed as part of the narrative in the text or recorded media. Although some students will skip these self-tests, most will take advantage of the opportunity to check their understanding of the material.

In most distance education courses, students have to hand in assignments for evaluation, and the communication technology used for this also allows them to ask and receive responses to questions. Giving feedback in this way allows the instructor, moderator, or tutor to establish a sense of participation in the course. Although many students can tolerate some delay, most people like feedback to be immediate, and few people find one-way communication with no feedback to be satisfying. The subject of interaction between student and instructor, student and student, and student and content will be taken up in the next chapter.

Designing Self-Directed Learning

The ability to undertake all or most of the design of one's own learning, to evaluate one's performance, and to make adjustments accordingly are the attributes of a self-directed learner. People who are good self-directed learners are able to: design their own learning objectives, identify resources that will help them achieve their objectives, chose learning methods to achieve the objectives, and test and evaluate their performance. Distance education is easier for people who have some degree of ability to direct their own learning than it is for people who are very dependent on a teacher's direction, encouragement, and feedback. Designers of distance education materials (like other educators) must keep in mind the desirability of encouraging and supporting self-directed learning, while at the same time giving the support needed by people at different stages of self-directedness. This range of ability to be self-directed and to exercise "learner autonomy" is a key concept in distance learning and is discussed further in Chapter 9. The most important thing to remember is that more autonomous, self-directed learners need less interaction with an instructor and need less structured materials than people who are less capable at managing their own learning. Bearing in mind that interaction costs money and time, it becomes important for designers to be able to estimate the extent to which their students are able to cope independently, and the extent to which they need interaction with the instructor and teaching institution.

Monitoring and Evaluation

In distance education, because the learner is separate from the instructor and the instructor is usually separated from the administering agency, success of the whole enterprise depends on an effective monitoring and evaluation system. For instructors, it is only by using evaluation materials and procedures designed by the teaching institution that they can know if their students are experiencing difficulty. With the right kind of evaluation data, it should be possible to determine precisely what kind of help is needed by a particular individual. It is the monitoring system that provides this data. A good monitoring system also tells administrators about problems experienced by instructors as well as students, and indicates if delays or breakdowns occur in the communication systems—while there is still enough time to take remedial action.

Effective monitoring requires a network of indicators that pick up the necessary data about learner performance and instructor performance; this must be done *frequently and routinely,* and the data has to be relayed with similar routine to a control center where it can be evaluated. Evaluation in this context is the process of analyzing the feedback data gathered by the monitoring system, reviewing it, and making decisions about how well the distance education system and its various parts are operating; as learners, instructors, designers, administrators, and communication resources work together to accomplish short- and long-term goals. For an educational system, the most important of these goals are learning outcomes; however, other goals are legitimate and may be monitored and evaluated (e.g., maintaining cost-effectiveness or rectifying demographic imbalances in the student population).

One of the few generalizations one can make about any distance education program—whatever the communications technology used, whatever the level of the content—is that a good monitoring and evaluation system is likely to lead to a successful program, while a poor system is almost certain to lead to failure. What, then, are some of the features of a good system? There are three key features.

The first is the preliminary specification of good learning objectives that we mentioned earlier. From the beginning of the course design process until the final summative evaluation of the project, no matter how large or small the course, or how long or brief its duration, the central questions are the same, namely: did each student produce evidence of having learned what was required as specified in the learning objectives, *and if not, why not?* All evaluation must ultimately address this question, and whether or not evaluators can show whether the project was effective will depend ultimately on how well the objectives of the project have been stated, at all levels of the course.

The second key to successful monitoring and evaluation is the construction and later the handling of the products submitted by students or trainees as evidence of learning, commonly referred to as *assignments*. It is the assignments that provide the indicators that were referred to earlier—they are the source of feedback signals that should alert authorities throughout the system whenever a problem arises.

In most courses, the assignment is a written document handed to an instructor in person at a study site, or sent by mail, either electronically or in hard-copy format. It may be an essay, a mathematical calculation, a report of observations of natural phenomena, an experiment, or a social event; it could be a multiple choice test, an analysis of a case study, a solution to a problem; it could be a work of art, a poem, or a piece of music. Use of tape recordings, audio or video, allows the student to report on an even wider range of learned accomplishments than text alone permits. All that is necessary in designing interesting and suitable assignments, besides a crystal clear awareness of the learning that the student is expected to demonstrate, is a creative interest in the task—worth stating because it is often missing when people constructing a course understand content far more than process—and an appreciation of the instructional value that really interesting and challenging assignments add to the course. A related awareness, the absence of which explains many unsuccessful assignments, is that of time limitations. Every lesson of every course has to be completed within a defined period of student time and that budget has to include the time needed to complete the assignment; if course designers ask for more in an assignment than can be accomplished within the time budget, obviously there will be a greater or lesser degree of failure, through no fault of the student, or perhaps the instruction. When failure occurs, evaluators need to look at several remedies, as will be discussed shortly, but it is worth saying here that one remedy is to consider whether the assignment itself is unachievable in the time allotted.

Many years of research provides some significant knowledge about assignments and assignment handling. We know that distant learners are more likely to continue and complete a course if they have frequent assignments. We also know there is a close relationship between students' propensity to continue or drop out of a course and the length of delay between assignment submission and its return. We know that early success in assignment completion is especially important, and that the capacity to tolerate frustration with assignments grows with experience as a distant learner. From such research and experience we know that in a typical course it may be desirable to require submission of assignments as frequently as once a week. When this is the case the instructor has two responsibilities: to respond weekly to the student and to make weekly reports of the results of the assignments to the agency's administration.

This leads to the third key to good monitoring and evaluation, which is a good data gathering and reporting system. Whether weekly or less frequently, after the instructor evaluates the assignment, the instructor must have procedures and documents to record such data as the date of the receipt of assignment and scores or grades given. In a major distance education system there is likely to be a regional administration as well as a central administration so that reports have to be provided for evaluation at a regional as well as central level. The region reviews reports from instructors and submits composite reports or reports of exceptional instances to the center. In a dual mode institution, reports of student progress may be presented to both the academic department as well as the distance teaching department. Whatever the particular administrative structure, however, what is common is the necessity for reports to be reviewed by senior staff in the system, who are able to recognize symptoms of system failure. At higher levels (i.e., beyond the instructor) monitoring is a default system; regional and central administrators do not normally review satisfactory assignments or look in-depth at instructors, or study sites where students show evidence of satisfactorily meeting learning objectives. Like a pilot in the cockpit who looks for red lights not green, their interest is not primarily in the indicators showing where the system works (i.e., the students are learning), but to look for the warning signals that indicate some part of the system is inoperative or operating below expectations. More specifically, if a student fails to complete an assignment while other students evaluated by the same instructor do so, the instructor is alerted to identify and rectify the problem experienced by the particular student. However, if all or many students of the same instructor have difficulty with an assignment, and students of other instructors do not, evaluators must ascertain what circumstances cause difficulty for that particular group of students. (Perhaps the instructor is misinterpreting evaluation criteria; perhaps the group of students did not receive a package of learning materials; perhaps an incorrect interpretation was given at a study site tutorial meeting.) At a more general level still, if all the students in a region fail to complete the assignment and those in others do it successfully, there is a suggestion of a regional breakdown (perhaps Internet connections failed, or a television broadcast that reached other regions was not received in the region in question; perhaps assignment packages arrived late and assignments were rushed, etc.; or perhaps a briefing and training session was missed in that particular region). Finally, evaluators have to deal with the situation in which large numbers of students across the whole system perform badly on an assignment; the administration then has to investigate if the teaching material was inappropriate, the objective was unattainable, or the assignment itself was an ineffective measure of the objective.

With clearly specified learning objectives and instructional materials and procedures developed to help students and trainees to achieve those objectives, with assignments designed to test exactly—no more and no less—what is expected from the learning program, and with a network of people knowing their roles in the monitoring system, where failure can be identified quickly and efficiently, the monitoring and evaluation subsystem plays a critical part in the success of any good quality distance education project.

For discussion of evaluation methodology relevant to distance education, see Cyrs (1998), Flagg (1990), Harrison et al. (1990), Horton (2001), Heinzen and Alberico (1990), Shaeffer and Farr (1993), and Thorpe (1988). Considerations associated with online evaluation are discussed by Achtemeier, Morris, and Finnegan (2003); and Hmieleski and Champagne (2000).

Copyright

Everyone who designs instructional materials has to comply with copyright laws. In general this means obtaining permission from a copyright owner (i.e., authors, publishers, institutions) to use or reproduce their work in teaching materials, and paying a royalty or licensing fee if requested to do so. Although teachers in a classroom may be able to claim the protection of the "fair use" exemption when they use copyrighted materials, this is hard to justify when the materials are packaged and distributed to students. Online learning makes copyright compliance even more problematic since it is so easy to copy and paste text or graphics from a Web site. In 1998, the Digital Millennium Copyright Act was passed to address the copyright implications posed by digital media. However, this act was quickly found to be too restrictive for teachers and institutions engaged in distance education. To rectify the situation and provide more flexibility with respect to the use of materials for distance learning courses, in 2002, the "Technology, Education and Copyright Harmonization Act," commonly known as the TEACH Act, was passed.

Besides the issues associated with copyright compliance, educational institutions are concerned about ownership rights for online materials. The long-standing tradition in the academic world has been for ownership of what a person writes to belong to that individual, but with many online courses being developed by teams, and paid for by the institution, this no longer seems so appropriate.

For a thorough discussion of legal issues in the development and use of copyrighted material in Web-based distance education, see Lipinski (2003) Intellectual property issues are discussed in an American Council on Education (ACE) policy paper at http://www.acenet.edu/washington/distance_ed/2000/03march/distance_ed.html. More details about copyright and how it applies to education can be found at http://fairuse.stanford.edu, http://www.copyright.iupui.edu or http://lcweb.loc.gov/copyright.

General Design Principles

It should be apparent from the preceding sections of this chapter that although there are different design considerations associated with the various technologies and media used in distance education, there are some general principles that apply to all of them. These include:

1. *Good structure.* The organization of the course and its components must be well defined and understandable for the student; there must be internal consistency among the different parts of the course; students should at all times know what they have to learn, what is expected of them to achieve the learning, and when they have arrived at the goal.

2. *Clear objectives.* Only when a course has clear learning objectives—unambiguous statements of what the student should be able to do as evidence of having learned—can instructional designers identify the most suitable learning experiences, make good technology and media selections, and design appropriate evaluation instruments.

3. *Small units.* The content of the course should be broken down and presented in small units, each of which might correspond to a single learning objective.

4. *Planned participation.* A fundamental mistake by inexperienced educators who become involved in distance education is to assume that students will participate. Participation and interaction have to be structured. Questions and assignments must be prepared to ensure that each student interacts with the instructor, other students, and the subject matter itself. It is not good enough to simply ask, "Any questions?"

5. *Completeness.* Course materials are far more than a textbook or informative Web site, and should contain instructional commentary, activities, and illustrations similar to those that would be provided, often extemporaneously, in a traditional classroom setting.

6. *Repetition.* Unlike some other media applications, in teaching it is acceptable for the text, audio, video, or computer based system to sometimes repeat key ideas and information (e.g., in online closure summaries) to provide reinforcement and to compensate for distractions and memory limitations.

7. *Synthesis.* Important ideas expressed in the materials or contributed by students should be woven together (especially in summaries). People don't learn as well from being told as when they discover for themselves and then are helped to synthesize or organize what they have discovered.

8. *Stimulation and variety.* Through the use of interesting formats, content, or guests, course materials need to capture and hold the attention of students. Information should be presented in a number of different formats and by different media to appeal to varying interests and backgrounds of the students.

9. *Open-ended.* Assignments, examples, and problems should, where possible, be open-ended to allow students to adapt content to their own interests or situations.

10. *Feedback and evaluation.* Students should receive regular feedback on their assignments and general progress in the course. The effectiveness of the media and instructional methods should be routinely monitored and evaluated.

Viewpoint: Randy Garrison

In distance education designed by an individual teacher, it is normally not possible to satisfy all of these design considerations fully, if only because of time and budget limitations. However the more factors that can be addressed, the more effective the course is likely to be. In single mode—and some dual mode—distance education institutions there is enough money and specialist personnel to attend more fully to all the design features, which is mainly why they are able to develop higher quality courses.

It is time to seriously consider how we design and deliver educational experiences considering the widespread adoption of communications technology in society at large. To date, these developments have not significantly impacted traditional educational institutions.

The current challenge for administrators, policy makers, and faculty of higher education institutions is to acknowledge and accept that there have been significant and irreversible changes in societal demands, funding shortfalls, competition, technological innovations, and student demographics. In higher education we must and can to do better than lecturing to students in 300-seat theaters. As has been demonstrated by some leading institutions, once there is clear policy and leadership, the transformation will be rapid. The only question is whether educational institutions will position themselves as leaders or risk their demise.

SOURCE: Randy Garrison, University of Calgary

Summary

This chapter has discussed a number of different facets of designing and developing distance education courses:

- Instructional Systems Design (ISD) is a widely accepted set of procedures used for the development of instructional programs.
- There are two quite different development approaches (i.e., author–editor and course team); each approach has its strengths and weaknesses.
- The major design characteristics of study guides include: organization of the content into units, a relatively informal writing style, and good document layout.
- Different factors are important in preparing an audio-conference, planning a satellite video-teleconference, and designing Web courses.
- Getting student participation is a challenge for all forms of distance learning.
- The quality of all courses is a function of the quality of the learning objectives.

- Evaluation is dependent on monitoring of student performance that is indicated by submission of regular assignments.
- Developers of distance learning materials must adhere to copyright laws; ownership of content is an increasingly problematic issue.
- A major challenge for institutions and individuals coming to distance education is knowing how to undertake the design tasks effectively. One of the greatest tests of effective management is to release the up-front resources needed for these design efforts.

Questions for Discussion or Further Study

1. How do the course design and development methods used at your organization (or perhaps the one you are currently studying at) compare to those discussed in this chapter?
2. What are the similarities and differences between planning an audio-conference, satellite video-conference, and computer conference?
3. What are the similarities and differences between a study guide to be delivered in print format and one to be delivered as a Web document? Do you agree that "even an online course can be considered 'a tutorial in text'"?
4. Imagine that you are asked to create a department to develop distance learning courses for a large organization. Prepare a list of the staff you will tell your boss you need if you are to take on the job.
5. Look at the Appendix to this chapter. Discuss the relative roles of the lead designer and the lead faculty.
6. Discuss Randy Garrison's view of the future.

Appendix   **Design Schedule for an Online Course at Penn State University's World Campus**

Open Enrollment Courses	Cohort Courses	Target Date (cohort courses only—where applicable)	Person(s) Responsible
Hold initial author meeting	Hold initial author meeting		Lead designer and lead faculty *Resource:* ID&D 101
Send Author Approval Form to department head	N/A		Lead designer
Generate Course Design Document	Generate Course Design Document		Lead designer
Set timelines for content generation, course development, and course delivery logistics	Set timelines for content generation, course development, and course delivery logistics		Lead designer and lead faculty (some aspects of timeline may have already been set by Program Manager or Program Team)
Initiation of Intellectual Property Agreements (requires "definition of work" and timeline)	Initiation of Intellectual Property Agreements (requires "definition of work" and timeline)	Before course development begins	Lead designer
N/A (at this point)	Pay faculty author(s) (if applicable—pay is typically funded as release time up front)		Program Manager
Create World Campus server space for course *(if applicable)*	Create World Campus server space for course *(if applicable)*		IT rep
Submit initial copy to lead designer	Submit initial copy to lead designer		Lead faculty *Resources:* Creating a Detailed Course Outline
Table of contents w/ Lesson titles	Detailed Course Outline		
Course introduction	Sample Lesson 1 ("first day of class")		
Sample content lesson, including activities and/or assignments	Sample content lesson, including activities and/or assignments		
Review/Revise initial copy	Review/Revise initial copy		Lead designer

Hold Course Launch meeting	Hold Course Launch meeting	Lead designer Lead faculty IMD Tech Typist IT rep Graphic Artist Production Specialists Program Manager
N/A	Review/Comment/Approve initial copy	Department head
Submit initial author payment form	N/A	Lead designer
Obtain desk copies of textbooks	Obtain desk copies of textbooks	Lead designer—provides list to production specialist Production specialist—obtains desk copies
Create listing of all anticipated copyright permissions and video licenses needed for course	Create listing of all anticipated copyright permissions and video licenses needed for course	Lead designer—drafts listing based on initial copy Lead faculty—double-checks draft list, adding/deleting as necessary; provides clean copies and source info
Initiate requests for all necessary copyright permissions and video licenses	Initiate requests for all necessary copyright permissions and video licenses	Lead designer and production specialist and/or Copy Center
Initiate request(s) for human research subjects clearance *(if applicable)*	Initiate request(s) for human research subjects clearance *(if applicable)*	Lead designer and lead faculty
Conduct Pre-implementation Meeting (if needed) (to work out logistics of proposed course format/delivery)	Conduct Pre-implementation Meeting (if needed) (to work out logistics of proposed course format/delivery)	Course development team plus "standard" implementation meeting members *Resource:* ID&D 101

(continued)

Appendix   *continued*

Open Enrollment Courses	Cohort Courses	Target Date (cohort courses only—where applicable)	Person(s) Responsible
Draft remaining course content, including course evaluation instruments *(if desired)* *Note: Drafts can be shared with lead designer either one at a time on a pre-determined schedule or in a "lump sum" on a single date in time—this is a decision made between the lead designer and the lead faculty*	Draft remaining course content, including course evaluation instruments *(if desired)* *Note: Drafts can be shared with lead designer either one at a time on a pre-determined schedule or in a "lump sum" on a single date in time—this is a decision made between the lead designer and the lead faculty*	(by the end of first semester for a two-semester development timeframe)	Lead faculty
Draft remaining exams *(if applicable)*	Draft remaining exams *(if applicable)*		Lead faculty
Obtain academic approval of unedited course content	N/A (at this point in timeline)		Lead designer
Submit author payment form	N/A		Lead designer
Pay faculty author(s)	N/A (at this point)		Manager
Develop remaining course materials *(Study guide, level 3 Web site, CD ROM, pdf documents, etc.)* *Note: This can be done as course content comes in from faculty member(s) or designer might wait to begin this process until all content is in*	Develop remaining course materials *(Study guide, Level 2 or 3 Web site, CD ROM, preliminary documents for pdfs, etc.)* *Note: This can be done as course content comes in from faculty member(s) or designer might wait to begin this process until all content is in*		Lead designer and, if appropriate, Technical Typist
Review/feedback of course materials *Note: This can be an ongoing process as the designer works with the author's draft content*	Review/feedback of course materials *Note: This can be an ongoing process as the designer works with the author's draft content*		Lead designer
Provide copy of all remaining course materials Welcome letter articles video masters etc.	Provide copy of all remaining course materials Welcome letter articles video masters etc.		Lead faculty *Resource:* World Campus Welcome Letter template

Review all remaining course materials Review/revise new materials Are articles and other existing materials "camera ready?" Should we create a readings book? Is audio and/or video of sufficient quality? Any additional copyright permissions needed? Required software? How will students get it? etc.	Review all remaining course materials Review/revise new materials Are articles and other existing print materials "camera ready?" Should we create a readings book? Is audio and/or video of sufficient quality? Any additional copyright permissions needed? Required software? How will students get it? etc.	Lead designer, lead faculty, and IMD
Edit ALL remaining course materials	Edit all non-Web course materials (with cohort courses, more time is available for Web-based course materials)	IMD and Tech Typist
Production of non-Web materials (like CD ROMs and pdfs, if applicable)	Production of non-Web materials (like CD ROMs and pdfs, if applicable)	Lead designer
Identify Instructor(s)	Identify Instructor(s)	Dept. head (with help from Program Manager)
Draft course Web site (promo; Level 1, 2, or 3)	Draft course Welcome Page site *(if applicable)*	Open enrollment—IT rep Cohort—Lead designer *Resource:* World Campus Welcome Page Template
Review/revise/approve course Web site *(promo, Level 1 or 2)*	Review/revise/approve course Welcome Page site *(if applicable)*	Lead faculty
Revise course Web site *(promo, Level 1 or 2)*	Revise course Welcome Page site *(if applicable)*	Lead designer
Edit course Web site *(promo, Level 1 or 2)*	Edit course Welcome Page site *(if applicable)*	IMD and Tec Typist
Finalize course Web site *(promo, Level 1 or 2)*	Finalize course Welcome Page site *(if applicable)*	Lead designer

(continued)

Appendix   *continued*

Open Enrollment Courses	Cohort Courses	Target Date (cohort courses only—where applicable)	Person(s) Responsible
Provide enrollment projections to lead designer # of RI students # of WC/DE students # of Campus Course Exchange students	Provide enrollment projections to lead designer # of RI students # of WC/DE students # of Campus Course Exchange students	15 weeks out	Program Manager
Generate preliminary Activity Sheet (include enrollment projections)	Generate preliminary Activity Sheet (include enrollment projections)	14 weeks out	Lead designer
Deliver "camera ready" student materials to Production Specialist, including welcome letter (in both print and pdf formats) masters for commercially-produced CD ROMS, videotapes, and/or audiotapes exams	Deliver "camera ready" student materials to Production Specialist (including welcome letter and exams, if applicable)	14 weeks out	Lead designer
Provide Welcome Letter in pdf format to Director of Learner Support	Provide Welcome Letter in pdf format to Director of Learner Support	13 weeks out	Production specialist
Welcome Letter (pdf format) sent to campus registrars for Campus Course Exchange courses	Welcome Letter (pdf format) sent to campus registrars for Campus Course Exchange courses	13 weeks out	Director of Learner Support
Provide MBS Direct liaison with information about a course and what items it requires, and enrollment projections if we know them	Provide MBS Direct with information about a course and what items it requires, and enrollment projections if we know them	13 weeks out	Production specialist
Order approximately 6 copies of PSU-produced print materials from Copy Center (this triggers the copyright permissions process) production specialists (2) lead designer Learner Support Tech Support instructor(s)	Order approximately 6 copies of PSU-produced print materials from Copy Center (this triggers the copyright permissions process) production specialists (2) lead designer Learner Support Tech Support instructor(s)	13 weeks out	Production specialist

Task	Timing	Resource/Responsible
Give enrollment projections to Copy Center and MBS Direct	13 weeks out	MBS Direct Liaison
Set tuition and materials prices; create stock numbers	13 weeks out	Tuition set by Program Manager Materials prices set by MBS Direct for items they stock; stock numbers given back to MBS Direct Liaison Other item prices set (for items PSU distributes) RR
Have Implementation Meeting	13 weeks out	*Resource:* ID&D 101
Produce final Activity Sheet	13 weeks out	BD
Create section for course (TCM = Term Course Master)		BD
Open course for registrations	12 weeks out	Learner Support
Welcome Letter sent to registered students (ideally everything else is ordered by student from MBS direct)		Learner Support
Notify Web Integrator that course Web site is ready for public		Lead designer
Link public pages to DE catalog and/or WC site		WC Web Master
Course made "active" in MBS Direct system (course shows up on Web site)	10 weeks out	MBS Direct
MBS Direct's Copy Center order sent to Production Specialist	10 weeks out	MBS Direct
PSU-produced masters for CD ROMs, videotapes, and/or audiotapes are given to Production Specialist	10 weeks out	Lead designer
PSU-produced masters for CD ROMs, videotapes, and/or audiotapes are sent to AVG for duplication	9 weeks out	Production specialist

(continued)

Appendix *continued*

Open Enrollment Courses	Cohort Courses	Target Date (cohort courses only—where applicable)	Person(s) Responsible
PSU-produced print materials are ordered from Copy Center Services	PSU-produced print materials are ordered from Copy Center Services	9 week out	Production specialist
Copy Center ships PSU-produced print materials to MBS Direct	Copy Center ships PSU-produced print materials to MBS Direct	7 weeks out	Copy center
AVG ships PSU-produced CDs/videotapes/audiotapes to MBS Direct	AVG ships PSU-produced CDs/videotapes/audiotapes to MBS Direct	7 week out	AVG
All necessary course materials ready at MBS Direct	All necessary course materials ready at MBS Direct	6 week out	IMD and Tech Typist
N/A	Edit of Web-based course materials		Lead designer
N/A	Finalize Web-based course materials		Lead designer
N/A	Obtain academic approval of final form of course. This includes review/revision/approval of all printed course materials, on-line course materials, CDs, videos, etc.—every aspect of the course!		
Train course instructor	Train course instructor		Lead faculty, Lead designer, and/or Tech support
N/A	Registration cut-off (ideal)	3 week out	Learner support
Registered students given access to password-protected on-line course materials	Registered students given access to password-protected on-line course materials	Open enrollment—upon registration Cohort—1 week out	Tech support
Course begins	Course begins		Instructor
N/A	Registration cut-off (actual)	1 week after course begins	Learner support
Tell MBS Direct to pull outdated materials	Tell MBS Direct to pull outdated materials		MBS Direct Liaison

Teaching and the Roles of the Instructor

In previous chapters, we have already introduced some ideas about the roles of instructors in teaching the distant learner. In this chapter we begin by looking more closely at the concept of interaction, and discuss the different roles of the distance teacher, the person who helps change information designed for a mass audience into the knowledge of each individual student.

How Distance Teaching Differs

There are several factors that make teaching a distance education course different from teaching in a traditional classroom. The most obvious difference is that, as an instructor, you will not know how students react to what you have written, or recorded or say in a broadcast (unless you happen to be using two-way interactive television) unless they choose to tell you through some feedback mechanism. For this reason alone, distance teaching remains a challenge for inexperienced instructors until they learn how to anticipate student responses to different events and how to deal with them.

A second factor making distance teaching a challenge for most teachers is the fact that teaching is conducted through a technology. All teachers have some experience of managing students in a classroom. Even if—as is still the case in higher education—most teachers have had no formal training, at least they can model their behavior after their own classroom teachers. However, until recently hardly anyone has had experience or training in how to teach through technology. People who become instructors in distance education in the United States must learn "on the job," with little or no guidance. Often the guidance comes from people who know little more than they do. They must find out for themselves the limitations and the potential of the technology and the best techniques for communicating through that technology. If you are teaching by television, you have to learn how to behave on-camera; in front of a radio or audio-conference microphone, to control (but vary) your rate and pitch of speaking; by correspondence or online, to interpret what the student writes and be able to write back "instructively"—without overextending the time you commit to each student!

The best distance teachers are empathetic, with an ability to sense their students' personalities, even when filtered through technologically transmitted communications. Students are often more defensive when taking a course from an unseen instructor than they would be in a conventional class, but are unlikely to express this anxiety. Some students are noticeably looking for a dependent relationship with the instructor, while others are noticeably counter-dependent—with most falling between the extremes. The instructor has to be able to identify such emotions and deal with them. The instructor must have ways of providing motivational support to those who need it, but also lead everyone to be as independent as they can be. Where peer interaction is possible, as it is in online courses, students can find it very sustaining; but it brings its own problems, which the instructor must be able to identify and intervene early rather than waiting until problems get out of hand.

Instructors must be able to guide students into being actively involved in the learning process, and for many students such involvement is counterintuitive. Many have been conditioned to think of *any* educational environment as one in which the student is expected to behave as a passive recipient of a teacher's knowledge, but even students who have a different perception of their role in the classroom are likely to take a more passive stance when faced with a television program, a Web site, or study guide. This is because the success of designers in making these packages well-structured and well-presented suggests a degree of certainty, if not perfection, that can be intimidating. A well-designed course will provide the instructor with many opportunities to engage students in discussion, criticism, and constructing knowledge. Nevertheless, the onus is on the instructor to establish an environment in which students learn to control and manage, and apply and engage with these materials, in the quest to relate them to their own lives, and thus to convert the designers' information into their personal knowledge.

Some Specific Functions of the Instructor

Table 6.1 lists the main functions of the instructor. They fall into four different types of activity. The first three items on the list are strictly "teaching" functions; that is to say, the instructor points out certain parts of the course content in a given unit of instruction (e.g., observing the discussion by students in an online bulletin board), intervenes to guide the discussion if necessary, and also interacts with individuals and groups of students as they prepare presentations or other projects for the class. The second set of activities pertain to "student progress," in which the instructor reviews each individual's

Table 6.1   Functions of Instructors in Distance Education

- Elaborating course content
- Supervising and moderating discussions
- Supervising individual and group projects
- Grading assignments and providing feedback on progress
- Keeping student records
- Helping students manage their study
- Motivating students
- Answering or referring administrative questions
- Answering or referring technical questions
- Answering or referring counseling questions
- Representing students with the administration
- Evaluating course effectiveness

regular assignment (see Chapter 5 regarding the centrality of the assignment in the distance education process), evaluates it, and communicates to each student regarding the extent to which that student has met the criteria of performance at that stage of the course. As discussed in Chapter 5, the data resulting from this student evaluation process must be entered into the system's records to provide the information needed by the program's managers in their monitoring of the system's effectiveness. The third cluster of activities consists of "learner support" functions. In most institutions, administrative, technical, or counseling questions will be answered by specialists in a student support service. In practice, however, we find that the great majority of students do not refer themselves directly to the specialists, but first raise their questions with instructors, who either may resolve the issue, or make the referral. The instructor must also be able to recognize the kinds of problems that are dealt with by the student support services so that they are often taken up before the student either recognizes them, or is ready to articulate them. For example, a student who consistently returns an assignment at the last minute may well be experiencing time management difficulties or may be excessively anxious about performance that a sensitive instructor will detect and will seek to resolve. The final activity listed in Table 6.1, evaluating course effectiveness, is undertaken on behalf of the institution in its effort to improve the quality of its programs. The instructor is the ultimate "eyes and ears" of the system. Course designers, technology experts, and administrators do not have contact with the students; each instructor on the other hand has—or should have—a truly intimate understanding of one small group of students, their progress, their feelings, and their experiences in the course. The instructor is therefore the most reliable source of information when managers of the system try to interpret the data flowing from the student monitoring (i.e., assignment) system.

Handling Assignments

The importance of the assignment has been mentioned already in this chapter and was discussed at some length in Chapter 5. The assignment is the *key component* that links the instructor to the student, the designer to the instructor, and even the student to other students. It is the key to program evaluation, as we have described, and is the means by which each individual student's progress is measured. Its importance cannot be exaggerated. Courses that are designed with good assignments and in which the assignment handling system works are likely to be good courses, while those that regard the assignment as less than the key component are likely to fail.

To summarize, and to reinforce the idea of the assignment's central role in the teaching system—which also serves to emphasis the importance of the instructor who supervises and evaluates each assignment—the relation of assignment to design and instruction and evaluation is illustrated in Figure 6.1.

Student Expectations

Here is what students say they expect in terms of grading and feedback on assignments (Cole, Coats, and Lentell, 1986):

- fair and objective grading
- to have their work treated with respect
- an explanation and justification of the grade awarded
- a clear indication of how they can improve both in terms of specific responses to questions and in general

Figure 6.1 **Central Position of the Assignment in Driving Monitoring of Performance and Training Interventions**

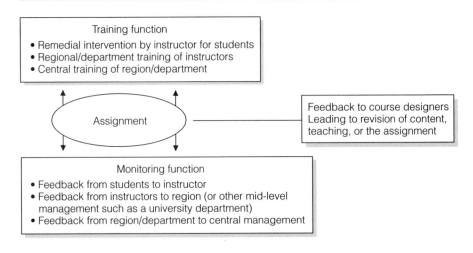

Reflections of a Correspondence Teacher

The following extract illustrates how similar the experience of correspondence edu-
cators was to those of us who teach online and suggests that we could learn from
the ways correspondence educators have dealt with their problems.

"I have been teaching Jewish studies in the School of Religion at the University
of Iowa for twenty-two years. For the past decade or so I have offered several guided correspondence courses through the Division of Continuing Education.

"Just as I had been brought up short in my initial attempts as a classroom
teacher, so too with my first efforts in correspondence courses. For instance, the
first assignment in "Quest" asks the student to submit an "outline" of the book of
Ecclesiastes. I had in mind a summary which would consist of a systematic listing
of the book's most obvious features. It quickly became apparent to me that most
students not only did not follow my argument but that many did not know what
I expected in terms of an outline. I received mail-in assignments ranging from a
few casual observations to virtual paraphrases. In the classroom, when this materials is assigned it is checked for conflicting interpretations by me and/or graduate teaching assistants, and we are able to respond immediately to questions about
our expectations. In one way or another the same problem, i.e. my failure to communicate with sufficient clarity, surfaced repeatedly. It is a truism that the success
of a correspondence course depends upon the instructor's ability to communicate
what is expected of the student with as much exactitude as possible.

"One more point. My correspondence courses have attracted both the best
and worst of students. Some students appear to take correspondence courses as
an end run around what they perceive to be a more difficult campus hurdle. They
are almost always mistaken, I believe, because of the great difficulty many of
today's students have in reading with care and writing with clarity. There are also
students, often nontraditional ones, who exhibit a depth of understanding that is
breathtaking. One of the best students I have ever encountered in any setting, a
housewife in Los Angeles, took the Holocaust course and displayed such intellectual acuity, curiosity, and integrity that I was left grasping for words of sufficient power to praise her. Were it not for my correspondence courses I never
would have encountered this woman and others like her."

SOURCE: Holstein (1992), pp. 22–33.

- encouragement and reassurance about their ability and progress
- constructive criticism and advice
- an opportunity to respond if desired
- a timely response (i.e., before the next assignment is due)

Satisfying these criteria takes considerable time and effort on the part of the
instructor, but from every point of view—student, designer, and program

manager—it is vitally important that this work is completed to the highest standard possible. Administrators who impede this work by imposing too large a student case load—that is, too many students per instructor—risk being responsible for serious damage to the quality of their program.

More about Interaction

Effective teaching at a distance depends on a deep understanding of the nature of interaction and how to facilitate interaction through technologically transmitted communications. Three distinct types of interaction have been identified. They are: interaction of the learner with content, interaction with instructor, and interaction with other learners.

Learner–Content Interaction

The first type of interaction that the teacher must facilitate is the interaction the student has with the subject matter that is presented for study. This interaction of student with content is a defining characteristic of education. Education is a process of planned learning of some content, assisted by a teacher or teachers. Every learner has to construct his or her own knowledge through a process of personally accommodating information into previously existing cognitive structures. It is interacting with content that results in these changes in the learner's understanding, what we sometimes call a change in perspective. In distance education, the content needed for this process is designed and presented by the course designers as explained in the previous chapter. The role of the instructor is to support and assist each student as he or she interacts with the content and converts it into personal knowledge.

Learner–Instructor Interaction

The second type of interaction, regarded as essential by most learners, and as highly desirable by most educators, is interaction between the learner and an instructor. After the content has been presented—whether it is information, demonstration of skill, or modeling certain attitudes and values—the instructors assist the students in interacting with it. Some of the ways they do this is by stimulating the students' interest in the subject and their motivation to learn. Next they help the students' application of what they are learning, as they practice skills that have seen demonstrated, or manipulate information and ideas that have been presented. Instructors are responsible for formal and informal testing and evaluation, designed to ensure the learner is making progress. Finally, instructors provide counsel, support, and encouragement to each learner, though the extent and nature of this support varies according to the educational level of the learners, the teacher's personality and philosophy, and other situational and organizational factors.

Where interaction between learner and a distant teacher is possible online, or through correspondence or teleconference, the learner is able to draw on the experience of the professional instructor while interacting with the content in whatever manner is most effective for that particular learner. This individualization of instruction is a long-recognized advantage of correspondence instruction and now extends to online versions. When the online instructor sits with a set of students' assignments, there is no class, but instead the instructor enters a dialogue with each individual. Although each student and the instructor attend to a common piece of content, usually in a set text, but quite likely on a Web site or audio or videotape, each student's response to the presentation is different, and so the response by the instructor to each student is different, too. To some students a misunderstanding is explained, to others elaborations are given, to others simplifications; to one analogies are drawn, and to another supplementary readings are suggested. The instructor is especially valuable in responding to the learners' application of new knowledge. Whatever self-directed learners may do alone when interacting with the content presented, they are vulnerable at the point of application, since they do not know enough about the subject to be sure they are applying it correctly, or as intensively or extensively as is possible or desirable, or that there are potential areas of application they are not aware of.

Learner–Learner Interaction

It is the third form of interaction that is a relatively new dimension for teachers in distance education. This is interlearner interaction, interaction between one learner and other learners. Two different kinds of interaction are included here; one is the interaction within groups and between groups that occurs in programs based on teleconferencing technologies. The other is learner-to-learner interaction in online settings where the individuals do not meet face-to-face and their group—if one is organized—is a virtual group.

In both settings, students generally find interaction with their peers to be stimulating and motivating. Real or virtual groups can be used by course designers and instructors for generating content, especially when students can be organized into project teams and given responsibility for making presentations to their peers. Generally, interlearner discussions are extremely valuable as a way of helping students to think out and test content that has been presented, whatever the means of presentation.

A Hierarchy of Interaction

Roblyer and Wiencke (2003) have developed the following rubric for evaluating different degrees of interactivity in distance learning courses (see Table 6.2). What is shown here is a hierarchy of interaction ranging from low to high. Each level defines interaction that is social, instructional, technological, learner driven, and instructor driven. We suggest you could study this as a

Table 6.2   **Hierarchy of Interaction**

Scale	Social/Rapport-building Designs for Interaction	Instructional Designs for Interaction	Interactivity of Technology Resources	Evidence of Learner Engagement	Evidence of Instructor Engagement
Low interactive qualities	The instructor does not encourage students to get to know one another on a personal basis. No activities require social interaction, or are limited to brief introductions at the beginning of the course.	Instructional activities do not require two-way interaction between instructor and students; they call for one-way delivery of information (e.g., instructor lectures, text delivery) and student products based on the information.	Fax, Web pages or other technology resource allows one-way delivery of information (text and/or graphics).	By end of course, most students (50–75%) are *replying to* messages from the instructor, but only when required; messages are sometimes unresponsive to topics and tend to be either brief or wordy and rambling.	Instructor responds only randomly to student queries; responses usually take more than 48 hours; feedback is brief and provides little analysis of student work or suggestions for improvement
Minimum interactive qualities	In addition to brief introductions, the instructor requires one other exchange of personal information among students, e.g., written bio of personal background and experiences.	Instructional activities require students to communicate with the instructor on an individual basis only (e. g., asking/responding to instructor questions).	E-mail, listserv, conference/bulletin board or other technology resource allows two-way, asynchronous exchanges of information (text and graphics).	By end of course, most students (50–75%) are *replying to* messages from the instructor and other students, both when required and on a voluntary basis; replies are usually responsive to topics but often are either brief or wordy and rambling.	Instructor responds to most student queries; responses usually are within 48 hours; feedback sometimes offers some analysis of student work and suggestions for improvement

(continued)

(continued)

Scale	Social/Rapport-building Designs For Interaction	Instructional Designs for Interaction	Interactivity of Technology Resources	Evidence of Learner Engagement	Evidence of Instructor Engagement
Moderate interactive qualities	In addition to providing for exchanges of personal information among students, the instructor provides at least one other in-class activity designed to increase communication and social rapport among students.	In addition to the requiring students to communicate with the instructor, instructional activities require students to communicate with one another (e.g., discussions in pairs or small groups).	In addition to technologies used for two-way asynchronous exchanges of information, chat-room, or other technology allows synchronous exchanges of primarily written information.	By end of course, all or nearly all students (90–100%) are *replying to* messages from the instructor and other students, both when required and voluntarily; replies are always responsive to topics but sometimes are either brief or wordy and rambling.	Instructor responds to all student queries; responses usually are within 48 hours; feedback usually offers some analysis of student work and suggestions for improvement
Above average interactive qualities	In addition to providing for exchanges of personal information among students and encouraging communication and social interaction, the instructor also interacts with students on a social/personal basis.	In addition to the requiring students to communicate with the instructor, instructional activities require students to develop products by working together cooperatively (e.g., in pairs or small groups) and sharing feedback.	In addition to technologies used for two-way synchronous and asynchronous exchanges of written information, additional technologies (e. g., teleconferencing) allow one-way visual and two-way voice communications between instructor and students.	By end of course, most students (50–75%) are *both replying to and initiating* messages when required and voluntarily; messages are detailed and responsive to topics, and usually reflect an effort to communicate well.	Instructor responds to all student queries; responses usually are prompt, i.e., within 24 hours; feedback always offers detailed analysis of student work and suggestions for improvement

Scale	Social/Rapport-Building Designs for Interaction	Instructional Designs for Interaction	Interactivity of Technology Resources	Evidence of Learner Engagement	Evidence of Instructor Engagement
High level of interactive qualities	In addition to providing for exchanges of information and encouraging student-student and instructor-student interaction, the instructor provides ongoing course structures designed to promote social rapport among students and instructor.	In addition to requiring students to communicate with the instructor, instructional activities require students to develop products by working together cooperatively (e.g., in pairs or small groups) and share results and feedback with other groups in the class.	In addition to technologies to allow two-way exchanges of text information, visual technologies such as two-way video or videoconferencing technologies allow synchronous voice & visual communications between instructor and students and among students.	By end of course, all or nearly all students (90–100%) are both *replying to and initiating* messages, both when required and voluntarily; messages are detailed, responsive to topics, and are well-developed communications.	Instructor responds to all student queries; responses are always prompt, i.e. within 24 hours; feedback always offers detailed analysis of student work and suggestions for improvement, along with additional hints and information to supplement learning.

means of thinking about what kind of interaction you would want to facilitate for different types of students and different subject areas you are familiar with, as well as evaluating your own or your students' interactions.

Interaction versus Presentation: Keeping a Balance

Some of the most common causes of failure in distance education result from a disregard of the multidimensional nature of distance teaching. We often notice a sometimes cavalier neglect of what should occur before and after the delivery of teaching materials to the learner. In the past this took the form of a view of teaching that regarded it as merely the presentation of information. Whether the primary communication medium is online or print, audio or videotape recordings, broadcasts or teleconferences, there is often an imbalance between the time and effort devoted to experts' presentations of information and the arrangements made for the learner to interact with the content thus presented, and the instructor-learner interaction and learner-learner interaction that we have discussed. Simply making a video presentation or putting lecture material on a Web site is no more teaching than it would be to send the students a book through the mail. As well as presentations of information, at least as much attention should have been devoted to finding out each individual's need and motivation for learning, giving each individual the opportunity for testing and practicing new knowledge, and for receiving evaluation of the results of such practice. If there is any one secret to good teaching it is summed up in the word "activity."

It is equally dangerous, however, to have an excess of interaction at the expense of presentation. Nowadays when it is so easy for an instructor to go online and engage in interaction with a virtual group of students, the trend of error is in the opposite direction from before. We now see extremely poorly designed presentation materials, hurriedly put together with a minimum of specialist assistance, and rarely with any audio or video media, as a preliminary to many hours of e-mail exchanges and bulletin board postings. It is a challenge to hold the healthy balance between these two dimensions of the teacher's role—whether the teacher is an individual or a course team. It is important to keep the balance of presentation and interaction, which is essentially the correct balance of resources invested in design and in instruction.

The Instructor's Role in Teleconferencing

Guidelines developed some years ago for by the Instructional Communications Systems group at the University of Wisconsin–Madison can be applied to online teaching as well as the audio or video media. These guidelines suggest that instructors should learn four sets of techniques:

1. *Humanizing.* The creation of an environment that emphasizes the importance of the individual and which generates a feeling of group rapport. This can be achieved by, for example, using students' names,

providing pictures of participants, and asking for personal experiences and opinions. In some programs, students are enabled to make their own Web sites where they enter personal information as a means of building a virtual community.

2. *Participation.* Ensuring that there is a high level of interaction and dialog, which is facilitated by such techniques as posing questions, group problem-solving activities, participant presentations, and role-playing exercises.

3. *Message style.* Using good communication techniques in presenting information including: providing overviews, use of advance organizers and summaries, variety, and using print materials for communicating information that has a lot of detail.

4. *Feedback.* Getting information from participants about their progress. Feedback can be obtained by: direct questions, assignments, quizzes, polls, and questionnaires.

Some elements specifically relevant to teaching by television are:

- Having background knowledge about: the strengths and limitations of television, the equipment and how it works, roles of the different people involved, general planning steps and procedures, copyright considerations, knowing television terminology

- Being able to prepare your own visuals for use with an overhead camera; how to use a blackboard on camera; using video, or slides

- Knowing on-camera techniques and appropriate behavior including eye contact, voice intonation and projection, clothing, and movement

- Knowing techniques to facilitate student participation and interaction within the range of cameras

- Knowing how to respond calmly and professionally on-camera to technical problems

A popular source of information about teaching by television is: *Teaching Telecourses: Opportunities and Options,* published by the Annenberg/CPB Project in cooperation with the PBS Adult Learning Service (Levine, 1988). Another faculty guide for television teaching is Cyrs and Smith (1990). For a research review of video-based instruction, see Wisher and Curnow (2003).

The Site Coordinator

As we saw briefly in an earlier chapter, when a distance education program is delivered by video or audio-teleconference, a local coordinator is needed at the receiving sites. Here we will look a little more closely at the characteristics we look for in a good site coordinator:

The first requirement is that this person is a *communicator.* We put communicating with the distant instructor as the top priority, because if communication should break down between the coordinator and the students or the larger community—provided the coordinator has sufficient trust to communicate the problem to the instructor—advice and assistance can be given and action taken to rectify the situation. The site coordinator must also have good communication with the local community. It is the coordinator who usually contacts the channels of information dissemination in the locality, such as the newspapers, radio, and bulletin boards, to spread information about a forthcoming course, and it is the coordinator who is approached by potential students with inquiries as they think about taking the course. When the course is being planned, the coordinator employs local resource people to undertake such production activity as copying printed materials, or the coordinator may arrange to make a videotape as part of a class project. Coordinators will negotiate the availability of rooms and teleconference equipment with administrators. They also communicate with administrators on such matters as receiving payment of fees when it is the local college or corporation that enrolls the students rather than the students paying tuition fees personally.

Coordinators should be *competent* in attending to technical details, to administration, and to instruction. Having technical competence means being able to either install technology themselves, or to negotiate and oversee the installation. With most technologies, there will be no technicians during the time of instruction, and the coordinators will therefore set up the technology, test it, and operate it during the session. They must have sufficient technical knowledge to recognize potential faults that may occur during the life of the course, or during a particular session of the course, and be able to take appropriate remedial action. An unexpected and uncorrected technical failure could result in an abandoned session; loss of students' confidence; and the collapse of an institution's presence in a site, a city, or a nation. This could all result from a very minor problem, perhaps just a loose telephone line that could have been easily dealt with by a coordinator with experience. A coordinator's competence also covers administrative procedures. Among the most important of these are efficiently receiving materials and distributing them to students, keeping records and reporting them to the instructor and perhaps to the institution that hosts the local site. Finally, it is helpful if the coordinator is competent in the content being taught in the course. It is better to appoint persons who have previously taken the course as students, so that they not only are familiar with the instructional procedures and have a long standing working relationship with the instructor, but that they know the subject matter better than the newly enrolled students at their sites. This helps them to interpret the instructor's explanations or questions when the need arises and also to help their students as they struggle to articulate their ideas.

Having made their best effort to recruit good local coordinators, distance teaching organizations and individual instructors should care for them well (which includes paying them well), because it is essential that they *continue* in the role and build up experience in the work. There are several reasons why this continuity is important. One is the time and experience needed to develop the effective working relationship with the instructor and community and the competence described in the previous paragraph. It is much more efficient when the instructor can send materials to a coordinator who has practiced what to do with them in previous iterations of the course; to make plans for a weekly program, or discuss a problem student with a colleague who shares memories of similar events in previous courses. Although each cohort of students consists of different individuals, their problems are usually similar to those of previous cohorts, and an experienced coordinator is likely to recognize problems and be able to explain them to the instructor with reference to previous experience, or on the basis of previous experience to solve them locally without recourse to the instructor.

The good coordinator has *control* of events at the local site, and the students have a comfortable awareness of this. Control is achieved as a result of the other characteristics just described. The technology is set up in advance of students' arrival at the site; the administrative work is done quietly and efficiently; the instructor communicates with the coordinator in ways that reinforces students' sense that they are in the care of a team that works together effectively. The environment at the site should be relaxed and friendly, but there should also be a sense that events are well-planned, that everything is under control, and that any problems can and will be resolved. During the sessions, coordinators and instructor handle any unexpected issues or problems with competent professionalism. This sense of control is more important in a distant learning environment than it might be in conventional settings, since it is especially important to instill confidence in the students. Many students are afraid of being separated from the instructor and others are skeptical about the viability of an environment in which there is no instructor present. To meet these emotional barriers to learning, it is important that the coordinator projects a sense of control, efficiency, responsibility, and authority.

Last but not least in importance, the coordinator has to be a person who *cares* about the comfort and welfare of the students, and be able to communicate this concern. No matter how skillful, the educator at a distance will not be able to establish as good an affective relationship with students as in a face-to-face environment. Although the instructor should do everything possible to establish an open, communicative, friendly, and caring environment as is necessary for learning, it will nevertheless be up to the local coordinator to make up for what the instructor will be unable to do. The coordinator does this in numerous ways: by greeting participants; by ensuring that everyone has freedom to participate in discussions; by privately conversing with anyone who is bruised during an oral exchange; or by voicing appreciation, approval, or congratulations at an individual's successes.

Instructing by Audio-Graphic Web Conferencing

Teaching via Web conferencing is more demanding than audio-conferencing alone because of the added dimension of the graphic and video. Training may be provided by vendors of Web conference systems in the form of demonstrations and "hands-on" practice sessions. In addition, universities offer training to their own faculty and students. Guidelines for Web conferencing are provided by Duckworth (2001), Driscoll (2003), and Hofmann (2000).

As with other teleconference technologies, it is challenging for the Web conference instructor to get students actively engaged in the class. Instructors must learn how to put students at ease with the system. One technique is to have everyone sign in at the beginning of class using the shared whiteboard and perhaps identify their location on a map. Using the annotation tools, you can have participants add comments or mark up slides presented via the whiteboard. Another strategy is to ask participants to draw a diagram to illustrate a concept being discussed. Students can also be directed to draw a question mark on the screen when they have a question, which is the equivalent of raising the hand in a traditional classroom.

It is probably a good idea to teach faculty how to use, create and modify their own slides, although a distance teaching organization should provide a graphics artist to prepare the slides for instructors, in order to save faculty preparation time as well as to ensure higher quality visuals.

Teaching Online

Bandwidth limitations prevent the Internet from being a useful means of transmitting audio and video media, and content designed for presentation in these media must usually be transmitted on CD-ROMs. For the same reason nearly all instruction online is dependent on text. The interactions in text are either synchronous or asynchronous. Most experienced online instructors find the asynchronous to be much more useful and effective than synchronous text-based interaction. As with audio and video technologies, getting online students to engage in discussions of pedagogical value and relevance to the course content is a challenge that requires instructors to develop good facilitation skills.

Conducting Asynchronous Discussions

The heart of the asynchronous online course is the discussion forum.
The basic pattern of the discussion forum is fairly standard:

1. *An opening message.* The course designers prepare a question requiring a response, the instructor gives an explanation or reflection on some item of content, or students post an assignment.

2. *Responding message.* Instructor or students are expected to reply to one person with an elaboration or alternative view, or question. To ensure that everybody receives at least one reply, the instructor may call for a response to a message that has not received a reply.

3. *Follow-up message.* Instructor or students reply to previous posting(s) with an explanation of how the second message was helpful in increasing understanding of the topic, and if possible building a further substantive comment.

4. *Summarize message.* Instructor summarizes the messages from all group members to include key points, similarities, and differences in the group's understanding.

Student Voices: The Value of Asynchronicity

Student A: My first language is not English. I am taking both face-to-face and distance courses in the United States. To tell you the truth, to me the online interaction is probably ten times more than that in the traditional classrooms. In the face-to-face classrooms, I could hardly catch up what everybody is saying not to mention respond to them or say something about my opinion immediately. In the online classes, on the other hand, I can read your postings, questions, thoughts, again and again until I totally got your points. The best part is I can "digest" what you said, and then respond to you after I've organized my thought. That is . . . so sweet!!

Student B: I teach math online, and I find that the asynchronous nature of the online discussion board is an advantage in that class as well. When the students ask questions, they need to show their work. Sometimes, as they do this, they find that they have been able to answer their own questions. Other students have been able to focus their questions. For example, instead of raising their hand and saying, "I don't get it" as they can in a face-to-face class, they have to start solving the problem and explain where they run into trouble in solving this particular problem. They do this under no time pressure. Other students can take the time to study the problem and offer solutions. I find the students asking the questions know that they understand some of the material, and the students answering the questions feel more confident in themselves because they can offer solutions. It has been a win-win situation.

Student postings in Penn State course ADTED 531 Fall 2003.

Tips for Online Instructors

The following are some tips for instructors teaching online, which should also be modeled for students:

- *Conduct an online conference like other teleconferences by "humanizing."* Have each student post a biography at the beginning of class. Deal with each student in as personal a way as possible. Aim to make students into a learning community. Establish a positive and helpful tone in replies to messages.

- *Conduct a computer-based conference like other teleconferences by asking good questions.* As students answer your question, be prepared to restate it to accommodate the fresh input. Encourage students to pose questions and also develop the habit of attempting to answer other students.

- *Control the number of messages.* With fifteen students in a class, a weekly posting of, for example, four messages is a substantial body of information to be processed by each student—and the instructor.

Define what is an acceptable number of postings, not in order to be pedantic in enforcing an arbitrary number, but so that students will know what is acceptable performance.

- *Control the length of messages.* In general it is a good idea to keep each message to a single idea or at least a single issue. When the course design calls for posting assignments as the basis for discussion, set a limit for their length. With graduate students, a maximum could be 200 words, but for some courses this would be excessive.

- *Occasionally provide summary messages that restate the major points already made.* This helps to minimize the risk of fragmentation and is a way of redirecting the discussion and keeping it on track.

- *Be careful to distinguish personal replies containing feedback for specific individuals from public comments intended for the entire class.* In our practice we tell students to send any private messages by e-mail, even complimentary messages such as "I liked your last posting." Our rule is that every posting must pass the criterion of "adding to the community's pool of knowledge."

- *Every message should be acknowledged.* Each student should receive personal feedback on assignments, explaining the strength and weakness of their answer. It is also very good practice to post a general summary after an assignment is completed that reviews the strengths and weaknesses of all responses.

- *Take advantage of tools now available in most online learning systems that enable the instructor to organize students in teams for group assignments and projects.* For example, students may need to be reminded to keep their discussion in their team subconference and also to use private messages when possible, to avoid "cluttering up" the general conference area.

- *Create a forum that explains discussion board procedures, and encourage students to add their own tips and comments during the course.* Post announcements to keep students up-to-date on class progress and special events.

- *Assuming participation is seen as essential (as it is by constructivist teachers) link it to course assignments and grades.* Scores can be given for assignments posted online and also for the quality of students' comments on each other's assignments.

- *Model good manners, and insist on good manners online.* Do not be sarcastic or insulting. Nearly all students online are volunteering their time and their money and nobody should find their learning experience an unpleasant one. Fortunately the vast majority of students are considerate and caring in their interactions with others.

For discussion of the facilitator role online, see Collison et al. (2000) and Salmon (2000). General guidelines for online teaching are provided by Hanna

Synchronous Online Instruction

Hints for Using Course Chat Room:
Example of Guidance Given by an Online Instructor

Chat is a modality all of its own . . . and its patterns of communication tend to be quite different from those we are used to. If you haven't used chat before, conversations might seem to be fragmented, speech bites truncated, and logic, at times, nonexistent. You will get used to it and it turns out to be quite an energizing modality.

Take time to get involved; write briefly, even dividing long sentences up into several bites; abbreviate where possible; use names to signal addressees; but above all, don't get frustrated. If it all seems to be too much, stop typing and watch, read, and get oriented again.

Enter the chat room area from the In Touch Menu page. Click once on the title to enter. You might need to wait a few seconds for the chat room to load. Be patient.

Type your message in the dialogue line at the top of the screen in the middle of the page. Then press enter or click on Send to the right of the dialogue line. Your message, along with everyone else's, will appear in the larger dialogue box below.

One of the first things you will want to do is click on Settings right under the beginning of the dialogue line and change the Message Life setting from 3 minutes to 30 minutes. If you don't do this, you will see only the postings put up in the last 3 minutes. After that, they disappear from the bottom of the dialogue box. Also, click on Refresh periodically to make sure you're seeing everything that is current.

If you want to send a message to just one person who is in the chat room, click on his or her name in the list on the right side of the page. The message to that person will appear with his or her name in blue in parentheses only in his/her dialogue box and yours. After sending a message to an individual, that person's name will now appear in the drop-down menu under "Everyone" in the upper left corner. OL! Have some fun!

Reprinted with permission from Ms. Kay Shattuck, instructor using ANGEL in teaching Penn State's ADTED 470 course.

et. al. (2000), Ko and Rossen (2001), Palloff and Pratt (2001), and White and Weight (1999).

See also:

http://www.spjc.edu/eagle/BEEP/BEEP4.htm

http://www.emoderators.com/moderators.shtml

http://onlinelearning.tc.cc.va.us/resource/discpatt.htm

http://www.ion.illinois.edu/IONresources/conferencing/chat.asp

For research about discussions in online education, see Winiecki (2003).

Questions for Online Teachers in the High School

In 2002, the National Education Association (NEA) published a document entitled "Guide to Online High School Courses." The guide outlined some of the major issues with respect to online learning at the high school level, posing them in the form of the following questions:

- Am I ready to teach online? What do I need to know and how can I learn this prior to teaching online?

- Do I have access to computers, Internet connections, and other resources necessary for teaching a course online? Will the school provide me with necessary access and support?

- Will this change what I teach and how I teach? Can I participate in the development of the curriculum? What is "academic freedom" in the online world? Am I required to use lessons that are designed by others for the online environment? How will the online environment affect my style of communication with students?

- How will this change my assessment of student learning? What kind of authentic performance works online? How can I ensure that the student is doing his/her own work?

- What are the students' rights and responsibilities for online classes? Are there consequences for inappropriate behavior or academic impropriety? Is there an appeal process for students who believe they have been treated unfairly? Are there criteria (such as level of participation) that

Social Aspects of Online Learning

As suggested in the rubric we studied earlier in this chapter, there is—as a result of the increasing use of Web-based learning—a great deal of interest in the social aspects of online interaction, especially in collaboration and in virtual group activities; see Wegerif, 1998, for example). The ability of students and teachers to establish "social presence" in an online course has been the subject of a number of studies (e.g., Gunawardena and Zittle, 1997; Rourke et al., 1999). A great deal has also been written about online learning communities (Carabajal et al., 2003; Palloff and Pratt, 1999; Roberts, 2003). Brown (2001) describes three stages of community building in an online class: comfort, conferment, and camaraderie. Conrad (2002a) describes the nature of etiquette in online learning courses, which she describes as "the art of niceness." Curtis and Lawson (2001) compared online collaboration with face-to-face collaboration and concluded that it

may affect grading regardless of how students perform on authentic assessments? Do students have access to counseling and other support services beyond what I can offer them?

- How will this change the way I interact with parents/guardians? Will I be able to contact my students' parents/guardians when needed or on an ongoing basis?

- What kinds of support structures will be in place to assist me to: (i) work with the technology, (ii) accommodate individual student needs (particularly students with special needs), (iii) enhance my professional skills, and (iv) collaborate with colleagues?

- How will teaching online change the way I am evaluated? Will administrators at other sites have access to my online class and interactions with my students and will they evaluate me? What standards will be used for my evaluation?

- What contractual rights and protections will I have?

- How will this affect my overall workload? Will adjustments be made in my other teaching assignments in order to accommodate the workload?

- Who owns the lesson materials and teaching ideas I use online? Will I be compensated if others use my designs and ideas or if they are marketed by the "provider"?

SOURCE: From the National Education Association (NEA), "Guide to online High-school Courses," 2002, pp. 7–8; http://www.nea.org/technology/onlinecourseguide.html. Reprinted with permission.

is similar in many ways, although more planning is required for online collaboration, and familiarity with the online system affects the nature of the collaboration. Bringelson and Carey (2000) studied the nature of participation in two online professional development communities, one called "Tapped-In" for K–12 teachers, and "TeleCHI" for researchers in the field of human–computer interfaces. Anderson and Kanuka (1997) found that educators using a Web conference system were satisfied with their online collaboration (though they still preferred face-to-face interaction). Hughes et al. (2002) discuss the obstacles to successful online collaboration; they include establishing trust in the technology, the instructor, and the other participants.

Carabajal, LaPointe, and Gunawardena (2003) provide a substantial research review of virtual groups in an online environment.

Examination and Test Security

Examinations and testing in a distance education setting present some special challenges with respect to security. If students take an exam or quiz at home or at a learning center with no supervision, it is not possible to guarantee the integrity of the test. Consequently, in most distance education programs, students must complete their main exams in a proctored setting at a learning center or school. Proctors are usually teachers or administrators who are selected by the student and approved by the distance learning institution. Another procedure, where the subject matter allows, is to use computer-based testing in which each student receives a different subset of questions randomly selected by the computer. In many adult learning courses, students complete a project report based upon a research study instead of a final exam.

With the advent of the Internet and Web, online testing tools have become available, and all integrated learning systems include testing capabilities (see Zhang et al., 2001). Not only do these tools make it relatively simple to create tests in a variety of forms, but they also make analysis and reporting of the results quick and easy. Integrated learning systems come with grade books that automatically display test scores for each student as soon as they have completed the test. Many options are provided in the test creation process including random ordering of items, display of correct answer, providing a time limit for the response, and allowing multiple attempts.

However, the availability of online testing does not solve the dilemma of ensuring test security. There is still no way to authenticate the learner, although use of desktop cameras (so-called "Web-cams") does offer the possibility of actually seeing the candidate to confirm their identity (matched against photo IDs). In the future, we may be able to remotely identify individuals using devices that scan finger, voice, or eye prints (technology which is already in use for security applications), but at present this seems a rather extreme measure. Probably a more serious element of online dishonesty than examination cheating is plagiarism in writing assignments. Plagiarism is a particular worry for educators in the online environment because material can be so easily located and captured electronically that the line between legitimate research and plagiarism is sometimes not easy for students to recognize. Additionally there is the threat posed by online companies that will sell term papers written by other students. To address this problem, a number of plagiarism detection tools have been developed (see http://www.plagiarism.org or http://www.plagiarism.com).

Faculty Perspectives: Some Findings from Research

Dillon and Walsh (1992) reviewed faculty perspectives about distance teaching. Here are some of their findings:

- Faculty believe that distance teaching requires a personal and empathic rapport with students.

Viewpoint: Lani Gunawardena

I believe that the theoretical challenges for distance education will center on issues related to learning and pedagogy in technology mediated online learning environments. One such issue is understanding and evaluating knowledge construction in online collaborative learning communities. Increasingly we are subscribing to a knowledge construction view of learning as opposed to an information acquisition view, as we design web-based distance learning environments. The knowledge construction perspective views computer networks not as a channel for information distribution, but primarily as a new medium for construction of meaning, providing new ways for students to learn through negotiation and collaboration with a group of peers. The challenge however, is to develop theory to explain how new construction of knowledge occurs through the process of social negotiation in such a knowledge-building community.

With the expansion and acceptance of the Internet and the World Wide Web across the globe for education and training, the significance of culture and its impact on communication, and the teaching and learning process at a distance will provide an impetus for further research and theory building. If we design learner-centered learning environments, how do we build on the conceptual and cultural knowledge that learners bring with them? How does culture influence perception, cognition, communication, and the teaching-learning process in an online course? How do we as instructors engage in culturally responsive online teaching? These types of questions need to be addressed in research and in theoretical frameworks as we move toward making distance education a more equitable learning experience.

Lani Gunawardena, Organizational Learning and Instructional Technology Program, University of New Mexico

- Communication skills are critical.
- Faculty who teach at a distance are generally positive towards distance education and their attitudes tend to become more positive with experience.
- Faculty motivation for teaching at a distance is intrinsic rather than extrinsic.
- Faculty believe that distance teaching experience improves their traditional teaching.

Blanch (1994) analyzed the barriers to faculty adoption of distance education. They were:

- lack of awareness on the part of the university community of the general benefits of distance education
- lack of incentives for faculty to be involved in distance education
- the unreasonableness of expecting faculty to commit themselves to a very different teaching approach without any trial period
- the faculty's sense that distance education was not integrated within the university's programs and plans

Rockwell et al. (2000) surveyed 207 faculty members in two colleges at the University of Nebraska to study the type of education, assistance, and support they felt they needed to develop distance education materials. The areas that faculty identified were: help in designing interaction, developing materials, applying technologies, and marketing their courses. An earlier study by Rockwell et al. (1999) examined incentives that encourage faculty and obstacles that discourage them. They found the primary incentives were intrinsic (e.g., taking up a new challenge, winning peer recognition) rather than extrinsic—such as monetary—rewards. The major perceived obstacles related to time requirements, developing effective technology skills, and general support needs.

Betts (1998) examined the factors that affected faculty participation in distance education at the George Washington University. She surveyed over 1,000 faculty and 8 deans and concluded that the faculty are more likely to participate in distance education if certain inhibiting factors are eliminated by the administration, and the intrinsic benefits involved in distance education are stressed by the administration.

Berge and colleagues have concluded that the perceived barriers are greater in the initial stages of an organization being in distance education, and that the view changes as the organization matures. See http://www.emoderators.com/barriers/index.shtml.

Lee (2002) surveyed faculty from 35 Western institutions to measure their views on instructional support for distance education. The study found that with the exception of one institution, Rio Salado College, the faculty seemed to feel that they were being asked to perform at a higher standard without receiving adequate support.

Figure 6.2 displays a selection of Web sites that illustrate the kinds of support given faculty in a number of university and K–12 systems. Figure 6.3 lists some of the best regarded professional development programs.

For more on faculty and their reactions to online distance teaching, see: Wolcott (2003), Taylor (2002), and Seay et al. (2001).

The Sloan Center for Asynchronous Learning Environments has developed a Web site where you can open media clips of instructors who are experienced in online asynchronous learning environments. See: http://franklin.scale.uiuc.edu/scale/presentations/aln_best_practices/faculty_satisfaction.html.

Figure 6.2   Institutional Support for Distance Teachers Online

The following are Web sites of institutions in higher education and K–12 school systems designed to support faculty teaching online:

Hawaii Community College—Faculty Teaching Tips
*http://www.hcc.hawaii.edu/intranet/committees/FacDevCom/guidebk/teachtip
/teachtip.htm*
Provides guidelines in over 20 areas including preparing a syllabus, teaching techniques, course design, assessment, and learning principles

Illinois Online Network—Online Education Resources
http://www.ion.illinois.edu/resources
A collection of articles on assessment, instructional design, communication, multimedia, intellectual property, online teaching, and many other areas

Maryland Faculty Online
http://www.mdfaconline.org
A course about online teaching that covers 12 major topics as well as other resource documents

Maricopa College—Maricopa Center for Learning & Instruction
http://www.mcli.dist.maricopa.edu/
Courses, resources, databases, and a learning exchange devoted to teaching online

Memphis City Schools—Teaching and Learning Academy
http://www.memphis-schools.k12.tn.us/admin/tlapages/academyhome.html
Provides professional development courses and online help for lesson design and planning as well as use of technology

Penn State WorldCampus—Faculty Development 101
http://www.worldcampus.psu.edu/facdev101/index.html
A course to prepare faculty to teach online and develop online materials

St. Petersburg College—Best Educational E-Practices (BEEP)
http://www.spjc.edu/eagle/BEEP/issues.htm
A collection of monthly annotated guides to e-learning topics

Summary

- Teaching in writing, by audio, video, or online is a different use of the technology than the other uses of that technology that the instructor may be familiar with. The instructor must learn the special techniques of the chosen technology (or technologies) for communicating teaching.

- In all forms of distance teaching, the ability to humanize the relationship with distant learners is important. Techniques to achieve this goal vary according to the technology. In real-time audio- or video-conferencing they include: (a) addressing each student by name, (b) having students who speak say their names, (c) starting class with an informal roll call and greetings, and (d) originating teleconferences

Figure 6.3   Professional Development Programs

The following are among the best professional development programs:

Indiana University School of Continuing Studies
http://scs.indiana.edu/nc/decert.html
"The program has eight modules that include readings, multimedia support materials, and individual projects that apply distance education concepts to real-world situations."

University of Maryland University College
http://www.umuc.edu/prog/gsmt/certificates/dist_ed.html
"The 12 credit-hour program consists of four courses and is designed to be completed within one year by the full-time working professional."

Penn State University Graduate Program in Learning and Performance Systems
http://www.worldcampus.psu.edu/pub/de/index.shtml
"This 18-credit graduate-level certificate program offered by Penn State's College of Education is designed to increase the knowledge and skills of those who work with adult learners at a distance."

State University of West Georgia
http://www.westga.edu/ ~ distance/certificate.html
"The program curriculum, developed by the State University of West Georgia, is based on cutting-edge distance education techniques and proven methodologies."

Texas A&M Center for Distance Learning Research
http://www.cdlr.tamu.edu/education/programs.asp
"The program provides an interactive, experience-based program leading to professional certification in distance education."

University of Washington
http://www.extension.washington.edu/ext/certificates/dld/dld_gen.asp
"This certificate program in designing and administering distance learning courses or programs focuses on the dynamics of teaching and learning at a distance."

University of Wisconsin-Madison Graduate Program in Continuing and Vocational Education
http://www.uwex.edu/disted/depd/certpro.html
"A Professional Development Certificate in Distance Education is earned upon completion of 20 Continuing Education Units (CEUs)."

---

from different sites so as to meet all students in-person at least once. In any technology the golden rule is to take opportunities to reflect a positive and caring attitude and appreciation of the student.

- A primary role of the instructor, as compared to the designer, is to facilitate interaction. It is necessary to learn how to manage interaction with individual students and to facilitate interaction between individuals and also between groups, whether by teleconferencing or virtual, online groups. Student participation is a core requirement of most successful distance teaching.

- Surveys of faculty show a demand for training in distance teaching methods. On the basis of the preceding discussion, it can be concluded that a good training program for distance teaching should have at least four ingredients: (a) ample "hands-on" practice with the delivery technologies involved, (b) practice with techniques for humanizing a course, and (c) practice with techniques for facilitating student participation. For faculty in institutions that require them to also design and produce their own courses, this will also be a necessary part of their training.

Questions for Discussion or Further Study

1. Is every classroom teacher capable of teaching at a distance? Do you think that online teaching is more difficult than other forms of distance teaching? Explain.

2. Discuss when content and students would make it appropriate for a course to be rated low on the Roblyer and Wiencke rubric and when a course should be rated higher.

3. Look at Figure 6.1 and discuss how a badly completed assignment might lead to teacher training and to changes in the design of the course.

4. Look at the extract from "Guide to Online High School Courses" and discuss how these questions might apply in a teaching context you are familiar with.

5. Discuss Gunawardena's viewpoint.

CHAPTER 7

The Distance Education Student

Because most distant learners are adults, this chapter begins with a brief review of adult learning, then moves to consider some of the characteristics of learning at a distance. We report some views about the value of distance education in opening opportunity and access, and review some research about predictors of success. The chapter concludes with a discussion of student support issues.

The Nature of Adult Learning

Although it is true that distance education courses are sometimes provided to school children to supplement or enrich the classroom curriculum, the overwhelming majority of distance education students in the United States are adults, typically between the ages of 25 and 50 years. Consequently, an understanding of the nature of adult learning is an invaluable foundation for understanding the distance learner. The best known description, now a classic, is that of Malcolm Knowles (1978).

Knowles's theory of adult education, what he called "andragogy" (the art and science of helping adults learn), can be reduced to the following propositions, expressed as differences between adults and children:

- Although children accept being dependent on a teacher, adults like to feel they have some control over what is happening and to exercise personal responsibility.

- Although children accept the teacher's definition of what should be learned, adults prefer to define it for themselves, or at least to be convinced that it is relevant to their needs.

- Children will accept the teacher's decisions about how to learn, what to do, when, and where. Adults like to make such decisions for themselves or at least to be consulted.

- Although children have little personal experience to draw on, adults have a lot, and they appreciate this being used as a learning resource.

- Children must acquire a store of information for future use. Adults either assume they have the basic information or need to acquire what is relevant here and now. Instead of acquiring knowledge for the future, they see learning as necessary for solving problems in the present.

- Children may need external motivation to make them learn; adults who usually volunteer to learn have intrinsic motivation.

Why Do Adults Enroll in a Distance Education Course?

For American children, going to school is the work of childhood. The adult is a person with employment, family, and social obligations; and so for an adult there are costs in enrolling in an educational course. The cost can certainly be measured in dollars but, more importantly, it costs time and effort that must be taken from the marginal time and energy remaining from what is spent on the normal demands of adult life. For most adults, therefore, there have to be specific and clear reasons for starting a learning program. These tend to be highly motivated, task oriented students.

Unlike younger learners, most adults have experience in employment, and many are seeking to learn more about fields of work in which they already know a great deal. Also unlike younger learners, they know a lot about life, about the world, about themselves, and about interpersonal relations, including how to deal with other persons in a class, and perhaps with a teacher and with an administrative system. To the adult student, teachers gain authority from what they know and the way they deal with their students, not from any external symbols or titles. Physical distance tends to further reduce the dominant psychological position of the teacher (probably one reason some classroom teachers do not enjoy being at a distance).

Some adults enroll in distance education courses to compensate for a neglected high school education; others are seeking college credit courses; many take noncredit courses in a plethora of subjects just to improve their general knowledge or to develop satisfying pastimes. Some seek practical knowledge when they first become parents, homeowners, or members of a school board. In America today education is presented primarily as a personal investment, with the return being improvements in employability or income. Therefore, the most common reason for taking a distance education course is to develop or upgrade the skills and knowledge needed in employment. However, the widely differing motivations for learning are suggested by recalling some of the organizations mentioned in earlier chapters in this book. They include Air Force personnel learning the mechanics of a truck by home study, the college drop-out trying to make up college credit through independent study, the professional engineer keeping abreast of new information through courses offered by NTU, the sales representative working on a company-sponsored program about a new product, and the group of home makers discussing gardening through a Cooperative Extension teleconference. It is impossible to summarize the topics that adult distant learners study; what is certain is that they cover just about every subject under the sun. And whatever the reason for taking a course and whatever the subject, it is also certain that adult distance students are always very serious, very committed, and highly motivated about what they are doing (see Table 7.1).

Anxiety about Learning

One reality that is not often talked about but something that needs to be kept in mind is that most adult distance learners feel quite anxious about studying, at least when they first begin a new course or especially a new institution (see, e.g., Conrad, 2002a). If this anxiety is revealed it's usually directed at the person who is the closest representative of the teaching institution—the instructor. It isn't really the instructor who is the source of the anxiety, but what underlies it is the student's concern about being able to meet expectations, both those of the institution and—just as important—self-expectations. This is a natural fear of failure that everyone experiences to some degree. Most students cover their anxiety, which of course makes it harder for others who feel they must be the only ones intimidated by the challenges of their course. The sensitive instructor tries to ensure the anxious student develops familiarity with procedures and that the institution's expectations are well understood. However, those adults who are inexperienced as distance learners may have a particularly high degree of anxiety at the beginning of the course. Their fear becomes concentrated when they have to turn in their first written assignment or present their views in a teleconference. The first assignment is especially critical; it is when an anxious student is most likely, statistically, to drop the

Table 7.1   Characteristics of Distance Education Students

In February 1998, the Distance Education and Training Council surveyed the 61 member institutions and found that:

- The average age of students was 31.
- 48 percent of students were male.
- 90 percent were employed at the time of enrollment.
- 31 percent had their tuition paid by their employers.
- 82 percent of the students had a college degree.
- The average non-start rate was 16 percent; the average rate for completing a course was 57 percent, and the average graduation rate was 38 percent.

SOURCE: DETC (1998).

course. Until this anxiety has been relieved by successfully taking the risk involved in handing in the assignment, students may not be able to enjoy the course, and in fact may not perform to the best of their abilities because of their nervousness. As they become accustomed to the system and have early positive feedback, confidence grows and anxiety comes under control.

Being aware of this anxiety, one of the first responsibilities of the instructor is to try to lower the level of tension. This does not mean that the work load or the standards required of the student are lowered, but it means first that steps are taken in the course design to deal with well-known causes of anxiety. Conrad's (2002b) study found that students were helped by having access to the course materials before the course began and they wanted to see a message from the course instructor when they first access the course. In setting the right climate for learning, the instructor should explain that mistakes are a natural part of learning and there is no reason to fear making them, risk-taking is approved, there is no such thing as a "dumb question," the instructor admires and approves effort and commitment, and the instructor cares about the student being successful and will work toward that goal (see Figure 7.1).

The statements in Figure 7.1 illustrate very typical responses of distant learners (and they also say something about the behavior of teachers at a distance, although that is not our primary focus in this chapter):

- *Enjoyment, excitement, pleasure.* All the students expressed these powerful, positive emotions. Adults who learn usually *enjoy* learning; adults who enjoy learning, learn! If they do not enjoy it, they are far more likely to give up the course, or not take another course. Enjoyment is a sign of high motivation, and of course it leads the student to be more motivated. In a distance education program, course designers try to make the program enjoyable; instructors try to sustain a sense of excitement and keep the virtual class pleasurable.

- Most students appreciated the convenience of learning at a distance, and being able to fit it into busy schedules. Loretta said "I could not otherwise be going to school"; Richard W. refers to a "time-efficient way to pursue a graduate degree"; Susan said, "There is no way I could have possibly taken graduate work."

- Not many of these students mentioned fear, partly because they are successful, experienced graduate students. Some fear and anxiety was reported by Loretta, "I found it stressful"; Richard F. had "anxiety about the final project"; Caroline "felt lost" at first.

- They like activity and learner-to-learner interaction. Caroline liked to "express my ideas and share opinions with the classmates"; Susan too commented, "I like the interaction on the BBS."

- They appreciate humor, which helps reduce tension and develops a playful environment, which is very conducive to learning.

- They like variety, expressed here by appreciation of the mixture of media and the number of different guest speakers.

Figure 7.1   Satisfaction with Distance Learning

Our experience is that the overwhelming majority of students taking—and completing—distance education courses are very satisfied with their experience. Here are some comments from such students in a distance education course that was delivered through cable television, videotapes, and a computer bulletin board system (BBS). The comments were posted on the bulletin board as part of the final course assignment.

I enjoyed the class very much. Distance learning is making a master's degree possible for me. I could not otherwise be going to school. I enjoyed the guests and felt that they add a dimension to the class that we could not get in a traditional classroom. I have never taken a traditional class with a guest speaker almost weekly. I find the application videos interesting to watch and useful for sharing with my colleagues to spark interest. Partnering for assignments was interesting, and it did have us communicate more with our classmates, but I found it a little stressful having someone else depending on me for part of their assignment.

—LORETTA A.

I also really enjoyed this course . . . my first in the distance learning format. The highlight for me was the video tapes which clearly showed techniques for using multimedia with children. Although most of the tapes seemed specifically designed to show the actual multimedia product themselves, I found that the teaching styles that were demonstrated along with them to be even more interesting. There was a continual emphasis on the role of the teacher as the facilitator of learning rather than someone who simply gives facts and answers. I also really enjoyed the format of the lessons. On the other side of the coin, there was always a lot of anxiety about the final project. I felt a bit in the dark for most of the course about what the expectations were. Although they became clear in the last few weeks, my blood pressure reading could have been helped a bit by having that information earlier.

—RICHARD F.

I am very excited about the prospects of distance education and graduate study. I think as the program matures it will just get better. It is a very time efficient way to pursue a graduate degree and you all are doing a great job. Your class preparation is obvious and instructor subject knowledge is outstanding. The guests are informative and the tape demos are good. I would like to see a little more topic specific information put out during the classes. Humor goes a long way in eliminating topic dryness. The BBS assignments were good and the instructor comments were prompt and to the point, amazing given the number of students in the class.

—RICHARD W.

There is no way I could have possibly taken graduate work in educational technology without this distance learning. The one criticism I have of most of the ed. tech. classes is that they are dry and lack humor. Bill and Greg have outdone themselves with their efforts to include this important aspect. I found the flexibility of the project requirements wonderful. I hate doing projects that I can not use in "real life." I like the interaction on the BBS. I feel pairing us in different groups of two for different assignments is great. I hate to sound like such a brown nose, but I even thought the video clips were good.

—SUSAN L.

(continued)

(continued)

> *In general, I found this class interesting, full of information and a real challenge for me. At first, considering that this was my first distance learning class, I felt lost. Using the BBS was a great way to converse with the class once I learned how to navigate through the system. Using the BBS for assignments and discussions proved to be one of the most valuable parts of the class . . . talk about hands-on . . . interactive learning!! It opened up a new form of interactive multimedia while allowing me to express my ideas and share opinions with the classmates and instructors. I've learned a lot!!*
>
> —CAROLINE B.

Perhaps the two most important, and typical, adult attitudes that these report show are: an appreciation of efficiency and an appreciation of an enjoyable learning environment.

Providing Access

One special feature of distance education and perhaps what most people think of when they first think about distance education is the capability for an institution or organization to provide access to education to some learners who could otherwise not have it. This in fact describes the professional people who we met in the previous section; although some of them lived in major cities, there was no access to the subject that they wanted at times and places convenient to them. However access is even more important to certain kinds of students: those who are disabled, elderly, or living in rural or remote areas. In Figure 7.2 you can see some stories about such students who took courses from Mind Extension University (MEU) delivered primarily by satellite or cable television.

Although the convenience and flexibility of distance education is a benefit to all students, the examples in Figure 7.2 and the case of California State University, Dominguez Hills (see Figure 7.3) remind us that for some students distance education makes all the difference between a richer and a poorer quality of life. These stories help also to illustrate the broad range of backgrounds and also the motivations that distance education students can have. Thousands of similar stories could be told by every distance education organization. We suggest that you might like to investigate the people behind the statistics, as a class project or as formal research. You will find it a very rewarding activity, because in every population of distant learners are found some very exceptional people.

Factors Affecting Student Success

As we saw in a previous chapter, one aspect of distance education that has been studied from several different angles involves the factors that affect student success and failure (e.g., Cookson, 1990; Dirr, 1991; Gibson, 1990).

Figure 7.2   Students Who Overcome Access Problems

Mico was a bright high school student who dreamed of becoming an engineer and attending MIT. But he lived in the tiny Texas town of Norheim (population: 369). Finding teachers who could provide the advanced science and math instruction he needed in order to compete for a spot at MIT would normally be impossible. However, his school arranged for him to take televised courses in these subjects provided by the TI-IN satellite. In his junior and senior years, Mico took 5 TI-IN classes, ranking as the top student nationally in two of them. He is now an electrical engineering student at MIT with a full scholarship. Mico credits the advanced science and math classes taken via TI-IN with giving him the background he needed to get into MIT.

• • •

Carolyn had plenty of free time and a love for learning. But she lived in rural Colorado, 150 miles from the nearest city and college. The 71-year-old Carolyn didn't drive and lived too far out in the country to receive radio or television signals. She loved the peace and beauty of her surroundings but longed for some intellectual stimulation. Things changed when she was given a satellite dish by her sister. Now she could pick up a broad range of television programming including courses provided by Mind Extension University (MEU). She enrolled in the "Humanities Through the Arts" course, which she found very rewarding and which helped her with an encyclopedia project she had been working on. She has gone on to take additional MEU courses.

• • •

Few people experience a more demanding full-time occupation than stay-at-home parents of small children. Yet while raising their children, many parents want to continue their education. Robin was an Ohio mother of three small children whose family responsibilities made it impossible for her to attend on-campus classes. However, she needed training that would enable her to manage the family business. In 1988, in the privacy of her living room she was able to go back to school for the first time in many years. She took an accounting course offered by the University of New Mexico via MEU. After completing this course, she was able to do the bookkeeping for the family business. She subsequently enrolled in other courses related to the business needs as well as her own personal interests.

• • •

Twyla was born with a physical disability that severely restricts her ability to move about. She completed public school in Woodleaf, NC, but when it came to attending college, she had trouble finding one that would accommodate her limited mobility. Twyla enrolled at the University of North Carolina at Greensboro, but had to withdraw after her sophomore year because of the physical burdens of trying to get to classes in buildings not designed for the handicapped. She was extremely disappointed and upset that she would not be able to complete her degree. Then she learned about MEU and began to take courses by television. She was able to complete her degree by distance education and work as an insurance clerk in the family business.

In most distance education courses and programs, since participation is usually voluntary, a proportion of the students who begin programs do not complete them. In the past it was not unusual for noncompletion (also referred to as "drop-out") rates for distance learning courses to be in the range

Figure 7.3   **Improving the Odds for Minorities**

In 1990, California State University, Dominguez Hills installed a two-way classroom-to-classroom compressed video television link at an inner city high school 15 miles from the campus. Both the university and the high school are located in south central Los Angeles and serve predominantly black and Hispanic populations. The primary goal in installing the two-way video link was to address a major problem for the university and the high school, which was the low rate of attendance at school and the poor preparation for college of many minority students. It was intended to use distance education to give students exposure to college-level courses and try to improve their motivation to attend college. Two-way video was selected as the delivery technology because it was felt that for this group of students, who generally had poor motivation, it was important to have a group learning environment, and also it was important for these students to see the instructors. Reading text on a screen would not be a good medium for these students.

Using the video link, professors at Dominguez Hills taught a number of college-level courses to the high school students; these courses included: advanced algebra, calculus, German, and Mexican-American studies. In addition, there were science demonstrations in physics and chemistry, and tutoring programs for help with homework and test-taking skills. The broadcasts were designed to augment regular class instruction and provide the students with enriched educational experiences. A single classroom at the school was used as a receiving site. Because of space limitations and security concerns, the equipment was keep locked in a closet and set up for each broadcast. The project involved 62 students, four high school teachers, and four college faculty. Students, teachers, and faculty were interviewed at the end of the school year to assess the success of the project. Students rated the courses as comparable to their high school classes and indicated a desire to receive credit for participation. Students complained about technical problems with the equipment (e.g., broadcasts were delayed or cancelled because no one was available to set up or operate the equipment), that the course content was too abstract and theoretical, and that there was not enough interaction during the classes. Teachers felt that the exposure to college courses had been beneficial to the students. They reported that getting students to interact during the broadcasts was a problem because they were too anxious or shy. They suggested that students needed to be given a better orientation to the use of the system and that teachers be given better training on how to set up and trouble shoot the system. A high degree of coordination between the teachers and college instructors was required to integrate the content of the broadcasts with regular classes.

The college faculty felt that the broadcasts had improved the self-esteem of the students, bolstered their confidence regarding taking college courses, and increased their interest in the subjects taught. However, they found it difficult to teach high school students, especially getting them to participate in the discussions. The instructors had no previous experience teaching at a distance generally, or via television in particular, and this almost certainly limited their effectiveness.

Did the system have any impact on college enrollment? Nearly all the students (93 percent) indicated that they wanted to attend college but only 8 percent applied and 3 percent were accepted. It appears that while the concept appeared sound and there were positive outcomes for some students, in general this project was too little and came too late in the students' high school careers to have any significant effect on their behavior.

SOURCE: J. McGowan (1992).

of 30–50 percent; nowadays the figure should be near the lower end of that range (and for university credit courses, it is comparable to traditional classes, i.e., less than 10 percent). For many years administrators and researchers have struggled to understand what causes some students to withdraw, in the hope of being able to improve their institution's completion rates.

One of the many methodological difficulties of this research is that dropout is usually a result of no single cause, but an accumulation and a mixture of causes. A number of researchers have developed formal models for predicting completion (e.g., Billings, 1988; Kember, 1989).

Research studies have identified a number of factors that are predictors of probable completion of a distance education course. They include:

- *Intent to complete.* Students who express determination to complete a course usually do. On the other hand, students who are unsure about their ability to finish are most likely to drop out.
- *Early submission.* Students who submit the first assignment early, or punctually, are more likely to complete the course satisfactorily. For an example of research, Armstrong et al. (1985) found 84 percent of the students who submitted the first assignment within the first two weeks successfully completed the course, whereas 75 percent who took longer than 2 months to submit the assignment did not complete the course.
- *Completion of other courses.* Students who successfully complete one distance education course are likely to complete subsequent courses.

Knowledge of factors such as these can be used by instructors or tutors to identify "at-risk" students who may need additional support or counseling in order to complete a course. As more and more classes are taught in a distance education form, a full understanding of the circumstances that facilitate student completion is critical to course developers, administrators, and instructors.

Kember's and Billings's Models of Student Completion

Kember (1995) presented a model for student progress that focused specifically on adult learners in distance education courses, using the term "open learning," which we have explained in earlier chapters. The model focuses on the factors that affect a student's successful completion of a distance education program with particular focus on the extent to which students are able to integrate their academic study with often conflicting employment, family, and social commitments (see Figure 7.4).

Kember's model suggests that students' entry characteristics (e.g., educational qualifications, family status, employment) direct them toward one of two pathways in a distance education course. Those with favorable situations tend to proceed on a positive track and are able to integrate socially and academically. Other students take a negative track where they have difficulties achieving social and academic integration, which affects their course achievement (i.e., GPA). The model also incorporates a cost/benefit decision step in

Figure 7.4   Kember's Open Learning Model

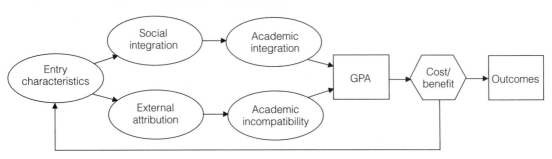

SOURCE: From Kember, 1995. Used by permission.

which students consider the costs and benefits of continuing their study. Those who decide to continue will "recycle" through the model for another passage. However, in each pass through the model, the students may change tracks due to their experiences in taking the course.

Kember's model is based on a large body of research and theory about student attrition in both traditional and distance education courses. Kember used empirical data collected via interviews and questionnaires from a number of sources in the formulation and validation of the model. These sources included students taking courses at the UK Open University, the University of Papua New Guinea, the University of Tasmania, Charles Sturt University (Australia), and seven different open learning programs in Hong Kong. In order to collect standardized data for the model, Kember developed and used the Distance Education Student Programs (DESP) questionnaire, which consists of 68 items pertaining to the variables in the model (plus demographic information for entry characteristics). Kember also collected student outcome data in the form of GPA and the number of course modules attempted and completed.

To validate the model, Kember used factor analysis on his questionnaire responses to determine the underlying factors. The factor analysis confirmed the four primary variables in the model: social integration, academic integration, external attribution, and academic incompatibility. Kember then used path analysis (multiple regression) to identify the causal relationships among the variables in the model. The results of the path analysis confirmed that the basic structure of the model is accurate: 80 percent of the total variance of student completions could be explained by the variables in the model.

Kember outlines the implications of his model as follows. The positive academic integration factor contains the subscales "deep approach" and "intrinsic motivation," while the negative academic incompatibility factor has "surface approach" and "extrinsic motivation" subscales. This suggests that student progress can be enhanced if the design of a course concentrates on developing intrinsic motivation and a deep approach to the subject matter. Academic integration can also be improved by developed collective affiliation and ensuring congruence between student expectations and course procedures. The model also identifies the difficulties students are likely to face in completing open learning courses and can therefore serve as a guide for counseling and guidance activities.

Kember's model is very compatible with the systems approach that is espoused in this book. Although Kember does not attempt to relate his model to a systems approach, the major variables of the model do map onto the primary subsystems we discussed initially in Chapter 1.

Billings's Model of Course Completion

Figure 7.5 illustrates Billings's model for the completion of correspondence courses. The links shown in the diagram represent the relationships among the variables (i.e., they are causal, additive, and correlational). Billings found that students who made the most progress were those who had the intention of completing the course in a specific period of time (3 months), submitted the first lesson relatively early (within 40 days), had higher entrance examination scores and high GPAs, had completed other correspondence courses, had a supportive family, had high goals for completing the program, lived relatively close to the instructor, and had good college-level preparation. The single most important predictor variable was the student's intention to complete, which suggests the importance of motivation over other factors.

Educational Background

Not surprisingly, one of the best predictors of success in distance education is the educational background of the student. In general, the more formal education people have, the more likely they are to complete a distance education course or program; see Coggins (1989), for example.

Personality Characteristics

Much less reliable as a predictor of success or failure, but clearly relevant, are the personality characteristics of the student (including what is often referred to as learning style). Early research (e.g., Moore, 1976; Thompson 1984) suggested that individuals who are more field independent (i.e., relatively less influenced by the surrounding environment, including social environment) are better suited to distance learning than people who are less field independent. Diaz and Cartnal (1999) found that students who selected an online version of a health class were more independent as learners and valued collaboration more for its intrinsic value than external incentives. Halsne and Gatta (2002) asked college students to take a survey that identified their visual, auditory, tactile, or kinesthetic learning preferences and found that those who selected online courses rated themselves higher as visual learners whereas those who selected on-campus classes were more auditory and kinesthetic in their learning styles. Another personality dimension that is often associated with distance education is introversion-extroversion, with

Figure 7.5   Model for Completion of Correspondence Course

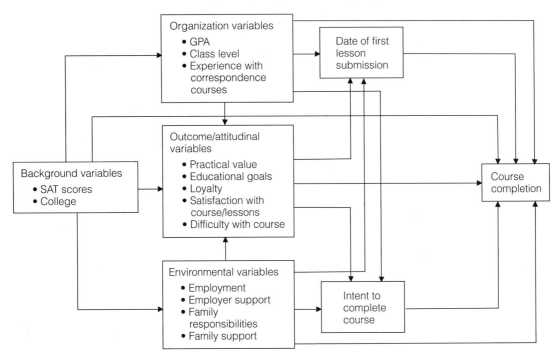

SOURCE: Billings, 1989.

introverted individuals being more predisposed to distance learning. Persistence, determination, and "need to achieve" are all qualities that would positively affect a student's success. The nature of the students' motivation for taking a particular course or program (i.e., intrinsic or extrinsic) is also likely to affect their success. For a series of articles on motivating and retaining adult learners online, see: http://www.geteducated.com/vugaz.htm.

Some other sources about learning styles are found at:

http://www.advisorteam.com/user/kts.asp

http://www.womensmedia.com/seminar-learningstyle.html

http://www.gwu.edu/ ~ tip/styles.html

http://www.d.umn.edu/student/loon/acad/strat/lrnsty.html

Extracurricular Concerns

A variety of extracurricular concerns—such as employment (e.g., job stability, workload), family responsibilities, health, and social interests—can positively or adversely affect completion of distance education courses. For example,

The Second Language Student

My first language is not English. I am taking both face-to-face and online distance courses in the U.S. To tell you the truth, to me the online interaction is probably ten times more than that in the traditional classrooms. In the face-to-face class-rooms, I could hardly catch up what everybody is saying not to mention respond to them or say something about my opinion immediately. In the online classes, on the other hand, I can read your postings, questions, thoughts again and again until I totally got your points. The best part is I can "digest" what you said, and then respond to you after I've organized my thought. That is . . . so sweet!!

SOURCE: *L.* (2003). Evaluation comment on a class bulletin board.

encouragement from employers, coworkers, friends, and family regarding distance learning can motivate the student to do well; conversely, lack of support from one or more of these groups can result in poor performance and noncompletion.

Course Concerns

Many features of the course or program itself affect the success of students. This includes:

- the perceived relevance of the content to career or personal interests
- the difficulty of the course and program (i.e., amount of time/effort required)
- the degree of student support available
- the nature of the technology used for course delivery and interaction
- the extent of the pacing or scheduling involved
- the amount and nature of feedback received from instructors/tutors on assignments and on course progress
- the amount and nature of the interaction with instructors, tutors, and other students

In summary, students are more likely to drop out of a course if they perceive the content as irrelevant or of little value to their career or personal interests; if the course is too difficult and takes too much time or effort; if they become frustrated in trying to complete the course or handling administrative require-ments and receive no assistance; if they receive little or no feedback on their course work or progress; and if they have little or no interaction with the instructor, tutor, or other students and hence become too isolated.

Cross-Cultural Considerations: Distance Education in Alaska

In Alaska, distance education courses are a highly valued service for that sparsely populated state. Approximately 12 percent of students are Native Alaskans who want to continue their education but do not want to give up their traditional lifestyle to attend university classes in a large city. Twenty-seven percent of the student credit hours at the University of Alaska, Southeast (UAS) during the 2001–2002 was delivered by distance education. The most common technology is online delivery (61.3 percent), audio-conferencing is the second most frequently used (48.8 percent), and 28 percent of courses have used videotape sent by mail. To participate in audio-conferencing, students have to go to a learning center. Many of the problems encountered in providing courses to Native students have to do with cultural issues. Here are some quotes from students at the University of Alaska that describe some of the issues:

> *It has allowed me to continue my education and stay with my family. I am free to go berry picking in the daytime and still go to college in the evening. I can't just leave and go to university to get a degree. What would my husband and family do?*

> *It was fifty below and I was a little late for class because of cooking dinner for my family. It was really snowing and I couldn't see anything. It was a whiteout. I used the rope that leads through the village to pull myself to the high school, but halfway up the rope broke. I got to class an hour late and I was freezing. It was hard to concentrate that night.*

> *It takes a lot of hard work to make these courses good for Native students. Lots of Natives are not accustomed to the academic life and don't know how to write papers and take tests. When they get to college they get stuck in remedial courses. I am so tired of always having to adjust to the system. The system should try to adjust to us, too.*

> *When we learn something in the Native culture . . . it's different . . . unless the instructor gives the student a second or third or fourth chance to learn. If you don't do it right the first time in the Native culture, you do it again a second time and you do it a third and a fourth time until you master it. It's more like long term observation.*

In addition to the cultural issues, there are also language considerations; many Natives are not highly proficient with English since they speak Eskimo (Yup'ik) at home. There is also a high percentage of hearing loss in Native populations, making it difficult for many students to participate fully in audio-conferences.

SOURCE: Sponder (1990), Franks (1996), and Schrum and Ohler (2003).

Study Skills

To a great extent, the study habits and skills of students determine their success in online classes and this is one factor under their control. Students who plan their study time and develop schedules for completing course work are more likely to do well in distance education. Procrastination is the number one enemy of distance learning—once students get behind in their assignments, it becomes very difficult to catch up and they invariably drop out. Of course a good program is one that has a structure that makes it hard to fall behind, and a student support system that intervenes if the student appears to be in difficulty.

There are lots of student oriented guides about distance learning (e.g., Gilbert, 2000; Stevenson, 2000; WICHE, 1998) and almost every distance education program provides guidelines to their students. Unfortunately, learning good study skills is not easy for students who have never practiced them, or perhaps have not used them in a long time. This is one area where counselors can make the difference between success and failure.

Student Attitudes

Researchers have examined student reactions from a number of perspectives. Most studies are concerned with assessing the level of learner satisfaction with a particular course or program, or the extent to which students perceive particular instructional media or teaching strategies to be effective. Some studies are concerned with changes in student attitudes to distance education that come about as a consequence of being distance learners.

Classroom versus Distance Learning

A common question that is examined is how students feel about distance learning relative to traditional classroom instruction. In many cases, student say they prefer traditional classroom learning even though they enjoyed their distance learning course and found it worthwhile. Sometimes there are problems (e.g., equipment failures, inexperienced instructors) that produce negative attitudes toward distance learning. Very similar problems occur in traditional classrooms, but the absence of the "father figure" or "mother figure" to take care of them is disconcerting for some students. Most students are able to cope with problems, and most students actually enjoy taking responsibility for solving their own problems. However this is obviously harder work than letting a teacher do it, so some of the negative attitude to distance learning comes from reluctance to take responsibility and make an effort. Fortunately this only applies to a minority of students. In well-implemented courses students can be very positive about their distance learning experiences and many prefer such courses over traditional classes.

Nelson (1985), for example, surveyed the attitudes of students taking classes via two-way video-conference and reported that 94 percent believed their level of achievement was as high, or higher, than regular classes, and 97 percent wanted to take further video-conference classes. On the other hand, Barker (1987) evaluated the attitudes of children who had taken classes via the TI-IN satellite video-conference system and found that 65 percent believed the video class to be more difficult than regular classes and 70 percent would prefer to take regular classes. It is worth noting that in this study, numerous problems were mentioned, including technical problems, difficulty contacting the instructor, and inadequate teacher preparation.

A number of research studies have examined the relationships between student perceptions and teaching strategies or program design characteristics. St. Pierre and Olsen (1991) found that the following factors contributed to student satisfaction in independent study courses: (1) the opportunity to apply knowledge, (2) prompt return of assignments, (3) conversations with the instructor, (4) relevant course content, and (5) a good study guide. Conversely, Hara and Kling (1999) reported the student frustrations in Web-based courses were caused by: (1) lack of prompt feedback from instructors, (2) ambiguous instructions for assignments, and (3) technical problems.

Maki and Maki (2000) in the journal *Behavior Research Methods, Instruments, and Computers* reported that young university students learned better when studying in a Web-based distance education mode than their counterparts who studied in a conventional class. Differences in pre-test and post-test scores were twice as high for the distant learners. Over a number of semesters and with different instructors, the distance learners in this study did better, but just as consistently they expressed less satisfaction with the course because getting better results went along with having to do more work than in a classroom course.

It is always worth keeping in mind when analyzing the results of student satisfaction surveys that that there is typically no relationship between these attitudes and actual achievement. Since students may do well in a course even though they may not enjoy it as much as being in a face-to-face classroom, the main use of measures of satisfaction is in predicting drop-out rate, advising on course choice at registration time, and also to trigger counseling intervention (see Figure 7.6).

Resistance to Distance Education

Since most students have little experience learning at a distance, they are unfamiliar with it and may be anxious about taking distance education courses. Indeed in some situations, this unfamiliarity is translated into resistance that must be overcome in order for the courses to have any hope of succeeding. Many students (as well as teachers and training managers) have misconceptions about distance learning that must be changed if they are to profit from it. For example, students may believe that distance education courses are easier than conventional classes and require less work. When they discover that this is not the case and that the opposite is true, they may be unhappy.

Figure 7.6   **"Students Can Be Very Positive about Their Distance Learning Experiences"**

The following are postings in one of our online courses.

Article No. 1207: posted by S.
Even though class officially ended only 1 day ago, I am already feeling a loss. I have no new assignment to look to. I have no pressing work that must get done. I must admit, it does feel kind of good to not have the extra pressure right now. This has been a tremendous learning experience. I want to thank all of my fellow students for your input, experience, stories, assignments, and everything else. I have learned so much from all of you. Everyone's combined effort made this the enriching experience that it was. Thank you. I hope to see you all in a future class.

Article No. 1210: posted by A.
I am glad that the classes are over, but also sad, because these courses have become part of my daily living. I will miss the interaction, but I am hoping to see you next semester, more important on graduation day. I am certainly grateful that I have the opportunity to study in this excellent distance education program.

Message No. 343: posted by W.
This course exceeded my expectations by far. Even though I have succeeded in all my other graduate courses, I didn't know I could handle this one. What a great experience. I was prepared to settle for a grad program that would give me an obligatory M.Ed. Lots of folks here do just that—get a degree that fits the bill but they say they didn't really learn anything. Your course and university is the antithesis of all that. I'm thinking beyond the horizons of being [her present employment] for the rest of my life. There just aren't words. Thanks.

Article No. 248: posted by L.
As my final send off for this class, I wanted to reflect on the subtlety of my progress. After several weeks of assignments and reading, I'm amazed at how much I've progressed. .... So, the point is this: after just one semester I feel more confident discussing instructional issues with senior faculty, particularly thorny issues like outcomes, assessment and cost-effectiveness. For that I thank [the professor] and my classmates. Hope to see you guys around!

Article No. 254: posted by R.
Good for you!! This was a very positive experience for me also in many ways. Like yourself, I have integrated the knowledge that I've gleaned from this course into my career goals already. My final paper is a draft business proposal to a continuing education company. I've been trying to talk the owner into online instruction for years and now I have the researched and documented proof that it doesn't have to be overwhelming and can be hopefully successful. I hope that our paths cross again. Thanks for the support and the many many references that I have stored in my database!!!

Article No. 256: posted by J.
This class has been an amazing experience in so many ways. The final paper was really an effort in putting all the pieces together and clarifying the relationships of all the component parts. When I thought I had learned enough, the last project brought new challenges. For example, in describing what a distance education program might look like, using a real example, I found that what I initially wanted to do was not

(continued)

Figure 7.6   *Continued*

feasible. It forced me to align my tacit knowledge with theoretical knowledge to come up with a workable plan. I only wish that all the faculty teaching online courses would be required to take this course. Working with them would be a pleasure.

Article No. 257: posted by D. L.
I have to agree with you. This class provided a challenge, but the benefits were worth it. Not only did I gain a better understanding of distance education, especially from the total systems view, but I also gained the confidence to speak-up and offer educated opinions and suggestions to faculty and management. Thanks to everyone who provided wonderful resources and this semester.

Students often assume that distance education courses will be of lesser quality than classroom offerings and thus avoid taking such courses. Students frequently do not understand that they must take a large degree of responsibility for their learning in a distance education course and not wait for the instructor or tutor to push them. This kind of misunderstanding leads to students falling behind and becoming dissatisfied. For these reasons it is very desirable to include an orientation session in any distance education course, where students can find out about how the delivery system works and what is expected of them. Granger and Benke (1998) report that a number of programs, recognizing that many of the adult students have been away from formal study for some time, provide a full orientation program to prepare them for their new study activities. This "Returning to Learning" activity can take various forms, from a face-to-face weekend session on campus to a term-long, credit-bearing study of adult learning strategies, including organization, time management, and study skills.

Another aspect that affects student receptivity toward distance education is the technology involved (Christensen, Anakwe, and Kessler, 2001; Irons, Jung, and Keel, 2002; Valentine, 2002). Much research has shown that comfort with the technology being used is a primary factor in determining satisfaction and success. If students are unfamiliar with the technology, they will be reluctant to use it creatively and adventurously, which will affect their experience quite severely. As students become familiar with the technology, this resistance erodes. However, if there are ongoing technical problems, frustration and resistance will continue and grow.

A research study by Perdue and Valentine (2000) of certified public accountants looked at the attitudes and reasons for reluctance to become involved as distance learners. Data gathered from 444 respondents revealed four main reasons why these professionals were unsure about taking professional development courses by distance education. They were: concerns about the effectiveness and their ability to handle electronically mediated communication, concerns about course quality, concerns about access to technology-based resources, and concerns about whether they could find the necessary personal resources.

In summary, research and experience suggests that the three main causes of dissatisfaction and resistance to distance education are:

1. Bad course design and teacher incompetence (the cause of most problems!)
2. Wrong expectations on part of students
3. Poor technology or inability to use technology properly

When properly conducted, however, distance education can be very satisfying. Figure 7.7 displays a letter written by a student who has been studying in his second language (he is from Finland) that expresses feelings about the freedom that being a member of a well-conducted distant learning group can provide.

Student Support: Guidance and Counseling Services

Traditional universities offer a variety of services to help students who have problems. Among such services are: walk-in counseling centers, financial aid offices, remedial tutoring, career development and placement offices, and facilities intended to boost peer support and social interaction. This is an area that is generally less well-organized in distance education, and less well-organized than the subsystems of course design and instruction. It is an area that deserves more attention since there is a direct relationship between students' failure and dropping out of a program and failure of the student support system.

The need for guidance and counseling can come at any stage of the distance learning experience. If guidance is available early in a course or program to help students make choices among various options, other problems are likely to be averted. Included in such admissions counseling should be an analysis of the student's knowledge and study skills to see if they match the expectations of the course. Ideally all students should receive some sort of orientation when they enter a program; this too will reduce the need for individual counseling later. It is particularly important to inform people of the time demands that accompany distance learning and to encourage them to think about how they will fit it in with their other interests and obligations. Within any group of learners there typically will be a considerable range in their aptitude for distance learning. Students with poor study or time-management skills, or poor communication skills, will usually have difficulty with distance learning. A common problem that every distance instructor runs into is that of the overoptimistic student who has successfully negotiated face-to-face classes with a minimum of effort but has a shock on discovering that the same avoidance techniques won't work in distance education, where there is no way of hiding in the back of a classroom!

Single mode institutions have specialist, full-time staff to provide student support services and use the full range of technologies, including face-to-face counseling sessions in study centers or such places as public libraries. Dual mode institutions might be able to use branch campuses in this way but usually their student support is provided by telephone and online. Many dual

Figure 7.7   What Students Find Satisfying in Distance Learning

The distance learning course was excellent. I would like to emphasize the word "learning" as opposite to the word "teaching." The whole attitude amongst most of us participants was something like this: "Those guys and gals, they respect our professional skills, they honor us. We want to co-operate not only with them but mainly with each other. This is and will be a good exercise/practice for all of us." In the very beginning, the "course masters" gave us the impression that we are here not for receiving highly authorized information but mostly for giving, relaying, distributing the information and skill that we hold. The class is the teacher!

All of us were not comfortable with the DE course. One of the participants wanted a more authoritarian or school style education. He disapproved the freedom given adult learners (it is possible that there were more of this kind, but he was the only one who told me so). He would prefer a style where the teacher has more authority. I myself hoped that the teachers or tutors would have gone deeper into my special interest areas.

The best or most lasting experience is in the cooperation. It was really exhilarating to be a member of a non-homogenous group (social workers, teachers, engineers, students). I could discuss my ideas and my ways of working with people who were total strangers to my profession, and could give me new views to my profession. The teachers taught me to teach and I taught the teachers to cooperate with the technology.

This course lasted half a year. When it was over, I felt sad. Is this all that there is? We have been a good team for a long time and now we must be separated—or must we? We grow together and then we depart; we will have a time to grieve, but the grief will pass by. Now I do not any more miss my fellow students or teachers, I only remember them. But still, I would like to stay in contact with the persons who were a part of my life for six months!

When I started to write this, I aimed towards "a cool and clean analysis." I gave up to my inner feelings. I still miss those people. Maybe this course will be something that I still miss when I am ten years older than now.

mode institutions have at least a skeleton staff of full-time counselors, but very often their services are not well-explained to students who as a result tend to turn to administrators and instructors when they need counseling support. In an attempt to reduce such calls, most institutions now provide Web-based support sites with some form of general orientation to distance learning, tips for online study, information on how to contact counseling and advising services, technical help, and programs to help potential students evaluate their own readiness for distance learning. Some examples are:

Brevard Community College
http://www.brevard.cc.fl.us/distlrn/virtual_ss.cfm

Montgomery College
http://www.mc.cc.md.us/Departments/distlrng/orient.htm

Penn State WorldCampus
http://www.worldcampus.psu.edu/wc101/

Rio Salado College
http://www.riosalado.edu/distance_learning/main.shtml

Santa Barabara City College
http://online.sbcc.net/success.cfm

Illinois Online Network
http://www.ion.illinois.edu/IONresources/onlineLearning/index.asp

DeAnza College
http://distance.deanza.fhda.edu/resources.shtml

University of Wisconsin
http://www.dcs.wisc.edu/classes/ed_web/ed_stusvc.htm

The advantage of providing these services online is that they are available around the clock, even when staff are not available. Furthermore, in dual mode institutions such as those just listed, providing student services online allows them to be better integrated with services to on-campus students (who also benefit from the online access). The more mechanized the student support, (i.e., not requiring a personal human intervention), the more cost effective also. Everyone likes support from a human rather than a Web site, but most people also want to have tuition fees held as low as possible.

Orientation

The following are some of the questions and information usually included in Web sites to orient potential or new students:

- What is distance education and how does it work online?
- What can I study?
- How do I learn?
- What do I need?
- Is distance education suitable for me (including self-assessment instruments)?
- Sample course materials
- Tour of the virtual campus
- Questions to gather data about educational background
- Questions about learners' expectations and motivations, time available for study, access to computer and Internet
- Learners' aptitude profile

One other important quality that institutions try to provide to their distance education students is a sense of belonging to the institution (Eastmond, 1998). On-campus students develop this feeling through their physical presence in clubs, sports, and other social events. It is not easy to do this at a distance, but creative student services can help establish some sense of relationship between distance students and the institution.

The social side of this class has demonstrated to me that attachments can occur despite distance and lack of physical presence. You have all invested so much virtual presence that I feel as though we have coexisted during the learning process, kidded one another and found our personalities, supported one another and discovered our strengths and need for support, and shown genuine camaraderie. I hope to meet each of you again in another class (Carol, Penn State student, Fall 2002).

In spite of all efforts to help students find the right level of course and to ease their entry into the distance learning experience, some students will encounter unexpected job-, family-, or health-related problems that threaten their academic progress. A student support service has to be proactive as well as reactive. If it only reacts to students who come forward to ask for help, many will be lost. Methods have to be developed for identifying problems early and by intervening to offer support, even though the student may not come forward to request it. The core method is careful monitoring of assignment productivity. If a student who normally produces good assignments begins to deteriorate, or not to produce on time, a "red flag" should alert student support personnel to a potential problem that may require at least an e-mail message to offer assistance. Failure to take such steps could mean that nonacademic problems will demand the student's complete attention, and there is a good chance the student will drop out of the course.

Administrative Assistance

Students sometimes get into difficulty, and therefore need assistance in dealing with the routine administrative aspects of being a student—registering, paying fees or getting tuition benefits, obtaining materials, receiving grades, taking exams, and so on. In the case of on-campus students, questions or problems can be resolved by visiting the relevant office. However, in the case of an off-campus student, all interaction is likely to be via e-mail or telephone. Students often have difficulty identifying and reaching the right person to talk to (especially in large institutions) and can become very frustrated. Ideally, students in distance education programs have a single person they can contact for all administrative problems. In addition, all administrative requirements and procedures should be described in a student handbook or Web page that students receive at the beginning of a course or when they first register in the institution.

Social Interaction

Most students enjoy interaction with their instructor and fellow students not only for instructional reasons but for the emotional support that comes from such social contact. Some institutions have developed electronic networking as a means of socializing in the form of real-time chat rooms (Brigham, 2001) where students "meet for coffee," discuss coursework, compare notes, or chat about noncourse or perhaps nonacademic matters. For many students this is a valued way of reducing their feeling of isolation.

A Realistic View of the Distance Learner

Although it is easy to talk about distance learners in general, in any specific distance learning program, it is essential (as we said in Chapter 5 when we talked about the ISD model) that designers and instructors take the time to understand their particular learners. It is very dangerous to proceed on generalizations because assumptions are then made that may be quite erroneous. Even groups that are thought—in general—to be ideal populations for distance training programs are not always. Here are some examples:

- *Professional development for classroom teachers.* Although they obviously appreciate the value of learning and education, many teachers feel very overworked, have little free time, and do not have a suitable learning environment during the day at school. Successful programs have been those where special arrangements have been made to provide time and facilities for professional development.

- *Management training.* Human resource managers tend to be "people oriented" and some may prefer to learn by informally talking to others on the phone or in person at a meeting, rather than studying alone reading what appear to be more messages on their computer.

- *Continuing medical education.* Even though all health care professionals accept the idea of continuing medical education, like school teachers, many find their daily routines, which often include exhausting evening shifts, too hectic to accommodate formal study.

- *Sales training.* To the sales person, the big sale is always just around the corner, so that any time taken for study carries the risk of losing the sale. Educators may have to convince the salesperson of the pay-off of taking time for study.

- *At-risk students.* Although they have the most need for extra educational opportunities, they usually have very poor learning/study skills and have a great deal of trouble with both the techniques and the self-discipline needed for distance learning.

- *Prisoners.* Individuals who are incarcerated may have more time than the average person, but may have limited access to equipment or facilities needed for learning (even obtaining specific books and frequent mail can be problematic).

- *Armed forces personnel, especially those on foreign assignments.* Such students have less control of their disposable time than in civilian life and may be sent on a mission that means special arrangements have to be made regarding the completion of their study assignments.

Viewpoint: Sir John Daniel

Distance education will include an increasing proportion of online activity. This will push institutions to return to the correspondence model of distance learning that allows students to enroll at any time and study at their own pace. Whilst this will increase flexibility for learners it will decrease success rates and throughput unless institutions improve student support. System costs will increase compared to the cohort-based approach of the previous generation of distance education exemplified by the mega-universities. Will this mean that distance education becomes less effective at increasing access to education?

SOURCE: Sir John Daniel, Assistant Director-General Education, UNESCO, Paris

- *Taking a broader perspective, it is always important to keep the possibility of cultural and gender differences in mind.* Again it is dangerous to generalize, but some groups of men and some groups of women may respond differently to certain program characteristics (Taplin and Jegede, 2001), as may different cultural groups (Thorpe, 2002). See also Blum (1999) and Ory (1997).

The point of mentioning these difficulties is not to say that programs should not be offered to these groups; of course there are thousands of successful programs with these groups, and there are other groups with challenges of their own. The reason for mentioning these challenges is to emphasize the importance of empathy—understanding how things look from the student's point of view—and not to make facile assumptions. Such assumptions can lead to unrealistic expectations that in turn lead to failure that could have been avoided with a little more understanding. Understanding these challenges is equally important for course designers, instructors, and administrators, but especially for student support personnel.

The Guide to Developing Online Student Services (see http://www.wiche.edu/telecom/resources/publications/guide1003/guide/wfdigest.htm) is a resource for administrators and others who need to provide student support services online. It provides:

- general tips for setting up online student services
- brief discussions on a range of student support issues
- guidelines for basic good practice in delivering student services via the Internet
- examples of practice in selected institutions.

⌐ Summary

This chapter has discussed a number of aspects related to the student in a distance learning setting:

- Most students involved in distance education are adults. Everyone involved in designing and teaching courses needs to understand the adult's motivation(s) for participating in a distance learning program, and what this means in terms of the design and delivery of such programs. Adults have many concerns in their lives (job, family, social life), and distance education must accommodate these concerns both as resources in design and instruction and also as potential sources of problems that may impede study.

- One of the unique benefits of distance education is that it is able to provide access to education for many students who would not otherwise have the opportunity. This includes rural populations, disabled individuals, parents with children at home, and the elderly. However, providing effective distance learning experiences to different types of learners requires a good understanding of their particular circumstances and limitations.

- Many factors affect the success of students in distance learning programs. These include: educational background, personality characteristics, extracurricular concerns, and course-related problems. Factors such as timely submission of assignments, history of previous course completion, and strength of intent to complete the course can be used to predict success.

- Students' reactions are a good source of information about the effectiveness of a particular course and help give ideas for how to design a course for a particular group. Student satisfaction with distance education courses can vary according to students' personalities and other characteristics, and depending upon the design of the course and how well it is taught.

- Having a means of providing student support if and when it is needed is critical to the success of distance education programs.

- Five categories of student support are especially critical: orientation and admissions, administrative assistance, study skills, crisis intervention, and social interaction with peers.

- After overcoming their initial anxiety, most adult learners find distance education that is well-designed and well-taught to be an exciting, even exhilarating experience because they have the structure and interaction provided by a teaching institution yet have freedom to conduct much of the learning themselves. When this happens in learning groups it leads to social bonding that for many learners provides great emotional satisfaction.

One fact that should have become clear to you in reading this chapter is how closely related matters involving the student are to teaching considerations as discussed in Chapter 6, and the design of distance education courses and programs as discussed in Chapter 5. As we said in Chapter 1, it is not a bad idea to try to separate the different components of distance education for the purposes of study and discussion, but in reality all the components impact each other.

For further discussion of learners and student support, see: Curry (1997), Gibson (1998), Carnwell (2000), Donlevy (2000), Rumble (2000), Tait (2000), Bothel (2001), Brigham (2001), Carnwell and Harrington (2001), Taplin and Jegede (2001), Thorpe (2002), Lynch (2002), and Simpson (2002).

Questions for Discussion or Further Study

1. Discuss the proposition that most adults are to some degree anxious when they begin learning at a distance. To whom would this apply more and to whom may it be less relevant?

2. Do you think that distance education programs make learning more accessible to cultural minorities? What about unemployed? Disabled? Why or why not?

3. Locate an online self-assessment for distance learning instrument and try it out. How accurate do you think it was?

4. Describe the student services available for a distance learning program or institution you are currently involved with (or pick one to research). How do they compare to services provided by other distance learning programs or those for on-campus students?

5. Discuss the viewpoint of Sir John Daniel.

CHAPTER 8

Management, Administration, and Policy

In this chapter, we describe some of the activities of the people responsible for managing and administering the human and other resources needed to deliver quality distance education programs. We also introduce some important examples of the kind of issues that have to be considered by those who set the policy framework within which managers and administrators have to operate, at institutional, state, and federal levels.

Strategic Planning

For the senior employees of an institution—its managers—one of the main responsibilities is strategic planning. This involves a number of processes, including:

- defining a vision and a mission, goals, and objectives for the institution or program regarding distance education
- choosing among options so that the priority goals can be achieved with acceptable quality and with the available resources
- continuous assessment of changing trends in student, business, or societal demands
- tracking emerging technological options that might make for greater efficiency
- projecting future resource and financial needs and taking actions to meet them

Defining the Mission

At the institutional level (and the same could be said of the state and federal levels) strategic planning begins with defining a mission, a long-term direction based on a concept of the place of the institution in society, usually based also on a self-awareness of its role historically. Not to have such a self-awareness leaves the administrative and teaching staff of an institution without a secure point of reference when faced with decisions to be made arising from the many changes that take place in the social and economic environment in which they have to plan and deliver their programs. Since there is an almost infinite variety of potential distance education markets, the organization's leadership needs to be explicit about who it is attempting to serve, how, and why. Otherwise, as they try to be "all things to all people," they are likely to spread their resources too thinly to survive in a competitive educational market. Certainly mission statements must not become a drag on flexibility and readiness to respond to new opportunities, and so should be reviewed periodically, especially by long-established institutions where the size and location of their student catchment area is likely to change as technology changes. A good illustration of the importance of the mission as both an anchor for policy making in the institution, as well as a guide to decisions about change, is seen in the state universities that have their distance education programs historically grounded in the Land Grant tradition of service and outreach to residents of the state. Look at the examples of statements in Figure 8.1 and ask yourself if you were on the staff of any of these institutions would you have great difficulty in deciding if a proposed course fits the mission of that institution.

It is the job of the institution's management to supply the resources (i.e., people, facilities, time, money) needed to achieve its mission, and to articulate policies that enable the administrators to select goals and objectives that are realizable within the limits of those resources.

Deciding Whether to Proceed

Before proceeding to invest in a distance education program, an institution's management must first consider if distance education is appropriate at all in fulfilling its mission, and if it is, then to make choices among the various alternative courses that could be offered.

One aspect of this is checking that there is a real demand (and one that is likely to be sustained) for it. Generally, this would be indicated by market research data showing that there is a sufficiently large number of interested students. It is also necessary to examine demographic and business trends to see what changes might be expected in the future that might impact courses and programs. For example, changes in immigration patterns that affect the multicultural makeup of the U.S. population mean that some colleges that have specialized in multilingual courses might see a new opportunity in distance education. Or the trend for more people to work at home or have home businesses may create a bigger market for locally developed programs of distance education in business topics specific to a particular region.

Figure 8.1   Examples of Mission Statements

The Distance Education Clearinghouse
http://www.uwex.edu/disted/about.html
Our mission is to produce a quality, highly maintained and frequently updated Web site that provides a wide range of information about distance education and related resources.

The Catholic Distance University
http://www.cdu.edu/
CDU's mission calls for transmitting faithfully and systematically the teachings of Sacred Scripture, the living Tradition of the Church and the authentic Magisterium, as well as the spiritual heritage of the Fathers, Doctors and Saints.

The University of Little Rock
http://www.ualr.edu/ ~ ddcherepski/mission.html
The mission of Distance Education is to provide the necessary curriculum to students across the State so as to meet their immediate post-secondary education needs.

In the past it was quite often found that a greater demand existed for educational courses than was revealed by normal market research procedures. In other words, by supplying new courses, an institution might stimulate demand for it. With the ease with which programs can be offered through new information and communications technologies, the challenge now is to correctly identify the "niche" in the market; that is, the subject or the population that an institution can serve better than any of its competitors.

Also, before deciding to proceed to design and to offer a course, the management must be convinced that it has both the technology and—more difficult than it may appear—the staff capable of designing and teaching the course. Unfortunately it is common for the decision to go ahead to be taken after there has been a check of the technology, but not of the human resources needed to use it properly. A surprising number of managers seem to think that faculty and trainers can simply add teaching at a distance to their existing workloads. An equally surprising number of faculty and trainers think so, too. The result can be a low-quality programs and eventual disillusionment that would have been best avoided by not going into the distance education field in the first place.

Further, before proceeding, managers have to decide if they will be able to recover the costs of investing in a course or program and how they would do it. We know that a considerable amount of investment costs will be involved as equipment is purchased, new staff hired, and others retrained. Some institutions have been able to obtain grants from philanthropic organizations, while others have to come up with the venture capital and work out how to recover this in tuition fees after the courses are produced. Some projection on this issue is essential, though, before the decision to proceed is taken. What is not possible is to expect income from tuition to pay for investment costs in the very short term. Again, such a policy is a recipe for low quality and disillusionment.

Before deciding to proceed, managers also have to consider issues relating to the faculty, particularly the effect on workload, compensation, and ownership of course materials. In a face-to-face institution considering moving to distance education, will a course be treated as equivalent to teaching a traditional class (even though more time in design and online interaction is likely)? At the most extreme, there are universities where faculty have gone on strike because the impact on their workload had been inadequately considered prior to the decision to set up a distance education program. Other problems have arisen (and are likely to arise in the future) regarding who should own the ideas and information contained in the course, the professor who created them, or the institution that published them. Various solutions to these questions have been arrived at, but whatever the solution, they are questions that are best tackled before the decision is made to proceed into distance education.

Finally, before deciding to proceed, managers must take a hard look at the problem of sustainability. As challenging as it is to get a distance education program started, it is an even bigger challenge to sustain it over the long term. This was demonstrated by a study (Berge and Kearsley, 2003) of 31 corporate, nonprofit, and government organizations that had previously been reported as having started online distance education programs. The authors described the problems that follow a successful start-up and reached the general conclusion that "distance education has grown more slowly than predicted over the past decade because it has not been sustained in many organizations—that is, it keeps getting 'reintroduced'" (p. 15).

Tracking Technology

The quality of the course delivered at a distance and the quality of the student's experience will to some extent depend on the particular delivery system used so that the management's decisions about what technology to purchase will have a significant effect on the cost effectiveness of an institution and its programs. In this period of intense development of Internet-based distance education, the decision concerns the relative merits of different course management systems (see Chapter 4). The administrators responsible for choosing from among various systems have to consider the merits of each system for presenting course materials and also for providing interaction between learners and teachers, but they also have to consider differences in costs. For example, Angel has an annual license fee determined by the number of users, while Blackboard's fee structure is not tied to the number of users in a course. For help in deciding which management system will be best for one's institution, managers and their advisers can use an online resource that compares different systems, such as http://www.edutools.info/course/compare/compare .jsp?product = 153,3.

For a research-based discussion of strategic planning issues see: Kaufman and Watkins (2003).

Administering the Program

The administration of a distance education program includes all the major events and activities that support any formal educational process. They include:

- deciding what courses to offer
- administering the process of designing and implementing the courses
- appointing, training, and supervising academic and administrative staff
- informing potential students about what courses are available and how to join them
- registering applicants and administering admissions procedures
- collecting fees, administering scholarships, and keeping accounts
- setting up and running instructional and counseling services to students
- administering student evaluation procedures, awarding grades, certificates, diplomas, and degrees
- locating and maintaining libraries and study centers
- obtaining and maintaining technology, especially servers and other computer hardware
- continuously monitoring the quality, effectiveness, and efficiency of the program

The extent and complexity of administrative activities will vary according to the type of distance education system. Thus, in many programs, instructors do much of the administration of their courses, linked to the resources of the campus administrative system. At the other extreme, in a single mode institution an entire department will deal with a group of different administrative activities—particularly recruitment, registration, finance, and evaluation. As traditional institutions convert to dual mode, they may decide the special needs of distance learners make it more efficient to set up specialist administrative units alongside such traditional departments as the bursar's office or registrar's office.

Staffing

Once the decision to enter the distance education field has been taken, one of the most important tasks for the administrators is to identify from the existing staff—or otherwise to recruit and then train—the individuals who will be needed to set up and run the program—or to set up and run an institution if it is a new institution that is to be established. The staff that is needed includes:

- subject experts, usually the academics of the teaching institution
- instructional designers
- instructors to teach the courses once they have been designed
- specialists in learner support
- technology experts and technicians who set up and maintain the communications systems

- administrators, such as program directors, course managers, and site coordinators
- clerks who process enrollments, grades, or materials
- managers such as deans, presidents, and other executives

Deciding on Full- versus Part-Time Staffing

One of the most challenging questions associated with staffing is whether to appoint full- or part-time employees, and what combination of each. In general, the higher the ratio of part time to full-time staff, the lower the average cost of providing the course to each student.

The principle of division of labor that we introduced in Chapter 1 supports the idea of having instructors whose primary professional skill is interacting with students, leaving other people to design, produce, and deliver the course learning materials. Such professionals become skillful at enabling each student to have a high quality personal relationship with a teacher in spite of distance. Because there is a limit to the number of students that an instructor can interact with, it becomes prohibitively expensive for an institution to maintain a large number of full-time instructors for this purpose as well as content experts, instructional designers, learner support staff, technologists, and administrative staff. It becomes more feasible to provide a good student-instructor ratio if part-time staff can be engaged in this instructor role. Having part-time staff also allows the organization to adapt its curriculum more quickly to changing needs than may be possible if it has a staff locked into a curriculum that may have been more relevant 10 or 20 years earlier. In general, therefore, hiring instructors on a part-time basis makes for better quality as well as greater cost-effectiveness. But it is a difficult policy to implement in many institutions.

In single mode universities, it is the normal practice to have full-time staff develop courses, usually supplemented with part-time consultants, and then to depend on part-time instructors ("tutors") to teach the course. In American universities it is more common for the full-time faculty of the university to provide both content and instruction, though it is increasingly common for part-timers, including graduate students and adjunct faculty, to act as instructors. Other organizations, such as a school district or corporate training department, may hire consultants as writers, editors, Web producers, graphic artists, and programmers to design and develop courses and use their full-time teachers or trainers to provide the instruction. Managers and administrative staff are usually permanent, full-time positions.

Training and Orientation of Staff

Whether full- or part-time, it is imperative that all staff understand the distinctive character of distance education, including an appreciation of the many positive characteristics of learning in a distant home or work environment. They need to appreciate the difficulties that distance education students experience, and must know how to be helpful, and *want* to be helpful. As compared with the past, there are fewer faculty in traditional institutions who disparage distance learners, but good intentions aren't enough to make good educators. Training is needed, and organizing this is an important responsibility of administrators. After initial training, staff should be monitored continuously and provided with ongoing, in-service training to enable them to develop their skills and keep up-to-date. Most training is likely to be in-house and on-the-job. Some members of staff might be enrolled in one of the various online training programs. (For a list of professional development programs, see Chapter 6.)

Staff Monitoring and Assessment

Once appointed and trained, both academic and other staff should be monitored and evaluated to ensure the quality and effectiveness of their work. The idea of being systematically monitored has not been understood in academia as long as it has been in the business and industrial worlds, or indeed in training departments of the armed forces or in school districts. It is an essential part of the systems approach, however. A means has to be set up for gathering data regularly and evaluating it, so that interventions can be made for remedial training where weaknesses in the delivery system are identified. Among the kind of data to be gathered are responses from students and from faculty themselves about how satisfied they are with course products and the teaching procedures as well as the learning accomplished.

We will return to this again when we discuss implementing policies for quality assessment later in this chapter. Also, refer to the discussion about assignments in Chapter 6.

Learner Support Centers, Libraries, and Teleconference Sites

Although an increasingly large range of learning materials and services for distance learners are now delivered by means of the Internet, there are still some that cannot be, and certainly there are some services that are better provided face-to-face and/or in group settings by audio- or video-teleconferences. A pure distance learning method may be unsuitable for teaching a subject such as interpersonal relations for trainee counselors, or for trainee teachers who need classroom practice, or where potentially dangerous results could occur without professional supervision, as in teaching chemistry. In such cases, administrators have to identify laboratory facilities, schools for teaching practice, and so on. Contracts may have to be drawn up, fees paid, and other responsibilities incurred in the use of these facilities that lie outside the immediate control of the distance teaching institution.

Setting up and maintaining learning centers require many administrative decisions, including:

- where learning centers should be located
- when they should be open
- what facilities and equipment are needed

- what staff (administrative and academic) they should have
- how they should relate to the "main campus"
- how they should be funded

Libraries

Most education, certainly at university level, requires students to undertake some research that uses materials beyond what is provided by the instructor. A great challenge for administrators of distance education has been how to provide library resources that could compare with what were available to students on campus. In 1967, the Association of College and Research Libraries (ACRL) released formal guidelines for providing for the needs of distant learners. The guidelines were updated in 1982, 1990, and in 1998 (ACRL Distance Learning Sections Guideline Committee, 1998). With the arrival of the Internet, the problem has become much easier to deal with. Academic libraries are beginning to add dedicated distance education librarians to their staffs. Central Michigan University, for example, employs seven full-time librarians for this kind of service (Kirk and Bartelstein, 1999). In Florida, distance learners anywhere in the state have access to dedicated distance education librarians at the Florida Distance Learning Reference and Referral Center (Guernsey, 1998). Another way academic libraries have responded to the needs of distance learners is through the formation of partnerships. Walden University, an accredited distance-based graduate school, formed an alliance with Indiana University to allow Walden students to make full use of the Indiana University Libraries resources (Kirk and Bartelstein, 1999). ILLINET, a consortium of 40 academic libraries in Illinois, provides cooperative borrowing arrangements for members' students as well as maintaining a common online catalog (Cooper et al., 1998). In California, nine campuses of the University of California formed the California Digital Library (CDL), which is accessible to the public, and provides online searches and a periodical database indexing over 800,000 titles available throughout the state. The Pennsylvania State University is part of several library cooperatives, including The Virtual Electronic Library (The VEL) and the Pennsylvania Academic Library Connection Initiative (PALCI). The VEL provides mutual borrowing among the Big Ten universities and the University of Chicago. Online catalogs, such as LibrarySpot, ECO (Electronic Collections Online), and the WorldCAT (both of which are maintained by the Online Computer Library Center (OCLC), provide online users with access to library resources, catalogs, and information systems. A 1996 survey of academic libraries found that of the 74 respondents, only 3 indicated they were not actively supporting their institution's distance education programs (Snyder, Logue, and Preece, 1996).

A few other examples of state-wide library collaborative initiatives are:

Colorado: http://www.aclin.org/

Maine: http://libraries.maine.edu/mariner/

Texas: http://www.lib.utsystem.edu/

Wisconsin: http://www.wils.wisc.edu/

From the Margins to the Mainstream: Developing Library Support for Distance Learning

The University Library has recently received a 3-year, $350,000 grant from the Bush Foundation to develop a comprehensive program of library services for distance learners.

Planning library services for distance learning will be guided by the principle that "What's good for on-campus students must also be good for distance learners." Conversely, library services developed with distance learners in mind must also work for on-campus students. This approach reflects the belief that, in time, the distinctions between distance and on-camps learning will diminish.

The Library plans to emphasize four major areas of development: 1) Faculty Liaison and Communications; 2) Expanded Access to Information Resources; 3) Reference and Consultation Services; and 4) Instruction in the Use of Information Resources.

SOURCE: John Butler, Project Director, *Libraryline: An Occasional Newsletter of the University of Minnesota Libraries—Twin Cities* (May 1997), Volume 8, Number 4. Available at: http://staff.lib.umn.edu/LibraryLine/LLvol8no4.htm.

Western Governors University: http://www.unm.edu/~wguclr/StuOverview/index.html

For more on the role of academic libraries in general, see McKnight (2003) and many online resources located at: http://www.uwex.edu/disted/libsupport.html.

Teleconference Learning Sites

With the arrival of the Internet there has been a decline in interest on the part of many institutions in setting up teleconference learning sites. It is certainly less trouble for the administrator in an institution that delivers instructional programs to the student's home computer than one that delivers by satellite—at least regarding the arrangements at the interface between the learner and the system. There are still many programs delivered to learning sites, however, and in a good system there would be an integration of both technologies. For an institution using this technology, the major problems for administrators are to ensure that the learning site is in a good location, that it is well run, and that the staff and equipment are working properly. The size of the learning site can range from a small conference room for a group of 4–5 participants to a large auditorium with hundreds of people. The most important administrative decision to be made is who is to be the coordinator. There are also many decisions needed about allocation of resources to this delivery system, levels of tuition fees, marketing strategies, and evaluation (see more about managing a teleconference in Chapter 5 and more about the coordinator in Chapter 6).

Budgeting

Of all the areas that administrators must deal with, budgeting is probably the most difficult. Budget decisions are basically about priorities and resource allocation. Administrators should always be concerned with the question of cost-effectiveness—are they getting the best value for the money they spend? This question comes in when making decisions at the most general level of policy (e.g., what types of course the institution will deliver), to the most specific (e.g., whether the price of a proposed textbook might have a negative effect on student enrollment).

When making up their budget, some of the most important decisions administrators must make are how much to spend on:

- developing new courses
- buying new technology
- hiring academic staff
- paying for student support services
- running learning centers
- running their administration
- marketing their programs

The main question is what relative proportion of funds and resources should be allocated to each of these categories. For example, should more of the budget go towards developing new courses, supporting the existing ones, hiring more academic staff, or improving facilities? In theory, allocating funds among the different items should be based upon a careful analysis of the needs of the distance education program, including current deficiencies and opportunities. For example, if student evaluation data indicates that students are dissatisfied with the level of interactivity in their courses, more money could be allocated to buying a new delivery system that allows more interaction, to workshops to train teachers in interactive techniques, or to simply hire more instructors to reduce the student-to-instructor ratio. On the other hand, if data from market research indicate that more students would enroll if more (or certain) courses were offered, it could be argued that course development should receive a larger share of the budget. Decisions have to be made, and in order to make the best decisions, it is necessary to have reliable evaluation data on all aspects of the organization's distance education efforts.

Budgeting at Different Levels

Budget decisions must be made at many different levels: institutional, departmental, programmatic, and in administering individual courses. Each level of decision making is likely to have different priorities. For example, senior administrators are likely to be concerned with reserving enough money to support marketing projects with a view to keeping up enrollments and thus revenue, whereas faculty are likely to take this background activity for granted and to be preoccupied with maintaining student support services or the number of academic staff, which they associate with maintaining quality. Differences like these mean that budget decisions are often accompanied by power struggles within the organization, as each constituency attempts to obtain as big a share of the budget as possible. To avoid these struggles turning into acrimonious conflicts, administrators must continually emphasize that budget decisions will be made on the basis of data, and that all groups wishing to influence the budget must present data to justify their requests or plans.

Budgeting the Administration

One of the most difficult budget categories for administrators to allocate funds to is administration itself. Most administrators feel pressure to run a "lean and mean" operation, having the smallest administrative staff possible. If taken too far, however, this can be counterproductive if it results in an administrative function that is understaffed and not able to run things efficiently. Money spent in running a good performance monitoring unit would, for example, almost certainly be a good investment. Similarly, good management means extensive planning, and this needs market research and other studies, which are more difficult to justify to the faculty or the public than creating new courses, hiring more academic staff, or buying new technology. On the other hand, it is true that institutions sometimes get "top heavy" with administrations that consume an inordinate amount of the budget while producing less than an equivalent benefit. Just like administrators in other units in the organization, senior administrators must continually collect cost-effectiveness data on their administrative operations to justify the portion of the budget that they are allowed to spend.

Scheduling

Budgeting the resources of time may seem a little strange to people who have only worked in traditional education, where all instruction is organized in a very familiar pattern of class sessions and semesters of fixed durations. In schools and colleges most of the attention given to budgeting time is a matter of developing and reorganizing schedules (timetables) for students and teachers. Indeed, formulae for funding and accrediting such schools are usually based upon student attendance in scheduled classes. In most forms of distance education, this kind of scheduling is far less significant. Instead, administrators have to budget the time of the many individuals that make up a course team during the often lengthy process of designing a course and then they have to schedule the instructional staff during its implementation.

Because course materials must be prepared in advance of their use—and some of these, such as video recordings, may need many months to produce—it is essential that a well-defined schedule be developed and maintained. Usually this takes the form of a work plan that lists all of the tasks that must be completed, the deadlines for each task, and who is responsible for completing the task. It is the responsibility of the administrator in charge of the distance education program to ensure that the development schedule is followed so the materials and programs all come together and are ready when the students and instructors appear to begin the interactive phase of the program. At that time there will need to be a widely distributed schedule for such activities as course registration and tuition payments; and a schedule of dates for the completion of course assignments, examinations, and graduation procedures. Other major scheduling tasks are involved if there is teleconferencing, such as booking of rooms at teleconference sites; and if the institution is delivering a program as well as receiving it, time on the satellite has to be scheduled with the telecommunications company.

Popular methods applied in scheduling design of courses are the Program Evaluation and Review Technique (PERT), the Critical Path Method, and the Gantt chart. Each technique results in a chart. PERT charts show each task and its planned duration, with each task connected to its successor in a network of nodes and connecting lines. A Critical Path Method chart is similar to a PERT chart, with a critical path showing the set of tasks that together take the longest time to complete and which receive special attention. A Gantt chart is a matrix with tasks listed on one axis and with the horizontal axis indicating such variables as the time to be given to the task, the skill needed to perform it, and the person responsible for it. For more on PERT see Taylor and Reid (1993). For a commercially available tool to help with the PERT process, see http://www.criticaltools.com/pertmain.htm.

Scheduling the Student

In correspondence courses, students usually set their own schedules and pace themselves towards completing the course. Most programs establish a maximum period (e.g., 6 months or 1 year) within which time a course must be completed. Within this time period, students can complete their assignments and examinations according to their own timetables. Some programs allow open enrollment, while others specify certain registration periods. On the other hand, programs that involve teleconferencing or television broadcasts usually have a fixed class schedule with well-defined beginning and end dates. The general practice with online distance education is to deliver a course according to a strict schedule, with groups of students enrolled very much like they do for a conventional class. Most students find this more rigid structure and pacing to be helpful in completing the course. It is important that such schedules are reasonably planned and take into account the amount of work involved and allow sufficient turnaround time for delivery of assignments.

Quality Assessment

Although everyone in an educational institution has a role to play in producing high quality instruction, administrators are responsible for its measurement and for using the data gathered in taking action to improve it. In one way

Some Data about Administration

- A survey of 61 North American college and university distance learning programs showed they offered an average of 65.9 distance learning courses per semester, ranging from as few as 2 to as many as 550 courses.

- Instructor salaries account for the highest percentage of the programs' total costs—31.72 percent.

- Programs spend an average of $19,046 on marketing and advertising. Private colleges spend $1,200 more than public colleges; 4-year colleges spend almost $4,000 more than 2-year colleges.

- For marketing, 75 percent of the programs use direct mail campaigns, 75 percent use the college or program Web site, 71 percent advertise in newspapers. Radio and television advertisements were used by 45 and 44 percent of the programs, respectively.

- 86.96 percent of the programs operate at a profit, and 13.04 percent operate at a profit of greater than 50 percent.

- 36.68 percent of distance learning instructors are adjunct faculty.

SOURCE: *The survey of distance learning programs in higher education,* 1999 edition; http://www.primary research.com.

or another all the administrative activities discussed can be evaluated in the search for data pertaining to quality. There are a number of other factors that might be monitored, including:

- number and quality of applications and enrollments
- student achievement
- student satisfaction
- faculty satisfaction
- program or institutional reputation
- quality of course materials

Each of these factors reflects different aspects of the quality of an institution's products and services.

Continually increasing or stable rates of applications and enrollments suggests the organization is doing a good job of tracking demographic and socio-economic variables and tailoring its offerings to real needs. It may also be considered to be an indicator of satisfactory teaching and good "word-of-mouth" promotion by satisfied students.

Student achievement should be one of the aspects of quality measurement that receives most attention. This is not difficult to monitor in the short term—

see the discussion of assignments in Chapter 6—but it is difficult to assess in the longer term. In professional fields where students have to take certification exams (e.g., law, medicine, engineering) it is possible to examine the achievement of students relative to other institutions. However, the kind of student achievement data that would be most valuable, namely job performance or work competency evaluations, is almost impossible to obtain, due to the complexities of conducting studies in the workplace. Most programs usually settle for anecdotal information about the impact of their courses, collected from interviews of graduates.

Student satisfaction data is important and relatively easy to collect. It is standard practice for students to evaluate a course at its conclusion, being asked to rate or comment on the content, course organization, the instructors, instructional materials, and the delivery system. Such data is usually scrutinized by the course manager and sometimes the department head or dean. This provides at least a minimal check on the quality of courses as far as the perceptions of students are concerned. However, student satisfaction data is far from an infallible measurement of how effective a course is in terms of students' learning, nor does it assess the validity or relevance of the content taught.

Similarly, faculty satisfaction may be a useful measure provided its subjective character is also kept in mind. Faculty can assess the extent to which existing teaching strategies and materials appear to be effective, whether student support services are adequate, and whether courses appear to meet the needs of students or their employers. Most faculty are concerned to be effective teachers and are likely to make recommendations that they believe will improve their effectiveness..

Taken together, the variables listed above add up to a general reputation for quality which is to a large extent reflected in an institution's enrollments. If graduates are satisfied with their courses, and employers who hire those graduates are satisfied with their job performance, they will all speak well of the program and this will result in further enrollments. Institutions may spend considerable sums of money on marketing and promotional efforts aimed at establishing a brand image of being a high-quality organization.

Finally, it is possible for administrators (and others) to assess the quality of their course materials or their teaching in terms of standards established by national associations. For example, the University Continuing Education Association has a Distance Learning Community of Practice, one of the purposes of which is to disseminate information about good practice. It encourages good practice with a series of awards, including a Distance Learning Course Award and a Program of Excellence award (see http://www.ucea.edu/dlhome.htm). The American Association for Collegiate Independent Study evaluates independent study courses for its annual awards (see http://www.aacis.org/awards/).

Benchmarks for Success
in Internet-Based Distance Education

In 2000, the Institute for Higher Education and Policy conducted a study to identify a set of factors (benchmarks) that could be used to assess the quality of online education. The study involved six institutions engaged in online teaching: Brevard Community College, Regents College, University of Illinois at Urbana-Champaign, University of Maryland University College, Utah State University, and Weber State University. The study examined 45 factors and determined the importance and presence of these factors in the online programs at these six institutions. Based upon this analysis, the following 24 factors emerged as significant benchmarks for quality.

Institutional Support Benchmarks

1. A documented technology plan that includes electronic security measures (i.e., password protection, encryption, back-up systems) is in place and operational to ensure both quality standards and the integrity and validity of information.

2. The reliability of the technology delivery system is as failsafe as possible.

3. A centralized system provides support for building and maintaining the distance education infrastructure.

Course Development Benchmarks

4. Guidelines regarding minimum standards are used for course development, design, and delivery, while learning outcomes—not the availability of existing technology—determine the technology being used to deliver course content.

5. Instructional materials are reviewed periodically to ensure they meet program standards.

6. Courses are designed to require students to engage themselves in analysis, synthesis, and evaluation as part of their course and program requirements.

Teaching/Learning Benchmarks

7. Student interaction with faculty and other students is an essential characteristic and is facilitated through a variety of ways, including voice mail and/or e-mail.

8. Feedback to student assignments and questions is constructive and provided in a timely manner.

9. Students are instructed in the proper methods of effective research, including assessment of the validity of resources.

(continued)

continued

Course Structure Benchmarks

10. Before starting an online program, students are advised about the program to determine: (1) if they possess the self-motivation and commitment to learn at a distance, and (2) if they have access to the minimal technology required by the course design.

11. Students are provided with supplemental course information that outlines course objectives, concepts, and ideas, and learning outcomes for each course are summarized in a clearly written, straightforward statement.

12. Students have access to sufficient library resources that may include a "virtual library" accessible through the World Wide Web.

13. Faculty and students agree upon expectations regarding times for student assignment completion and faculty response.

Faculty Support Benchmarks

14. Technical assistance in course development is available to faculty, who are encouraged to use it.

15. Faculty members are assisted in the transition from classroom teaching to online instruction and are assessed during the process.

16. Instructor training and assistance, including peer mentoring, continues through the progression of the online course.

17. Faculty members are provided with written resources to deal with issues arising from student use of electronically accessed data.

A Realistic Assessment of Quality

Following a study of six selected colleges and universities, Compora (2003) arrived at what is probably a realistic conclusion about quality beyond the specific cases he studied and pointing to areas in which all institutions could probably do better. He reported "there appears to be a discrepancy between the literature cited and the actual practice of the institutions surveyed" (p. 15) and concluded:

- Program specific mission statements are inadequately developed.
- Programs are often implemented in the absence of a needs assessment.
- Programs generally target and tailor programs to a certain type of distance education student.

Student Support Benchmarks

18. Students receive information about programs, including admission requirements, tuition and fees, books and supplies, technical and proctoring requirements, and student support services.

19. Students are provided with hands-on training and information to aid them in securing material through electronic databases, interlibrary loans, government archives, news services, and other sources.

20. Throughout the duration of the course/program, students have access to technical assistance, including detailed instructions regarding the electronic media used, practice sessions prior to the beginning of the course, and convenient access to technical support staff.

21. Questions directed to student service personnel are answered accurately and quickly, with a structured system in place to address student complaints.

Evaluation and Assessment Benchmarks

22. The program's educational effectiveness and teaching/learning process is assessed through an evaluation process that uses several methods and applies specific standards.

23. Data on enrollment, costs, and successful/innovative uses of technology are used to evaluate program effectiveness.

24. Intended learning outcomes are reviewed regularly to ensure clarity, utility, and appropriateness.

The full report on the study is available at http://www.ihep.com/Pubs/PDF/Quality.pdf.

- Institutions overwhelmingly are creating their own online courses.
- Courses are approved for distance delivery with little consistency; there is little use of a hierarchical approval system.
- Delivery methods are often selected based on availability of technology as opposed to a systematic design process.
- Instructors generally teach distance education courses based on their willingness rather than their expertise.
- Students do not appear to be getting the support they need.
- Little data about matriculation is being gathered making evaluation of effectiveness of program difficult.
- No specific trends are noted regarding a dedicated budget for distance education programs.

- There is an absence of marketing strategies.
- There is little consistency on how evaluation information is used.

For more on quality measurement in distance education, see Sherry (2003) and for more on evaluating distance education programs, see Thompson and Irele (2003).

Regional Accrediting Commissions

In higher education, the Regional Accrediting Commissions have published guidelines for institutions offering electronically delivered distance education that can be useful for administrators in their internal quality assessments. Most of the guidelines would apply equally well in fields of practice besides higher education.

The Regional Accrediting Commissions are listed in Figure 8.2. The publication that carries the guidelines agreed to by these accrediting agencies is: *Distance Learning Programs: Interregional Guidelines for Electronically Offered Degree and Certificate Programs* (2002) (http://www.msache.org/msache/content/pdf_files/distguide02.pdf).

Accrediting Commission of the Distance Education and Training Council (DETC)

The DETC Accrediting Commission was established in 1955 and is recognized by the U.S. Department of Education and the Council for Higher Education Accreditation (CHEA) to accredit distance education in postsecondary programs, including the first professional degree level.

The Commission establishes educational, ethical, and business standards; it examines and evaluates distance education institutions in terms of these standards; and accredits those who qualify. Its accrediting program employs procedures similar to those of other recognized educational accrediting agencies (see http://www.detc.org/acredditHandbk.html). More on accreditation of distance education in higher education can be obtained from the Council on Postsecondary Accreditation, Washington, DC, at their Web site and specifically at: http://www.chea.org/pdf/fact_sheet_2.pdf. Finally, Lezberg (2003) gives a research-oriented discussion of accreditation.

Policy: Institutional, State, and Federal

Some of the decisions that managers face mentioned earlier in this chapter, such as determining and modifying an institution's mission or deciding when to proceed in a particular programming direction, are policy decisions. An institution's policy (or that of a state, regional organization, or federal authority) is a relatively general set of principles against which administrators can

Figure 8.2   The Regional Accrediting Commissions

Middle States Commission on Higher Education
http://www.msache.org

New England Association of Schools and Colleges
http://www.neasc.org

North Central Association of Colleges and Schools
http://www.ncahigherlearningcommission.org

Northwest Association of Schools and of Colleges and Universities
http://www.nwccu.org

Southern Association of Schools and Colleges
http://www.sacs.org

Western Association of Schools and Colleges
http://www.wascweb.org

test plans, proposals, or ideas for specific actions. If, for example, an institution has a policy agreed to with its faculty that there will be a certain ratio of full- to part-time teachers hired at that institution, distance education administrators know the limits of the options open to them in planning the human resources needed for the delivery of a new course. Or, to take another example, if the institution makes a policy that all its programs will be delivered on the Internet and there will be no video-teleconferencing, a boundary has been set within which they have to make their administrative decisions regarding the purchase of new technology.

Making policy and ensuring it stays up to date requires a concentrated effort on the part of an institution's management. In fact it is too easy for managers to become so distracted by day-to-day administration that the attention they should give to renewing the policy framework on which everything else is founded can too easily become neglected. In dual mode institutions where distance education involves, for example, new working arrangements that depend on collaboration among previously separate departments, or where it might be necessary to divert resources of money and people's time from conventional teaching, it will be essential to have a systematic way of engaging the staff in the process of formulating new policies and for reviewing old ones on an ongoing basis.

At the state and federal levels there is a similar need for policy review and for setting up new policies that are appropriate to the electronic age. Since elected officials are likely to be involved in this process and they are, of course, not expected to be educational professionals, a process of explaining and educating has to go on to prepare them to consider the policy changes needed at those levels.

For broader reviews of policy issues, see Dirr (2003), and Pacey and Keough (2003).

Policy Barriers to Distance Education Are Falling

In the first edition of this book, we explained that among the reasons for the slow rate of development of distance education were barriers thrown up by policies that were designed to support an older model of education, which actually have impeded the evolution of new systems. These policy barriers could be found at federal, regional, state, and institutional levels. It is now apparent that the situation has improved significantly.

At the Federal Level

THEN: Barriers include the criteria used to determine what programs are eligible for federal funding, which are biased toward traditional provision.

NOW: More generous treatment of distance education exists. In particular, there have been changes in U.S. Department of Education policy on the infamous "12 hour rule," which stated that financial aid can only be given to students who attended a face-to-face classroom at least 12 hours a week.

Another policy area at the federal level where there has been progress concerns changes in the copyright laws. Both the Digital Millennium Copyright Act of 1998 and The TEACH Act (Technology in Education and Copyright Harmonization Act) of November 2002, sets policy to ease restrictions on using materials in distance education courses (see http://archive.ala .org/washoff/teachdrm.pdf).

At the Regional Level

THEN: Criteria applied in giving institutions their official accreditation to teach are based on the practices of campus-based learning, faculty-centered teaching, and classroom-based instruction.

NOW: *All* Regional Accrediting Commissions have adopted distance education criteria in their procedures for evaluating distance education programs when institutions in their jurisdictions undergo the accreditation process.

At the State Level

THEN: "There are mechanisms that drive continuing investment in bricks and mortar education, and prevent the expenditures that would establish virtual universities based on a telecommunications network. The typical funding formulae the states use to decide on allocation of resources, being based on numbers of traditional day-time students, systematically generates on-campus classroom space for 8:00 a.m. to 5:00 p.m. teaching, and underprovides not only the communications technology but also the building facilities needed for off-campus learner support and instruction for distance learners" (Moore and Kearsley, 1996, pg. 192).

NOW: Most states are investing in state-wide virtual delivery systems (see the subsequent examples).

At the Institutional Level

THEN: ". . . the barriers include some of the administrative structures and procedures that are supposed to serve students but are often inappropriate for distance learners. They are found in the rules and regulations concerning registration, tuition payment procedures, student support services, library services, examinations, and most especially the provision of instruction at times and places convenient to the learner" (Moore and Kearsley, 1996, p. 192).

NOW: Huge improvements at the institutional level (see subsequent examples and throughout the book).

Policy is obviously a dynamic concept; the following are some of the areas where policy is still unsettled and is being made as you read this.

Institutional: Faculty Policy

Among the most difficult areas regarding distance education policy in educational institutions concern faculty, especially their compensation, workload, and intellectual property rights. Policy varies considerably between institutions and even within institutions regarding the rights and responsibilities of faculty regarding both course design and subsequent teaching of the course. At some institutions, the policy on compensation for design is for the full-time faculty to develop courses for no additional payment, with this effort considered part of their normal workload. Other institutions recognize that the level of effort and creativity in designing distance education courses is greater than preparing for a course in residence and have established an "additional compensation" policy. When it comes to the delivery of courses, one option is for full-time faculty to provide the instruction as part of their load, some institutions treat it as an overload for extra compensation, while others depend on part-time faculty to do this.

The impact of all distance education work on the regular workload is a matter of concern to most faculty. In particular at the university level, faculty have to give a high priority to their research and to having the results of that researched published. This is usually required for faculty to obtain a tenured position and to qualify for promotion. Whereas traditional measures of teaching, scholarship (publications in refereed journals), and service are included in the promotion and tenure formulae, work related to innovative instructional products, including those for distance education, are not generally given comparable recognition. Thus it becomes necessary, if an institution is serious about distance education, that it modifies its promotion and tenure policies to give credit for the time spent in designing and delivering courses. Another aspect of the workload problem is the instructor's need for additional training

Intellectual Property Policy: The Example of Brigham Young University

Pursuant to law and university policy, and without an express agreement specifying otherwise, any work (whether a technical work or a creative work) prepared by university personnel within the scope of their employment is work for hire owned by the university. When works are commissioned to an individual who is not an employee of the university or when the commissioned individual is an employee but the work to be created falls outside that person's scope of employment, the university will proceed with a written agreement, signed by the university and the individual, stating that the resulting intellectual property is owned by the university and assigning to the university all intellectual property rights to the work held by the individual.

The university retains ownership rights to all technical works but relinquishes ownership rights to the developer(s) of creative works when "nominal" use of university resources are involved in the production of the intellectual property. When "substantial" university resources are used in the production of creative works, however, the university will retain its ownership position, and income from the project will be shared with the developers. The conditions that differentiate between nominal and substantial use of university resources are discussed below (see sections IV.A and IV.B). Decisions based upon the extent of the utilization of university resources are to be negotiated with developers by the deans, in consultation with the appropriate Intellectual Property Services support office and within these general guidelines prior to approval by the academic vice president's office

SOURCE: http://www.byu.edu/ ~ ttdata/documents/ippolicy.htm

on use of technologies and learning the pedagogy of teaching at a distance. As the need for training becomes apparent, a policy is needed that rewards participation in training and allows the allocation of resources for this.

State Policy on Funding and Administration of K–12 Programs

Clark (2000) has identified the following alternative policies regarding funding in state-wide distance education programs:

- Funding should be from state agencies.
- Funding should be based on per-student tuition fees.
- Funding should be based on a barter system in which each school district pays an up-front fee and contributes resources.

In a survey of online programs, Clark reported that 73 percent of programs charged tuition and received an average of roughly $1 million in nontuition funding (typically state or federal funds) per fiscal year. Funding from state agencies allows programs to charge below cost, thus increasing equity of opportunity for poorer districts. The barter system allows for schools and districts to supply teachers and other resources in place of higher tuition fees, but is logistically more difficult to administer.

A California Virtual School report offers the following recommendations on finance: To establish a state virtual school program, initial start up monies will be needed, which could come from the state legislature, federal grants, corporate grants, or corporate partnerships. Start-up funds in other states ranged from $2–15 million. Depending on the policy chosen by the state, $5 million would be needed in the first year of operation. This would include establishing a state virtual school office, staff, and the technology infrastructure needed to support the implementation of the program.

The California Virtual School Report also provides the following information about funding policies and the establishment of virtual high schools in other states as follows:

Illinois Virtual High School (IVHS) was created on the basis of a series of state and federal investment grants totaling roughly $800,000 between late 1999 and 2001. IVHS policy is to establish a revenue model that gives priority to sustainability of the programs and to this end charges a $300 fee per student that covers operating costs (i.e., technology and support fees to a vendor, and teacher pay).

Policy for the Michigan Virtual High School has a similar financial model. Operating costs are covered by tuition fees, which are paid by schools in one of two ways. Schools may pay a fee for a single course, which is $335 per student per course. Alternatively, they may become "members" by paying a fee that is determined by the size of the school, up to a high of $5,000 plus $.50 per student for the largest schools in the State, which entitles the member to 60 course seats.

The policy in Florida is for the state to provide all the funding, so that there are no tuition charges. Total funding over the 5-year period of 1997–2002 was approximately $23 million, with funding for the 2003 fiscal year at $5.7 million. In the 2002–2003 school year, Florida Virtual had 62 courses and 8,200 students, with additional demand of at least 1,000 students.

For more on state policy issues, see Simonson and Bauck (2003).

Implementing Institutional Change

Most educational and training institutions share three significant problems in introducing distance education. They are:

1. An academic culture that views teaching as an individual's act in a classroom.

2. A policy-making structure dominated by staff who are satisfied with the system that gave them power.

3. An administrative system in which technological and human resources are fragmented in a multilayered structure of faculties and departments, each of which guards its own interests.

There is no simple strategy for change for administrators faced with these issues, but there are some steps that seem to be productive.

The first step is to *identify the innovators* in the organization, the small number of people at every level who are interested in change. These people should be encouraged, with money and in other ways, to organize themselves and to develop a consensus of ideas about distance education and strategies for bringing change to their organization. This recognition of potential stakeholders is critical. The kind of change needed to establish a distance education system cannot be brought about entirely from the bottom of the institution and definitely needs leadership from the senior management. On the other hand, lower level support for senior management has to be generated, though it is likely to be in a limited number of areas within the institution.

The second step is for the innovators to be enabled to *undertake a demonstration project.* Institutional change will not occur as a result of argument, reasoning, or persuasion alone. The majority of members of the institution will not become persuaded of the viability of distance education until they see the process at work, see that it can provide a good standard of teaching, and see the achievements of the students. They will lose fear of change as they see the professional satisfaction of their peers who engage in the distance teaching activity.

It is vital that the demonstration projects are of the highest possible standard, since failure or mediocre results will have exactly the opposite effect from what is desired. For this reason it is imperative that financial, technological, and human resources are ruthlessly focused. The temptation to spread resources over a number of projects must be resisted. For that to happen the organization needs what is probably the most important ingredient if change is to occur, which is a high-level manager with a strong vision of distance education and courage to implement it. Given such leadership, and a team of innovators, resources can then be organized with the aim of showing how a distance education system works. *All* the technologies of the institution must be brought into play; in an institution that aspires to deliver programs on a national or even state level, several million dollars are likely to be required to design, produce, and deliver a single demonstration project of sufficient quality.

A National Policy Issue: The Digital Divide

A relatively new problem that has been getting attention from policy makers at all levels is that of the digital divide—defined as the gap between those who have and those who do not have access to the digital technology that is an

Penn State: Developing a Policy
for an Institution-Wide System

The Pennsylvania State University is widely recognized for its leadership in developing and implementing a distance education policy. This success has been the fruit of an institutional change strategy that was worked out over a 10-year period, beginning with the creation, in 1992, of a task force made up of selected innovative members of the faculty representing stakeholders from across the university.

The report from the Task Force presented a vision to the faculty:

> In our view, distance education will become a substantial part of the University's future regardless of this report or any actions that are taken as a result of it. We believe that the external forces of an evolving student population, the revolutionary advances in technology, and the changing economic picture for all of higher education will eventually bring an enhanced and expanded use of distance education methodologies into the central strategies of most major universities. . . . However, the Task Force believes that, at this moment, there is a "window of opportunity" that is open to the University that will allow it to capitalize on existing strengths and assume a position of national leadership in distance education. We believe that this could ensure the future viability of our distance education efforts, increase the quality and efficiency of many of our academic programs, bring national recognition and prestige to the University through accomplishments in this area, and serve as a source of both cost-savings and revenue generation.

To implement the vision, the Task Force recommended a set of policies:

- the creation of a university-wide unit to facilitate the development of distance education at the university
- the rewriting of tenure and promotion procedures to recognize distance education activities as being equivalent to all other categories of teaching
- the assignment of substantial resources to the distance education unit to support program development and a significant portion of revenue or cost savings generated by distance education efforts be returned to the unit
- the proposed distance education unit develop demonstration projects throughout the university to establish the potential benefits and applications

This is the policy foundation for Penn State's World Campus. Coopting stakeholders into a task force or similar consensus-shaping group, and building a policy on the basis of its findings is illustrative of the kind of policy-making procedure most likely to succeed in any large educational organization.

SOURCE: The Report of the Task Force on Distance Education. University Park: The Pennsylvania State University, November 1992.

essential prerequisite for online learning. As described by Damarin (2000), there are several classes of access to digital technologies:

- Those who own state-of-the-art computers and subscribe to an Internet service.
- Those who have access to computers and the Internet at work, libraries, or other locations, and know how to use them.
- Those who have rare or minimal access to computing technologies and little facility with them.
- Those who experience their everyday lives untouched by computer and information technologies.

The National Telecommunications Information Administration (NTIA) has reported on specific groups in the United States affected by the digital divide. The 1998 report, "Falling Through the Net: Defining the Digital Divide," describes accessibility by race, income, education, and geographic areas. The 1999 report also identified trends in connectivity from 1984 until the time of the study. Although the NTIA found that the number of connections is on the rise, the number of connections for the "haves" are growing at a faster rate than the "have nots" and thus the gap has continued to grow. See http://www .ntia.doc.gov/ntiahome/fttn99/contents.html.

A study by the Progressive Policy Institute (Dunham, 1999) ranked the 50 states on how well they were adapting to the New Economy. Using criteria such as the number of high-tech jobs, quality of educational technology, percentage of population online, commercial Internet domains, and available venture capital, the report identifies a clear geographic pattern. The West Coast and eastern seaboard from New Hampshire to Virginia are the most privileged, and the Deep South and the upper Midwest lag far behind.

Policy Initiatives to Reduce the Digital Divide

Federal Government

U.S. Federal Government policy initiatives have included:

- The Department of Commerce has a strategy for making computers and the Internet accessible, and monitoring the levels of connectivity in relation to income, education, race, gender, geography, and age; encouraging applications that enable low-income Americans to start and manage their own small businesses.
- The Department of Education's Community Technical Centers program has provided money to develop model programs to demonstrate the educational effectiveness of technology, especially in economically distressed communities.
- The Star Schools program has allocated more than $125 million since 1988 to support demonstration projects that use technology to provide programs and activities in underserved areas.

- The Technology Literacy Challenge Fund is allocating $2 billion over five years to help states and local districts meet the administration's educational technology goals.
- Lessons learned from grant programs and educational technology initiatives are disseminated, with an emphasis on underserved citizens.
- Giving tax advantages for businesses providing technology to schools libraries, community centers, and individuals in low-income areas (the "E-rate") (Damarin, 2000).

Private Sector

Policy initiatives from the private sector include:

- providing low-cost Internet access and computers
- funding community computing centers
- encouraging IT professionals to do volunteer training (Tapscott, 1998)

Examples include:

- Companies such as Ford Motor Company and Delta Air Lines offer low-cost Internet access and computers to their employees (Peirce, 2000)
- Joint Venture—a group organizing a Silicon Valley network. "Through the Digital Divide initiative and workforce initiatives, Joint Venture worked with local communities within Silicon Valley to distribute information, facilitate dialogue, educate stakeholders, and gain insight and understanding on issues and potential solutions." (http://www.joint venture.org/workforce/history.html)
- High technology companies like Intel and Cisco Systems, taking computers and computer education to the schools. See: http://newsroom .cisco.com/dlls/philanthropy/ and http://www.raft.net/

Nonprofit Sector Examples

- *Executive Leadership Foundation Transfer Technology Project* A program to enhance computer courses at traditionally black colleges (Hill, 1999)
- *The College Board* (http://www.collegeboard.org) Formed a national coalition of educators, civil rights leaders, technology executives, and elected officials to bring computers and Internet access to children in low-income homes
- *The Institute for Women and Technology* (http://www.iwt.org) Started in 1997, working with research universities and women's colleges to bridge the digital divide between men and women
- *Benton Foundation* (http://www.benton.org/Library/LowIncome/one .html) Published a series of studies to promote awareness of the digital divide
- *The Gates Learning Foundation and the Gates Center for Technology Access* Provided computers and Internet access to public libraries in

low-income communities, in schools and community organizations; by the end of 1998, the Learning Foundation had awarded grants of more than $22 million

Community Level Examples

- *Boston, MA.* "Technology Goes Home"—a program to provide free technology training, computers, modems, printers, and Internet access to 1,000 low-income families. Also, through a partnership with 3Com, the city launched a "Kids Computer 2001" effort and became the first major urban school system in the country to become fully wired to the Internet (Brennan, 2000).

- *LaGrange, GA.* The city provided free Internet access to all cable television households in the city. The "LaGrange Internet TV" initiative was funded by the city through a $9.2 million bond issue without federal or state support, and involved a collaborative effort between the city and Charter Communications, Inc., using WorldGate's Internet on EVERY TV service (Brennan and Maltese, 2000).

- *Taos, NM.* Community leaders formed La Plaza Tele-community, training more than 5,000 people to e-mail, surf, and search the World Wide Web by offering free classes to the public and by opening three facilities to those without Internet access at home. It also offers Web design courses and has helped more than 50 nonprofit agencies generate their own Web sites (Conour, 2000).

For more on the digital divide, see: http://www.ntia.doc.gov/ntiahome/digital divide/index.html.

Case Study in National Policy Making

To obtain an idea of the difference in approach to policy about distance education in the United States compared to that of some other countries—where it is not only the availability of technology that occupies policy makers, but the development and improvement of a system of program design and delivery—consider the following, which contains extracts from an official government document from the Republic of South Africa. There, the national Ministry of Education was considering a proposal to merge the country's single mode distance education university, the University of South Africa (UNISA) (see Chapter 11), with its largest technical school (Technikon) and a teacher training program (Vista) into a single organization. The student body of the new organization would be over a quarter of a million students, distributed nationwide. The difference between American priorities that focus on technology ahead of organizational change could hardly be more striking.

National Planning in South Africa

Extracts from Ministry of Education response to recommendations of Council on Higher Education, October 2002.

The Ministry agrees with the Council on Higher Education's recommendation that:

> a single predominantly dedicated distance education institution that provides innovative and quality programmes, especially at the undergraduate level, is required for the country. The opportunities that the present distance education institutions have created for students in Africa and other parts of the world must be maintained and expanded (CHE: 45).

The establishment of a single dedicated distance education institution would have many advantages for the development of the higher education system. These include:

- Developing a clear focus and strategy for the role of distance education in contributing to national and regional goals
- Developing a national network of centres of innovation, which would enable the development of courses and learning materials for use nationally, thus enhancing quality within the higher education system
- Developing a national network of learning centres, which would facilitate access and co-ordinate learner support systems
- Enhancing access and contributing to human resource development within the SADC region in particular and the continent as a whole
- Enabling economies of scale and scope; in particular, ensuring that advantage is taken of the rapid changes in information and communications technology, which are expensive and where the additional investment is unlikely to be within the capacity of any one institution

The Ministry therefore proposes to establish a single dedicated distance education institution through merging UNISA and Technikon South Africa and incorporating the distance education centre of Vista University into the merged institution. Such a merger would allow for some rationalisation of resources, but still make available a formidable infrastructure and array of technical expertise. The Ministry will establish a Working Group to facilitate the merger, including the development of an implementation plan. The Working Group will also be asked to advise on the role of a single distance education institution in South Africa; in particular, the role the latter could play, as the White Paper suggests, in the development of a "national network of centres of innovation in course design and development, as this would enable the development and franchising of well-designed, quality and cost-effective learning resources and courses, building on

(continued)

continued

the expertise and experience of top quality scholars and educators in different parts of the country" (White Paper: 2.61). In addition, the Working Group will be asked to investigate the broader role of distance education in higher education in the light of current and future international trends and the changes in information and communication technology. This would ensure that distance education is well placed to contribute to the development and transformation of the higher education system and its role in social and economic development.

SOURCE: http://education.pwv.gov.za/DoE_Sites/Higher_Education/HE_Plan/section_4.htm

Viewpoint: Michael Beaudoin

Those of us who have played various roles as activists and scholars in the field of distance education for the past two decades or more are, for the most part, quite encouraged by the exponential growth in online course enrollments, and we are likely to view this phenomenon as confirmation of earlier predictions by many that, within a relatively short time into the new century, traditional educational institutions would undergo dramatic transformation, even to the point where all or most instruction would be provided by virtual teachers.

But does this heightened activity reflect any real change in the way we structure our institutions and how the professoriate functions? Are most, in fact, truly engaged in distance education, or are they essentially appropriating selected aspects of instructional technology to enhance traditional courses while preserving conventional attitudes and behaviors regarding pedagogy?

It seems to me that, unless we attract or develop transformative leadership that can create conditions for genuine innovation in academe, conventional organizational arrangements and traditional teaching methods will remain the rule well into the new century, and that the authentic practice, understanding, and acceptance of teaching and learning at a distance will, despite burgeoning online enrollments, continue to be an elusive goal.

Michael Beaudoin, University of New England.

Summary

This chapter has discussed a number of major issues related to the management and administration of distance education and the development of policy regarding distance education at institutional, federal, regional, and state levels.

- Strategic planning is one of the critical responsibilities of management at all levels—institutional, state, and national. This includes: formulating a vision and a mission, having goals and objectives, balancing aspirations with currently available resources, assessing changes in student, business or societal demands, tracking technology alternatives, and projecting future resource and financial needs.

- Some of the staffing issues of concern to managers in distance education are: whether to hire permanent or part-time employees; their knowledge and understanding of distance education; their training and formal qualifications; monitoring and supervising their work.

- Administrative issues include: choosing the best delivery system, the proper use of local facilities; budget decisions relating to allocation of funds to different components of the system, dealing with priorities at different levels of the institution, and how much to spend on administration itself. Scheduling concerns include student completion dates and pacing as well as the development of materials and programs.

- Quality assurance is a primary function of administration. Components that can be evaluated for quality include: number of applications or enrollments, student achievement, student satisfaction, faculty satisfaction, program and institutional reputation, and course materials/offerings.

- Policy issues to be addressed at institutional, state, and federal levels include: program accreditation, the process of deciding to offer distance education courses, and influencing and responding to policy initiatives at higher governmental levels.

- Policy barriers to distance education have been lowered at institutional, state, and national levels. Further change depends on innovation strategies such as that adopted at Penn State to lay the foundation for its WorldCampus.

- An example of policy related to distance education that is being tackled in the United States is the problem of the digital divide. The United States could benefit from study of national policy making in other countries; the example of Republic of South Africa was given.

Questions for Discussion or Further Study

1. Try to locate a statement of the mission of a distance education institution you know about and discuss how helpful you think it would be to managers in deciding how to spend $1 million on a new distance education program.

2. Imagine you are a senior manager in that institution and make an argument *against* that institution developing a new distance education program.

3. Imagine the program is going ahead; make an argument for employing only part-time faculty and list what you think would be the objections to your argument.

4. Discuss the criteria used by the Regional Accrediting Commission that oversees an institution in which you teach or study.

5. Why does the United States not have a national distance education policy and what do you think should be done about it?

6. Discuss Beaudoin's viewpoint.

CHAPTER 9

The Theory and Scholarship of Distance Education

If you want to do research in distance education, you must first know the theory. We will begin this chapter with a short history of the scholarship of distance education, and then describe one of the main theories.

The Importance of Theory

Everything that is recorded in the literature of a field is the theory of the field. Somebody, sooner or later, organizes and summarizes this body of knowledge, or parts of it, and as these summaries are found useful by more and more scholars and researchers, they becomes authoritative. Then, instead of reviewing all the literature yourself you can refer to this summary. It is like a map. A map summarizes what is known about a place, and if there are any empty spaces it shows them. That is the clue to knowing where new exploration (i.e., research), is needed. The accepted facts and concepts that make up theory also provide a shared perspective for those who have studied it, and a common vocabulary for discussing, analyzing, or criticizing it. People who go on journeys of discovery who have not read the theory—either exhaustively in its long form (the literature) or in its summarized forms—are traveling without a map. In research they ask questions that have been answered, or that are unanswerable, and because they don't understand the vocabulary they are confused and they cause a great deal of confusion. In education, a lot of the information about technology that is collected and reported as "distance education" is not really about distance education at all and is rather trivial in significance, while questions that do need to be researched are often overlooked. Knowing the theory, then, is very valuable for everyone who wants to practice in distance education; for researchers it is indispensable.

A Very Short History of Scholarship

Scholarship can be defined as research grounded in theory. It should be sur-prising—but it is a fact—that while whole departments of professors in hun-dreds of colleges of education have for decades studied teaching and learning and how these are organized *inside* the campuses and classrooms of schools, universities, and training organizations, what goes on when communications technologies extend teaching *outside* the classroom and campus has been ignored by nearly all of them. What little research was done in this area was, until very recently, undertaken by people who were engaged in the *practice* of teaching at a distance and took it on themselves to attempt some analysis of and reflection on what they were doing. Even when they produced research reports, they had difficulty in sharing them, since the editors of the journals of education had little interest in publishing what they were writing about.

Probably the first person to suggest there was a need for research in dis-tance education was J. S. Noffsinger, first Director of the National Home Study Council,(NHSC) who went on to produce the first systematic description of American correspondence education (Noffsinger, 1926). This was followed a few years later by another landmark survey by Bittner and Mallory, published in their *University Teaching by Mail* (1933). In 1956, a major survey was undertaken by the National University Extension Association (NUEA), gather-ing information from 34 institutions and 69,519 distance learners. In 1968 another national survey was undertaken jointly by NHSC and NUEA and was disseminated in *Correspondence Instruction in the U.S.* (Mackenzie, Christensen, and Rigby, 1968). The *Brandenburg Memorial Essays,* a collection of contributions from the leading thinkers and practitioners of the years fol-lowing World War II, edited by Charles Wedemeyer, appeared in two volumes (1963 and 1966). Among the few outlets for publication were the newsletters of the NUCEA and the NHSC, and the newsletter of the ICCE, which Wedemeyer started in 1971. Matters improved when two foreign journals entered circulation: *Distance Education* (an in-house organ of the UK Open University) and *Epistolodidaktica,* a journal published by the European Home Study Council. However these were hard to obtain in the United States and their editorial policies meant they were unlikely to publish American research. In the 1980s, as interest in using telecommunications for distance education became of considerable interest, a growing number of people began to engage in research. They received a significant stimulus in 1986 with the establish-ment of The American Center for Study of Distance Education (ACSDE) and the founding of the *American Journal of Distance Education* (AJDE), "one of the most significant events affecting university independent study in the past 15 years" (Wright, 1991, p. 57). Providing a foundation for scholarship, along-side the AJDE, was a unique event that occurred in 1986. That was the First American Symposium on Research in Distance Education. This was an invita-tional meeting of 50 American academics who had shown an interest in research in distance education, convened specifically by the ACSDE to review and discuss a research agenda. From the symposium came a book, the first scholarly collection on American distance education (Moore et al., 1990). A similar key event opened the 1990s when an international workshop was held in Caracas, Venezuela under the auspices of the ACSDE, bringing American researchers to meet with other researchers from all five continents for the purpose of formulating a global research agenda (Paulsen and Pinder, 1990). In 1991, the history of the field was recorded in a book sponsored by the Independent Study Division of the National University Continuing Education Association, *The Foundations of American Distance Education* (Watkins and Wright, 1991).

The first formal courses of instruction began in the early 1970s when Charles Wedemeyer began his graduate seminar in "independent study" offered in the adult education program at University of Wisconsin–Madison. His research assistant in this was Michael G. Moore, who took over teaching the seminar on Wedemeyer's retirement in 1976 and continued teaching it each year as a special summer course until 1986. After moving in that year to the Pennsylvania State University, Moore instituted his own program of graduate courses. By 1987 Holmberg was able to list a number of universities where distance education was being taught, and felt able to assert that "it is evident that a research discipline of distance education has emerged" (Holmberg, 1987, p. 20).

History of a Theory of Distance Education

In the summer of 1972, Moore made a presentation to the World Conference of the International Council for Correspondence Education (ICCE) meeting in Warrenton, Virginia on the topic of "Learner Autonomy: the Second Dimension of Independent Learning." It began as follows:

> We started by postulating that the universe of instruction consisted of two families of teaching behaviors, which we referred to as "contiguous teaching" and "distance teaching." After describing conventional, or "contiguous teaching" Moore defined distance teaching as: "the family of instructional methods in which the teaching behaviors are executed apart from the learning behaviors, including those that in contiguous teaching would be performed in the learner's presence, so that communication between the learner and the teacher must be facilitated by print, electronic, mechanical, or other devices." (p. 76)

This was the first attempt in America to define distance education and it went on to propose a general theory of the pedagogy of distance education. For two years, while working with Wedemeyer, Moore had studied educational theory, and noticed what had not been noticed before: that there was no systematic theory to account for education in which "the teaching behaviors are executed apart from the learning behaviors." He explained to the ICDE conference (1973):

> As we continue to develop various non-traditional methods of reaching the growing numbers of people who cannot or will not, attend conventional institutions but who choose to learn apart from their teachers, we should direct some of our resources to the macro-factors: describing and defining the field; discriminating

between the various components of this field; identifying the critical elements of the various forms of teaching and learning; building a theoretical framework which will embrace this whole area of education. (p. 661)

History of the Term *Distance Education*

The term *distance education* that Moore chose to define the universe of teaching–learning relationships characterized by separation between learners and teachers was one he first heard in a conversation with the Swedish educator, Borje Holmberg. Holmberg was Director of the Hermods Correspondence School in Sweden, and being fluent in German, he had read about the work of a group of researchers at the University of Tubingen. Instead of talking about "correspondence study" these Germans used the terms *Fernstudium*, or *distance education*; and *Fernunterricht* or *distance teaching*. Prominent among these were K. H. Rebel, M. Delling, K. Graff, G. Dohmen, and Otto Peters. Since they only published their work in German, it only became known to English-speaking scholars in later years, mainly due to the efforts of Desmond Keegan (1980, 1986).

Otto Peters

In 1967, Peters published a seminal work, "Das Fernstudium an Universitaten und Hochschulen," which was translated into English in 1983 with the title "Distance Teaching and Industrial Production. A Comparative Interpretation in Outline" (Sewart, Keegan, and Holmberg, 1983). In this article Peters explained how "it becomes clear that distance study is a form of study complementary to our industrial and technological age" (p. 95). His thesis was that distance education is best understood as the application of industrial techniques in the delivery of instruction, and that *unless industrial methods are used, distance education will not be successful.* These techniques include: systematic planning, specialization of the work force, mass production of materials, automation, standardization, and quality control, as well as using a full range of modern communications technologies. This application of industrial practices will result in high quality; the high cost of this is amortized when courses are distributed to a large number of students—what is known to economists as the economies of large scale production.

Toward a Pedagogical Theory

Peters' theory was an organizational theory, and it did not circulate in English until the 1980s. The nearest to a theory in English was Wedemeyer's (1971) attempt to define the independent learner as a person not only independent in space and time but also potentially independent in controlling and directing learning. Moore was attracted by this idea of learner independence and the possibility that distance could actually be a positive force, in helping adult learners, individually and in groups, to have greater control of their learning and more independence from the control of educational institutions. Although working with Wedemeyer, he was more influenced than Wedemeyer by the writings of Carl Rogers, Abraham Maslow, Charlotte Buhler, and other so called "Humanistic" psychologists. Also at this time the ideas of andragogy promoted by Malcolm Knowles, and the self-directed learning research of Alan Tough (1971) were at the height of their popularity.

In searching for the "macro-factors," Moore gathered and analyzed the structure and design of several hundreds of courses in which "the teaching behaviors are executed apart from the learning behaviors" and on this empirical basis, offered his theory at the 1972 Conference. The theory was intended to be global and descriptive. In other words, it was to be of sufficient generality to accommodate *all* forms of distance education as defined, and to provide a conceptual tool that would place any distance education program in relationship to any other. "You are creating an equivalent of the periodic table," advised University of Wisconsin adult education professor Robert Boyd. "Follow Linnaeas," said Charles Wedemeyer; just as that 18th century scientist sought to identify the characteristics that would differentiate living creatures and also assist in classifying them, the aim was to create a system for classifying this special type of educational program. What emerged combines both the Peters' perspective of distance education as a highly structured industrial system, and Wedemeyer's perspective of a more learner-centered, interactive relationship between learner and teacher. Since 1986 it has been known as the theory of Transactional Distance.

Theory of Transactional Distance

The first core idea of the theory of Transactional Distance is that distance is a pedagogical phenomenon and is not simply a matter of geographic distance. Although it is true that all distance education learners are separated by space and/or by time from their teachers, what is important for both practitioners and researchers is the *effect* that this geographic distance has on teaching and learning, communication and interaction, curriculum and course design, and the organization and management of the educational program. When we speak of distance learning, we do not speak of an educational experience that is no different from "contiguous" courses except for the physical separation of learners and teacher, but we describe a family of programs that have distinctive, qualitative differences. Transactional Distance is the gap of understanding and communication between the teachers and learners caused by geographic distance that must be bridged through distinctive procedures in instructional design and the facilitation of interaction.

Distance Education as a Transaction

The concept of transaction was derived from John Dewey, and developed by Boyd and Apps (1980). As explained by Boyd and Apps it "connotes the interplay among the environment, the individuals and the patterns of behaviors in a situation" (p. 5). The transaction that we call distance education is the interplay between people who are teachers and learners, in environments that have the special characteristic of being separate from one another. It is the physical distance that leads to a communications gap, a psychological space of potential misunderstandings between the instructors and the learners that has to be bridged by special teaching techniques; this is the Transactional Distance.

Transactional Distance is a continuous rather than a discrete variable; a program is not *either* distant *or* not distant, *more* distant or *less* distant. In other words, Transactional Distance is relative rather than absolute. As has been pointed out, for example by Rumble (1986), there is *some* Transactional Distance in any educational event, even those in which learners and teachers meet face to face in the same space. What is *normally* referred to as distance education is that subset of educational events in which the separation of teacher and learner is *so* significant that it affects their behavior in major ways. The separation actually dictates that teachers plan, present content, interact, and perform the other processes of teaching in significantly different ways from the face-to-face environment. In short, the Transactional Distance is such that special organizational and teaching behaviors are essential. How special will depend on the degree of the Transactional Distance.

These special teaching behaviors fall into two clusters. We can describe Transactional Distance by looking at these teaching behaviors. Similarly, if we are designing courses we can think about how much to invest in each of these clusters of teaching behaviors; or, in other words, how much Transactional Distance we, or our students, will tolerate. The two sets of variables are labeled dialogue and structure.

Dialogue

Dialogue is a term that helps us focus on the interplay of words and actions and any other interactions between teacher and learner when one gives instruction and the other responds. Dialogue is not the same as interaction, though interactions are necessary for creating dialogue.

> The term "dialogue" is used to describe an interaction or series of interactions having positive qualities that other interactions might not have. A dialogue is purposeful, constructive and valued by each party. Each party in a dialogue is a respectful and active listener; each is a contributor, and builds on the contributions of the other party or parties . . . The direction of a dialogue in an educational relationship is towards the improved understanding of the student. (Moore, 1993)

The extent and nature of this dialogue is determined by the educational philosophy of the individual or group responsible for the design of the course, by the personalities of teacher and learner, by the subject matter of the course, and by environmental factors. One important environmental factor that affects dialogue is the existence of a learning group and its size. It is probable there will be more dialogue between an instructor and a single learner than between an instructor and a particular learner in a group of learners. Another environmental variable that influences dialogue is language; it is found that persons working in a foreign language are likely to interact less with an instructor than those who share the instructor's tongue.

One of the most important environmental variables is the medium of communication. For example, in a correspondence course or an online course, each individual learner has a dialogue with the instructor through either electronic or surface mail. Because it is in writing, this is a rather highly structured and—in the case of surface mail—a slow dialogue. A greater degree of dialogue is likely in a course taught online because of the speed and frequency of responses by teacher and student to the inputs of each other. Audio conferencing by telephone is usually a highly dialogic process. However, as indicated before, since the audio conference is group based, there will be less dialogue for each individual student than in an online course. Also, foreign students usually feel more comfortable and engage in more dialogue by the text-based, asynchronous communication methods than they do in the faster, synchronous audio-conference.

Some courses, such as those using video-telecourses, have very little or no dialogue. It is possible to learn a foreign language, for example, from a video-telecourse. When watching these television tapes, a student might actually speak out loud, giving a response to something the televised teacher says, but since there is no feedback to the instructor, the instructor is not able to respond to the student, and no dialogue occurs.

Guided Didactic Conversation

Working as Professor at the Fernuniversitat, or Distance University, in Hagen, Germany, Borje Holmberg selected the learner–teacher dialogue as the fundamental characteristic of distance education. Distance teaching, suggested Holmberg (1981), should be a conversation, what he called a "guided didactic conversation." Distance education, he said:

> . . . implies that the character of good distance education resembles that of a guided conversation aimed at learning and that the presence of the typical traits of a conversation facilitates learning." (Holmberg, 1986, p. 55)

And also:

> the feelings of personal relation between the teaching and learning parties promote study pleasure and student motivation and that such feelings can be fostered by well-developed self-instructional material and suitable two-way communication at a distance. (Holmberg, 1989, p. 43)

The Growing Importance of Dialogue

In the decades since the formulation of the idea of dialogue in Transactional Distance, there has been considerable research on the social and language based nature of the teaching–learning relationship, casting further light on the importance of the concept. This perspective is based on Vygotsky's (1978) theory of learning, which explains the centrality of language as a medium by which the learner constructs a way of thinking. The relation to "learner autonomy" is shown by the Vygotskian notion of "handover." Through the exchange of meanings and the development of a shared understanding within what Vygotsky calls the "zone of proximal development," learners gradually come to take control of the process of learning. They enter a community of shared discourse as novices and, supported by a teacher (or other more competent person) primarily through their growing competence in using the tool of language, progressively take charge of their own learning. In this Vygotskian perspective on learning, a dialogue between teacher (more competent other) and learner is accompanied by a shift in control of the learning process from teacher to student.

Course Structure

The second set of variables that determine Transactional Distance are elements in the course's design. The term used to describe this is "structure." A course consists of such elements as: learning objectives, content themes, information presentations, case studies, pictorial and other illustrations, exercises, projects, and tests. Quality depends on how carefully these are composed, and how carefully structured. A design team might pilot-test parts of their course on an experimental group, and thus ascertain exactly how long it will take each student to accomplish each objective. They may measure the reading speed of their potential students and then tailor the number of pages of reading required for each part of the course. Instructors may be provided detailed rubrics and marking schemes to help them ensure all students meet standard criteria of achievement. They may monitor the learning performance of each student with great frequency, providing remedial activities for those that need them, and so ensure that every student has accomplished each step of the course in a tightly controlled sequence. The students may be admitted into the course as cohorts, and none may be permitted to move into any content area except at the pace of the whole group. In an online course or in using a printed study guide, each student might be required to follow the same sequence of study and activity; audio and video materials may be synchronized very tightly to specific pages in the study guide or on the Web; and online discussions may be carefully organized so that each student is included in an online chat room, according to a carefully scripted plan.

By contrast, a different course may permit students to explore an undefined set of Web pages and/or tapes at their own speed, study a set of readings, and submit assignments online only when they feel ready. They may be told to call or e-mail an instructor or a help desk if, and only when, they wish to receive advice. Such would be a course with much lower structure than the former course just outlined.

Like dialogue, structure is determined by the educational philosophy of the teaching organization, the teachers themselves, the academic level of the learners, the nature of the content, and by the communications media that are employed. Since structure expresses the rigidity or flexibility of the course's educational objectives, teaching strategies, and evaluation methods, it describes the extent to which course components can accommodate or be responsive to each learner's individual needs. A recorded television program, for example, not only permits no dialogue, but it is also highly structured, with virtually every activity of the instructor and every second of time provided for in a script, and every piece of content predetermined. There is little or no opportunity for any deviation according to the personal needs of any student. This can be compared with many Web-based courses, which can be structured in ways that allow students to follow many different paths through the content.

Structure and Dialogue Measure Transactional Distance

The recorded television course program is very highly structured, and teacher-learner dialogue is nonexistent. This means the Transactional Distance is high. In the correspondence course mentioned earlier, there is more dialogue and less structure, so it has less Transactional Distance. In those live audio- or video-teleconference programs that have much dialogue and little predetermined structure, the extent of Transactional Distance is even lower. In online settings those courses that have little or no dialogue, asynchronous or synchronous, are of higher Transactional Distance than those that have such dialogue. Again and again it must be emphasized that these are generalizations, *and the analysis has to be done on specific programs,* because so much more is involved than merely the technology being used. The extent of dialogue and the degree of structure varies from course to course, from program to program. In a course or program with little Transactional Distance, learners receive directions and guidance through ongoing dialogue with their instructors and by using instructional materials that allow modifications to suit their individual needs, learning style, and pace. In more distant courses where there is less dialogue and more structure, learners have some guidance; if there is neither dialogue or structure, then they must be entirely independent and make their own decisions about study strategies, decide for themselves how to study, what to study, when, where, in what ways, and to what extent.

Learner Autonomy

The greater the Transactional Distance, the more such responsibility the learner has to exercise. Calling his 1972 ICCE presentation "Learner autonomy: the second dimension of independent study," Moore declared that a theory of distance education that only considered the variables of teaching would be flawed. This was at a time when all education, including correspondence teaching, was under the influence of behaviorist learning theory, and the idea of learners being autonomous individuals constructing their own knowledge based on their own experience received little notice outside some adult education circles.

In the behaviorist view, since distant learners were beyond the immediate environment of the teacher, the main problem was how to optimally *control* them. Instructors were urged to identify their goals in very specific behavioral terms, to prescribe a *highly structured* regime of presentation, practice, and reward; and to test and measure achievement of all students according to the precise standards built into the objectives. The purpose of *interaction* was to test the extent to which learners were achieving the instructor's objectives, and to give the successful learners positive reinforcement. The challenge for the educator was to produce a perfect set of objectives, techniques, and testing devices, one that would fit every learner, in large numbers at a distance so that no one would deviate or fall between the cracks. The parallel of a distance education pedagogy described in this way with the "industrial model" for delivery of education that Peters was working out at that same time is obvious.

Having identified the importance of structure as a key element of distance education, Moore believed that in the theory of distance education, a balancing perspective was needed, one that accepted the *idiosyncrasies and independence* of learners as a valuable resource rather than a distracting nuisance. In addition to highly structured courses in which passive learners were trained by irresistibly elegant instructional tools, it was necessary to conceptualize a dimension that accommodated more collaborative relationships between teachers and learners, which would allow for the fact that many learners chose their own learning objectives and conduct, construct, and control much of the learning process and that some teachers and teaching institutions encourage this.

The concept of *learner autonomy* is that learners have *different capacities* for making decisions regarding their own learning. The ability of a learner to develop a personal learning plan—the ability to find resources for study in one's own work or community environment, and the ability to decide for oneself when progress was satisfactory, need not be conceived as extraneous and regrettable noise in a smooth running, instructor-controlled system. Instead, the degree to which these learner behaviors exist can be seen as an important dimension for the classification of distance education programs. It is a fact that some programs allow for the greater exercise of learners' autonomy than others. Therefore programs can be defined and described in terms of what degree of autonomy learners are expected or permitted to exercise. This is not to say that all students are fully autonomous, or ready to be autonomous, or that all programs and teachers should treat them as such. Like dialogue and structure, learner autonomy is a relative concept. For an elaboration of learner autonomy, see Moore (1986).

Since the original theory, a number of important researchers have elaborated on the idea of learner autonomy, particularly Candy (1991) Brookfield (1985), Pratt (1988), and Long et al. (1989). One of the most comprehensive discussions of autonomy in the context of distance education theory is that of Munro (1991, 1998).

Desmond Keegan

When he founded the Australian journal *Distance Education* in 1980, Keegan published, in the first issue, an analysis of what he called "four generally accepted definitions of distance education." The four definitions were those of Holmberg, Peters, Moore, and (perhaps rather strangely) the July 1971 Law of France, which regulated distance education in that country. From this analysis, Keegan concluded that the following six elements "are to be regarded as essential for any comprehensive definition":

They are:

- separation of teacher and student
- influence of an educational organization, especially in the planning and preparation of learning materials
- use of technical media
- provision of two-way communication
- possibility of occasional seminars
- participation in the most industrial form of education (Keegan, 1980)

Keegan's summary of the "four generally accepted definitions" became the most widely cited definition of distance education. In 1986 he repeated his technique, this time analyzing Holmberg, Peters, Moore, and Dohmen. He did not change his list of key elements, but he did state them in a longer form. The first element for example was: "The quasi-permanent separation of teacher and learner throughout the length of the learning process; this distinguishes it from conventional face-to-face education." The "possibility of occasional seminars" became: "the quasi-permanent absence of the learning group throughout the length of the learning process, so that people are usually taught as individuals and not in groups, with the possibility of occasional meetings for both didactic and socialization purposes" (Keegan, 1986, p. 49).

Randy Garrison

Further insights into learner autonomy and its relationship to dialogue and structure are found in a model developed by a group of Canadian researchers (Garrison, 1989; Garrison and Shale 1987; Garrison and Baynton, 1987; Baynton, 1992; and Anderson and Garrison, 1995. This group focuses the discussion of the learner–teacher relationship in terms of "control." Another important term is "proficiency," which is the student's ability to construct meaning and the disposition needed to initiate and persist in a learning endeavor. The educator's aim is to arrive at an optimum balance of control among facilitator, learners, and curriculum. The resulting learning outcome will be socially worthwhile as well as personally meaningful, if the three dimensions of control are in dynamic balance. Meaningful means the learners assume responsibility to "make meaning" of the content by assimilating or accommodating new ideas and concepts into their existing knowledge structures. In addition, "socially worthwhile" knowledge is that "knowledge which has been consensually confirmed and which has redeeming social values" (Gibson, 1998, p. 100). What is being described here is a collaborative constructivist perspective of teaching and learning, where the individual has the responsibility to construct meaning and participate in reciprocal communication for the purpose of confirming understanding and generating worthwhile knowledge. Until recent times, such collaborative constructivist approaches to learning at a distance were limited by the character of the technology. However, new Internet networks make it possible to offer collaborative learning experiences at a distance in a cost-effective manner. Technological advances are allowing more distance education institutions to choose delivery methods that are "transactional" rather than "transmissive" (Burge, 1988; cited in Munro, 1998).

Garrison's (1989) model proposes six types of transactional relationships, building on Moore's (1989) three-part model of interaction. Thus, in addition to learner–content, learner–instructor, and learner–learner interactions, Garrison added: teacher–content, teacher–teacher, and content–content. With the incorporation of computer-mediated conferencing (CMC) into program design to support interaction, Hillman, Willis, and Gunawardena (1994) added a fourth type of interaction, which they called learner-interface interaction. Garrison (2000) argues that the focus of distance education theory has shifted from structural constraints (overcoming geography) to transactional issues (optimizing teaching-learning strategies). Recent research has been concerned with the cognitive and social presence that occurs in computer mediated interaction. (e.g., Garrison, Anderson, and Archer, 2001; Anderson, Rourke, Garrison, and Archer, 2001).

Collaborative Learning and the Social Construction of Knowledge

Conceptualizing learning as socially situated, some researchers argue that group-based collaborative learning enables development of learning communities in the short term and potential communities of practice in the longer term. Since, in distance settings, normal communication is conveyed through an artificial medium, we must find ways to achieve "social presence" (Gunawardena, 1995). One seminal study (Gunawardena and Zittle, 1997) developed an interaction analysis model to examine the social construction of knowledge in computer mediated instruction. It was concluded that the dynamics of the virtual group pulled all the participants toward various forms of compromise and negotiation on the way to socially constructing a commonly acceptable knowledge. Research suggests that the affection, inclusion, and sense of solidarity of the group, the ease of expression and synthesis of multiple viewpoints with no one student dominating, are important characteristics in this successful social construction of knowledge online. In an earlier study of computer mediated instruction, Cheng et al. (1991) reported a higher completion rate for those learners who worked collaboratively (90 percent) than for those who worked independently (22 percent).

System Dynamics of Saba

With his colleagues and students, Farhad (Fred) Saba has elaborated the theory of Transactional Distance by using computer simulation modeling. (Saba, 1988; Saba and Twitchell, 1988; Saba and Shearer, 1994).

In the first project, Saba and Twitchell used a computer simulation method based on Systems Dynamics modeling techniques that demonstrates and explains the interactions of different forces in a distance education system. Next, Saba employed the model to describe the interrelationships of the variables that make up structure and dialogue.

Here is how he describes the model (1988):

> Integrated systems provide a flexible means for decreasing structure through increased dialogue. They also expedite increased structure so dialogue can be kept to a desirable level. This defines a dynamic relationship between dialogue and the level of required structure. This relationship can be displayed as a negative feedback loop in a system dynamics causal loop diagram.
>
> The negative flow diagram represents an inverse relationship between levels of dialogue and structure. As dialogue increases, structure decreases, and as structure decreases dialogue increases to keep the system stable. In negative feedback loops, the stability of the system depends on interventions from outside the loop. The level depends on the action of teacher and learner. In a plausible scenario, the need for decreasing structure is communicated to the teacher. Consultation automatically increases dialogue; then adjustments in goals, instructional materials, and evaluation procedures occur and the learner achieves the desired level of autonomy. (p. 22)

Saba expanded the systems model in a third project (Saba and Shearer, 1994), when he ran simulations of distance students' exchanges with instructors to measure relationships of Transactional Distance and autonomy. Using a technique for coding speech called "discourse analysis," the researchers identified the speech content of a number of educational transactions at a distance and classified them into ten main categories and twenty subcategories. In this way they operationalized Dialogue, Structure, and Teacher/Learner Control and measured the effects that changes in any of these had in the others.

Other Applications of Theory of Transactional Distance

At the University of Hawaii, Bischoff et al. (1996) surveyed 221 students' perceptions of structure, dialogue, and Transactional Distance in a course mediated by interactive television. Data were generated by a 68-item questionnaire and items were measured along a five-point Likert scale. As expected, results showed that "dialogue" and "Transactional Distance" were inversely proportional; that is, as dialogue increased, Transactional Distance decreased.

Chen and Willits (1999) studied the experiences of 121 learners in a video conferencing environment. They found that the greater the Transactional Distance between instructor and learner, the students perceived their learning outcomes lower. What had the most significant effect on the learners' perceived learning outcomes was the frequency of in-class dialogue. They found that the larger the learning group, the greater the Transactional Distance between instructor and learners (as perceived by the learners).

In research on factors that affect online dialogue in computer mediated instruction, Vrasidas and MacIsaac (1999) emphasize the relationships of the structure of the course, class size, feedback, and prior experience. Prior experience with CMC, along with access to appropriate technology, is relevant to the quality of dialogue, a point noted by Wegerif (1998). Hopper (2000) undertook a qualitative study of life circumstances and Transactional Distance in a video conferencing environment and found that even students who reported a perception of high Transactional Distance were satisfied with their experience and the level of their achievement. Gayol (1995) used Transactional Distance theory to explore the transactions that occurred in the computer-mediated communication learning environment of students in a course with participants in four different countries, with four different languages. Posted assignments and messages of the students and the instructors were analyzed to measure the changes in the degrees of dialogue, structure, and learner autonomy. Bunker, Gayol, Nti, and Reidell (1996) examined the effect of changes in structure on dialogue in an audio-conferencing course connecting nine sites internationally. In another study Chen (2001) measured the impact of individual and instructional variables on learners' perceived Transactional Distance in a World Wide Web learning environment and recommended the further development of instruments for measuring Transactional Distance.

Theory and the Student

These examples indicate how researchers can base their study on a theoretical platform, and how the result of each study then, in turn, makes the platform more helpful for the next researcher. You can see how the theory serves as a tool to help specify variables of structure, dialogue, and learner autonomy, and then suggests questions about the relationships among these variables. Unfortunately there is far too little research that is theoretically oriented in this way. After an extensive review of the research on Web-based instruction (WBI), Jung (2001) concluded: "WBI research showed little resemblance to established pedagogical theory in general or distance education theory in particular. While some studies raised their research question and discussed the findings in theoretical frameworks, other studies had little relationship to established learning theories." (page 532). She went on to suggest questions for future research, including:

Viewpoint: Farhad Saba

Traditional educational institutions from K–12 schools to colleges and universities were primarily organized in the industrial age, and were structured to serve an industrial society. In recent years, distance education has moved from a peripheral activity in these institutions to the mainstream of their operation. A major challenge of distance education, as a professional field, is how to reconcile its contemporary post-industrial nature with the structure of traditional institutions. Judging from the current trends, it is highly unlikely that traditional educational institutions would take the necessary steps to change their structure to meet the demands of the post-industrial era. In the next decade, distance education will either emerge as a distinct enterprise that will have the potential to serve the post-industrial society, or it will be co-opted by traditional institutions. These institutions will merely use technology to reach students at a distance, but will not provide the learner with requisite autonomy through addressing his/her individual needs, thus compromising the essence of distance education in practice. Alternative educational models, such as home schooling, and charter schools that can take advantage of distance education will grow. In higher education, schools of extended and continuing education that show more flexibility will emerge to be more effective to address the needs of students. The battle between these alternative models and traditional institutions will reach epic proportions as the 21st century unfolds.

Farhad Saba, Ph.D., Professor of Educational Technology, San Diego State University

- "Does the extent of rigidity or flexibility in the structure of a WBI course affect dialogue and Transactional Distance as is the case in other distance education modes?"
- "What WBI structure best supports interaction and learning?"
- "What are the effects of different types of interaction on learning and satisfaction in WBI?"
- "How can we balance learner autonomy and course structure in WBI?" (p. 533).

Following Jung, we would agree that there is a need for much more research of an empirical nature to identify the many variables that lie *within* structure, dialogue, and autonomy; and to explore them more thoroughly. There are rich opportunities for graduate students in this unexplored field, especially with the rapid growth of Web-based instruction. But, as Jung emphasizes, when students look into the possibilities for research, it is important they first read as much as possible of the existing distance education literature. The journals mentioned in this book will provide the basis of this reading. It is also necessary for students to think how they can connect their thinking about research in distance education with their study of the more general body of educational research and theory. There are many aspects of traditional learning theory that are relevant to distance learning. Likewise, there is a great deal of research in instructional design and technology-based delivery systems that is directly applicable to distance education efforts.

The Theory and the Practitioner

What determines the success of distance teaching is the extent to which the institution and the individual instructor are able to provide the appropriate structure in design of learning materials, and the appropriate quantity and quality of dialogue between teacher and learner(s), taking into account the extent of the learners' autonomy.

The more highly autonomous the learners, the greater is the distance they can be comfortable with (i.e. the less the dialogue and the less the structure). For others, the goal must be to reduce distance by increasing dialogue (ranging from online asynchronous to synchronous interaction, perhaps using the telephone, or at the most extreme, face-to-face contact), while providing the security of sufficient structure.

Summary

- For most of the history of distance education there was very little research and no formal theory. Practitioners who did research found it difficult to have their work published or acknowledged. Major changes occurred in the 1980s with the establishment of journals, conferences, graduate study and professional training courses.

- There have been a number of efforts to develop theoretical frameworks. The oldest in English is Moore's theory of Transactional Distance, which suggests that there are two critical underlying variables: structure and dialogue, and these are in relationship to learner autonomy. This is a pedagogical theory that explains the nature of programs and courses, and can help understand as well as guide the behaviors of teachers and learners.

- Subsequent theorists have focused on the role of technology, the significance of student versus teacher control, the system dynamics of Transactional Distance, social relationships in online courses, and causal relationships among factors affecting student success. Future developments in the theory of distance education need to be empirically based rather than philosophical or ideological exercises.

Questions for Discussion or Further Study

1. If you were to gather data about either dialogue, structure or learner autonomy, which would you choose to study and what question would you ask about it?

2. What kind of data would you need to collect in order to answer your question? Where would you find such data?

3. Do changes in the technology available to us affect distance learning theory? Why or why not?

4. List some ways that you think theories of distance learning are related to more general theories of learning? (For a database of learning theories, see http://tip.psychology.org.)

5. Discuss Saba's viewpoint.

CHAPTER **10**

Research and Studies of Effectiveness

In this chapter, we introduce some of the questions that have attracted research about distance education, particularly questions about its effectiveness. We provide examples of the research about effective course design and teaching, research on cost-effectiveness, and policy issues.

Most of the research that has been done in distance education has been about its effectiveness. Effectiveness has been studied to a degree that has rarely been matched with regard to teaching in conventional classrooms. The main areas for this effectiveness research are:

- How effective is teaching at a distance in terms of learner achievement and learner satisfaction?
- What is the relative effectiveness of different communications technologies? Which technologies are more effective for particular teaching processes?
- What course designs are most effective?
- What interaction strategies are most effective?
- Do particular types of learners find some technology, course designs, or interaction strategies more effective than others?
- Are some technologies, course designs, or interaction strategies more effective in teaching a particular subject than others?
- What are the main student support issues and how are they handled?
- What are the most effective administrative procedures to use for designing courses, and what are effective for implementing courses?
- What are the main problems in managing faculty for distance teaching?
- Is distance education cost–effective? Under what conditions?

- What policies at the institutional, state, or national level have been effective in developing and sustaining distance education?

These are very general questions, and within them lie a host of specific researchable questions. There have been several attempts to draw up lists of specific questions. Dirr (2003) has a particularly valuable list of more than 50 such questions organized under the headings:

- Quality issues
- Equity and access issues
- Collaboration and commercialization issues
- Globalization issues
- Ownership and intellectual property rights
- The role of technology
- Faculty issues
- Student issues
- Research and evaluation issues

For students looking for a researchable question for their thesis or dissertation, we recommend a review of Dirr's list.

The General Situation Regarding Research

Other good ways to get an overview of the research is to look at a full set of one or more scholarly journals and to review the doctoral dissertations (caution—it is necessary to think carefully about key words when searching the abstracts of dissertations since not all research relevant to distance education is labelled as such). Occasionally you find a helpful meta-analysis of journal articles, such as that by Berge and Mrozowski (2001) who provide a picture of the state of research for the years 1990–1999 by reviewing both the dissertation abstracts and the four principal distance education journals: *The American Journal of Distance Education, Distance Education* (Australia), *Journal of Distance Education* (Canada), *and Open Learning* (UK). They discovered that 85 percent of the journal articles were descriptive reports or case studies. They also found that certain questions were asked over and over again (suggesting a lack of knowledge of theory by those who formed the questions—and the doctoral committees that approved them!). The most popular questions had to do with teaching and learning, including design issues, learner characteristics, and questions about teacher-learner and learner-learner interaction. There were far fewer questions on policy and management, technology selection and adoption, and questions of cost and benefit.

Research in distance education has often been criticized for being devoid of theoretical foundation (Saba, 2003; Perraton, 2000) and the situation has not improved in recent years. What this means is that many studies gather data that is of little or no value to the field as a whole, even though they may be useful to a particular practitioner or meet the need of an institution to evaluate its program. To do research that has general value, it is necessary to pose a previously unanswered question and gather data that can be generalized beyond a particular case. However, you can only know what questions have *not* been answered by first knowing what is already known. The sum of what is known is the theory. Too many researchers ask questions that have already been answered, or which are unanswerable given the present state of knowledge, and they would not have done this if they knew the theory. A theoretical foundation for research can be laid by undertaking a thorough review of what has been published in the scholarly journals and in dissertations; alternatively, in some areas, the literature has already been organized by previous scholars, whose analysis has been sufficiently accepted that reference to their theory can serve as the foundation for a new question. The theory of Transactional Distance that is described in Chapter 9 is such a summary, as is the definition of distance education provided in Chapter 1. A researcher does not have to scour the literature and produce a defensible definition, since the definition in this book has the validity of being widely accepted over many years. Similarly, one can do research on learner characteristics and interaction by connecting the question to the dimensions of dialogue and autonomy in the theory of Transactional Distance. A prominent theoretician, Saba (2003), explains that the "building blocks" of distance education theory have been provided with "exceptional conceptual clarity in understanding core concepts" (p. 3). To take another, very specific example to illustrate this important point, Bunker (1998a, 2003) reviewed in her doctoral dissertation for the first time, all the proceedings of the International Council for Distance Education (ICDE) from 1938 to 1995, and identified significant themes addressed at the conferences during that period. It would be folly, would it not, for a new researcher, ignorant of Bunker's work, to spend months or years undertaking a study of the main themes in the ICDE conferences from 1938 to 1995? However, after careful study of Bunker's research, a successor would make a valuable contribution by identifying a specific theme, and focusing in greater depth on that topic than the first researcher was able to do. Thus, on the theoretical foundation of Bunker's work, the new researcher would identify an unanswered question, answer it, and thus build the theory.

Effectiveness as Dependent on a Technology

The single largest group of research studies in distance education focuses on how effective it is as a way of learning, with the principal focus being on a particular communications technology. There are two main types of this technology-effectiveness research: descriptive case studies and comparative achievement studies.

Descriptive Case Studies

First there are a lot of simple descriptions of particular programs, and how a teacher or an institution used one or more communications technology to teach a group of distant learners. Descriptive reports can be found about programs that use every kind of technology, including correspondence, audio teleconferencing, computer conferencing, broadcast television, interactive video, and the Internet. In these reports, even though there may be some sophisticated data analysis, all that is being reported is the researcher's personal experience of teaching at a distance, and the extent to which the teaching was effective. This research is a bit like that of the anthropologists or geographers who "discover" a new tribe or a new land, and proceed to write descriptive "travelers' stories" about their discovery. Such stories may be interesting, especially if they describe a previously untested technology application or a student population or content that has not been described already. However, this is rare. At best, such anecdotal descriptions and case studies only point the way for research that is more controlled and systematic and that might give results that could be generalized beyond the particular case.

Here is just a small sample of a host of descriptive reports:

- Falk (1998) described student comments and his own impressions about the results of teaching his undergraduate biology course by means of the Web.

- Fredericksen et al. (2000) reported on student satisfaction and perceived learning in State University of New York online courses, and the implications for course design and faculty training.

- Schrum and Benson (2000) described the first year of a pilot program which included online and face-to-face components from faculty, administrative, and student perspectives.

- Shapley (2000) described her experiences in teaching an upper-level organic chemistry course in an online environment.

- Sener and Stover (2000) discussed how online interaction was added to independent study courses at a community college and made suggestions about the instructional design considerations for effective online learning.

- Deubel (2003) provided a reflective piece on implementing a new online course, based on her own experience and made recommendations for other new online teachers.

- Canning (2002) conducted case study research of a distance education vocational program in northern Scotland.

- Morse (2003) conducted case study research into implications of cultural context on the effectiveness of computer mediated asynchronous learning.

Comparing Learner Achievement

One step in sophistication beyond these "one-shot" descriptions and case studies are studies that compare the effectiveness of teaching through one technology with another. Most often these studies compare the results of teaching in a conventional classroom with teaching in a distant environment. Others compare learning outcomes in two or more distant environments. Occasionally in these studies, subjects are randomly assigned to the two treatments, which leads to more valid conclusions. But although desirable, use of this basic experimental technique is rare.

The following are some examples of these studies:

- In the first (so far) recorded study of this kind, Crump (1928) published findings from his doctoral study in which he reported there were no significant differences between test scores of Oklahoma students in a classroom compared with those who studied the same subjects by correspondence. (We mention this just to show how old a question this is!)

- Phelps, Wells, Ashworth, and Hahn (1991) looked at the effectiveness of Army resident courses converted to distance study by computer-mediated communication and found that any differences favored the latter.

- Chute (1996) compared the final exam performance of a regular class and a Web-based class in an undergraduate statistics course and found the Web-based class scored an average of 20 percent better.

- Gray (1996) studied achievement levels of students of Japanese taught in a traditional high school and by interactive video and concluded that those in the distance learning environment achieved academic success at a rate equal to or better than those in the traditional environment.

- Hislop (2000) compared the grades and completion rates of graduate students in an online systems analysis course with those of traditional classes and found no significant differences.

- Freeman, Grimes, ands Holliday (2000) compared the performance and satisfaction of graduate students taking an introductory statistics course via audio-graphics, satellite television, live in the television studio, or live in a traditional classroom, and found no significant differences in learning performance among these groups (although there were some differences in student satisfaction).

- MacGregor (2001) conducted a study with 158 students, in five online and five classroom groups, and compared students' perceptions of workload, satisfaction, comfort, learning, and anticipated grades. Although students rated similar learning achievement and satisfaction, the online students thought their courses were more rigorous and expressed lower levels of comfort.

- MacDonald (2001) found that print-based and CD-ROM based instruction were equally effective, and students in the CD-ROM group were additionally satisfied at improving their computer skills in addition to the main content of the course.

- Wisher, Curnow, and Seidel (2001) investigated knowledge retention of two different military occupational specialties—air traffic control operators and battle staff non-commissioned officers—when the training was provided via interactive video. Results demonstrated that knowledge retention was equal.

- Collins (2002) compared learning outcomes of community college students in a two-way interactive video course with a traditional face-to-face course and also a video telecourse, with students having the same instructor and syllabus. Students in the interactive video course demonstrated higher learning outcomes than the other two groups.

- Neuhauser (2002) compared two sections of the same course, one taught online and the other face-to-face. Learning styles/preferences, retention rates (84 percent in both formats), test scores, and final grades, along with students' evaluations of the effectiveness of course activities, were comparable.

- Thomson (2002) compared the performance of 168 individuals learning to use Excel spreadsheets either online, in a blended class, or as self-directed learners. The online participants performed real-world spreadsheet tasks with 99 percent more accuracy than the self-directed learners, and the performance in the blended class was 30 percent more accurate than the online group.

Because of the large number of comparative effectiveness studies that have been conducted, several metastudies have presented a summary of what has been learned. For example:

- Valore and Diehl (1987) summarized studies of the effectiveness of home study courses and concluded: "All of the research published since 1920 has indicated that correspondence students perform just as well as, and in most cases better than, their classroom counterparts" (p. 3).

- Cavanaugh (2001) conducted a meta-analysis of 19 studies of the effectiveness of distance education on K–12 student achievement, reporting which technologies and teaching strategies appeared more effective.

- Olson and Wisher (2002) reviewed 47 reports of evaluations of Web-based courses in higher education published between 1996 and 2002. Most of the studies compared groups of students taking the same course face-to-face or online. They concluded that Web-based instruction appears to be at least as effective as classroom instruction.

- Neumann and Shachar (2003) did a meta-analysis of 86 experimental and quasi-experimental studies conducted between 1990 and 2002. Data represented more than 15,000 students. Analysis showed that by a two-thirds margin students taking courses via distance education were reported to have outperformed students taking traditionally delivered courses.

- Machtmes and Asher (2000) conducted a meta-analysis study of 30 experimental studies that examined methods used in video and one- or two-way audio courses. Learner achievement was affected by: type of interaction during the broadcast, type of course, and type of remote site.

- Over 350 studies done since 1928 (Russell, 1999) show that when you measure the average differences between students in a face-to-face group and a distance education group, there is usually no significant difference(see http://teleeducation.nb.ca/nosignificantdifference/).

Given the evidence of research illustrated by these examples, if you want to do research, it should be obvious that there is little point in gathering data to see if distance education courses can be as effective as conventional classroom instruction. The evidence already shows that: (1) instruction at a distance *can be* as effective in bringing about learning as classroom instruction, and (2) the absence of face-to-face contact is not *in itself* detrimental to the learning process.

Beyond "No Significant Difference"

In most of the studies just mentioned, the question was: which learning environment or which delivery technology is more effective when the outcome variable is the average score of groups of learners? These studies show that the environment in which learning occurs, and the technology of communication between teacher and learner, are not *in themselves* predictors of achievement.

The question that is much more important than differences *between* groups is differences *within* a group. We would like to know what *types* of students learn best in one environment, or from one technology or teaching strategy, and what characterises those who learn better from the alternatives. Similarly, we may ask, what are the types of information or other educational messages that can better be communicated by one technology and one medium than another?

Here are some examples of studies that begin to ask these kinds of questions:

- Biner, Bink, Huffman, and Dean (1995) have concluded that the personality characteristics of students who enroll in televised college level courses differ from those of traditional students. (But they have not yet discovered *which* students were more suited to each treatment *within* each group.)
- Fjortoft (1996) looked at adult learners' persistence in distance learning programs. Specific career-related factors, such as job security, better career mobility, competitive advantage when applying for job, competitive advantage when being considered for promotion, and enhanced salary were found to be the main motivators to completing a course.
- Osborn (2001) constructed an instrument to assess the ability of students to complete their courses. Students found to be less likely to complete had less stable study environments, lower motivation, less computer confidence, and poorer time management skills.
- Peters (1999) found no connection between learning styles and dropout from Web-based courses. Drop out rates were primarily related to technical problems, such as computer or Internet connection problems.

- Sparks (1997) found that Myers-Briggs Personality Temperaments, gender, or grade level did not significantly affect attitudes of students in a two-way video course.

- Michel (1999) found no difference in satisfaction resulting from course development methods across Myers-Briggs preference types.

- Jung, Choi, Lim, and Leem (2002) investigated the effects of different types of interaction (academic, collaborative, and social) on learning achievement, satisfaction, and participation in Web-based instruction. They concluded that social interaction with instructors and collaborative interaction with peers have significant effects on learning.

- Picciano (2002) studied the relationship between performance in online courses and social presence; that is, the ability of learners to project themselves socially and affectively into a virtual community. Students with higher levels of social presence did better on the written assignments, but there was no difference in their performance on objective tests.

- Shin (2002) found that the view a student holds about the institution; in other words, the degree to which the student perceives the availability of, and connectedness with, other parties involved in the distance education setting, has a significant effect on performance and satisfaction.

Effective Course Design

Many research questions can be asked about the techniques of designing courses such as:

- How can academic content be most effectively structured and presented for study by the distant learners?

- How can we design the course to obtain each student's optimum participation in interaction with the instructor and with other students?

- How is a Web site or study guide to be laid out, a television program to be scripted, or an audio-conference to be structured, in order to obtain maximum results in student understanding?

- What learning objectives are best achieved by use of video (either in broadcast or interactive modes), text (either printed or online), or by audio?

- How can you effectively link printed materials with the electronic, and each of these with an instructor?

- What are the most effective methods of monitoring to obtain optimum feedback about learner progress?

- What problems arise from, and how can we provide for, the different pace at which students learn?

- What are satisfactory criteria for the summative evaluation of learning and how can you measure them?

- What are the most cost-effective methods of producing and distributing course materials?
- What are the procedures by which technologies are chosen by distance teaching organizations? By whom are they selected, and by what criteria?
- What training, if any, is given to the administrators and other decision makers who make these selections?

Examples of course design studies:

- Vrasidas and McIassc (1999) found that flexible course structure, quick and frequent feedback, visual layouts, and multiples zones of content knowledge were factors influencing interaction in an online course.
- Hashim (1999) examined instructional and technical design elements used in writing self-instructional models.
- Bi (2000) conducted a series of interviews and examined course materials to identify instructional design attributes of online courses from three universities. She concluded that courses must be designed specifically for that environment, be designed for both immediate and long-range use, be part of a systems approach to distance education, and focus on learning goals and outcomes. The importance of teams working together during the planning process was highlighted.
- Swan, Shea, Fredericksen, Pickett, and Pelz (2000) identified consistency in course design, contact with course instructors, and design of discussion opportunities as key factors in student satisfaction with design of online courses. The study included 1,406 students enrolled in 264 courses offered through SUNY Learning Network.
- Swan (2001) found student satisfaction and perceived learning were correlated with higher perceived levels of interaction with course content, instructors, and other students.
- Murphy, Mahoney, and Harvel (2000) experimented with effectiveness of signed contracts by online group members.
- Koory (2003) discussed the characteristics of an online learning environment that result in better student outcomes in an English literature course.

Course Design Teams

The two main approaches to the development of distance education courses and materials—the course team model and the author-editor model—are discussed in Chapter 5. There are many unanswered questions about the effectiveness of these models, especially the course team. For example:

- How much specialization is really needed in a course team? What is the cost-benefit of each specialist?
- What is the most effective division of labor between the content expert and the Web designer, television producer, or other media specialists?
- How do you best organize and control the work of specialists?

- Are such teams really cost efficient? Under what conditions?
- How has document sharing and other online techniques impacted course team procedures?

Although there are strongly held opinions on the advantages of different ways of organizing the course design process, very little research has been done to compare the two main approaches.

- Olson, Olson, and Meader (1995) investigated the use of video and audio conferencing by design groups. With audio only, groups spent more time talking about how to manage their work, and the quality of the work suffered. When using video, the work was accomplished differently from the face-to-face environment and the quality of work was just as high.

Media and Technology Selection

As part of the course design process, what technology and which forms of the different media to use—be they text in print or online, recorded audio or video, interactive audio, video, audio-graphic, or online—will have a major impact on effectiveness. Here are some relevant studies:

- Dutton and Lievrouw (1982) compared the media then available, on the basis of the kind of communication provided (one way, reactive, and two way), ease of modification, expense, complexity, and potential fit with different types of learning objectives (i.e., cognitive, affective, and psychomotor). They conclude that considerations of instructional content, the need for student involvement, and the particular learning outcomes desired should provide the basis for choosing technology and media.
- Wagner and Reddy (1987) described the characteristics that make for greater effectiveness of interactive audio (effective for discussions of abstract concepts), audio-graphic conferencing (the combination of verbal messages and visual materials is effective for both abstract and concrete learning objectives), interactive video (permits both oral and visual interaction that enhances learner "satisfaction"), and computer conferencing (allows convenient transmission of text and graphics while asynchronicity encourages reflective discussions).
- Norenburg and Lundblad (1987) developed two matrices to help planners make good choices in their choice of technology and related educational and management decisions. The first presents learner, teacher, and pedagogical considerations for each technology; the second matrix presents technology costs, advantages, and limitations.
- Dillon and Gabbard (1998) examined the findings of experimental studies of hypermedia that emphasize quantitative methods of assessing learning outcomes. Three themes were used to categorize the research: studies of learner comprehension, effects on learning outcome, and individual differences in learner response to hypermedia. The authors conclude that the benefits of hypermedia are limited to learning tasks

that are reliant on repeated manipulation and searching of information, and are distributed across learners depending on their learning style and ability.

- Valentine (2002) (as cited in Deubel, 2003) noted students' comments that not all courses are appropriate for an online format, especially those requiring mastery of physical skills. Course designers might do better by choosing video and audio delivery technologies.

Combining Media and Technologies

Experience has shown (though there is not enough research evidence to provide support beyond the most general level), that the "best" medium and technology varies from student to student. This being the case, a mixture of media is more effective for providing instruction to a large and varied student body, since this allows different types of students to find the combination that suits them best. A useful line of research is into the synergistic effects of the media, that is to say, how text of different types, audio and video, reinforce each other, and the effectiveness of using one medium as a complement to another. Over 30 years ago, Ahlm (1972) and Beijer (1972) investigated the effect of combining audio (telephone tutoring) and text (correspondence instruction). Lauzon (1992) recommended adding synchronous computer conferencing to enhance asynchronous computer-based instruction. Gunawardena (1992) advocated combining audio-graphic conferencing with computer based (asynchronous) instruction. Eastman (2002) looked at the impact of adding gaming simulation on the effectiveness of a distance course offered in a military setting, and found that trainees in the course section supplemented with a gaming simulation reported a greater level of effectiveness that those in the control group. There are many opportunities for students to build on the older studies as theoretical foundation in proposing new investigations regarding combining media on the new Internet delivery technologies.

Effective Teaching Strategies

The kind of questions about how to be an effective distance teacher include:

- What are the techniques needed to be effective in interacting with learners asynchronously in text?
- What techniques can be used to be effective in interacting synchronously online? By audio-conference? By interactive video?
- Are there skills that are generic to all the above, and if so what are they?
- How can teachers be most effectively trained in these skills?
- Are there identifiable characteristics of teachers who are effective in teaching in this way?
- More specifically, are there recognizable "triggers" for intervention in interstudent dialogue online? What are they?

Research hasn't discovered anything regarding the online forms of distance education that would change the general principles about teaching previously identified by research into teaching by print or audio and video technologies. From that research it has been clear that one of the keys to effectiveness is that the instructor takes full advantage of the interactive nature of whichever technology is being used. This means bringing learners frequently into action by asking questions, encouraging student presentations, getting students to talk to each other, and in other ways involving them fully in the teaching-learning process. (Another key is that the teaching institution provide a solid, high-quality program to present content, so that the instructor is able to attend to the interactive phase of the program; this caveat is widely ignored.)

Further research is needed, however, especially of an experimental kind, concerning these and other techniques of facilitating interaction.

Here is a sampling of studies on teaching strategies in distance education delivered online:

- In an early study of computer conferencing, Boston (1992) compared the interactive potential of this technology and traditional delivery, and lists the special skills needed by instructors to be effective.

- Hiltz, Coppola, Rotter, Turoff, and Benbuanan-Fich (2000) discuss the significance of using collaborative techniques in online teaching.

- McIsaac, Blocher, Mahes, and Vrasidas (1999) investigated teacher–learner and learner-learner interactions. They found that teachers perceived that their responses to student messages and their other online interactions enhanced their effectiveness; that student-initiated interactions with teachers were primarily task oriented; that without immediate feedback, students felt isolated; and that students felt dissatisfied without both structured and informal opportunities to interact with their peers.

- Youngblood, Trede, and DeCorpo (2001) studied 6 teachers and 89 graduate students and identified four phases of the ways in which teachers facilitate learning in an online environment.

- Hiltz et al. (2000) describe three studies that examine the effect of collaborative learning strategies on success in online teaching. Grades and other academic performance measures, student self-assessments of perceptions of the quality of learning, and faculty perceptions about interaction and learning outcomes were analyzed. The results demonstrated that when students were actively involved in collaborative learning, the outcomes were as good as or better than those of traditional classes. However, when students only received posted material and sent back individual assignments with little or no collaborative work, their results were poorer than in traditional classrooms.

- Vandergrift (2002) conducted a case study and as a result proposed a refinement of the theory of Transactional Distance to include the concept of a teacher's "restrained presence." This technique is a deliberate effort to facilitate students' autonomy and personal responsibility for their learning, as well as for community building in an online learning environment.

- Hong (2002) looked at the relationship between instructional variables in a Web-based course and students' satisfaction and learning. Findings showed student satisfaction was related to the extent and quality of student-instructor interaction, which in turn affected student grades.

- Chang (2003) found that students with different characteristics were found to have different preferences for different types of guided online activities—preparing assignments, accessing networks, holding online discussions, having group activities, and accessing other course materials.

As we have noted previously, interactive video conferencing nowadays gets less attention from researchers as well as practitioners because of the enthusiasm for online technology. Examples of some studies of teaching by interactive video include:

- Kelsey (2000) investigated the interactions of 73 students and 5 site facilitators in an interactive video course delivered to 5 sites. Findings indicated that students had the most frequent and enjoyable interaction with the site facilitators.

- Baker's (2002) investigation of the effectiveness of compressed video at high school level found that while instructors perceived video conferencing to be effective, those who were more favorable were those who had received training.

Table 10.1 lists some of the variables that have been shown to influence the effectiveness or outcomes of distance education courses (without taking into consideration either subject or technology factors).

Cost Effectiveness

The research questions of primary interest to educational administrators involve strategies to organize resources of people and money in ways that will produce good results at the lowest cost. Rumble (2003) charted the research in this area and noted that it was not until the emergence of the "big budget" single-mode systems that questions about costs became a high-profile research issue. Then, from the mid-1970s until the early 1980s, research in this area focused on technologies and finding out the actual and comparative costs of using these technologies, often linked to interest in broadcasting systems. At about the same time, there was increasing interest in whether or not distance education universities were more efficient than traditional universities.

Variables to Include in Cost-Effectiveness Analysis

As Rumble and others (e.g., Jung, 2003; Inglis, 2003) have observed, a number of different models have guided the study of the cost effectiveness of distance education so that a determination of whether a course or program is cost effective can be arrived at in different ways.

Table 10.1   Variables Determining the Effectiveness of Distance Education Courses, Requiring Further Research

- Number and distribution of students (individuals, small groups, large groups)
- Whether in "real" groups by teleconference, or virtual groups online
- Length of course (hours, days, weeks, months)
- Reasons for student taking course (compulsory, personal development, certification)
- Educational background of student (especially experience with distance learning)
- Nature of instructional strategies used (lecture, audio/video presentation, discussion/debate, problem solving)
- Kind of learning objectives (concepts, skills, attitudes)
- Type of pacing (student determined, teacher defined, fixed or flexible completion dates)
- Amount and type of interaction and feedback provided
- Role of tutors or site facilitators
- Preparation and experience of instructors and administrators
- Extent of learner support provided

Batey and Cowell (1986) proposed the following as elements to be included in any evaluation of costs:

- overall costs, component costs, and per student costs
- comparison with the cost of conventional delivery methods
- a record of all cost data, including "already paid for" costs
- relating costs to educational gains including increased student enrollments

Jung (2003) reviewed the work of Cukier (1997) who identified the following approaches to investigating the cost-effectiveness of distance education:

- a value-based approach (the institutions' pedagogical needs and values)
- a mathematical modeling approach (quantifiable costs and benefits)
- a comparative approach (same course delivered by different technologies)
- a return on investment approach (monetary gains described in relationship to cost of technology)

A favorite measure in the corporate training area is to calculate the savings due to lowered travel expenses or the hiring of fewer teachers. In higher education the latter is too politically sensitive to be addressed openly and the former is a cost passed onto students.

Morgan (2000) has provided a detailed discussion of the cost elements associated with the development and delivery of online courses as well as a cost calculation tool that projects costs and revenues over a 7-year period (see http://www.marshall.edu/distance).

Some Examples of Cost-Effectiveness Studies

- Studies addressing travel-cost saving by using interactive video and audio teleconferencing (Showalter, 1983; Rule, DeWulf, and Stowitschek, 1988; Hosley and Randolph, 1993) and in related work-time saving (Chute, Hulik, and Palmer, 1987).

- Studies comparing costs to those of traditional delivery (Ellertson, Wydra, and Jolley, 1987; Fredrickson, 1990), as well as converting traditional classroom courses to a distance format—also in the teleconference environment (Phelps et al., 1991; Project NETWORC, Nevada State Department of Human Resources, 1990).

- Studies of online technology have started to emerge. For example at Penn State University it was estimated that converting an undergraduate statistics course to online delivery saved $125,000 and resulted in improved student performance (Harkness, Lane, and Harwood, 2003).

A report issued by the General Accounting Office on cost effectiveness of programs developed for military training provided the following examples:

- The battle staff noncommissioned officer course conversion to a distance education format resulted in a $2.9 million annual cost avoidance while maintaining student performance.

- The Air Force saved an estimated $16.6 million by using CD-ROM training for hazardous material incident response for Department of Defense firefighters and law enforcement personnel.

- By introducing online distance education, the Defense Acquisition University instructional time increased from 15,750 hours to 1.4 million hours, the number of graduates attending training courses increased 38 percent, and the program management curriculum reduced annual student training weeks from 36,120 to 10,000—a savings of 300 annual work years or $17.4 million (United States General Accounting Office, 1997).

- Due to the Marine Corps' distance education application of a terrorism awareness course, training time was reduced from 11 hours to 6 hours and average exam scores increased by seven percentage points (Chisholm, 2003).

Economies of Scale

A standard assumption in distance education is that it is rarely possible to provide programs that are of both high quality and cost effective unless done on a fairly large scale. This is because heavy investment is required to set up production facilities and to pay for materials' production in publishing departments, Web production, broadcasting and recording, production of other media, as well as instructional design. All these add up to costs that have to be incurred before the enrollment of any students, regardless of how many students are to be enrolled. These up-front fixed costs of a distance education system are higher than those of the conventional university, while the variable (or direct) cost per student is lower. In a good distance education system, large numbers of students can take the course and the more that do so, the lower the average costs of the course. This is what is meant by economy of scale.

Research in the early days of the UK Open University (UKOU) by Laidlaw and Layard (1974) showed that the threshold at which the university became more cost-efficient than the average campus-based university was when it enrolled 21,691 students. Wagner (1977) showed that the average cost per student at the UKOU was about one-third of that at the conventional universities, and the cost per graduate was about one-half. More recently in the United States, Turoff (1997) has provided an analysis of the costs of creating a virtual university and illustrates how economies of scale apply to this form of distance education. In the United States, where there is no large single mode university, the economies of scale might be achieved by collaboration among dual mode institutions (Feasley, 2003). An example of the kind of collaboration that can bring economies of scale is a consortium of 39 state-supported colleges and universities in the Commonwealth of Virginia which was able to achieve around $74.5 million in cost avoidance over an eight-year period (1994–2002) by coordinating and sharing online library resources (see http://www.sloan-c.org).

Faculty Time and Other Hidden Costs

Rumble (2003) and others have suggested that a fuller understanding of the cost-effectiveness of distance education in dual mode institutions requires consideration of the cost of faculty time and other hidden costs (e.g., the travel costs for students attending face-to-face classes usually ignored in comparative studies). In particular, there is need to examine more carefully the costs of faculty time. Among studies so far in this area are:

- Visser (2000) found that faculty needed nearly twice as much time to teach at a distance compared to traditional teaching. However, DiBiase (2000) contradicts this finding, since his analysis showed that he needed less time. Lazarus (2003) reported a similar finding to DiBiase saying that the time range for teaching online "falls within the range of reasonable expectations."

- The University of California, Davis (see http://www.sloan-c.org) compared instructor costs of an undergraduate course online and in the classroom. Using a time log, costs were measured by the time spent: (1) working with project staff, (2) planning the course, (3) preparing the course for online delivery, (4) delivering the course, (5) interacting with students, (6) evaluating student performance, and (7) training and supervising teaching assistants. The findings from this study revealed that the instructor spent more time on the traditional course than the online (112 hours compared to 107 hours, respectively) and that the overall cost per student who passes the course is less for online courses ($99) than those face-to-face ($105).

It is necessary to be very cautious—indeed, to be skeptical—in reviewing all cost-effectiveness studies. As Rumble, the leading authority on this issue, has pointed out (Rumble, 2003) it is very hard to find truly comparable data, particularly because some evaluators ignore certain costs that others include. There is a tendency in dual mode institutions, for example, to overlook many capital costs (e.g., who paid for the faculty parking lot?) and other shared costs such as equipment, telephone, and Internet access costs. Furthermore, the Davis study mentioned here illustrates very well the need to identify the kind of distance education organization where the study occurs, since in this case it seems to be one of the "distance education by instructor" situations that are, by definition, very labor intensive, and employ costly labor.

Research on Policy

Institutions and governments have never given more attention to policies about distance education than in the last decade. Nevertheless, policy and how policies are arrived at is the most underdeveloped of all areas of research.

The following are some examples of research on institutional policy:

- In a doctoral dissertation, Irele (2002) studied the written policies about distance education in four Land Grant universities to identify the dynamics by which distance education becomes what she termed a "mainstream activity." She found that barriers to such mainstreaming included administrator's desire to use distance education to generate additional revenue, and other conflicts of values between faculty and administrators.

- Nelson (2000) conducted a study of chief academic officers in the University of Wisconsin system. In their view, effective distance education policy would provide institutional flexibility, enable competition, and be firmly rooted in institutions' missions. Good policy-making processes included: engagement and management of the expectations of both internal and external stakeholders, taking into account the fluid and ambiguous environment in which policymaking occurs, and recognition of the need to move from "prescriptive policies to broad principles."

- Smith, Eddy, Richards, and Dixon (2000) used a two-phase process in their case-study to expose "a broad array of business risks" (p. 5) that can result from higher education institutions partnering with businesses. They concluded that the majority of the top higher education institutions maintain control of their distance education programs as well as of their copyright and intellectual property policies, but they noted there is a "large learning curve involved in dealing with these polices" (p. 11).

- Schauer (2002) surveyed academic department chairs at Land Grant universities regarding their decisions to implement distance education courses and programs. As a result she recommended the following policy guidelines:
  - Focus distance education in the institution's strategic plan.
  - Develop a set of written strategies that can serve as reference points.
  - Review tenure and promotion guidelines.

- Develop a "set of creative strategies for generating or obtaining" resources for course development.

- Develop an evaluation plan especially designed to obtain student feedback.

- Staffo (2002) investigated the influence of government's instructional technology policy on decision making in rural Alabama schools and concluded that although those policies encouraged technical advancement, they did not result in expanded partnerships or in addressing certain digital divide issues (between rural and non-rural schools).

- In a case study of six metropolitan universities, Eastman (2003) found that Web-published distance education policies contained mostly institutional administration items, and that although faculty support and legal components contained relatively the same number of policies, student support contained the least number of policies.

- Levy (2003) reviewed the distance education plans of 108 community colleges and found that only 48 had any documented planning. Only two plans referred to the mission statement of the college; 33 percent referred to curriculum and/or program development; 27 percent referred to staff training and support; 28 percent referred to student services; 7 percent to student training and support; and 8 percent referred to the law, the Americans with Disabilities Act, and accreditation.

- Rockwell, Furgason, and Marx (2000) conducted a study on policy using as sources: a distance education steering committee, a panel of state (Georgia) policy makers, and participants in a distance education conference. Four themes emerged:

  1. Need for policy regarding interinstitutional collaboration, including funding formulas

  2. Need for basic research on learning and teaching at a distance

  3. Need for policies on faculty including teacher preparation

  4. Need for research on completion rates and other outcomes

- Howell, Williams, and Lindsay (2003) identified 32 trends in the distance education literature that provide "an informed foundation for strategic planning" (p. 1). Policy regarding each of these trends is needed. Note that any of these could be the subject of a doctoral or other research study. They are:

  1. Student enrollment trends

     - Distance education programs are necessary because current higher education infrastructure cannot support the demand.

     - Students are shopping for flexible courses.

     - Higher education learner profiles are changing.

     - Adult, female, and minority learners are increasing.

     - Retention is of concern to administrators and faculty.

2. Faculty trends
   - Traditional faculty roles are shifting or "unbundling."
   - The need for faculty development, support, and training is growing.
   - Faculty tenure is being challenged, allowing for more nontraditional faculty roles in distance education.
   - Some faculty members are resisting technological course delivery.
   - Instructors of distance courses can feel isolated.
   - Faculty members demand reduced workload and increased compensation for distance courses.

3. Academic trends
   - Knowledge and information are growing exponentially.
   - The institutional landscape of higher education is changing: traditional campuses are declining, for-profit institutions are growing, and public and private institutions are merging.
   - There is a shift in organizational structure toward decentralization.
   - Instruction is becoming more learner-centered, nonlinear, and self-directed.
   - There is a growing emphasis on academic accountability.
   - Academic emphasis is shifting from course-completion to competency.
   - Education is becoming more seamless between high school, college, and further studies.
   - Higher education outsourcing and partnerships are increasing.
   - Some advocate standardizing content in learning objects.

4. Technology trends
   - Technological devices are becoming more versatile and ubiquitous.
   - There is a huge growth in Internet usage.
   - Technological fluency is becoming a graduation requirement.

5. Economic trends
   - With the economy in recession, there are fewer resources for higher education and higher education initiatives, such as distance education.
   - Funding challenges are the top IT concern for many.
   - Lifelong learning is becoming a competitive necessity.

6. Distance learning trends
   - More courses, degrees, and universities are becoming available through distance education programs. The Internet is becoming dominant among other distance education media.

Viewpoint: Curtis Bonk

I predict a distinct shift from courseware tools that warehouse students to ones that engage them in collaborative, interactive, and motivational activities. Open source courseware will force major course management vendors to develop more pedagogically engaging tools and resources. In terms of course content and delivery, there will be enormous growth in online certification and recertification programs, associate and master's degrees, and blended learning. Learning objects on different topics will be something you can grab like magazines and newspapers on the way into a plane, bus, or train.

Paralleling the explosion in online learning, there will be increased attention on courses and degrees granted in how to moderate or mentor within online learning. At the same time, professor rating sites will evolve into global online teaching ratings on every online instructor on earth, complete with sample teaching videos, course evaluations, and testimonials. With the continued rise in part-time and non-tenured instructors, freelance instructor matching or exchange sites will annually help millions find scholarly jobs. Collaboration, case learning, and problem-based learning will be the preferred methods of the online instructor, with few relying solely on lectures, modeling, or Socratic instruction. Finally, most will see the potential of the Web in the coming years as a tool for virtual teaming or collaboration, critical thinking, and enhanced student engagement, not as a tool for creativity and idea expression.

SOURCE: Curtis Bonk, Professor, Indiana University, and President of SurveyShare, Inc.

- The distinction between distance and local education is disappearing.
- The need for effective course management systems and Web services is growing.
- There is an increasing need for learning and teaching strategies that exploit the capabilities of technology.

Conclusion

It should be apparent from the review of literature in this chapter that with the emergence of online technology and the huge increase in participation by faculty and their institutions, that more research is needed, especially research that is based on theory and explores beyond the level of short-term program description and evaluation.

⅃ Summary

- The single largest group of research studies in distance education focuses on the effectiveness of the communications media.
- There are a lot of simple program descriptions about the effectiveness of a teacher or an institution that used one or more communications technologies.
- Other studies compare the effectiveness of teaching in one medium with another. Most often these studies compare the effectiveness of teaching in a conventional classroom and teaching through an electronic technology. More recent studies compare learning outcomes in two or more distant learning settings.
- There is need for more research to find out what is the most effective medium for different types of students and what media are most effective for different types of distance teaching strategy and content.
- Other areas of research about effectiveness include: effective media selection, effectiveness of different aspects of course design, effectiveness of various teaching strategies, cost effectiveness and effective policies and policy making.
- Research is ineffective when it is not set in a theoretical framework. Researchers are not able to build on the work of others, they are less likely to identify the really significant questions, and their results are of limited generalizability.

Questions for Discussion or Further Study

1. Of the many research studies mentioned in this chapter, which one(s) do you find most compelling or relevant? Why?

2. Discuss the implications of the *italicized* words in the statements: "Instruction at a distance *can be* as effective in bringing about learning as classroom instruction," and "The absence of face-to-face contact is not *in itself* detrimental to the learning process."

3. How would you design a study to assess the effectiveness of a distance learning course or program you are currently (or were previously) involved with?

4. Specifically, regarding a course you are familiar with, what items could you include in evaluating its cost? Think of a conventional course and try to list all the items that go into its cost. How do they compare, in total cost and in cost per student?

5. Discuss the viewpoint of Curtis Bonk; what research needs does it suggest?

C H A P T E R 1 1

The Global Span
of Distance Education

In this chapter, we would like to give you an impression of the amazing worldwide scope of distance education. It is impossible to do more than give an impression, because today distance education is found in every country of the world, and a book could be written about the history and scope of every one of these. What we will do here is give a short description of a few examples, taken from each continent.

Historically, distance education has always been a very international field. This becomes apparent if you look at its principal professional organization, The International Council for Distance Education (ICDE). ICDE started in 1938 in Canada with a strong U.S. participation, and was known as the International Council for Correspondence Education (ICCE) until it was renamed the ICDE in 1982. ICCE organized a World Conference in 1938, and since then, conferences have been held about every 4 years. Now there is a World Conference every 2 years as well as regional conferences in all parts of the world. At these ICDE conferences you can be sure of meeting distance educators from virtually every country in the world. For more information, see: http://www.icde.org.

Thanks to the Internet it is easier than ever to keep informed about distance education in other countries, and one of the benefits arising from this is it helps us get a better perspective on practices in our own country. Thanks to the Internet, too, it is possible to do more than just study what goes on in other countries. It is now quite easy to *take part* in what goes on there, as a growing number of programs in other countries are made available online to American students. Similarly, a growing number of American institutions are enrolling distance learners from other countries; our own students tell us that being in such a course is much more interesting than most traditional classes.

The potential of distance education as a means of transferring knowledge, especially from developed to developing countries, has attracted the interest of international agencies like the World Bank and UNESCO, both of which have policies regarding distance education for international development and even offer some courses of their own. These and other trends towards internationalism are likely to accelerate in the years ahead, and make it important that we all have at least some idea of the global scope of distance education.

We should not overlook the fact however that most people in the world do not have access to sophisticated technology. Some data about the technology in developing and industrial countries is given in Table 11.1 and a comparison of media is in Table 11.2.

A Brief World Tour

To help you get a taste of what distance education looks like in different national contexts, we will give some examples from the following countries, representing five different continents: China, Korea, Brazil, Finland, Norway, Australia, South Africa, United Kingdom, and Turkey. After that we will provide very short introductions to more than a dozen other countries having either single mode universities or a distance education consortium. There are many more institutions in every country and we hope you will use Web sites to examine more closely those that you are most interested in.

China: A National System

The People's Republic of China is vast in size, about the size of the whole of Europe, with a population (about 1.3 billion people) five times that of the United States. More than 65 percent of these live in rural areas, often remote from major cities. The income per person has doubled in a decade to about $1,000 U.S. Under these circumstances, it is not surprising that there is both a need for distance education—which has already played an important role in national development—and that it continues to be extensively developed. Beginning in the 1940s with correspondence study and radio broadcasting, a key development came in the 1960s; this was the establishment in a number of cities of local "TV universities." Educational broadcasts were provided in the early morning and late at night for people to watch in study groups set up in their workplaces. In 1979 a nationwide system of regional Radio and TV Universities (RTVUs) was set up, and in that year 400,000 students were enrolled at such universities all round the country (Wei and Tong 1994, p. 19). In 1982 when the first RTVU students in engineering and technology graduated, there were 92,000 of them, which equaled half the number of such students graduating from conventional universities.

In 1986 China started to transmit educational programs by satellite, and in 1987 satellite television became the communications channel for a national distance education system, known as the China Central Radio and TV University (CCRTVU). The CCRTVU delivery system combines satellite, cable

Table 11.1 **Comparative Use of Technology in Distance Education in Developing and Industrial Countries**

	Developing countries (%)	Industrial countries (%)
Mail and physical delivery	86	87
Public service telephone network	57	83
Radio	29	6
Direct broadcast TV	16	9
Terrestrial broadcast TV	11	13
Integrated services digital network	7	20
Specialized links (unspecified)	2	17
Digital specialized links	5	11
Public data network	2	12
Cable	2	11

SOURCE: Von Euler, M and Berg, D. (1998). *The use of electronic media in open and distance education.* Paris: UNESCO.

Table 11.2 **Comparative Use of Learning Media in Distance Education in Developing and Industrial Countries**

	Developing countries (%)	Industrial countries (%)
Printed documents	100	99
Audio	86	67
Video	77	82
Computer-based media	43	50
Multimedia	7	30

SOURCE: Von Euler, M and Berg, D. (1998). *The use of electronic media in open and distance education.* Paris: UNESCO.

and broadcast television, radio, Internet, computer programs, and correspondence instruction to deliver over 350 courses in most subject areas. About 9,000 teaching hours per year are transmitted over three dedicated channels. CCRTVU has published more than 1,000 textbooks.

Organizational Structure of China's Distance Education System

Figure 11.1 shows the organizational structure of distance education in China. At the national level, the Central RTVU reports directly to the State Education Commission; that is to say, the Ministry of Education, which establishes

Figure 11.1   The Organizational Structure of Distance Education in China

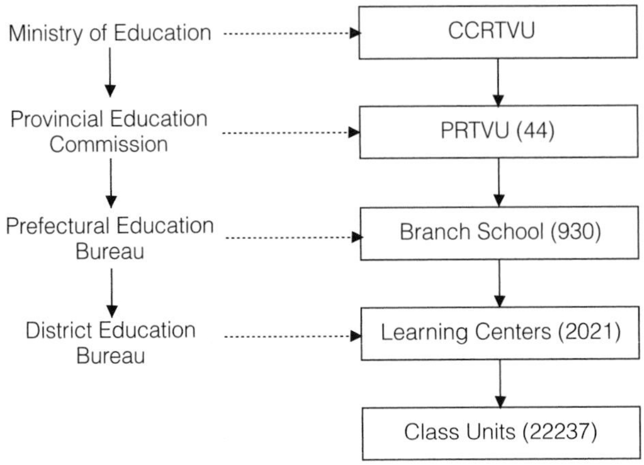

SOURCE: Based on Li and Li, 2003.

national policy, direction, and standards. The Provincial Radio and TV Universities (PRTVUs) in turn are under the auspices of the provincial governments and are responsible for developing courses and programming to meet local needs. The Branch Schools come under the control of prefectural or municipal agencies, and are responsible for supervising the activities of the learning centers. Learning centers organize classes, register students, collect fees (tuition), distribute course materials, and appoint tutors. The "class units" are the point of contact of students with the system, and where they receive supervision of and support.

Looked at from the point of view of distance education as a system, this is a model system, which ensures efficiencies and quality through centralized design and delivery of courses and programs, but also allows for considerable decentralization and local application of the subject matter.

By 2001, the China Radio and TV Universities had graduated over 3.06 million college graduates, making up 12.3 percent of the total graduates in higher education institutions in the same period and 25.6 percent of the higher education institutions for adult learners. There have been more than 1 million secondary and vocational school graduates. Non-degree students completing continuing education and in-service training courses number over 35 million; tens of millions of farmers have received training in practical agricultural courses. Initial training has been provided to 710,000 elementary school teachers and 550,000 high school teachers and in-service training to 2 million teachers and 1 million school principals. For more statistics about the CRTVU, see Table 11.3.

In addition to the Radio and TV universities, 66 universities have been authorized by the Ministry of Education to develop as dual mode distance education institutions. For more information about distance education in China, see Wei (1991), Li and Chen (1999), Li and Li, (2003) and visit: http://www.edu .cn/HomePage/english/education/disedu/index.shtml. For more on CCRTVU, see: http://www.crtvu.edu.cn/english/introduction/k1.htm.

Table 11.3   **Growth of CCRTVUs' Graduates, Entrants, Enrollment, and Staff**

Year	Graduates	Entrants	Enrollment	Staff (full-time)
1999	171,200	202,800	497,100	57,500 (28,200)
2000	190,000	395,600	734,600	62,100 (31,300)
2001	217,600	495,600	1,039,000	65,500 (33,600)
2002	279,000	593,900	1,509,600	69,400 (36,900)

SOURCE: Based on Li and Li (2003).

Korea: A National Policy

The 1960s and 1970s saw a huge expansion in Korean education, which in turn gave rise to rapid economic expansion and also to changes in politics, society, and culture. During this period as part of a process of reforming the school systems, several important institutions were founded. They include the Korean Air and Correspondence University (later renamed the Korean National Open University KNOU), the Air and Correspondence High School (ACHS), and the Korean Education Development Institute, the national research and development institute for education. In 1990, the Educational Broadcasting System (EBS) was opened as an affiliate of the Korean Education Development Institute. EBS now has its own broadcasting TV channel, two satellite TV channels, and one FM Radio channel for delivery of formal and non-formal distance education programs at all academic levels. Since the mid-1990s Korean governmental policy have been based on recommendations of the Presidential Commission on Education Reform (1997). The Commission defined the goal of the Korean education system in the 21st century as an "Edutopia," meaning "an education welfare state—a society of open and life-long education to allow each and every individual equal and easy access to education at any time and place."

To build this Edutopia, several strategies have been implemented. These include setting up a national credit bank and the establishment of a Bureau of Educational Information and Technology to promote the use of information and communication technologies. In 1997, The Korean Research and Information Center (KRIC) and the Korean Multimedia Education Center were founded. KRIC provides online journal articles, research papers, academic databases, and other academic materials. The Korea Multimedia Education Center (KMEC) supports application of information technologies in K–12 schools and provides online teacher training. In 1999, KRIC and KMEC were integrated into the Korean Education and Research Information Services.

In 1998, the government initiated the Virtual University Trial Project. Sixty-five universities and five companies have participated in the project; eight universities participate independently without forming a consortium, and fifty-seven universities and five companies have formed seven consortia. Each of the eight conventional universities has established its own virtual campus and each of the consortia has established its virtual institution. In the second semester of 1998, about 45,000 students registered in 536 courses in the Virtual University Trial Project.

Korea National Open University (KNOU)

Korea has 156 universities, 158 junior colleges, 11 teachers' colleges, 18 poly-technics—and *one* single mode, national distance teaching university (KNOU). Founded in 1972 the KNOU (http://www.knou.ac.kr) now has a student population (2002) of 207,440 and has graduated over a quarter of a million successful students. It offers courses in 18 major areas of study and is the only distance teaching university to offer a 4-year degree. Its origin as the Air and Correspondence University is reflected in the continued heavy emphasis on broadcast and recorded television. KNOU requires participation in face-to-face tutorials, and relies heavily on video-conferencing between groups of students at study centers and centrally located faculty. The Digital Library System holds audio and videotapes on 580 subjects and these are available for borrowing or for downloading from the Internet. There are 242 full-time academics, 5,779 part-time academics, and 511 administrative and technical employees. There are 14 regional study centers and 35 other study centers in major cities. KNOU receives about 35 percent of its budget from the government.

Trends in student profiles show that the number of KNOU students who attended other higher education institutions prior to KNOU increased each year. In 1999, more than 40 percent of new KNOU students already had either a college certificate or a bachelor's degree. A graduate school was opened in 2001. For more on KNOU, see: http://www.knou.ac.kr/english/index.htm.

Brazil: A National System of Teacher Training

Brazil is exceptional in having in its Ministry of Education a special department called the Secretariat of Distance Education. It is this Secretariat that has been responsible for developing and implementing PROFORMACAO—the Program for Training of In-Service Teachers. This is a national project that uses distance education to provide training for unqualified elementary school teachers, most of whom are in rural schools in the most underdeveloped parts of this huge country. Improving their skills and knowledge is seen as a major contribution to national policy aimed at improving the lives of millions of the nation's poorest people. The program has been underway since 1999 and has successfully trained over 27,000 teachers. It is an excellent example of a systems approach, applying all the most important of the principles that have been discussed in this book.

Course Design

PROFORMACAO course materials were designed by national teams of the country's best subject specialists, working with instructional designers and contracted companies specializing in production of high quality video and textual materials. They are designed to deliver 3,200 hours of training, organized in four modules. A set of learning objectives and training procedures for every component of the national curriculum was worked out by the course team, over more than a year of intensive negotiation. Each module begins with a 2-week residential orientation workshop. The remaining weeks are organized into 8 units of study of 2 weeks each, consisting of independent study, a Saturday all-day workshop, classroom practice, and preparation activities for the bi-monthly tests. Each unit is organized around a study guide and a series of video programs. Other printed materials provides the trainee with administrative information; there is a tutor manual and supporting texts, a video for tutor training, and a guide for the state teacher training agencies that supervise local tutors.

Implementation

Implementing the instruction and providing learner support depends on a network of tutors recruited in each locality, supported at regional level by instructors in teacher training colleges, who are supported in turn by a manager-coordinator and technical assistants at the state level. The tutors are the direct point of contact between the trainee and the system. They were selected from experienced trained teachers in local schools and are responsible for guiding the trainee teachers' work and overseeing the supervised practice and Saturday activities. They also generate the data needed for the monitoring function. Each student's assignment is evaluated by the tutor and a score is entered into a data base at regional level. This data enables national and regional trainers to intervene with any student or tutor needing special attention and this is done at the point of training (i.e., the trainee's own school). This implementation system contributes to the important policy goal of involving local authorities in the process of improving their own schools. Training of the tutors is designed by the central management and implemented by the teacher training colleges in association with state and municipal authorities.

At the national level, a management unit at the Secretariat of Distance Education is responsible for managing the design process, production, and distribution of instructional materials; coordinating the implementation process; providing training and technical support to the states; and monitoring and evaluating processes and results.

Performance data from the first intake to the program show that 85.6 percent of trainees were successful in meeting the criteria for promotion, 3 percent required further training, and 11 percent dropped out. The total cost of the program was US$30 million and the estimated cost per trainee was about $1,100 for the 2-year course.

PROFORMACAO is an example of the kind of system that will be the model of distance education system in the 21st century. Its main administrative components are shown in Figure 11.2. Although exhibiting all the important features of the best single mode distance teaching institutions, it does so *without the establishment of an institution.* It employs the best human and technical resources in the nation in a collaborative, *virtual* system. The spe-

Figure 11.2   PROFORMACAO Components of a Twenty-First Century Virtual System

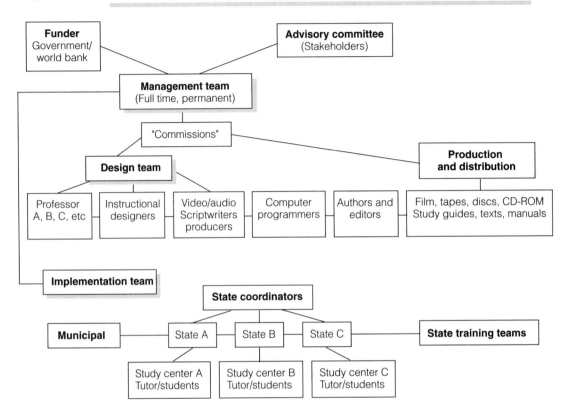

cialists who designed the courses have returned to their institutions and the specialists who support the trainees at the municipal and state levels remain in their home institutions. Only at the national level is there a very small team of coordinators to oversee and facilitate the monitoring, training, evaluation, and logistical procedures. Thus, although it invests large sums to produce materials and instruction of a high quality, it is also a very cost effective program. See http://www.mec.gov.br/seed/proform.

Finland and Norway

The Scandinavian countries of Sweden, Norway, Denmark, and Finland are a direct contrast to the other three countries we have looked at so far. They both have small populations (totaling altogether less than 20 million people), which are dispersed over a wide area; outside the cities, people are isolated due to both geography and a harsh winter climate. These countries are among the richest in the world, and education, like other social services, receives high priority in national policy. Since the level of basic education is very high, people have good study skills and are therefore able to adapt to distance education quite readily.

In Finland, the first correspondence schools started in 1908; radio and television were used to deliver programs to primary and secondary schools and to support voluntary adult education. In the 1980s with the success of innovation in high technology by companies like Nokia, the Finns became eager users of audio and videoconferencing. Early on there was a consensus on the benefits for such a small country of institutional cooperation and coordination. Recent examples of collaborative projects are the Finnish Virtual University (http://www.virtuaaliyliopisto.fi) and the Finnish Virtual Polytechnic (http://www.virtuaaliamk.fi).

Progressive policy leadership is provided by the National Board of Education (http://www.oph.fi) and the Ministry of Education (http://www.minedu.fi)—especially in promoting the use of new technologies.

Although the emphasis in the 1980s and 1990s was on creating the technical infrastructure, there was also strong interest in these years in creating new content and developing new teaching processes. Finnish institutions were among the first in the world to engage in close collaborative relationships with institutions in other countries, particularly for purposes of professional development. The universities of Helsinki and Turku, later Yvaskylla and Tampere, all worked in partnership with the Pennsylvania State University (and several universities in Latin America) in an extended series of professional development courses from the late 1980s until the mid 1990s, transmitted by audio-, video-, and computer-based conferencing. The country's largest insurance company also took part in these activities, and subsequently other financial companies have been active in using distance education for employee and customer training. One of the leading providers in Finland is the Tax Authority.

After joining the European Union (EU) in 1995, Finland turned primarily to European institutions for its collaborative relationships. In turn, it is said that the European Social Fund (ESF) and the numerous EU-funded programs have strongly influenced the development of Finnish distance education practices.

Norway's distance education has been dominated throughout its history by two private institutions. The first distance education institution in Norway, the Norsk Korrespondanseskole (NKS), was established in 1914. Today, the NKS has 70,000 enrollments a year in a wide range of courses, from secondary school to university degree levels (see http://www.nks.no). Another major private school, the Norsk Korrespondanse Institute (NKI), has 20,000 active students, and mainly provides technical, vocational, and administrative courses. Nettskolen is the name of its Internet College. See http://www.nki.no/in_english.xsql.

The Norwegian government was one of the first in the world with a national policy to support distance education, with laws passed as long ago as 1948. In 1977 it set up the Norwegian State Institution for Distance Education (NFU) to coordinate the development and distribution of distance education programs by the national broadcasting system, businesses, publishers, and the public schools and university systems.

The Norwegian Association for Distance Education (NADE) was established in 1968 as an association of accredited correspondence schools, and in 1984 was reorganized to include all institutions in Norway involved in distance education (as well as representatives of the NFU and SOFF). In 1988, the Norwegian Center for Distance Education (SEFU) was created by NFU, NKI, and NKS to conduct research projects. Also in 1988, the Norwegian government established—and continues to support—the permanent Secretariat of the International Council for Distance Education, with its offices in Oslo.

In recent years distance education programs have been started by conventional Norwegian universities and colleges. This post-secondary provision is coordinated by the Norwegian Executive Board for Distance Education at University and College Level (SOFF) (http://www.soff.uit.no).

Australia and New Zealand

Australia is geographically massive, with the land mass equivalent of the United States, and has a small population equivalent to that of Pennsylvania. Over 80 percent of this population lives in the cities; the remainder is distributed over huge areas. By comparison, New Zealand is a small land mass with a small population (4 million). In both countries, distance education has always been an accepted form of teaching and learning. Today, many school systems and universities provide distance education courses as part of their regular activities.

Australia is truly one of the pioneer nations in distance education. At the school level, Education Acts were passed in the 1870s that mandated the provision of education to children in remote and isolated places as a right to be comparable to what was available in the urban areas. Consequently, by the early 1920s, all the States had adopted a system of correspondence education to serve children from preschool to the end of secondary education. Teachers in rural areas received their professional development courses by correspondence through State Teachers Colleges. From the 1930s, schools used radio broadcasts to supplement their teaching. By the early 1960s, Departments of Education established "Schools of the Air" to provide two-way interactive learning opportunities. Note that these "schools" were not using one-way broadcasting; exchanges between teachers and students, or the parents of school children, were by means of the two-way short-wave radios that provided the main means of communication in what was called the "Outback." In the 1990s the States of New South Wales and Queensland began to decentralize their distance education programs for children, establishing regional centers in order to establish teaching as close as possible to student's homes.

At the university level—to take one example—when the University of Queensland was established in 1910, it was required by an Education Act to offer correspondence programs. Such programs were also established at the founding of other universities and they were usually known as external studies departments. Today, entry qualifications for accredited distance education courses are the same as for on-campus courses, so it is common for students to take a mix of on-campus and off-campus courses. This means that Australian distance education students tend to be younger and full-time, rather than older and part time, as is more usual in the United States. Australian degrees taken through distance education are not distinguished from the on-campus offerings either by title or their cost.

Australia incorporates a wide range of technologies into distance education. The most common materials are print, audio, and videotapes, with increasing use of the Internet as well as computer conferencing, video-discs, audio and audio-graphic conferencing, and satellite delivered video/audio conferencing. Many remote rural primary schools have high speed Internet connections.

One of the distinctive characteristics of Australian distance education is the significant involvement of the federal and state governments in the planning, implementation, and evaluation of distance education at all levels, including targeting of publicly funded courses to meet specific occupational needs. Since almost all college and higher education in Australia is federally funded, the government exerts considerable influence on the direction and development of distance education programs. However, each State's school system, as well as individual universities, operate fairly autonomously and implement distance education to meet the needs of their own constituencies.

In the comparatively small island nation of New Zealand, distance education began with the New Zealand Correspondence School in the 1920s. It was established to provide education to primary school children who lived in remote, rural areas unable to attend a conventional school. During the 1940s, adults were also able to enroll as part-time students, and in later years, the school also became well known for specializing in providing education to children who had special education needs. Today, the New Zealand Correspondence School is the largest school in New Zealand, providing courses to students from early childhood to secondary levels. Student numbers vary throughout the year and are usually between 20,000 and 30,000 students. Many students attend their local residential school and take additional subjects that are not offered locally through the Correspondence School. It has grown from being a one-teacher operation that relied on handwritten letters for correspondence, to one that now uses a full range of technologies.

At the tertiary (post–high school) level, distance education has been lead by Massey University. Until 1960, universities in New Zealand made their own *ad hoc* arrangements to provide for external or "extramural" students. Massey, at that time, formalized and systematized the development of a correspondence service for such students and began to officially enroll extramural students from all over the country. Since then, enrollment numbers for students studying by distance have grown to 21,000—just over half of the total enrolments at the University.

While the Correspondence School catered for early childhood to secondary education, and Massey catered for post-secondary, tertiary education, distance education training for trade specialists was developed by the Technical

Correspondence School, now known as the Open Polytechnic of New Zealand. It began by providing resettlement training for men and women returning from service during the World War II, and over the years has developed expertise in vocational education by distance, focusing on workforce up-skilling, nationally and internationally.

The New Zealand government has had, and continues to have, a strong commitment to ensuring equality of educational opportunity. The above three key players in the development of distance education in New Zealand were state-funded teaching institutions. Today, the national government funds distance education at the same levels as conventional campus-based delivery. Advances in digital communication technologies have resulted in every higher education provider in New Zealand having differentiated levels of e-learning provision. In response to these strategic developments, the University of Auckland—a traditional campus-based university—became the first university in New Zealand to establish a dedicated Centre for Flexible and Distance Learning. An e-Learning Collaborative Development fund has also been established under the auspices of the Tertiary Education Commission to allow higher education providers to access funds for the development of e-learning capability.

The Republic of South Africa

The Republic of South Africa (RSA) has a long history of distance education, incorporating a range of providers. This includes a single mode distance education university, a large single mode "Technikon" (a college focusing on vocational training), a number of private colleges, and an increasing number of traditional campus-based universities moving into dual-mode provision. The South African higher education system is currently (2004) undergoing a process of structural transformation to improve the efficiency of the system and to eradicate the duplication of institutions. If successful this should set an example for other countries throughout the world.

University of South Africa (UNISA)

The story of distance education in the RSA begins with what is almost certainly the oldest single mode distance education university in the world, The University of South Africa (UNISA). Originally founded as the University of the Cape of Good Hope in 1873, UNISA became a federation of colleges in 1916. As each of the colleges became independent universities, UNISA focused increasingly on what it called "external studies," which meant teaching primarily by correspondence, and was formally constituted as a solely distance education university in 1946. The whole educational system of South Africa is influenced by this long-established acceptance of distance education. Governments at national, provincial, and municipal levels have many graduates of UNISA or one of the other national distance education institutions. Nelson Mandela, South Africa's first democratically elected president, is one of UNISA's most famous graduates, obtaining a qualification while imprisoned on Robin Island. This widespread familiarity with distance education means the methods of distance education are more readily considered among options by policy makers than is the case in many other countries.

In 2002, UNISA had more than 150,000 students, which represents one-third of South Africa's university students. UNISA offers diplomas, certificates, and degrees at both the undergraduate and graduate levels in a variety of content areas. It employs around 3,300 permanent staff, about half of whom are teaching staff. There is a central counseling service and a limited number of regional learner support centers located in the principal cities. Like many other publicly funded single mode universities, UNISA's main mission has been to provide a "second chance" for university study for people who: are unable to obtain admission to conventional face-to-face campuses, cannot afford the higher residential university fees, reside in remote areas, or are unable to attend residential classes because of employment or other commitments. UNISA predominantly uses a model of print-based, independent study with the incorporation of audio- and videocassettes in some courses. Face-to-face discussion classes are presented once or twice a year for courses with large enrollments at five regional locations in South Africa. Video-conferences are used in place of discussion classes for courses with lower student enrollments. An Internet interface called Student's Online, allows students to register for courses, submit assignments, obtain assignment results, and access study materials electronically.

For more on UNISA, visit http://www.unisa.ac.za/.

Other Systems in RSA

Another large distance education institution is the Technikon SA, established in 1980 and focused on career education (e.g., police administration, community services). Technikon SA began with 5,039 students in 1986 and had an enrollment of more than 60,000 students in 2003 with a faculty of 716. Another university, VISTA University, was created in 1981 and dedicated to providing higher education to the urban black population. In 2003 it had an enrollment of 19,978 students organized around seven regional campuses and a distance learning centre, the Vista University Distance Education Centre (VUDEC). VUDEC focuses primarily on the upgrading of underqualified school teachers, and in 2003 had 9,045 distance learners. Finally, Technisa is a technical college that provides distance education for vocational and technical training in engineering, business, and general studies. It was founded in 1984 and had an enrollment of 7,607 students in 1992–1993. Like UNISA, Technikon SA, Vista, and Technisa serve a national constituency, primarily through printed correspondence, with other technologies used when the student population has access to the necessary equipment. For most South African students, this means the correspondence text is still the most common medium of instruction. South Africa also has a number of private distance education colleges. Five of these dominate the private market and together they enroll more than 177,000 students a year. With regard to South Africa's attempts to apply new technology, some important policy foundations were laid in its Technology Enhanced Learning Program and its Telematics for African Development Consortium. Projects such as the Shoma teacher development program (using satellite TV and Internet technology to support in-service training for under-qualified teachers) demonstrate the potential of partnerships between private companies and national and provincial Departments of Education.

An interesting phenomenon in South Africa is the explosion of numbers of distance learners at previously single mode institutions. According to the Council on Higher Education, enrollment in UNISA and Technikon SA dropped by 41,000 students, or 21 percent, from 1995 to 1999 as a result of the growth of new dual mode institutions. These drew 31,000 new distance students—an increase of 111 percent. The 6 campuses with the largest distance-education programs have about 65,000 students in distance courses. Most of those students are school teachers trying to upgrade their qualifications, in pursuit of promotions. At the University of Pretoria there are now 30,000 distance learners, about 25,000 of whom are studying for a further diploma in education management taught through correspondence courses. About 3,500 postgraduate distance learners receive study material electronically, via e-mail, Web sites, and television. With 27,000 full-time residential students, the University of Pretoria, not long ago a fully residential university, now has fewer residential than distance students. A similar pattern has emerged at the University of Port Elizabeth where 13,863 students have enrolled in distance programs offering undergraduate diplomas, further diplomas, and master's degrees—more than double the 6,000 students registered for conventional classes. The majority of distance students are unqualified or underqualified teachers who are upgrading their certification. Rand Afrikaans University has more than 7,000 students registered for distance courses and about 13,000 students in traditional instruction. Eighty-two percent of the distance students are registered for a further diploma in education, and their average age is 36. About 6,000 of the distance-education students are black Africans.

A Major Policy Development

Distance education is set to change in South Africa in a way that is likely to find a place in the history books beyond that country. As is usually the case when major change occurs in distance education, this is a result of a government prepared to take hard policy decisions. The policy in this case is contained within the framework of a sweeping top-to-bottom rationalization of all higher education (see http://www.che.ac.za/documents/d000009/index.php).

As far as distance education is concerned, the South African government has ordered that UNISA, Technikon SA, and VUDEC will merge into a single institution. (Vista's regional face-to-face campuses will be incorporated into one of the local campus-based institutions.) This merger will result in a very large, single national distance education system. It is anticipated there will be significant savings in administrative costs, further savings from economies of scale in course development and implementation, and improvements in stu-

"Open University courses are delivered as an integrated combination of media and methods, each chosen for its unique contribution to the learning experience. It is essential to provide the appropriate balance of media—text, audio, video, interactive simulations, database resources, IT tools and communication environments."

SOURCE: The Learning and Teaching Strategy, the Open University, 2000.
For updated information about the OU's evolving learning and teaching strategy visit: http://www.open.ac.uk/pdg/lto/p3_2.shtml.

dent support as a result of combining regional and local infrastructures. The new single institution to be created by this merger of UNISA, Technikon SA, and VUDEC will be known as the University of South Africa. The merger date is set for 1 January 2004 (http://www.che.ac.za/projects/distance_edu.php). We suggest you visit the Council for Higher Education website to find out about progress (http://www.che.ac.za).

The United Kingdom: The Open University

The British (more correctly, the United Kingdom) Open University (UKOU) is, as you already know, the premier model of distance education in the world. Today, it continues to be one of the largest single mode institutions, with more than 200,000 students. Three-quarters of these study for an undergraduate degree; 26,000 reside outside Great Britain. There are 25,000 graduate students. Since it began teaching in 1971 it has allowed over 2 million people to access higher education through distance education. In line with its original mission, which was to open opportunity for adults who had been denied the chance of entering a conventional university (and thus giving rise to its name), the UK Open University has no prerequisite qualifications for admission. Applicants must only be more than 18 years old and pay a modest tuition fee (about $7,000 for a Baccalaureate degree in 2003). Approximately 70 percent are employed and study on a part-time basis.

Courses of Quality

The UK Open University offers more than 360 courses, mostly at undergraduate level, in arts, social sciences, mathematics, science, education, technology, and in many professional areas. According to the evaluation of the government's Quality Assurance Agency, when compared to all other universities in the country, the OU is rated in the "Excellent" category on 17 of 23 subjects. Although the main focus is on individual students, the OU does work directly with businesses and corporations in meeting staff development needs. There is a large academic research program. Recent additions to the curriculum include a range of new foreign languages and a bachelor's degree in law.

Course Design and Learner Support

The UKOU's administrative center is in the (planned) city of Milton Keynes. This is where all courses are designed and materials produced. Courses are designed by course teams consisting of as many as 20 content, design and media specialists. Full-time academics spend most of their time on these course development teams. For day-to-day instruction, the university depends on part-time tutors. The country is organized into 13 regions each with its regional administrative center, which among other things manages approximately 300 local study centers, monitors instructors, and has immediate oversight of student progress. A tutor's interaction with students may be in local face-to-face tutorials, as well as by correspondence, online communications, or by telephone. This breakdown of the teaching roles is one of the systems principles that helps distinguish the UKOU from traditional higher education providers. The University's first vice chancellor stated the principle succinctly as follows: "the academic staff who created the courses would not necessarily know anything about the problems of adult education, of which many of them had had no previous experience. It was therefore considered vital that the regional tutorial and counseling services should be undertaken by (people) with a long experience of the particular problems involved in that kind of work" (Tait, 2002, p. 155).

Technology

The UKOU's courses are delivered through a wide range of technologies, most commonly study guides written by OU faculty, textbooks, broadcast television and radio programs, computer software, CD-ROMs, audio and videotapes, and home experiment kits. Approximately 40 percent of the courses use new information technologies for online tutorials, discussion groups in "chat rooms," electronic submission of coursework, multimedia teaching materials, and computer mediated conferencing.

The university is home to the Knowledge Media Institute (http://kmi .open.ac.uk), a laboratory for study of new technology housing some 60 researchers, technologists, and designers; and The Institute of Educational Technology (http://iet.open.ac.uk), which undertakes research into the pedagogical aspects of distance education.

For more information on the UK Open University, visit: http://www.open .ac.uk.

Turkey: The World's Largest Distance Teaching University

With 760,859 students (2003), Turkey's Anadolu University (http://www.aof .anadolu.edu.tr) is the world's largest distance teaching university. One in every three students in higher education in Turkey is a student in the Anadolu Open Education system, and more than 550,000 of its students have graduated with a bachelor or associate degree. Students are admitted to Turkey's universities on the basis of results in a standard national examination and Anadolu's Open Education Faculty was established to provide an alternative opportunity for students for whom there were not enough places on residential campuses. With the passage of time, Anadolu, like many other open universities, has become popular with working professional people as a means of continuing education. Anadolu University reaches its students through printed materials, TV courses, face-to-face academic counseling, radio programs, video education centers, newspapers, computer centers, CD-ROMs, and the Internet. Television and radio broadcasting are carried by the state owned Turkish Radio and Television Corporation. All the materials are produced by course design and production teams at the central campus in Eskisehir. Face-to-face sessions are offered in certain courses and videocassettes of these classes are available. In each course a required text is produced to be compatible with television-based instruction. There are no assignments, and assessment is by means of multiple-choice tests. Students may use interactive software in computer laboratories provided by the university in major cities. A counseling center responds to students' questions by phone, e-mail, or fax. Turkey also has a Film, Radio, and Television Education Directorate in its Ministry of National Education, which provides distance education at secondary school level. Beginning with 41,000 students in 1992, there are now more than 600,000 students.

Some Other National Institutions

India

The Indira Gandhi National Open University (http://www.ignou.ac.in) was established in 1985 with two functions; while primarily offering distance education programs leading to certificates, diplomas and degrees, it also coordinates and monitors other distance education institutions throughout the country and provides training programs for their personnel. In 2003 it was reported to have 430,832 students. The instruction and learner support system is organized in 48 regions with 1,135 study centers.

Pakistan

The Allama Iqbal Open University (AIOU) (http://www.aiou.edu.pk/) was created in 1974. Teaching is through correspondence, radio and television broadcasts, special textbooks, and printed study materials, along with part-time tutors and a system of study centers. By 2003 it was the biggest university in the country with around 1 million course enrollments, more than 700 courses, 9 regional campuses, 23 regional study centers, and 1,400 local study centers. Increasingly, traditional technologies are giving way to the satellite and Internet. Among open universities, Allama Iqbal is outstanding in the extent to which it has emphasized nonformal adult education, for improvement of rural literacy and skills needed for employment in rural villages.

Another major thrust of activity in the AIOU's early years was teacher training and teacher continuing education, but this is giving way to such subjects as business administration, computer science, and information technology.

Thailand

The Sukhothai Thammathirat Open University (STOU) (http://www.stou.ac.th/Eng) has some 200,000 students in about 400 courses. 382 of the 1,272 permanent employees are academic staff. A bachelor's degree is normally awarded after a 4-year program. Other programs focus on professional and vocational training and continuing professional education in such areas as education, management, science, and law. Teaching is primarily through study guides and textbooks, tapes, and other materials delivered by the postal service, supported by radio and television programs and local tutorials.

Malaysia

The distance education program of Universiti Sains Malaysia (USM) (http://www.usm.my/en/) was launched in 1971 and was considered experimental until 1982, when it became a permanent part of the university. The distance education program still maintains a separate faculty. USM has enjoyed a government-endorsed monopoly on adult distance education, based on a policy that this is the best way to get a high-cost benefit where financial, infrastructural, and human resources are limited. USM offers degree programs across a range of academic areas to 20,000 enrolled students. A Centre for Educational Technology (CET) produces the print, radio, audio, and videocassette materials. In many courses, students must attend an annual 3-week residential school and there is a requirement to live on campus for the final year of study for the bachelor's degrees.

Germany

The FernUniversitat (http://www.fernuni-hagen.de/) was established in Hagen in 1974 as an institute of higher education of the state of Nordrhein-Westfalen. There are six faculties offering 1,700 courses in 85 subject areas. The student body is around 58,000. The main teaching medium is print, supplemented by audiovisual media. In 2003, a comprehensive "virtual university" was under development. There are 68 study centers where students use study materials and receive tutoring and counseling from one of 470 "mentors." Full-time academic staff number about 500.

The Netherlands

The Open Universiteit of the Netherlands (OU-NL) (http://www.ou.nl) was founded in 1984. It offers degree programs in law, economics, business and public administration, engineering, environmental science, cultural studies, and social science. There are short courses in vocational and postgraduate subjects, developed in cooperation with other universities and professional groups, and a scheme by which students can study from over 300 course modules on a noncredit basis. One of the less common features of OU-NL is that study is self-paced; that is, there is no cohort of students following a prescribed study pattern, as in most open universities. Students can enroll at any time and generally decide for themselves when to take an examination. Learning materials can be downloaded from the university's electronic network, Studienet.

Portugal

The national distance education university is the Universidade Aberta (http://www.univ-ab.pt). Founded in 1988, with headquarters in Lisbon, it has 6 academic departments and some 10,000 students, in undergraduate courses, teacher education and continuing education. All teaching is in Portuguese; the basic delivery technology is print, complemented by recorded audio and video materials, broadcasts, and Internet. There is a small number of graduate students in face-to-face courses and there are plans for putting these courses online.

Spain

Founded in 1972, the Universidad Nacional de Educacion a Distancia (UNED) (http://www.uned.es) in Spain was one of the first open universities, and with around 200,000 students it remains one of the world's major national systems. UNED describes the "keystones" of its teaching methodology as "printed and audiovisual teaching material, tutorial teaching, and an ever-increasing use of new information and communications technologies." The faculties are: Law, Sciences, Economics and Business Administration, Philosophy, Education, Geography and History, Philology, Psychology, Industrial Engineering, and Political and Social Science. There are 75 study centers including 15 overseas, one of which is in Washington, DC. Admission requirements to undergraduate courses are similar to conventional universities, but there is a preparatory program for adults who do not have these prerequisites. Admission to the large teacher education program is open to all practicing teachers.

Canada

The principal distance education institution in Canada is Athabasca University (AU) (http://www.athabascau.ca) in Alberta. Founded in 1970 as one of the first of the single mode universities, AU now has around 26,000 students. It offers around 500 courses in baccalaureate degrees in a dozen major fields as well as a range of certificate and diploma studies, and graduate degrees in several professional fields, including a Masters in Distance Education. Students can enroll year round. Sixty-six percent of students are female. Admission is offered to any person 18 years or older residing in Canada, the United States, or Mexico. Technology takes the form of individualized study packages (student manual, study guide, textbooks, and if appropriate CD-ROM, audiocassettes, and video tapes) and the Internet.

Venezuela

The Universidad Nacional Abierta (UNA) (http://www.una.edu.ve) was founded in 1977 on the lines of other open universities. It has a national center in Caracas and 21 regional centers. Total number of distant learners is about 60,000. It provides over 250 courses in degree programs in various "professional studies." These are in Administration, Education, Engineering, and Mathematics. Before entering the Professional Studies programs, every student must pass an Introductory Course aimed at orienting them to the practice of learning at a distance and a General Studies Course. In addition to the 21 regional centers, 45 study centers provide opportunities for students to consult with full-time counselors, meet in study groups and participate in face to face tutorials. UNA has a declared policy of incorporating Web technology into its delivery system, previously primarily dependent on printed text.

Costa Rica

When it was founded in 1977, the Universidad Estatal a Distancia (UNED) (http://www.uned.ac.cr) in Costa Rica concentrated on developing a series of professional degrees, especially programs for the Ministry of Education for teachers in secondary schools. It is now organized in faculties of Administration, Sciences, Social Science, and Education, as well as Postgraduate Studies. As in most autonomous institutions, especially in developing countries, the basic teaching medium is the printed course. Course texts are written by external authors who are contracted by full-time academic producers. About 80 television programs are produced each year, and around 4 hours are broadcast each week. Tutorials take place at the regional centers, of which there are 22 throughout the country.

Arab States

In the Arab world there are three full-fledged, single mode open universities—in Palestine, Algeria, and Libya—and fifteen dual mode universities.

The *Palestinian* al-Quds Open University (QOU) began teaching in 1991. Set up to meet the needs of Palestinian students in Gaza and the West Bank, the University initially operated out of Amman, and in 1993 moved its headquarters to Jerusalem. It now offers five academic programs at the baccalaureate level. Teaching materials are supported by tutorials in some twenty study centers in the major Palestinian cities. QOU has branches to support Palestinian students in Riyadh and Jeddah in Saudi Arabia and in Dubai and Abu Dhabi in the United Arab Emirates.

In Algeria, the Centre National d'Enseignement Generalise offers general and technical education to baccalaureate level, and specialist professional training. Courses are offered through print, audio- and videocassettes, radio, telephone, and group study. Some 100,000 students are enrolled.

In one of the poorest countries of the world, the Sudan Open Learning Organisation (SOLO) has operated since 1984 to provide educational programs in Somalia, Ethiopia, and Sudan, including basic adult education to refugees from civil war. It offers a literacy program, a primary health care program, income generating and small business skills for women, and training courses for basic level teachers employed in the refugee schools.

In Saudi Arabia, where tradition requires men and women to study in separate environments, distance education enables women to engage in higher education by studying at home (Al-Rawaf and Simmons, 1992). Some universities use closed-circuit video to transmit lectures simultaneously to both genders, without which "thousands and thousands of girls in Saudi Arabia would not have the chance to pursue their higher education studies" (Alsunbul, 2002, p. 59).

An ambitious multinational Arab Open University (http://www.arabou .org) has recently been established, with headquarters in Kuwait and participation by Kuwait, Bahrain, Egypt, Jordan, Lebanon, and Saudi Arabia, with the possibility of other countries to follow. The university offers BA and BS degrees in business studies, computer studies, education, and languages. The AOU is affiliated with the UKOU for purposes of licensing of materials, consultancies, accreditation, and validation of its programs.

A growing number of conventional universities in the Arab Gulf Region have started to use electronic course management systems to extend their face-to-face teaching. For example, Oman's Sultan Qaboos University and Bahrain University are using WebCT, while Zaid University in the United Arab Emirates has launched an online course titled "Study Skills" using Blackboard. With this exception, these universities do not yet conduct courses fully at a distance, but local innovators believe this will happen as confidence grows in the method.

Consortia and Virtual Systems in Some Other Countries

Just as consortia are important in United States, so has this alternative to establishing single mode national distance education systems been preferred by a number of other countries. Here are some examples.

In France, the National Centre for Distance Learning (CNED) (http://www .cned.fr) was created in 1939 when war broke out in Europe, to cater for the needs of young refugees. The CNED is the distance education provider for the Ministry of Education. It comprises a central directorate, eight institutes, and a center for training staff in professional skills for distance education. The 350,000 students taking CNED courses include 37,000 in more than 200 foreign countries. Courses range from preschool to higher education; there are over 500 complete training programs and 3,000 modules. CNED provides the infrastructure for delivery of the courses that are developed in collaboration with more than 50 universities. Among recent developments is the Campus Electronique on the Internet.

Italy's Consorzio Per L'Universita a Distanza (CUD) was founded in 1984 as a consortium for designing learning materials and providing student support services for students who register with those Italian universities, corporations, and governmental organizations that were members of the consortium. The first programs were in informatics and modern languages (both 3-year part-time diplomas), a 4-year full-time degree in economics, and continuing education courses for school teachers. For enrollment in undergraduate level courses, standard university entrance requirements apply. The part-time student's workload is estimated at 20 hours a week, with one-third spent at a study center. In 2003 the status of CUD was not clear, specifically in relation to a new and larger consortium called Nettuno (http://uninettuno.it). This has a larger membership than CUD with a heavy technology bias, with courses broadcast on satellite channels, "280 courses produced by the Nettuno network, for a total of 14,000 hours of university video lessons" supported by "didactic books, workbooks, multimedia software and products and didactic Internet web sites linked to the video lesson" (see http://www.open.ac.uk/pdg/lto/p3_2.shtml). Courses are in engineering, social psychology, informatics, business, and economics.

The Irish National Distance Education Centre (OSCAIL) (http://www.oscail.ie) was established in 1982. Its remit is to work cooperatively with universities and colleges throughout the country in developing a coherent national distance education program. Courses have been developed by course teams made up of members from the various cooperating institutions. The Centre offers baccalaureate degrees and diplomas in Arts, Information Technology, Internet Systems, Operations, and Nursing Studies, as well as graduate qualifications in several Management disciplines. The total number of students is in the region of 3,500. The main teaching medium has been a printed text, supplemented by recorded audio and video materials, but in new course development there is a strong emphasis on "e-learning."

In Canada, "Contact North" is The Northern Ontario Education Access Network. In 1986 the Ontario government granted $16 million, to set up a network of primarily video and audio conference facilities for the delivery of programs to mostly isolated rural communities in northern Ontario. Working through coordinating centers in colleges and universities, Contact North enables any nonprofit group to deliver courses using print, audio and video media, teleconferencing, and computer communications. The Network has been used, for example, to provide a degree program in nursing and others in public administration, forestry, and teacher upgrading. More than 320 courses were included in the 2003 calendar of offerings. There are now 145 distance education and training centers, in over 100 communities serving about 13,000 enrolled students (http://www.cnorth.edu.on.ca).

In Mexico, the Universidad Virtual of the Systema Tecnologico de Monterrey (http://www.ruv.itesm.mx/) is an extension of the Monterrey

Institute of Technology. In the late 1980s, "Monterrey Tech" became heavily committed to using satellite video technology, and continues to provide programs in this medium across Mexico and abroad. The Universidad Virtual specifically targets overseas markets with its graduate courses in engineering and technology and in education, with some programs delivered in about 10 other Latin American countries. Although the Internet is now also used, there are still over 1,000 satellite downlink sites in Mexico itself and over 100 overseas. While the parent institution has some 80,000 students with a large proportion in undergraduate education, the Universidad Virtual has an enrollment of some 50,000 students with nearly half in the "business channel" and only a small number of undergraduate students.

Mexico's Telesecundaria Project (http://www.telesecundaria.mx) is a broadcast television system that was started in 1968 to provide courses for rural high school students. In 2002 its enrollment was 1,022,901 students in over 1600 schools. It had 23,000 students enrolled in Costa Rica, the Dominican Republic, El Salvador, Guatemala, Honduras, and Panama. The system broadcasts a 15-minute lesson followed by a structured 35-minute local teacher–student discussion. There is a 10-minute break between each lesson session and the next broadcast. A rural community can initiate a new Telesecundaria program by enrolling a minimum of 15 primary school-leavers and providing a place to study. The Education Ministry provides a teacher, a television, decoder and satellite dish, the broadcasts, written materials and training for the teacher. The learning materials are supplied free of charge to students and include a study guide for each lesson. The study guide includes activities designed to help students synthesize and apply new knowledge. Teachers are also supplied with a teacher's guide and receive training via the same broadcast system. The programs are broadcast twice each day to accommodate a morning stream and an afternoon stream (as is quite common in developing countries where school places are scarce). Although Telesecundaria is usually thought of as a teacher-supported program, it can just as easily be described as a distance education program in which the local, poorly qualified teacher provides the learner support and tutorial functions.

Africa

Sub–Saharan Africa is where both the "knowledge gap" between rich nations of the (mainly) northern hemisphere and poor nations of the (mainly) southern hemisphere are most obvious. Here, distance education is mainly used to widen access to basic education and to improve quality in the conventional school system through in-service training of teachers and then by supporting teaching in schools. It is also used to supplement very limited opportunities for higher education. Correspondence education has been the main medium of instruction, with radio also widely used. Radio transmitters reach over 60 percent of the population, whereas television coverage, like other technologies, is usually confined to major towns (UNESCO, 1999). Internet technolo-

The Global Digital Divide[1]

- The United States has more computers than the rest of the world combined.
- 80 percent of Web sites are in English—less than 1 percent of the world's population reads English.
- A personal computer costs about a month's salary in the United States—it costs eight years of salary in Bangladesh.

[1]One word of caution is necessary, however; most data related to technological innovation must be considered indicative of the situation rather than exact; it is often impossible to acquire precise information, and even where this exists, the picture changes very quickly. The statistic cited in the panel regarding the proportion of websites in English has changed since the data was gathered for the 1999 report. We urge students to visit the UNDP Web site and similar sites to ascertain more up-to-date information.

SOURCE: United Nations Development Program: 1999 Human Development Report, p. 62. See http://www.undp.org/hdro/report.html.

gies have been of limited value in a region in which the availability of telephone lines is about five times lower than the average low-income country and where they are concentrated in urban, relatively privileged, areas. Estimates for the number of personal computers in Africa in put the average at about 3 per 1,000 people. Some of the wealthier countries such as Botswana, Mauritius, and South Africa have higher levels of penetration, at least 5 per 1000 (Jensen, 1999). In 1996, only 11 countries had Internet access even in the cities, but by 1999 only the Republic of Congo (Brazzaville), Eritrea, and Somalia were still without urban Internet service (see http://www.bellanet.org/partners/aisi/nici/nici%20indicators.htm).

It is not possible to mention every country in Africa, so the following cases have been chosen to illustrate the general picture.

In *Tanzania* (http://www.saide.org.za/worldbank/countries/tanzania/tanoverview.htm), distance education is co-coordinated through The Distance Education Association of Tanzania (DEATA), a national association established in December 1992. Its membership includes the Ministry of Education and Culture, the Open University of Tanzania, the University of Dar Es Salaam, the Vocational Education and Training Authority, the Muhimbili University College for Health Sciences, the Southern African Extension Unit, the Institute of Adult Education, and the Cooperative College Moshi. Between them these organizations enroll over 18,000 students. In addition to higher education courses, programs have been offered to Burundian refugees, for training local councillors, and offering various programs of civic education.

The Open University of Tanzania (OUT) is the only successful single mode distance teaching university south of the Sahara, outside the Republic of South Africa. OUT was established in 1993 to provide the people of Tanzania (among the poorest of the countries in Africa) a "second chance" to obtain higher education, since only about one-third of Tanzanians with the qualifications for university admission were able to obtain a place in the conventional face-to-face universities. The OUT provides degree and non-degree programs in arts and social sciences; education, science, technology, and environmental studies; and educational technology. Two of its degrees are intended mainly for teachers. By 1998 OUT enrolled approximately 6,000 students. Though print is used as the basic technology of communication, other technologies including motion pictures, audio-systems, satellite video and radio, and new digital technologies are being experimented with. There are 21 regional centers each having a resident tutor. Smaller units are established in the local districts where students organize their own study groups. During the first seven years of operations, OUT has made it a priority to cooperate with other educational institutions both in and outside of Tanzania, especially focusing on developing a national library network, science laboratories, and information services.

In *Botswana* (http://www.saide.org.za/worldbank/countries/botswana .htm), the flagship distance education provider is the Botswana College of Distance and Open Learning (BOCODOL). BOCODOL offers courses for the Junior Certificate, which is the culminating qualification in basic education, constituting ten years of formal schooling. BOCODOL also offers distance education courses for the General Certificate in Secondary Education (GCSE). BOCODOL has been charged with offering school equivalence programs and additional vocational and non-formal courses for adults and youth. It uses printed materials, which are distributed in the post; regional offices are used as study centers for students to meet tutors. Some counseling and advice services are available, and there is a weekly 30-minute slot on national radio.

Malawi (http://www.saide.org.za/worldbank/countries/malawi.htm) has two established dedicated distance education providers, one a private school and the other a department of the Ministry of Education, Sports and Culture. MIITEP, an in-service program run by the Teacher Development Unit, trains underqualified teachers. International providers, such as the Rapid Results College, have also operated in Malawi for many decades. Institutions developing plans include the University of Malawi, the newly established Mzuzu University, and the Domasi College of Education, which plans to offer a Diploma in Education through distance education.

In *Zimbabwe* (http://www.saide.org.za/worldbank/countries/zimbabwe/zimoverview.htm), the Centre for Distance Education was established by the University of Zimbabwe in 1993, and in 1999 was transformed into the Zimbabwe Open University. The University offers programs leading to Bachelors degrees in Education, a BA in English and Communication Studies a B.Sc in Agriculture and Undergraduate Diploma in Classroom Text and Discourse (DCTD).

In *Namibia,* a semigovernmental agency, the Namibian College of Open Learning (NAMCOL), was set up in the Ministry of Education and Culture in 1997. Its goal is to provide access to out-of-school youth and adults who want to complete their secondary school studies. NAMCOL provides a Certificate of Education for Development (CED), which targets community development officers, adult educators, and extension workers from various Ministries. NAMCOL mainly uses printed textual materials, audiocassettes, and radio broadcasts. For the CED program course, materials were adapted from UNISA course materials. Student support entails one week's face-to-face orientations every year and exam preparation towards the end of the academic year plus occasional workshops. There are plans for telephone tutorials between regional centers and the local study centers (Nyirenda et al., 1999).

Distance Education, International Agencies, and National Development

Poor countries are poor not only because they don't have enough capital—machinery, roads, telecommunications and other productive capacity—but also because they don't have as much knowledge as richer countries or the resources to create knowledge, such as schools and well-qualified teachers. A major challenge for developing countries is to obtain knowledge. The relationship between knowledge and economic development has been well-documented by organizations like the World Bank.

For instance, in its 1999 report, the World Bank gave as an example the role played by knowledge in the development of Korea, one of the countries we looked at earlier in this chapter. According to a World Bank report (1999): "Forty years ago Ghana and the Republic of Korea had virtually the same income per capita. By the early 1990s Korea's income per capita was six times higher than Ghana's. Some reckon that half the difference is due to Korea's greater success in acquiring and using knowledge." More generally, the World Bank report continues: "[S]tarting as low income economies in the 1960's, a few economies in East Asia managed in a few decades to bridge all or nearly all of the income gap that separated them from the high income economies of the Organization for Economic Co-Operation and Development (OECD). Meanwhile many other developing countries stagnated. What made the difference? Comparative studies indicate it was not growth in land, or in the labor force; there were investments in heavy capital and in education, but so were there in other economies where similar growth did not occur. . . . Perhaps the difference was that the East Asian economies did not build, work, and grow harder, as much as they built, worked and grew smarter. It is working smarter that leads to growth in productivity. A study that analysed variations in growth rates across a large number of countries showed that the accumulation of physical capital explained less than 30% of those variations. The rest was attributed to intangible factors . . . the most important among which is knowledge" (p. 19).

The World Bank emphasizes the importance of technical knowledge. This is knowledge of information, facts, and skills that people can apply in economically productive ways. Examples of technical knowledge are nutrition, software engineering, and accountancy. The Bank states: "Typically developing countries have less of this know-how than industrial countries and the poor have less than the non-poor" (p. 1). Closing such knowledge gaps is not easy, since developing countries and poorer regions—indeed, poorer individuals—pursue a moving target, as the high-income countries push the knowledge frontier further outward. It is the countries, regions, and individuals with the greatest technical knowledge that have the knowledge investment necessary to make more knowledge. They can use knowledge to make knowledge; as they ask and answer new questions; pose and solve previously unrecognized problems; and create new ideas, theories, and concepts. Some rather old data from the European Commission (1991) showed that high income economies spent twice as much on research and development as did the Asian economies and 200 times that of the poorest countries. As a strategy for tackling this gap in knowledge and all that it implies in terms of economic development, the World Bank proposes that "poorer countries have the option of acquiring and adapting much knowledge already available in the richer countries. With communications costs plummeting, transferring knowledge is cheaper than ever" (World Bank, 1999, p. 2). Delivery of information and generation of knowledge through distance education is a key part of this strategy.

UNESCO

A report from the United Nations Educational, Science and Cultural Organization (UNESCO)'s Division of Higher Education suggests policies and strategies to help developing countries make the best use of culturally-relevant and affordable information and communication technologies (ICTs). UNESCO argues that because of lack of resources, demographic trends, and the HIV/AIDS pandemic, it is no longer realistic to expect traditional educational structures to provide an adequate basis for knowledge development in poor countries. In efforts to meet the new and changing demands for education and training, distance learning should be seen as a complementary approach, which under certain circumstances, says UNESCO, can be an appropriate substitute.

The paper highlights ongoing UNESCO initiatives, including:

- encouraging partnerships between business, professional bodies, and distance teaching institutions
- focusing on the special needs of people with disabilities, migrants, minorities, and refugees
- supporting distance learning for in-service teacher training and for training of trainers

- cooperating with international and regional development banks, private and public sector partners, and non-governmental organizations

UNESCO calls on policy-makers to join its efforts to:

- generate public interest in distance learning and make decision makers aware of its potential
- undertake cost studies which do not simply compare the costs of single mode distance-learning with that of conventional systems, but also take into account the broader qualitative and social benefits that distance learning can bring to marginalized people and to workers whose skills are upgraded
- balance funding for distance education within general education expenditure—taking care to remedy any unjustified economic discrimination between distance learners and other students
- critically examine the common assumption that students in open and distance learning can afford to pay a higher proportion of the costs than conventional students increase access to learning and training and provide increased opportunities for updating, retraining and personal enrichment (UNESCO, 2002a).

In 2002, UNESCO's Institute for Information Technologies in Education (IITE) designed a special course "Information and Communications Technologies in Distance Education" for training policy makers and practitioners in distance education in developing and emerging economies. The course was offered in Tanzania in 2002 and South Africa in 2003. For further information, see: http://www.iite.ru/iite/publications/publications?id=48.

The World Bank

The World Bank was created in 1944 to help countries build up their economic and technological infrastructures and fight poverty. It has always focused on improving countries' educational systems as a way of achieving its goals, and it has also run training programs itself, through a training department called the World Bank Institute (WBI). In recent years it was agreed that the has been decided that the WBI approach was no longer cost effective since it required experts to be flown around the world to set up classes, and even then it was not able to teach more than 40 people at a time, so although the Bank was spending a lot of money on transportation and living expenses, it was reaching only a small number of people. As an alternative, around 1996, Bank officials began to focus on distance education, and in the next 2 or 3 years they spent some $20 million to get a distance-education program started. The main technology was satellite delivered, interactive video-conferencing. In the first phase the Bank set up some 20 study "distance learning centers" in different developing countries and signed agreements with some 200 universities and other institutions to provide content for courses enrolling as many as 150 students each. What is now called the Global Development Learning Network gives certificates of completion in each of the 70 courses and seminars it offers. The Bank delivers its courses to its distance learning centers, which have cameras, computers, satellite equipment, and Internet capabilities. These centers are owned and operated locally. For more on the World Bank's Global Development Learning Network, see Foley (2003).

The World Bank has another project, called the Global Distance Education Network, which is part of its knowledge dissemination strategy. It is managed in partnership with the Vancouver-based Commonwealth of Learning and consists of a carefully selected set of resources chosen for use by practitioners and policy makers involved in distance education in developing countries. It includes readings and other resources assembled by teams in countries in Asia, Latin America, and Africa—as well as North America—organized in blocs that deal with technology, pedagogy, management, and policy. For more information see: http: http://www1.worldbank.org/disted/.

The African Virtual University

One of the most high profile World Bank projects in distance education is the African Virtual University (AVU) (http://www.avu.org/). The idea for the AVU arose in 1995, and it started offering courses in 1997. The AVU provides satellite/technology-based distance education through public and private tertiary education institutions in sub-Saharan Africa in the disciplines of science and engineering. AVU offers a mixed package of programs (video transmission of lectures using digital compression technology from teleports in the United States, Ireland, France, Belgium, and Switzerland), courses online, and other asynchronous conferencing facilities (e.g., e-mail, exercise, exam questions, access to libraries, etc.). A satellite capacity was obtained from Intelsat; the installation of equipment at the participating African universities was completed in the first half of 1997. In 2000, the World Bank made the African Virtual University an independent nonprofit institution. The university now operates 25 centers in 14 countries and has taught more than 12,000 students on topics ranging from computer science to business journalism (see http://www.worldbank.org/html/emc/documents/afvirtual.html).

Experience with projects such as the African Virtual University project has underscored a number of important challenges that must be faced regarding distance education between developed and developing countries. In particular, when teaching spans cultures, especially when the delivery medium is synchronous, making the presentation relevant for foreign communities is a challenging problem. There are technical problems also. Satellite broadcast time is expensive and the benefits are limited by the number of students that can be present at the specific times of the broadcast and the numbers of students that can be accommodated according to the size of the receiving sites. Critics have pointed to the AVU as an example of an approach to education for development in which a technological solution (i.e., satellite broadcasting), was allowed to determine answers to problems that might have been answered bet-

Viewpoint: Michael Foley

One of the growing areas for the use of distance education is its application to ensuring the effective implementation of aid projects in developing countries, many of which suffer from a lack of capacity on the part of the implementing teams. But it will not be distance education as we know it in the traditional sense. Distance learning methods and technologies will be used, not only for education and training, but as a way to integrate learning with performance on the job in implementing aid programs. The new emphasis will be on designing activities such as: knowledge sharing, knowledge management, action learning, team learning (as distinct from individual learning for diplomas), performance support, "just-in-time" learning. These learning programs will move beyond the setting of learning objectives to attempting to reach practical performance outcomes for teams of development practitioners. Much of the knowledge will not be provided by experts in training and education institutions. It will be provided by those who have direct experience of implementing similar programs, shared in "south-to-south" dialogues, using a variety of technologies as they emerge. The aim will be to mine the implicit knowledge of practitioners rather than the explicit knowledge of the textbook, through a process of storytelling and the building of communities of practice.

SOURCE: Michael Foley, Lead Distance Learning Specialist, The World Bank, Washington DC.

ter if the leaders of the initiative were more pedagogically astute and less technically driven. It remains an open question whether using technology to replicate classroom pedagogy is as cost effective as investing the same money in courses delivered in methods closer to the independent study tradition.

For a discussion of these and other issues related to globalization and international distance education, see Mason (2003), Visser (2003), Gunawardena et al. (2003), and Evans and Nation (2003).

Summary

- Distance education is found in some form in every country of the world. All countries are interested in applying new technology, but all less developed countries rely heavily on print, radio, and to some extent, television as the main forms of communication.
- Many countries have set up national open universities on the pattern of the UK Open University, in which systems principles are applied to achieve the most cost-effective delivery of distance education programs.

- Many other countries are developing cooperative arrangements among a number of institutions, into consortia and virtual systems.

- The sophistication of the distance education delivery systems is closely related to the wealth of the country, with the weakest systems in sub–Saharan Africa (except for the Republic of South Africa). Some of the largest systems are in Asia.

- Cases in the chapter are only examples; readers should not underestimate the importance of countries not mentioned.

- One of the biggest problems facing the world is to bridge the gap in knowledge and knowledge creation between wealthy countries and poorer countries, since this gap reinforces economic inequality which in turn has an effect on disaffection and political instability.

- The international agencies are increasingly involved in distance education; examples given are the World Bank and UNESCO.

Questions for Discussion or Further Study

1. Chose a country from the African list and find out what distance education programs are offered. Compare the organizational structures—the procedures used to design and delivery courses—with those in the American institution you know best.

2. If you had the opportunity of advising the ministry of education in the African country about developing its distance education programs, what changes would you suggest, if any?

3. Research online the World Bank and UNESCO and make a list of some of their programs related to distance education. Try to find one or more other international agencies that use distance education. What is your assessment of the appropriateness of their programs for their mission?

4. Visit the World Bank's Global Distance Education Network and browse some of the resources at the South African and Hong Kong sites.

5. Discuss the viewpoint of Michael Foley.

CHAPTER 12

Distance Education
Is about Change

The beginning of the new millennium has been described variously as an Information Age, a Digital Age, or a Knowledge Society. Global changes are—to a significant extent—the result of changes in technology. We have arrived at a point in history where these technological developments as well as economic, demographic, and pedagogic trends converge and reinforce each other to provide momentum for an accelerated rate of change in the years ahead. We will close our study in this book with brief discussions of some of these issues—some of which will be reflecting earlier discussions—before we leave you to your own dreams about where the field is going—and the part you will play in taking it there.

The Changing Supply of Information

Although we are accustomed to talking about the "information explosion," few people know what this means in quantifiable terms. At the University of California-Berkeley School of Information Management and Systems researchers have tried to calculate how much information is being produced. They tell us it is between 1 and 2 exabytes of new information per year; an exabyte being a billion gigabytes, or 10^{18} bytes. This is roughly 250 megabytes for every man, woman, and child on earth. Each letter of the English alphabet and each number takes eight bits, so it looks as if every person on earth is producing the equivalent of about 15,000 pages of typed manuscript every year. There is not really that much manuscript, because new information includes visual images, which use a lot more data than does text. But by using a familiar medium we can understand that the volume of new information is vast. Of this information, about 25 percent of all the textual information, about 30 percent of the photographic information, and about 50 percent of the content stored on magnetic media are produced in the United States. Most of this information is stored magnetically, and the capacity of our computer hard drives to store it is doubling every year, while the cost is falling; at the end of 2000 a gigabyte of storage cost $10 and is predicted to drop to $1 by 2005.

The UC-Berkeley researchers comment on two striking facts emerging from their estimates:

1. The first is the "paucity of print." Printed material of all kinds makes up less than .003 percent of the total storage of information. Most information is now digital and it is information in digital form that is the most rapidly growing. While content on print and film is hardly growing at all, optical and digital magnetic storage shipments are doubling each year. Most textual information is "born digital," and within a few years this will be true for images as well. Digital information is inexpensive to copy and distribute, is searchable, and is malleable.

2. The second striking fact is the "democratization of data." Roughly 55 percent of hard drives are installed in personal computers. Whereas just a few years ago the average person could only create a very small amount of information, now ordinary people not only have access to huge amounts of information, but are also able to create gigabytes of data themselves and publish it to the world via the Internet. Some indication of how the world is changing in regard to the origination of information can be gathered from the estimate of e-mail exchanges— some 610 billion e-mails being sent each year (see http://www.sims .berkeley.edu/research/projects/how-much-info/summary.html).

Changing Access to Information

It is of course the availability of the Internet and the use of the World Wide Web for accessing and sharing information that has been driving educators in the direction of distance education. At any given time it is impossible to say exactly how many people are able to access the Internet. One estimate (March 2004) indicates there are 800 million people online (see http://global-reach .biz/globstats/index.php3). By some estimates, about 50 percent of the U.S. population has access to the Internet, but most still do not have access to broadband delivery. Broadband technology is essential to take advantage of the vast volume of information in storage, with emerging technology enabling transmission of the equivalent of 90,000 sets of encyclopedias per second. Access can be expected to accelerate worldwide as cost continues to fall. By some estimates, a dollar's worth of bandwidth needed to send data in the mid-1970s would buy twice as much in 1980, 30 times as much in 1990, 200 times as much in 1995, and nearly 1,000 times as much in 2000.

There are about 2 billion static Web pages and the number is doubling every year. Most Web sites are in the English language (35.8% percent); other European languages make up 37.9 percent of users, and Asian languages 33 percent. The proportion of sites originating in English is falling, from about 70 percent in 1998 to about 66 percent in 1999, and from 40.2 percent in 2002. (http://global-reach.biz/globstats/index.php3). It is informative to compare the geographical distribution of providers and users of content on these Web sites (see Table 12.1).

One of the most obvious conclusions we can make from the data in Table 12.1 is that half of all people on the Web are reading North American content, and half the people accessing information on the Web are in North America. The cultural and political implications of this should be cause for your reflection, analysis, and perhaps research. Because the picture regarding Web usage changes so quickly we recommend you visit the sites mentioned here to check on the latest statistics.

Changes in Relation of Knowledge to Economic Development

Technology, however, isn't the only factor driving change; economics does as well. At the same time as the cost of electronically processing, storing, and transmitting information has been falling, the cost of conventional education and training has been rising. And this is when the need to continue learning for effective employability in the "information age," coupled with an aging of the labor force, has led to an increase in demand for new ways of accessing knowledge.

At the national level, access to information and the skills needed to convert that information into knowledge has become the key driver of economic development, social development, personal development, and, some would say, political development, too. We have quickly become accustomed to speak of knowledge industries, knowledge systems, knowledge tools and knowledge workers—all important resources for helping people organize and employ an exponentially expanding volume of information.

One of the most immediate results of this explosion of information is that the *information part* of what we know becomes out of date very quickly and must either be replaced with new information, or at least will need frequent "topping up." Half of what has been learned by the student of engineering, for example, is out of date 18 months after graduation; every doctor is challenged to keep up with the flow of new information from the research laboratories, brokered as it often is through vendors of pharmaceuticals; consider how assiduously new information is sought in fields such as competitive sports or the production of movies and popular music. One effect of this continuous expansion of information is that the process of turning information into knowledge—that is, learning—must also be continuous. Education is no longer a process of acquiring knowledge in preparation for life and work, but a process of first preparing and then "repairing" knowledge throughout the life span. The fastest-growing job categories (managerial, professional, and technical) that account for 28 percent of new job openings in the United States are the

Table 12.1   Users and Providers of Information on the World Wide Web

Region	Users (Percent of Total)	Content Providers (Percent of Total)
Africa	0.9	0.5
Asia/Pacific	16.7	10.1
Europe	23.5	25.2
Middle East	0.4	0.4
Canada and United States	55.9	59.5
Latin America	2.6	4.2

SOURCE: http://www.nua.ie/surveys/how_many_online/index.html.

most in need of continuing education. The trend is towards a population of older workers and older learners too. Whereas in 1975 half the U.S. workforce was aged 16 to 34 (and what they recently learned in school was fairly relevant to their adult tasks), by 2005, as the volume of new information continues to expand, half the workforce is expected to be between 33 and 55 years of age, with 53 million people older than 55 years. Responding to the information explosion, half the U.S. adult population has engaged in some formal learning activity, whether it is a training session at work, a community-based adult education program, or a formal degree or certificate program. More than half of these had a bachelor's degree (see http://nces.ed.gov/pubs2000/coe2000/section1/indicator10.html).

Clearly, some of the developments we have discussed in this book have been in response to these pressures for more continuing education and training for older, well-educated adults. As we have seen throughout this book, educational institutions are no longer simply *places* where young people come to prepare for work and adult life, but now they are also providers of continuing education *services,* made accessible to students who must continue to fulfill all the other responsibilities of adult life. Some of this adult, continuing education can, it is true, be provided in traditional residential and other face-to-face situations, but in future the majority of such learning will occur, inevitably, through distance education.

The data already points in this direction. One survey concluded that among adults who accessed the Web in the United States, one-fifth participated in some sort of online learning program, be it training for work, a graduate-level university course, or preparation for standardized tests. Traffic to Web sites serving adult learners increased by 60 percent between 1997 and 2002. Visitors to these sites spend more time online than the average Internet user, an average of 15.3 hours per week compared with 11.5 hours (http://www.medialifemagazine.com/news2002/feb02/feb18/3_wed/news5wednesday.html). By 1998 nearly all Fortune 1000 companies were already offering some type of online training, with much of the delivery through their own "corporate universities" (Meister, 2000).

Changes in Technology

When we wrote the final chapter of the first edition of this book we included some predictions about the technology that would impact on distance education. Among our projections were:

1. "The most significant development in the late 1990s is ISDN . . . enabling transmission of multi-media communications."
2. "Computers are . . . likely to replace telephones as the primary communications device for learning and teaching."
3. ". . . cost or lack of awareness . . . could lead to a severe deterioration of the under-class of already illiterate. . . ."
4. ". . . automated video-conferencing will become more popular."
5. ". . . cellular telephone service will become ubiquitous."
6. ". . . storage capacity for computers will continue to offer more capacity for less money."
7. "If every person owned a computer (preferably handheld) that contained a CD-ROM drive, we would have a very satisfactory technology for learning."

Although we were not too wrong in our expectations about the growth of the major trends, there were other developments. Some of these technological developments since the first edition of this book are shown in Table 12.2.

The effect of these technological developments on education have been dramatic in some ways, disappointing in others. As we have noted many times, Web technology has been adopted widely for both distance and traditional forms of education, but so far it has done little to change the balance of investment in distance education compared to traditional, or indeed to change the ratio of capital to labor (i.e., the technology has had only a marginal effect on the number of students served by each teacher). Most instructional programming is limited to text and simple graphics, with interaction by e-mail and its derivatives (electronic fora, bulletin boards, chat rooms). There remains considerable interest in "room-based" or desktop-based video-conferencing, usually with relatively small groups involved and low production values, but the quality of instruction has not been enhanced by the integration of high-quality audio and video presentation delivered on the Web. It is not only narrow bandwidth and high telecommunications costs that limit the use of streaming video and audio of good quality on a large scale, but the failure of educational institutions to invest in developing programs for delivery by these media. We can hope that in the fairly near future, as high-speed access to the World Wide Web becomes more generally available, course designers will be given more opportunity to offer a richer variety of media with much higher quality video and audio programming. These will include multipoint full-motion video-conferencing, broadcast television-quality netcasting, and high-resolution image transfer.

Table 12.2   Technological Developments since the First Edition

- Internet, broadband, high speed access achieves mass market
- Rich multimedia presentations are delivered by broadband and CD-ROM
- Widespread adoption of DVD players and recorders
- Real-time streaming audio and video
- USB memory sticks
- Online data storage
- Wireless internet and home networks (e.g. Bluetooth)
- Online gaming and games designed for Java-enabled mobiles
- Growth of games consoles
- MP3 music and MP3 players
- Interactive digital television
- Video on demand and wide-screen monitors
- Digital cameras and Web cameras
- Handheld computers, thin laptops, flat-screen monitors
- E-mail taking over from surface post
- Text messaging, picture messaging, video-phones

SOURCE: British Telecommunications. For further information visit: http://www.btexact.com.

What Technological Changes Lie Ahead?

Instead of trying to predict the future in the area of technology ourselves, we are going to point you to a source that is more authoritative in this regard. Futurists at one of the world's major telecommunications companies make regular forecasts and we have reproduced a few of the predictions that seem to be of greatest interest to educators in Table 12.3.

Does Technology Add Value and If So, What Is It?

It was reported in 2004 that the Virginia Polytechnic Institute and State University (Virginia Tech) has built a mini-supercomputer called Beowulf, which is the second most powerful supercomputer on the planet. It has the power of 1,100 dual-processor Macintosh G5 computers (hence 2,200 parallel processors). It has been said that the Beowulf represents a breakthrough in constructing huge computing power at a low cost, because it was built entirely from off-the-shelf components. It cost a bargain-basement price—only $5.2 million; compare that with the cost of $40 million for most supercomputers, up to the $350 million price tag for the Earth Simulator. Beowulf, so it is claimed, points the way for research groups, high schools, colleges or small business to build or buy their own low-cost clusters, realizing the promise of a supercomputer in every basement (see: http://www.wired.com/news/technology/0,1282,60821,00.html).

Table 12.3   **Some Predicted Technological Developments (with Suggested Dates)**

- Tactile sensors comparable to human sensation (2004)
- Full voice interaction with machine (2005)
- Voice synthesis quality up to human standard (2005)
- TV Internet users overtake computer-based users (2005)
- Emotionally responsive toys and robots (2006)
- "Smelly TV" using chips with small reservoirs of chemicals (2010)
- 3D TV without need for special glasses (2012)
- Holographic displays for continuous video (2015)
- 3D video conferencing (2015)
- 85 percent of American management personnel are knowledge workers (2005)
- 80 percent of U.S. homes have PCs (2005)
- Third World teleworkers use clockwork PCs (2005)
- Virtual reality used to teach science, geography, art and history (2005)
- 95 percent of people in advanced nations are computer literate (2010)
- Artificial Intelligence (AI) entity gains bachelor's degree (2013)
- AI entity gains Ph.D. (2016)
- Learning is superseded by transparent interface to smart computers (2025)

SOURCE: British Telecommunications, BTexact. For more information visit: http://www.btexact.com.

We have, of course, heard extravagant claims for particular technologies before and this may or may not be one of them. But the question we want you to think about when you read about technological breakthroughs like this is *so what?* What value if any, can this technology, and the others suggested in this chapter, add to distance education? The example of technological power of cable television, which provides some cities with hundreds of channels to deliver hundreds of equally mediocre programs, reminds us to keep at the forefront the imperative need for investment in the Beowulf kind of super technology to be equaled, we repeat *equaled,* by investment in the quality of designing instructional programs and supporting their teaching. Otherwise, from an educator's perspective, the technology has little or no value. In future, as we are offered new technology, how do we evaluate its potential value? Addressing this question, adult educator Liz Burge recommended McLuhan's four Laws of Media, converted into questions in the following way:

- What does it (the technology) enhance or intensify?
- What does it render obsolete or displace?
- What does it retrieve that was previously [made obsolete]?
- What does it produce or become when [pushed] to an extreme? (McLuhan and McLuhan, 1988, p. 7)

Commenting on the first of these, Burge (2001) offered a point of view we would recommend to you:

> When the functions of any new technology don't create drastic changes in the fundamentals of good learning and teaching, i.e., the technology effectively enhances or amplifies my practice, I am driven back to reflecting on the generic principles that support adults' learning and then figure out how and where the technology fits. (p. 3)"

Going back to basic principles as preparation for deciding where technology fits is exactly the perspective on the relation of technology to pedagogy/andragogy that we have attempted to reflect consistently in this book. If you think about the value added to distance education by arrival of the Internet, you might agree it does little to change "the fundamentals of good learning and teaching" but you might also agree that it has proven a valuable way of enhancing distance learning in those programs in which the generic principle of respect for learner's propensity for constructing knowledge is attached to the technological power of the browser to enable learners to access a vastly greater wealth of information than was previously available.

We suggest that the other three questions just listed should be equally helpful when facing difficult personal and professional decisions about adopting new technology. First, consider what will be "displaced"—not only by technological hardware; but software too, and remember that often, perfectly good teaching materials and methods have been pushed aside in the rush of enthusiasm for something new, the attraction being merely the novelty, not the usefulness. To return to the Internet example, the wonderfully rich learner-to-learner interactivity generated in well-managed audio-conferences has been widely abandoned as administrators have pushed to justify their investments in online technology. As bandwidth problems are overcome, we should certainly consider whether the next generation of technology might help us "retrieve" the benefits of real-time interstudent discussions. Consider lastly the *unintended* effects of adopting each new technology; for example, the deterioration in the quality of video production that is partly a result of the spread of cheap personal video cameras, which led administrators to run down specialist production facilities (and save money) on the assumption each professor could be his/her own camera operator (and producer, editor, and scriptwriter, too!).

Changes in Program Design: Learning Objects

One of the important trends in the area of design and instruction, with enormous implications for how distance education is organized in the future, is the movement to design learning objects.

From a social or policy perspective, one of the many unsatisfactory consequences of the fragmented nature of our distance education resources at the national and state levels, but even within large institutions, is the multiplicity of courses and course materials and services that are delivered by thousands of independent providers at the national level. These courses are usually very similar, but because of underinvestment they often fall short of the highest quality. Also, because there are no common standards, even an innovative institution that would like to adopt materials made elsewhere, rather than waste money in further replication, has difficulty in transferring them into its curricular or administrative structure. One development that indicates the beginning of a move towards dealing with this lack of standards, and eventually to help bring about some rationalization of resources and improvements in quality and costs, is the work of the International Standards groups, prominent among them being Instructional Management Systems. A related initiative in this gradual progress towards rationalization is the U.S. Department of Defense's Shareable Content Object Reference Model (SCORM). SCORM is a member of another consortium of government agencies, corporations, and educational institutions called the Advanced Distributed Learning Initiative (ADL—see http://www.adlnet.org). The aim—and thus the trend we need to observe—is the development of a universe of marketable "learning objects." These are products which in the future could be bought and sold by different institutions for assembling into their different educational programs (Resmer, 1998).

Learning objects are, we might say, the bricks out of which an institution could construct a program according to its own preferred architecture. By using the standard bricks, every institution would save the cost of manufacturing their own, and—just as important—would have raw materials that were of a common standard. That would allow—to stay with the analogy—for a small organization to build its course offerings module by module rather like adding rooms to a home, or to pick up the whole house and merge with another! Learning objects include educational content as well as procedures that help students locate and use the content, but also activities that help teaching institutions track learner progress, report learner performance, and facilitate better interaction between administrative systems. Among many advantages of standardizing operations into learning objects, compare, for example, the cost of training an administrator or instructor who moves from one institution to another before there are standard procedures and after such standards are agreed and implemented. Even more interestingly, think of the saving in instructor time if and when we have a standard set of learning objects based on standard learning objectives for, let us say, Introductory Biology. Then it would no longer be necessary for every instructor to try to be an expert in designing learning objectives, or to structure the content for a given length of course at a given learner level. All the pieces would be available for assembly by the instructor. Then, think of the rich opportunity—in the time saved from such unnecessary chores—to scour the market for learning objects that you, as an individual instructor or as administrator in an institution, could knit together to make up a course, constructed with materials that came from a range of vendors; and that, because of the principle of "interoperability," could be linked together in your own unique way. Following the theme of Independent Study mentioned previously, we can see the possibilities from the point of view of the learner, who should be able to put together a personally constructed learning package using materials from a variety of providing institutions, possibly using advice from student support services from other, different, agencies, all operating of course to common standards. The advantages in such areas as certification and transfer of credits are also fairly obvious. Though the goal of producing standardized learning objects makes economic sense as well as educational sense, the procedures for harmonizing the interests of academics, administrations, and vendors are likely to remain difficult and time consuming. With so many competing interests involved it is hardly surprising that achieving the development and implementation of common standards will be challenging. If the result of all this effort is to fulfill the promise of an almost infinite number of modularized resources that can be aggregated and disaggregated at will to create courses or whole programs of study, it would give the returns to scale that are so missing in American distance education. That would lead to an enormous increase in both efficiency and quality.

Organizational Change

"To get the bad customs of a country changed and new ones, though better, introduced, it is necessary first . . . to convince them that their interests will be promoted by the proposed changes; and this is not the work of a day" (Benjamin Franklin, quoted in Rogers (1983, p. 1)).

According to Rogers's well-known work on the adoption of innovations, a new idea or a new practice is more likely to be adopted when it is perceived to have a relative advantage over its predecessor; when it is compatible with the needs and value system of the adopters, is relatively simple and easy to understand, can be tested and tried prior to commitment, and can be seen by the adopters prior to adoption i.e., have observability (Rogers, 1983, p. 211).

Adopting the innovation of distance education has, as we have acknowledged throughout this book, been driven by the emergence of new digital technology. It has been technology that led to such changes as have occurred in how educational institutions are organized; how they see their missions; the types and numbers of students they serve; the curricula they offer; how they employ human resources; how they support learners, provide instruction, evaluate learning; and even how highly their programs are regarded. Institutions *ought* to have made changes in access, and ought to have made teaching more learner-friendly a long time ago, but it was technological innovation that made most move at least a few cautious steps in these directions. However, as we have repeatedly stated, meeting the challenges and opportunities offered by the Information Age will not be possible by technological innovation alone. Change and innovation will certainly be needed in curriculum and instructional methods, and even though these are much more difficult to implement than bringing in new technology, there is at least a body of knowledge about how to effectively train and teach in a distance education system. As we have seen, the response so far by teachers and their employers in dual mode institutions has been conservative. Courses delivered on the Internet are very similar in content to what is taught by the same teachers in their conventional classrooms and the teachers from conventional classrooms persist in projecting classroom practice as the norm. In fact, in many universities this is a deliberate policy. The same instructor who teaches in the classroom also teaches the course on the Internet, and the same person provides most of the content, the design of instruction, and the interaction with the learner. This approach does not require significant changes in resource allocations or the role of the teacher, and is popular with professors and administrators for those reasons. It resembles the response to the first cinematography, in which producers placed a camera in front of the stage to film actors as they performed in ways they had always performed! Teaching at a distance is to the classroom as the movie is to the stage play; there are basic similarities, but also very different technologies, different crafts, different economics, and different forms of organization.

The programs that in the future will benefit from innovations in technology, and survive the challenges of competition in a global market, will come from those states and organizations that are able to support the most distance-appropriate ways of presenting information and enabling learners to interact with facilitators as they process that information into personal knowledge. They will be able to achieve this only marginally through new technology and associated changes in an extended classroom type of instruction. The institutions that will benefit in significant ways, with results that are more than marginal additions to current outputs, will be those that either change how they organize and manage their human resources, or that are set up from scratch to manage these resources according to a distance education systems approach. It will take political vision and political leadership to bring about the redistribution of resources and reorganization of long-entrenched departments within institutions and institutions within national systems. Before it will be possible to deal with the serious macroeconomic implications of the knowledge gap between social classes and between regions and nations, it will be necessary to deal with the inefficiency and inequity of distribution of education and training resources at a macro-level. This means fundamental change in how we organize the delivery of education and training, moving from parochial supply to global, from labor intensive to technology intensive, from monopolistic and protected to competitive, from small scale capitalization to large investments, and from entirely supplier dominated to one marked by rich consumer choice and rich consumer support.

A New Supply Model of Distance Education Organization

One such model, which we have called a "commissioning model," is a virtual agency that follows the systems approach to design and deliver programs without setting up a permanent institution. Instead of locating all the specialist human resources and technologies in one location (go back to look at one of the Open University's Web sites if you need to remind yourself what such a center looks like) the same individuals and services are employed, but without leaving their home base. They are linked together by communications technologies, regardless of where they are located, in a network to provide the kind of services previously delivered by dedicated institutions. This is managed by a central contracting agency that commissions their services. The general principle is that institutions, states, or nations can draw on their best resources wherever they are located—the content experts, instructional designers, the full range of communications technologies, and all the resources needed to provide a learner support system—and configure whatever mixture is needed for a particular program or project on a flexible, open, "mix and match" basis. Only a small management unit is permanent, consisting of specialists in design, technology and learner support, whose responsibility is to commission the mixture of personnel and other resources needed for each particular project. This permanent, experienced, management team is one of two essential requirements for a successful commissioning system; the other is a significant funding resource. The only way the management team can obtain the quality resources needed on a *pro-tem* basis; guarantee quality; and monitor, train, and in every way maximize the human and other resources available is by the power of funding. Very large amounts of money can be saved from not having the fixed costs of a traditional institution. What this approach leads to is a very versatile, responsive system, producing high quality without commitment to ongoing institutional costs, and without the tendency to conservatism that blocks continued innovation within established educational agencies. It has the dual effect of stimulating partnerships while employing the comparative advantage of each institution in a country or region. As suggested by Venkatraman and Henderson, as summarized by Woudstra and Adria, such "virtual organizing can result in a living organization that is inter-organizational in scope and that contains customer (student) communities, resource coalitions, and professional communities of practice. Sustained innovation and growth are made possible by virtual organizing" (Woudstra and Adria 2000, p. 539). One of the best examples of this approach that has emerged so far is the PROFORMACAO project of the Brazilian Ministry of Education described in Chapter 11.

A New, Demand-Driven Model of Distance Education

Another emerging organizational model is a system based on Independent Study. The key difference between this and other models is that in an Independent Study system, the "supplier"—that is to say, the university, training department or other provider—is *not* the decision maker regarding what is to be learned, when, how, or even to what extent. These determinations lie with the "consumer," the learner. You will see the concept of Learner Autonomy (Chapter 9) coming into play here, although since "consuming" implies being informed, there may be a key role for advisory and learner support services in such a "demand-driven" system.

In this new model of distance education there is another factor at work, converging with the digital technology that makes it possible. This is the reinvention by a number of scholars of the basic concept of education, moving away from the idea of education as a standard process originating from any single geographic location and thus moving beyond the idea of distance education being limited to what is provided *by any single institution or any single agency.* Under the new concept, the provision of education is seen as an open system. A student's faculty in future will no longer be limited to those who assemble in any one place any more than a teacher's students would have to assemble in one place. Students can learn wherever they are located from instructional resources wherever *they* are located. No student would need to take instruction from exactly the same teacher as any other; students could have access to teachers from any state or country at any time and in any combination; they could have access to information resources from any state or country at any time and in any combination. Students also could have universal access to advice and guidance. The explosion of knowledge, increasing specialization, and of course new digital technology are all accelerating this trend toward deconstruction of the educational processes, an "unbundling" of the functions traditionally performed by educational institutions and opening of resources to access on demand. As well as a key role for advisory and learner support services in such a "demand-driven" system, another vital component that has barely arrived on the policy agenda is the need for a more powerful credit banking and transfer system. In the recent past, educational institutions have been able to assert a near-monopoly over the supply of teaching to each student because of its control of generally accepted certification. Once this monopoly of control of the certificate is broken, the student will have almost complete freedom to draw instructional programs into a personal portfolio, with access via the Web to whatever institutions best meet his or her needs, wherever located. The move towards construction of curricula based on learning objects is a reinforcement of the trend to learner-controlled program management.

Globalization and Commercialization

Like other aspects of globalization, changes in the role of education in society are driven by policies that are beyond the responsibility and control of educators. A significant example of this is the World Trade Organization's General Agreement on Trade in Services (GATS). The GATS framework promotes a free-market orientation to the supply and trade in services. Education is considered such a service. Thus GATS will in the future continue to accentuate and promote the transition of education, from being a publicly owned and funded cultural service that is central to the social and cultural goals of each nation, to being a private good subject to the market orientation of suppliers and consumers on an increasingly transnational scale (Department of Education Training and Youth Affairs, Australia, 2000).

There are two ways of looking at this. As the growth in telecommunications and private entrepreneurial activity globalizes the delivery of distance education, it will have the positive effect of enabling education consumers to choose more widely. Edwards (1994) predicted that "in the realm of distance education, modularisation and the plethora of innovations to increase 'openness' can be constructed as developments to satisfy the demands of consumers for educational products" (p. 9). For him, it is the power of consumer choice that will force educators to acknowledge and allow for student needs and to loosen a range of academic constraints—staffing, semester time-frames, credit accumulation and transfer, and course modularization. In this view, students will benefit from the emergence of a commercial global marketplace where they can shop for courses and where "the expertise of the few can be made available to the many, such that those in remote areas can have the same access to educational resources, specialist courses and renowned experts as those located in large cities and developed parts of the world" (Mason, 1998, p. 5).

There is an alternative perspective, however: when "the needs of the economy have precedence, market solutions are the rule and educational consumerism flourishes" (Usher et al., 1997, p. 38). This educational consumerism reduces teaching to a process of training workers for the productive economy and training them to become consumers of mass-produced goods and services—especially services. The core aim of education in this culture is supporting *continuous production* and continuously *unsatisfied and uncritical* consumers. Consumerist values already dictate a growing part of the curriculum, instruction, and educational policy in many countries. It may be exported abroad through their distance education programs. This export will be accomplished not simply through the sales of particular products, or even by promoting the ideal of productivity and consumption as ultimate and overriding social values, but more subtly by promoting consumerist attitudes to nation, race, gender, family, and use of national and personal resources, including time. In education it promotes learning as a competitive process, teaching as labor rather than vocation, sets up professional managers in control of academics at universities, evaluates educational programs by the income generated (i.e., the number of satisfied "customers").

The pursuit of a marketable diploma, and the higher consumer status it endows, replaces older ideas about personal enlightenment and the reward of intellectual achievement or the vision of education as a means of community and social development. Education is spoken of solely in terms of supply, demand, and costs; students are increasingly referred to as customers; many institutions of higher education regard themselves as competitors trying to attract "business," rather like competing movie theaters. Increasingly, higher education as a consumer service may be available to almost anyone—but only those able and willing to pay a price. Legislators, having themselves graduated through such self-serving educational programs are increasingly reluctant to raise public funds for education and reinforce the dogma that education is a personal investment, with the purpose of individual self-advancement. Educational services are offered in a mass market, with a concomitant effect on the quality of what is provided since the primary aim is to maximize "throughput" and volume. In the consumer society, even ideas are regarded as objects to be marketed, to be "sold." Ideas are less for the purpose of debate, examination, analysis, and perhaps compromise than for packaging and selling in a pervasive marketing culture of "spin" and hyperbole. The consumerist view of distance education leads to individual educational programs being treated as cost-centers that have to become profitable at relatively low levels in the delivery organization (i.e., if a course can not pay for itself in student tuition fees, it is cancelled) and also to focus on producing a financial profit, usually in the short term. One effect of this on the curriculum has been for institutions to drop non-vocational programs and to only provide programs that workers or their employers are willing to pay for. More serious perhaps is the effect on instruction. Just as the American radio station maximizes profits by spending as little as possible on creative programming while selling as much advertising as possible, so the distance education institution may in future have a profit-driven interest in spending as little as possible on program design as well as hiring the cheapest instructors. The issue you have to deal with as you look to the future is the position you will take with regard to policies that push further the establishment of systems of distance education that are increasingly controlled and directed by the values of the producer-consumer complex of business organizations, for whom the primary, perhaps sole, purpose of education is to support the mechanisms that lead to the production of consumer goods and their consumption.

The voices of those who object to the commercialization within nations, as well as the voices of those with alternative educational values, have to be heard. In the network systems of the future, we can hope that the flow of information will no longer be unidirectional from one teacher or teaching organization to narrowly targeted and contained sets of learners, nor exclusively from certain countries, the "developed countries" to "the underdeveloped." On the one hand, the new network systems will certainly have to support expanding knowledge for economic development in those countries where there is still insufficient food, insufficient shelter, and insufficient medical care. On the other hand, these same networks must also help educators working in cultures that hold values other than mere consumerism to bring their different forms of knowledge to the global meeting. The developed economies must learn greater sensitivity to the negative effects of their overeager and naive intrusion into other cultures. More conscious efforts will have to be made to identify what can be learned from those cultures. The new network systems must allow, indeed require, content and process to be contributed by teachers, scholars, students and lay people in the less developed countries. Students in the advanced economies have to learn to question the assumptions continuously promoted by domestic marketing media that tells them the good society is found only in their country and their culture. This is not to say they are asked to denigrate or reject their culture. On the contrary, by coming to a much better understanding of other cultures and other societies, they may come to a better understanding and appreciation of their own. Distance education is equipped to facilitate this exchange of knowledge on a scale that no previous forms of education could equal.

Changes Needed in Use of Terminology

It should have been apparent to you from the beginning of this book that there is serious confusion about concepts, and—reflecting this—a muddled use of terminology in the field of distance education. We have noted the plethora of terms competing for attention and have tried to pick our way through them in the different chapters of this book. Some of these, you will remember, such as "telelearning," "asynchronous learning," and "e-learning" emphasize a particular communications technology; others such as "distributed learning" and "distant learning" emphasize the location of learners; still others, such as "open learning" and "flexible learning" emphasize the relative freedom of learners to enter an educational system more easily and to exercise a greater degree of control over their learning than in conventional education. We have seen how different authors use different terms to mean essentially the same thing, as for example the use of "distance learning" as a synonym for "distance education," but also such terms as "virtual education," and "distributed learning." Similarly, at times the same term, such as "virtual university," is used to refer to very different types of educational arrangements.

This conceptual confusion is of more than pedantic interest, since it has a direct effect on the quality of research, practice, and the making of policy. As we have seen in discussing effectiveness, much of the current enthusiasm for new technology is based more on opinion and anecdote than on solid empirical evidence. And this is, as we discussed in Chapter 10, in large part because the right kinds of questions are not being asked as a result of enthusiasts for new technology not knowing the research about teaching and learning at a distance prior to, as well as since, the emergence of that technology. This sober evaluation of research quality suggests problems from both a practical administrator or policy maker's point of view, as well as that of academia. In developing policy, even such a simple matter as a report on growth in programs may be untrustworthy if the definition of what is included in a study in a base year differs from that in the subsequent year; or, for example, the NCES, by excluding primarily print-based distance education in the study mentioned in Chapter 3, can lead to the unwary reader seriously underestimating the actual numbers of distance learners by at least 3 million. Thus, as distance education changes from the margins to the mainstream of educational provision, any organization proposing to develop a distance education program must appreciate the need for its personnel to become knowledgeable about the field. This means providing at least enough professional training for them to be able to read research and other literature critically and enter dialogue with others in the field more constructively than has generally been the case in the past. For those, like you, who have studied distance education at least at the foundation level, it is essential that you use terms carefully, and in that way not add to the confusion caused by those who have not read the foundation literature.

While thinking about issues concerning language, we would like to draw attention to an issue that goes beyond the important need to communicate in a more disciplined and precise way. This is the need to develop a critical awareness of the implications, assumptions, and the values portrayed by our choice of terms. This has been an introductory text and we have not entered into discussion beyond the level of explaining terms, but as you go forward we hope you will reflect on the value issues that are engaged as we use apparently valueless, technical terminology. For example, consider the expression "teaching-learning system" and consider the implications of the way that term is constructed with

Viewpoint: Neil Postman

". . . every culture must negotiate with technology, whether it does so intelligently or not. A bargain is struck in which technology giveth and it also taketh away. The wise know this well and are rarely impressed by dramatic technological change, and never overjoyed."

SOURCE: Postman, N. (1992). *Technopoly: The surrender of culture to technology.* New York: Knopf, p. 5.

regard to the acceptance of power relationships, control of knowledge, dependence, and learner autonomy. Consider what are the long-term effects of changing the order of these words to "learning-teaching system." We have previously alluded to a "Copernican revolution"—when distance education casts the learner to become the center of the educational transaction, and not the teacher, conceiving teaching as behavior that *follows* the actions of a learner as contrasted to the traditional view of the teacher as *driving* the learner. What does this imply for program design? Instruction? Evaluation? Organization? Or consider the habitual assumption that "education" means "classroom," and always includes a person in the role of "teacher." What happens if we can abandon the association of "education" with those terms and the entities they represent and see learning as a self-managed disciplined activity that a learner does, in his or her total life context (e.g., work, family, society, community) supported by helpers who are available from anywhere through all kinds of communications channels?

We feel this is a good point at which to leave you. Usually the best class is the one where the student leaves with questions unanswered, with "food for thought." We hope this last paragraph will give you much food for thought—but in case you want a little more, see below the final Viewpoint, and then some questions for discussion.

We wish you well as you move to your further study of distance education.

Summary

- The volume of information is expanding, and the means of accessing it is expanding also, and improving, especially for people away from centers where information was traditionally stored, and for people with specialist interests.
- The character of information is changing and changes continuously, so knowing how to manage this changing information and convert it into knowledge is a key determinant of personal and national economic effectiveness.

- Because information is continuously changing and people have to cope with this even while carrying out their roles as adult workers, when people need structured learning resources and dialog with instructors, it can only be accessed through distance education.
- There will be new technologies and some of these innovations are predicted. However, principles of learning and teaching at a distance are relatively stable; it is necessary to evaluate the value of each technology for how it contributes to improving the application of these principles.
- Good practice of distance education, as well as research and theory, will depend on more training of educators and others about the field; to contribute to better communication on which good practice and research depends, there has to be more understanding of distance education theory as a means of getting less confusion in terminology.
- Changes are anticipated in the organizational structures that provide distance education with a shift from supplier control to consumer control and from permanent institutions to virtual systems, with the most effective being where a strong management entity is able to commission inputs from a wide range of sources.
- Changes are anticipated in how distance education is designed and implemented, increasing use of learning objects (whether under that name or something different).
- Globalization raises many issues. On the one hand it offers the possibility of more choice and so greater freedom and better resources for distance learners. When driven by commercialism there is danger of degradation of both curriculum and instructional programs.

Questions for Discussion or Further Study

1. How do you see the changes in information in future affecting distance education?
2. What about the technologies we listed? How might they change distance education? Can you suggest other technological changes that may have more effect?
3. In a field of practice known to you, describe how a "commissioning" model might work; think of who would provide the management and budget. Where would the different expert resources be found?
4. Do you think globalization will have a more beneficial or damaging effect for American distance education? Why?
5. Discuss Postman's viewpoint. How realistic do you think our society has been regarding the application of technology in distance education? Have we taken full advantage of it, and if not, what should we do differently?

Sources of Further Information

You now have a good introductory level of knowledge about distance education. We hope you are sufficiently interested to move on from here, to do your own research and pursue certain aspects in more depth. To help with this, we will point you to some resources that we have found useful.

U.S. Centers and Organizations

Here are a few of the organizations in the United States that specialize in distance education or closely related fields:

American Association for Collegiate Independent Study (AACIS)—AACIS is a membership organization with the mission of advancing understanding about independent study, and providing collegiality and professional development opportunities for its members. Activities include an annual conference, a newsletter, and an online listserv, AACIS-L.
http://www.aacis.org/

American Center for the Study of Distance Education (ACSDE)—The ACSDE was founded in 1986 by Michael G. Moore, who served as Director until 2001. The first center of its kind in the United States, ACSDE organized seminal conferences and research symposia and published a variety of monographs. It sponsors "DEOS," the Distance Education Online Symposium, an online discussion group/newsletter.
http://www.ed.psu.edu/acsde/

The American Distance Education Consortium (ADEC)—ADEC is a non-profit consortium of approximately 65 state universities with a mission to develop high quality, economical distance education programs and services for delivery by the Land Grant colleges and universities.
http://www.adec.edu/

Annenberg/CPB Project—Established in 1981, Annenberg/CPB, a partnership between The Annenberg Foundation and the Corporation for Public Broadcasting (CPB), demonstrated the use of media and telecommunications in K–12 schools as well as the development of programs (especially television-based) at the college level.
http://www.learner.org/

Association for Media-Based Continuing Education for Engineers (AMCEE)—AMCEE is a consortium established in 1976 that brings together more than 25 educational institutions and provides hundreds of videotape-based courses on engineering and related topics, derived mostly from university classes. AMCEE also offers televised workshops and seminars through NTU.
http://www.amcee.org/

Center for Academic Transformation—The Center for Academic Transformation is a program of the Pew Foundation that serves as a source of expertise and support for those in higher education wanting to use information technology to transform their academic practices.
http://www.center.rpi.edu/

Consortium for School Networking (CoSN)—The purpose for which the Consortium for School Networking is organized is to advocate access to, and facilitate the evolution of, national and international electronic networks as resources to K–12 educators and students.
http://www.cosn.org

Consortium of Distance Education (CODE)—The mission of the Consortium is to acquire and share knowledge about state-of-the-art distance learning in higher education focusing on college telecourses.
http://www.codenetwork.org

Council for Adult and Experiential Learning (CAEL)—CAEL is a national organization dedicated to expanding lifelong learning opportunities for adults.
http://www.cael.org

Council for Higher Education Accreditation (CHEA)—CHEA is the largest institutional higher education membership organization in the US with approximately 3,000 colleges and universities and offers a list of monographs about quality assurance and accreditation in distance education.
http://www.chea.org/

Defense Activity for Non-Traditional Education Support (DANTES)—DANTES is a tuition assistance program run by the Department of Defense with a strong distance education component to provide off-duty voluntary education programs to military personnel.
http://www.dantes.doded.mil

Educause—Educause is a nonprofit association whose mission is to advance higher education by promoting the use of information technology. The current membership comprises nearly 1,900 colleges and universities, more than 180 corporations, and 13,000 member representatives.
http://www.educause.edu/

Federal Government Distance Learning Association—The FGDLA is a nonprofit association formed to promote the development and application of distance learning and to actively foster collaboration and understanding among those involved in educational and training within the federal government.
http://fgdla.org/

International Association for Continuing Education and Training (IACET)—IACET authorizes educational providers to award the IACET Continuing Education Unit (CEU). IACET has developed its Distance-Learning Guidelines to help developers of distance and online learning to apply the IACET Standard to their specific situation.
http://www.iacet.org

Learning Anytime Anywhere Partnerships (LAAP)—LAAP is a federal grant program to encourage innovative, scalable, and nationally significant distance education projects. Eligibility requirements for LAAP include at least two partners and a one-to-one matching of requested federal funds.
http://www.ed.gov/programs/fipselaap/applicant.html?exp = 0

Sloan Consortium (Sloan-C)—Sloan Consortium encourages the collaborative sharing of knowledge and effective practices to improve online education in regard to learning effectiveness, access, affordability for learners and providers, and student and faculty satisfaction.
http://www.aln.org

The Distance Education and Training Council—The Council was founded in 1926 to promote sound educational standards and ethical business practices in for-profit correspondence schools. The DETC is a non-profit educational association and sponsors a nationally recognized accrediting agency called the Accrediting Commission of the DETC.
http://www.detc.org/

University Continuing Education Association (UCEA)—Founded in 1915, the University Continuing Education Association (formerly the National University Continuing Education Association) is a professional association for everyone involved in continuing education at all levels, with a special interest group for those involved in using technology. UCEA has six regional associations.
http://www.ucea.edu/

U.S. Distance Learning Association (USDLA)—USDLA is a member organization concerned with distance education at all levels, with a strong representation in corporate training contexts. It has an online journal and organizes annual conferences.
http://www.usdla.org/

Web-based Education Commission—The Commission was established by Congress to develop policy recommendations geared toward maximizing the educational promise of the Internet for pre-K, elementary, middle, secondary, and postsecondary education learners.
http://www.hpcnet.org/webcommission

Get Educated—This is a consulting firm with a Web site that provides links to its informative newsletters.
http://www.geteducated.com/index.htm

The Distance Learning Resource Network (DLRN)—The Distance Learning Resource Network (DLRN) is the dissemination project for the U.S. Department of Education Star Schools Program, a federally funded program offering instructional modules, enrichment activities and courses in science, mathematics, foreign languages, workplace skills, high school completion, and adult literacy programs.
http://www.dlrn.org/

Advanced Distributed Learning (ADL)—ADL—an initiative sponsored by the Office of the Secretary of Defense (OSD)—is a collaborative effort between government, industry, and academia to promote the interoperability of learning tools and course content. http://www.adlnet.org/index.cfm?fuseaction = home

Instructional Technology Council—The Instructional Technology Council provides leadership, information, and resources to expand and enhance distance learning through the effective use of technology. http://www.itcnetwork.org/default.htm

The International Center for Applied Studies in Information Technology (ICASIT)—The focus of ICASIT is on policy issues related to Information Technology (IT). ICAS-IT has projects in over 20 countries, in partnerships with foundations, research centers, and universities. http://www.icasit.org/index.html

International Multimedia Telecommunications Consortium (IMTC)—IMTC is an international community of companies working to facilitate the availability of real-time, rich-media communications between people in multiple locations around the world. Members include Internet application developers and service providers, teleconferencing hardware and software suppliers, telecommunications companies and equipment vendors, end users, educational institutions, government agencies, and non-profit corporations. http://www.imtc.org/

Journals, Magazines, and Directories

The following are the principal scholarly journals in distance education:

The American Journal of Distance Education http://www.AJDE.com

Distance Education (Australia) http://www.tandf.co.uk/journals/carfax/01587919.html

The Journal of Distance Education (Canada) http://www.cade-aced.ca/en_pub.php

International Review of Research in Open and Distance Learning (Canada) http://www.irrodl.org/

Open Learning (UK) http://www.tandf.co.uk/journals/carfax/02680513.html

The following publications specialize in distance education, or carry articles on related topics.

The Journal of Library Services for Distance Education http://www.westga.edu/ ~ library/jlsde/

Online Journal of Distance Learning Administration http://www.westga.edu/ ~ distance/jmain11.html

Quarterly Review of Distance Education
http://www.aect.org/Publications/default.htm

The USDLA Journal
http://www.usdla.org/html/membership/publications.htm

Distance Educator.com
http://www.distance-educator.com

Educational Technology
http://www.bookstoread.com/etp/

Technological Horizons in Education Journal
http://www.thejournal.com/

The Technology Source
http://ts.mivu.org

Sloan Foundation publications: Sloan-C View, Journal of Asynchronous Learning
Networks, Sloan consortium Series, and ALN Magazine
http://www.aln.org/publications/index.asp

The Chronicle of Higher Education
http://chronicle.com/

The Institute for Higher Education Policy Recent Reports
http://www.ihep.com/Publications.php

EDUCAUSE Quarterly (formerly CAUSE/EFFECT)
http://www.educause.edu/pub/eq/

International Journal of Instructional Media
http://www.adprima.com/ijim.htm

Interpersonal Computing and Technology Journal
https://www.aect.org/Intranet/Publications/index.asp

TechKnowLogia (International Journal of Technologies for the Advancement of
Knowledge and Learning)
http://www.TechKnowLogia.org/

First Monday
http://www.firstmonday.org

Educational Technology Research and Development
http://www.aect.org/Intranet/Publications/index.asp

Journal of Research on Technology in Education
http://www.iste.org/jrte/36/1/index.cfm

Some English language journals published in other countries are:

European Journal of Open and Distance Learning
http://www.eurodl.org

International Journal of Educational Technology
http://www.outreach.uiuc.edu/ijet

Journal of Interactive Learning Research (JILR) (Switzerland)
http://www.aace.org/pubs/jilr/

International Journal of E-Learning
http://www.aace.org/pubs/ijel

E-JIST (Australia)
http://www.usq.edu.au/electpub/e-jist/

Turkish Online Journal of Distance Education (TOJDE)
http://tojde.anadolu.edu.tr/

Journal of International Forum of Educational Technology and Society (New Zealand)
http://ifets.ieee.org/periodical

British Journal of Educational Technology (UK)
http://www.blackwellpublishing.com/journals/BJET/descript.htm

The Journal of Distance Learning (New Zealand)
http://www.deanz.org.nz/jour.htm#anchor1

Directories

Here is a selection of directories that describe distance education courses, programs, or providers:

Directory of Courses and Materials for Training in Distance Education
http://www.col.org/train.htm

The USDLA Funding Sourcebook
http://www.usdla.org/html/resources/eStore.htm

Going the Distance
http://www.learner.org/edtech/distlearn/topten.html

World Lecture Hall
http://wnt.cc.utexas.edu/ ~ wlh/index.cfm

Maricopa's
http://www.mcli.dist.maricopa.edu/tl/

Distance Learning Projects in the United States (K-12)
http://www.ed.gov/bulletin/summer1995/tech.html

The Diversity Directory: Distance Learn
hhttp://www.excelsior.edu/pub_rcey.htm

The Independent Study Catalog (compiled by the UCEA)
http://www.amazon.co.uk/exec/obidos/tg/stores/detail/glance/-/books/1560794607/026-1441464-3487651

The Business Television Directory & Multimedia Database
http://www.irwincom.com/web/publications.htm

Directory of Accredited Home Study Schools
http://www.detc.org/theaccrediting.html

Campus-free College Degrees
http://www.college-distancedegree.com/

Accredited College Degrees by Correspondence
http://collegeathome.com/index.html

Multimedia Education Resources for Learning and Online Teaching (MERLOT)
http://www.merlot.org

Selection of Conferences and Training Opportunities

In addition to the conferences and workshops conducted by the organizations listed previously, here are some others:

Annual Conference on Distance Teaching and Learning Conference, organized by The Graduate Program in Continuing and Vocational Education, and sponsored by University of Wisconsin-Madison
http://www.uwex.edu/disted/conference/

Annual Conference organized by American Association for Collegiate Independent Study (AACIS)
http://www.aacis.org/

Annual Distance Education Conference, organized by the Center for Distance Learning Research of Texas A&M University
http://www.cdlr.tamu.edu/information/index.asp

Annual Online Learning Conference and Expo
http://www.onlinelearningconference.com/

Annual K–12 School Networking Conference organized by The Consortium for School Networking (CoSN)
http://k12schoolnetworking.org/presentations.html

Online Educa Berlin (Germany)—Online Educa Berlin is organized by ICWE GmbH, a German company. OEB is the world's largest international e-learning conference and Europe's leading annual gathering of distance education professionals, with 1,127 participants from 64 countries worldwide in 2002.
http://www.online-educa.com/en/

Conference & Expo (formerly Telecon East/International Distance Learning Conference (IDLCON))
http://www.usdla.org/html/aboutUs/majorAchievements.htm

First Friday (monthly distance training), organized by Teletraining Institute
http://www.teletrain.com/Index.htm

All Partners Conference (annual), organized by the Indiana Higher Education Telecommunication System (IHETS) on behalf of the Indiana Partnership for Statewide Education
http://www.ihets.org/progserv/education/apc/index.html

Distance Education and Related Programs
of Study at Graduate Level

University of Alaska
Area of Study: Education/Rural Education
Degree or Emphasis: Master of Education
http://www.uaf.edu/educ/coursepages.html

Florida State University
Area of Study: Instructional Systems
Degree or Emphasis: Master's or Doctorate
http://www.epls.fsu.edu/

University of Iowa
Areas of Study: Instructional Design and Technology Planning, Policy & Leadership
Studies
Degree or Emphasis: M.A. and Ph.D.
http://www.uiowa.edu/ ~ ccp/

Iowa State University
Area of Study: Curriculum and Instructional Technology
Degree or Emphasis: M.A. and Ph.D.
http://www.ctlt.iastate.edu/

University of New Mexico
Area of Study: Training and Learning Technologies
Degree or Emphasis: M.A. and Ph.D.
http://www.unm.edu/ ~ olit/index.html

University of Oklahoma
Area of Study: Adult and Higher Education, integration with educational technology
Degree or Emphasis: M.A. and Ph.D.
http://www.ou.edu/education/elps/edah/

Oklahoma State University
Area of Study: Mass Communications
Degree or Emphasis: M.S.
http://gradcollege.okstate.edu/programs/masscomm.htm

The Pennsylvania State University
Area of Study: Adult Education
Degree or Emphasis: Master's, Ph.D. and Ed.D.
http://www.worldcampus.psu.edu/pub/home/studserv/index.shtml

San Diego State University
Area of Study: Educational Technology
Degree or Emphasis: M.A.
http://edweb.sdsu.edu/EDTEC/EDTEC_Home.html

University of Wisconsin
Area of Study: Continuing and Vocational Education
Degree or Emphasis: Master's and Ph.D.
http://www.soemadison.wisc.edu/cave/

University of Wyoming
Area of Study: Instructional Technology, Adult Education
Degree or Emphasis: Master of Science
http://ed.uwyo.edu/Departments/depalt/index.htm

International Research Centers and Organizations

UNESCO.ORG—The UNESCO Web site, like UNESCO itself, is huge; and like
UNESCO is a vast resource of information about everything to do with education,
particularly in developing countries and emerging economies. At the Web site you
can search for "open and distance learning" and you will find distance education in
the area that deals with Information and Communications Technologies. There are
links to training activities, documents, publications, statistics, activities, and partners.
http://www.unesco.org

EDEN (European Distance Education Network)—Founded in 1991, EDEN is an association open to networks, institutions, and individuals with a wide variety of conferences, workshops, and other professional development activities.
http://www.eden.bme.hu

Athabasca University Centre for Distance Education—Established in 1986, its primary
interest is systematic research and development in distance education. The Centre
also teaches a Master of Distance Education and an Advanced Graduate Diploma in
Distance Education (Technology).
http://cde.athabascau.ca/

Central Institute for Distance Education Research (ZIFF)—Part of the FernUniversitat
located in Hagen, Germany, established in 1975, ZIFF has the task to do basic and
applied research on distance education and to teach about the methods of DE.
Results of all projects and studies are published in ZIFF Papiere.
http://www.fernuni-hagen.de/ZIFF/welcome.htm

The Communication Initiative—The Communication Initiative is a partnership of
development organizations seeking to support advances in the effectiveness and
scale of communication interventions for positive international development.
http://www.comminit.com/

German Institute for Distance Education (DIFF)—One of the longest established
(1967) centers of research on teaching and technology, located at the University of
Tubingen, Germany.
http://www.uni-tuebingen.de/uni/qvr/e-30/m30-01.html

Instituto Universitario de Educacion a Distancia (IUED)—Located at the Universidad
Nacional de Educacion a Distancia (UNED) in Madrid, Spain.
http://www.iued.uned.es/index.html

International Centre for Distance Learning (ICDL)—Located at the British Open University, the ICDL was established in 1978 to serve as a documentation center for distance education. It maintains a computer database listing courses available worldwide that is accessible via Internet. The searchable database includes over 11,000 abstracts on books, journal articles, research reports, conference papers, and dissertations.
http://www-icdl.open.ac.uk/

Asociacion Iberoamericana de Educacion Superior a Distancia (AIESAD)—
Organization of approximately 50 institutions interested in developing distance teaching programs in Spanish and Portuguese. Sponsored by UNED and based in Madrid, Spain.
http://www.uned.es/aiesad/

Asian Association of Open Universities (AAOU)—AAOU was founded in 1987 and today represents a significant number of the world's major distance teaching universities.
http://www.ouhk.edu.hk/ ∼ AAOUNet/

Commonwealth of Learning—The Commonwealth of Learning (COL) is an intergovernmental organization that facilitates dissemination of knowledge about distance education as a means of helping developing nations improve the quality of and access to education and training. Its headquarters is in Vancouver, Canada.
http://www.col.org/
http://www.col.org/forum/forum.htm links to forum papers/abstracts that are rich with information about "open and distance learning" from Commonwealth countries.

Consorcio-Red de Education A Distancia (CREAD)—CREAD was founded in 1990 to facilitate cooperation about distance education in the nations of North, Central and South America.
http://www.cread.org/

The South African Institute for Distance Education (SAIDE)—SAIDE was formed as an educational trust in 1992 with the mission of promoting the use of quality distance education methods and the appropriate use of technology in South Africa.
http://www.saide.org.za

European Project of Advanced Continuing Education (EuroPACE)—A non-profit organization primarily supported by high-tech corporations that delivers technical courses (mostly engineering) via satellite to members (currently 70 organizations) in Europe. Established in 1989. Headquarters in Paris, France.
http://www.europace.org/portal/index.html

GLOSAS/Global University—A private organization to promote the efforts of corporations, universities, and other groups to exchange educational and training courses across international boundaries via computer and telecommunications technologies, including the establishment of a global electronic university (GU). Headquarters in Flushing, New York.
http://www.friends-partners.org/GLOSAS/

International Association for Continuing Engineering Education (IACEE)—The International Association for Continuing Engineering Education (IACEE) is an international, non-profit, and non-governmental organization. Its purpose is to improve the quality of engineering education worldwide with over 500 members representing 71 countries. Headquarters are in Espoo, Finland.
http://iacee.asee.org/default.htm

International Council for Distance Education (ICDE)—A worldwide organization dedicated to distance education at all levels. ICDE affiliated with UNESCO as a specialist non-governmental agency. Originally founded in 1938 as the International Council for Correspondence Education (ICCE) and changed its name in 1982.
http://www.icde.org/

International Institute for Capacity Building in Africa (IICBA)—IICBA was officially established by UNESCO in 1999. IICBA is utilizing distance education programs in Africa and other parts of the world for training and upgrading teachers.
http://www.unesco-iicba.org

The Global Distance EducationNet—It is a product of the Education Group of the World Bank's Human Development Network. It is a set of information management tools designed to provide information about distance education and training primarily focused on developing nations.
http://www1.worldbank.org/disted/home.html

The Department for International Development (DFID), United Kingdom.—DFID's mission is to promote the development of education, health, and human rights through economic development. Enter the Web site and search for "open and distance education."
http://www.dfid.gov.uk/

The Norwegian Association for Distance Education (NADE)—Established in 1968, NADE aims to spread knowledge of distance education, to heighten its professional and pedagogical standards, and to strengthen the position of distance education within the Norwegian educational system.
http://www.nade-nff.no/nade-nff/nade.html

The European Association of Distance Teaching Universities (EADTU)—EADTU is an institutional member organization whose activities and projects support and advance goals towards achieving its mission: to promote and support the creation of a European network for higher level distance education.
http://www.eadtu.nl/

Australian Agency for International Development (AusAID)—AusAID is responsible for the management of the Australian Government's overseas aid program. Search for "distance learning" on the site.
http://www.ausaid.gov.au/

International Development Research Centre (IRDC)—IRDC is a Canadian aid agency. Here is one example of their development projects related to distance education: go to the following site and search for "distance learning."
http://www.idrc.ca/pan/pr040416_e.htm.

The Canadian Association for Distance Education (CADE)—CADE is the national association of distance educators in Canada. Their Web site includes information regarding conferences, workshops, publications, member services, and links and resources.
http://www.cade-aced.ca/

Canadian International Development Agency (CIDA)—CIDA is the international aid department of the Canadian federal government. Search for "distance learning" on the site.
http://www.acdi-cida.gc.ca/index.htm

International Telecommunication Union (ITU)—Headquartered in Geneva, Switzerland, ITU is the United Nations specialized agency for telecommunications. ITU has focused on the need for formal collaboration of those engaged in promoting the use of distance learning internationally.
http://www.itu.int/home/index.html

The British Association for Open Learning (BAOL)—The BAOL exists to promote quality and the best practices in "open, flexible and distance forms of learning" throughout the education and training sectors of the United Kingdom, Europe, and internationally.
http://www.baol.co.uk/

The Global Development Learning Network (GDLN) (international)—The Global Development Learning Network (GDLN) is a delivery system sponsored by the World Bank and several partner institutions. GDLN counts over 50 centers around the world, and more than 30,000 people participate in GDLN events every year.
http://www.gdln.org/

The Open and Distance Learning Quality Council (ODL QC) (UK)—ODL QC lists all currently accredited colleges and the courses these colleges offer in United Kingdom.
http://www.odlqc.org.uk/odlqc.htm

The Finnish Association for Distance Education (FADE) (Finland)—The Finnish Association for Distance Education (FADE) is an association for distance education institutions or organizations. FADE arranges meetings and conferences and supports contact between institutions at the national and international level.
http://www.fade.fi

European Study Centre Network North-West Germany (ESCN) (Germany)—European Study Centre Network North-West Germany (ESCN) is an organization of five centers for distance education and open learning at the universities of Bremen, Hamburg, Hildesheim, Lüneburg, and Oldenburg in Germany.
http://www.uni-oldenburg.de/zef/escn-gb.html

Easy Access to Software and Information (EASI)—Easy Access to Software and Information (EASI) is a provider of online training on accessible information technology for persons with disabilities, reaching more than 4,000 people in over 3 dozen countries since 1993.
http://www.rit.edu/ ~ easi/index.htm

A Selection of Online Reference Resources

Distance education resources from Auburn University—This Web site includes:
(1) Distance Learning on the Net, (2) The Boston College Center for International Higher Education (provides information about international initiatives in higher education), (3) the American Educational Research Association homepage,
(4) Edupage Newsletter, published by the American Educom Consortium (a summary of news items on information technology), (5) The Globewide Network Academy (an educational and research organization for distance learning courses and programs), and (6) The Apple Virtual Campus.
http://www.auburn.edu/administration/horizon/sept_www.html

Distance Education Clearinghouse—The site, managed and produced by the University of Wisconsin-Extension, provides definitions and glossaries, which are particularly useful to those of you who are those new to distance education.
http://www.uwex.edu/disted/overview.html

The Distance Learning "Getting Started" Booklist—A reading list aimed at people who are "getting started" in distance learning.
http://pages.prodigy.com/PAUM88A/

The WWW Virtual Library—This meta–Web site provides links to Internet sites including resources for education technology offerings.
http://vlib.org/Home.html

The Online Distance Education Learning Resource for Adult Students—Includes access to many resources, including free distance education catalogs, computer training tutorials, daily online learning news, free online courses, and the EdSurf Newsletter.
http://www.edsurf.net/

The Official alt.education.distance FAQ (Frequently Asked Questions)—This page links information that makes up the alt.education.distance newsgroup FAQs, and is presented as a complement to the details posted periodically by the MIT Usenet Server.
http://personalpages.tds.net/ ~ rlaws/dlfaq.html#one

EdSurf BookShack—Part of the EdSurf site, EdSurf BookShack provides information about online learning and distance education guides for students and educators. It allows users to search a specific area of interest.
http://www.edsurf.net/bookshack/

ERIC Database—A meta-database. One may find it helpful to search the Eric database using such terms as "distance education," "distance learning," and "open learning."
http://askeric.org/Eric/

International Forum of Educational Technology & Society—Provides information regarding formal discussions, which are theme-based and take place for a predefined time period of one to two weeks; and informal discussions, which take place any time.
http://ifets.ieee.org/discussions/discuss.html

Center for Distance Education (University of Oldenburg)—This site contains papers about the theory of distance education developed in their Foundations of Distance Education course by Ulrich Bernath and Thomas Hülsmann of the Carl von Ossietzky University of Oldenburg, and Eugene Rubin at the University of Maryland University College.
http://www.uni-oldenburg.de/zef/cde/found/
http://www.uni-oldenburg.de/zef/cde/found/w7essays.htm contains sample answers to essay questions focusing on theory of Transactional Distance.

Distance Learning in Higher Education—Available from the Council for Higher Education Accreditation (CHEA), Washington, DC. Updates are published approximately once every six months.
http://www.chea.org/Commentary/distance-learning/distance-learning-3.cfm

Report of the University of Illinois Teaching at an Internet Distance Seminar (December, 1999)—This widely cited document is the product of the University of Illinois Teaching at an Internet Distance Seminar.
http://www.vpaa.uillinois.edu/reports_retreats/tid.asp?bch = 0

The "No Significant Difference Phenomenon"—This site provides selected entries from the book "The No Significant Difference Phenomenon" as reported in 355 research reports, summaries and papers.
http://www.nosignificantdifference.org/

A companion site features comparative studies that *do* document significant differences at http://teleeducation.nb.ca/significantdifference.
Degree Programs Available through Distance Education—This site provides links to U.S. colleges and universities with distance degree programs.
http://www.angelfire.com/fl/AtHomeDegrees/

How to Find Online Courses in Higher Ed—The site provides information on various ways to search for institutions offering college courses and degrees via distance education.
http://www.dlrn.org/adult/higher.html

Ed-X LLC (Distance Learning Channel)—Ed-X.com is a search engine and Web resource for distance learning and online education with comprehensive information on over 20,000 online courses and degree programs from 700 online colleges worldwide.
http://www.ed-x.com

The International Distance Learning Course Finder—The International Distance Learning Course Finder is the world's largest online directory of e-learning courses from 130 countries. This universal distance education resource has information on over 55,000 distance learning courses and programs offered from a multitude of universities, colleges, and companies.
http://www.dlcoursefinder.com/US/index.htm

Links of Issues on Distance Education (Canada).
This is a list of hot issues on distance education.
http://ccism.pc.athabascau.ca/html/ccism/deresrce/issues.htm

Collection of Distance Education Resources (UK).
Here is a collection of distance education resources, links, and contacts assembled in Great Britain.
http://www.fae.plym.ac.uk/tele/resources.html

GLOSSARY

This is a glossary of terms used in this book. Part I is a list of educational terms. Some technical terms are in Part II.

Part I: Educational

Andragogy The art and science of facilitating learning by adults, as contrasted to pedagogy, the teaching of children. This concept is associated with Malcolm Knowles, and is based on assertions about how adults learn, including: (1) adults want to know why they need to learn something, (2) adults like to learn experientially, (3) adults tend to approach learning as problem-solving, and (4) adults tend to learn best when the topic is of immediate value. See http://www.learnactivity.com/andragogy.html or http://tip.psychology.org/knowles.html.

Anecdotal Research A form of descriptive case study in which untested findings lead the way to more controlled and systematic research. Findings are not generalizable beyond the immediate program being studied.

Assignments A course should be designed to achieve specific outcomes by each learner, and this achievement is evidenced by presentation of a product, usually written, called an assignment. Assignments should be required at frequent intervals and form the basis of dialogue between the instructor and student(s). Assignments are the key ingredient in all evaluation, being the principal means of tracking student progress and monitoring program quality.

Behaviorism The view developed by Pavlov, Watson, Thorndike, and Skinner that regards learning as behavior driven by reward and punishment, on which much early distance education was based, and which still has an appropriate place in course design and instruction.

Cognitive Theory Follows the interest in the internal processes of the brain and processing of information. Theory tends to focus on learners' prior knowledge and on learning styles. After behaviorism, cognitive theories were a major underpinning of distance education in the past and they still have an appropriate place in course design and instruction.

Collaborative Learning A learning environment in which individual learners support and add to an emerging pool of knowledge of a group; emphasizes peer relationships as learners work together creating learning communities.

Constructivism View of learning that regards knowledge as resulting from an active process of subjectively building a system of meanings. The concept is related to notions of independent learning in the early history of distance education.

Content Expert The specialist in a course design team who is responsible for contributing the subject matter to be taught and learned. Also referred to as a Subject Matter Expert.

Correspondence Education Teaching and learning that was (and is) based on use of the first generation of communication technology. With the advent of postal delivery in the mid-1880s, interaction between learners and teachers at a distance was possible for the first time. In the United States, correspondence became known later as "independent study" and "home study" before being recognized as part of the expanding field of "distance education."

Cost Effectiveness Relationship of results in terms of students' learning to investment by the teaching organization. Distance education is potentially very cost-effective because of economies of scale.

Counselors Specialists in a distance education system who concentrate on helping individual students with academic or personal problems that might interfere with learning. In North America the term "advisors" is more commonly used. Quite often, course instructors are required to provide advising.

Course Design Setting learning objectives, choosing technology and media applications, and preparing instructional strategies and evaluation procedures, all in advance of student recruitment.

Course Team Group of specialists in content, instructional design, learning, and technologies convened to produce distance education course.

Craft Approach The traditional approach to teaching in which it is not a team, but an individual teacher who is entirely responsible for all the processes of course design as well as instruction.

Dialogue One of the three "macro-factors" in the theory of transactional distance, being the interplay of words, actions, and ideas between teacher and learner; determined by the educational philosophy underlying the course, communications technology, and the size of learning group *inter alia.*

Distance Education (DE) Teaching and learning in which learning normally occurs in a different time and/or place from teaching. DE is "planned learning that normally occurs in a different place from teaching, requiring special techniques of course design, special instructional techniques, special methods of communication by electronic and other technology, as well as special organizational and administrative arrangements" (from Chapter 1).

Distance Education Consortium Two or more distance education institutions or units that share in designing distance education courses, teaching them, or both.

Distance Education Courses Structured programs of instruction for learners in a different place from the teacher, having learning objectives, one or more teachers, a medium of communication, and subject matter.

Distance Education Institution College, university, or school system organized exclusively for distance education. Also referred to as a "single mode" system.

Distance Education System All the component processes that result in distance education, including learning, teaching, communication, design, and management.

Distance Education Unit A special unit dedicated to distance learning within a conventional educational or training system.

Distance Learning A term often used synonymously with distance education, which isn't strictly correct since distance education includes teaching as well as learning. All distance learning is characterized by: (1) separation of place and/or time between learner and instructor, and (2) interaction between the learner and content, with an instructor, and possibly between learners, conducted through one or more technologies.

Distributed Learning A term used loosely as a synonym for distance education.

Economies of Scale Average costs decrease with increases in units of production. In distance education, average costs fall with increases in the number of students taking the course because the "fixed costs" of designing and producing the course are divided among larger numbers. Instruction is a "variable cost" that rises in proportion to increases in student numbers.

Educational Objects Interoperable learning units that can be aggregated (and disaggregated) to construct larger (and smaller) modules of instruction or courses.

Effectiveness Measures of performance, to be evaluated against costs. The most important effectiveness measure in distance education is students' learning, but satisfaction, faculty sustainability, and institutional reputation can also be considered. Relates to quality assurance.

Facilitation Assisting, guiding approach ("guide-on-the-side") to teaching; can be contrasted to the directive teacher-instructor ("sage-on-the-stage") approach. Heavily influenced by Humanistic psychology, as well as andragogy and ideas about learner autonomy.

Feedback The response transmitted to the sender of a message by the receiver (learner to teacher in a distance education context), which should lead in turn to modification of the message if needed.

Formative Evaluation Evaluation taken during the implementation of a course to monitor progress; often used to improve segments of the course as data gathered from current course members reveal weaknesses in the design.

Humanistic Psychology Follows the traditions of Abraham Maslow and Carl Rogers in emphasizing human growth potential and a constructivist/subjective view of knowledge. Leads to the view of learner as active agent and teacher as facilitator.

Independent Study Term used by Wedemeyer and taken up in North American universities in the mid-1960s in place of "correspondence study," partly to accommodate emerging, non-text media and partly to emphasize the greater autonomy and responsibility of the student in the teacher-learner transaction.

Industrialized Techniques The basis of the systems approach. Applying planning principles, division of labor, mass production, automation, standardization, and quality control; applied by Wedemeyer in distance education and theorized by Otto Peters in *Distance Teaching and Industrial Production: A Comparative Interpretation in Outline.*

Instructional Systems Development (ISD) Systematic approach to the planning and development of a product to meet instructional needs and goals. All components of the system are considered in relation to each other in an orderly but flexible sequence of processes.

Intellectual Property Ownership of works resulting from a person's original ideas. This is an important concept in distance education as courses become widely accessible via the Internet. Copyright legislation provides for protection of intellectual property.

Interaction Exchange of information, ideas, and opinions between and among learners and teachers. A widely cited interpretation discriminates between learner–teacher interaction, learner–learner interaction, and learner–content interaction.

Instructors Specialists in learning who interact through technology with students as they learn content in programs that may be designed by a course team or by the instructors themselves. See also *Content Experts, Tutors.*

Just-in-time An approach to educational delivery in which segments of learning material and instruction are delivered on the job, in response to specific problems.

Knowledge Transfer A view of education in which content is packaged and organized sequentially with visual clues to enable information transfer from the teacher to the student, usually with little or no interaction. More familiar to behaviorist or cognitivist practitioners than humanistic or constructivist.

Learner Autonomy Concept that people have capacities for making decisions regarding what, how, and to what extent they learn. People differ in these capacities but they can be developed, and their exercise is particularly beneficial when instructors are at a distance. The greater the transactional distance, the greater the need for learner autonomy. In transactional distance theory, programs can be classified according to the degree of learner autonomy exercised.

Learning The process of acquiring knowledge. Although a natural process, there are skills that can be practiced to make learning more efficient. Knowing the skills and training learners to use them is a job of educators. There are different theories about learning, the most important being humanistic, behavioristic, cognitive, and social learning theory; each supports a different approach to teaching and therefore to distance education.

Learning Style Relatively stable and developed ways in which a person perceives, behaves, and interacts in a learning environment

Lifelong Learning Learning throughout the lifetime, with emphasis on developing autonomous learning determined by contextual personal needs.

Modularization Breaking ideas and information up into "chunks," or distinct instructional components. It is good practice to design distance education programs in smaller and larger "chunks" of content (i.e. units and modules that approximate inputs of students' time).

Needs Assessment A management process aimed at identifying priorities for the most cost-effective allocation of resources. A needs assessment might precede the decision to establish a distance education organization; at another level it would precede the decision of which courses to offer. Needs assessment is an ongoing part of the design process, taking into account the results of formative and summative evaluation.

No Significant Difference The most common outcome of media comparison studies, no significant difference refers to the fact that the statistically evaluated difference of average results when two treatments are compared is not significantly different from chance (see http://teleeducation.nb.ca/nosignificantdifference).

Objective A statement describing the instructors' aims in terms of learners' achievements. A good learning objective contains one action, the conditions under which the action should be observed and a criterion for its evaluation. Although developed by Behavioristic psychologists, learning objectives can be applied in distance teaching that follows other learning theories. Students can be facilitated in developing their own objectives as autonomous learners.

Open Education An imprecisely defined term often used synonymously with distance education in countries that have had a very closed and elitist higher education system, to indicate the kind of freedom of access and choice of routes to course completion usually offered by distance education.

Open Learning Uses synonymously with Open Education to emphasize removal or lowering of barriers to access to education, including admission standards.

Organizational Culture An organization's "personality"; patterns of shared and normed meaning and behavior.

Paradigms of Education Models or systems of education influenced by different values about knowledge, learning and the role of the teacher. Distance education represents a shift from the traditional educational paradigm which was teacher and institution-centered, rigidly scheduled, and traditional-aged student-centered.

Pedagogy A term associated with teaching; specifically teaching children, but often used interchangeably with andragogy.

Quality Assurance The arrangements by which an institution monitors its teaching and promotes improvement.

Research Investigation based on theory aimed at extending existing knowledge; answers a question demonstrated from theory to be of general interest. Answers a question demonstrated by analysis of what is known in existing literature to be an unanswered question.

Seat-time Traditional basis for documenting inputs by teachers and learners; face-to-face class time; associated with "Carnegie Unit," established in 1906 by the Carnegie Foundation for the Advancement of Teaching as an academic bookkeeping device.

Self-assessment A process within a distance learning course by which learners are assisted in checking their own progress towards achieving course objectives.

Self-directed Learning The ability to exercise "learner autonomy" and a goal of most educational philosophies. The teacher aims to transfer to the learner the skills associated with teaching—that is, to decide what to learn, the most effective way of learning it, and to know when the learning has been achieved.

Staff Development Various, usually formal, forms of training or activities, funded by employers to enhance the attitudes, knowledge, and skills of current employees; also referred to as "professional development."

Structure Organized framework of the distance learning course consisting of "chunks" of information and teaching strategies, with internal consistency in regard to objectives and evaluation.

Study Guide Material presented to the distant learner prior to the interactive phase of instruction, with content and teaching strategies structured as considered appropriate for the target population of learners; traditionally delivered by print but also may be delivered by electronic media.

Summative Evaluation Concluding evaluation determining the final success of the project, relevant to accountability to stakeholders and potential development of future projects.

Systems Approach Application of industrial principles, including the division of labor where specialists work in teams to produce educational materials and services. Technologies are also linked, to benefit from the special qualities of each. Management is responsible for ensuring people and technology are used to full cost-effectiveness.

Theory A summary of what is known, providing the basis for research into what is unknown.

Transactional Distance Theory of distance education developed by M.G. Moore, which describes distance as a pedagogical/andragogical phenomenon having the "macro-factors" of structure and dialogue. Programs can be described as having greater or lesser distance. Course designers determine the appropriate degree of structure and dialogue for a given student population, giving particular attention to its capacity to exercise learner autonomy.

Tutors Term used in open universities for the specialists who provide instructional guidance to students during a distance education course, usually in terms of reviewing and grading assignments. Should have a knowledge of the content as prerequisite but not at the level of content specialists in the course design team.

Part II: Technical

Advanced Distributed Learning (ADL) Initiative A project aimed at developing software for training with emphasis on creating reusable content as "instructional objects." (see http://www.adlnet.org). ADL developed the SCORM standards for learning objects.

Asynchronous Literally "not synchronous"; in other words, not at the same time and thus communication with a delay that allows participants to respond at a different time from when the message is sent.

Asynchronous Learning Networks (ALN) A term popularized by the Sloan Foundation to describe distance education using Internet resources with emphasis on the merits of asynchronicity. See http://www.aln.org.

Audio-conference In distance education, a class in which an instructor and students in different locations use telephones with or without additional microphones and speakers to communicate in real time. The number of participants may be as small as two or as large as 100 or more.

Audio-graphic conference An audio conference that is accompanied by graphic materials for purposes of both presenting information and allowing interaction among participants at the different sites. This required the availability of two telephone lines at each site and has fallen out of use since the development of Web-conferencing.

Authoring Software/Tools High-level computer programs designed for use by non-programmers in the creation of computer-based training, interactive presentations, and multimedia. The commands are presented as simple terms, concepts, and icons. The authoring software translates these commands into the programming code needed by the computer and related hardware devices. See also *Integrated Learning Systems.*

Bandwidth Maximum frequency that can be used to transmit a communication signal without excessive distortion. Measured in bits per second (bps). The more information contained in a signal, the more bandwidth it requires for distortion-free transmission. High capacity bandwidth (in excess of 56Kbps) is called broadband and is highly desirable for Web applications, especially multimedia.

Chat Two or more individuals connected to Internet have real-time, that is, synchronous, text-based conversations by typing messages into their computer. As you type, your words are immediately displayed to the other members of the chat group.

Computer-assisted Instruction (CAI) Teaching process in which a computer is used to assist students in gaining mastery over a specific skill. Does not necessary involve the use of a network (e.g., can be CD-ROM based) and so can support learner-content interaction.

Desktop Video-conferencing Video-conferencing on a personal computer equipped with a fast Internet connection (at least 56Kbps modem), a microphone, and a camera. It can be two-way or multi-point, depending upon the hardware and software of participants. Only appropriate for individuals or very small groups.

Digital Communication A communications format that transmits audio, video, and data as bits ("1s" and "0s") of information, and allows communications signals to be compressed, which makes for more efficient transmission.

Electronic Bulletin Boards Information that can be reached via computers connected by modem and/or Internet. Users can place and read electronic messages from other users, and download available files. Most popular features are threaded discussion forums.

Electronic Mail More often called e-mail. E-mail is a fast, easy, and inexpensive way to communicate with individuals or groups on networked computers and computers equipped for Internet access. Besides basic correspondence, with most systems you can attach and send documents and other files.

Http Hypertext transfer protocol (http) is the standard method used to transfer data in HTML format from server to a remote computer. Web addresses often begin with http://, indicating that the documents you will access are written in HTML.

Hyperlinks Text or images on a Web page that, when clicked with a mouse, cause your browser to load another page of HTML. Because a simple mouse click allows the user to easily go from one page of hypertext to another, these pages are said to be "hyperlinked." Text links are usually (but not always) underlined, while hyperlinks that are images often take the form of "buttons."

HyperText Markup Language (HTML) HTML is the code used to write most documents on the World Wide Web. HTML codes (called "tags") tell your browser how to arrange/place text, images/graphics, and sound on the computer screen. You can write the code yourself using any text editor, or can use any one of several commercially available HTML editors to create a document.

Instructional Management Systems Project (IMS) IMS (http://www.imsproject.org) is developing and promoting open specifications for facilitating online learning activities such as locating and using educational content, tracking learner progress, reporting learner performance, and exchanging student records between administrative systems.

Instructional Multimedia A form of computer-based training that incorporates a mix of media as the stimulus to the student. Possible media elements include sound, animation, graphics, video, text; whatever it takes to get the instructional message across to the target audience. See *Multimedia.*

Integrated Services Digital Network (ISDN) Digital network with higher speed than found on the traditional telephone network. Even though ISDN uses existing phone lines, it does require specialized equipment. Because the network is entirely digital, it can send voice, data, and video over the same line simultaneously.

Integrated Learning Systems (ILS) Software systems designed for the development and delivery of Web-based courses. These systems generate courses that are compliant with standards such as SCORM. Popular examples include Blackboard, LearningSpace, and WebCT.

Internet A worldwide network of computer networks. It is an interconnection of large and small networks around the globe.

Learning Management Systems (LMS) Software systems used to manage student data and records for online and classroom learning. May be combined with Integrated Learning Systems (ILS) to provide complete online education environment. Popular examples include Banner, PeopleSoft, and Saba.

List-servs Electronic mail-based discussion groups. Users submit their names to the LISTPROC server via e-mail and are added to the list. Users then receive all e-mail messages that are sent to the list. List-servs are a convenient way for people to electronically discuss a common interest.

Media Messages that are distributed through technologies, principally text in books, study guides, and computer networks; sound in audio-tapes and broadcast; pictures in videotapes and broadcast; and text, sound, and/or pictures in a teleconference.

Meta-Data A definition or description of data, information embedded on Web pages and educational objects that facilitate retrieval for specific purposes through search engines or other tools of modern library science. See *IMS, SCORM.*

Multimedia Systems that support the integration of text, audio, still images, video, and graphics. Before they can be used in a computer application each of these elements must be converted from analog form to digital form. See also *Streaming Media.*

Network A configuration of two or more computers linked to share information and resources.

Sharable Content Object Reference Model (SCORM) A reference model that defines a Web-based learning "content model" developed by the ADL initiative. SCORM incorporates many emerging standards (developed by IMS and various other organizations) into one content model that continues to evolve.

Streaming Media Digital transmission of video or audio on the Internet/Web. Large multimedia files can be transmitted in highly compressed format. Makes multimedia on the Web possible with relatively low bandwidth.

Synchronous Interactive communication with no time delay. Also, a system in which regularly occurring events in timed intervals are kept in step using some form of electronic clocking mechanism. See *Asynchronous.*

Technology Mechanisms for distributing messages, including postal systems, radio and television broadcasting companies, telephone, satellite, and computer networks.

Telecommunication The process of transmitting or receiving sound, video or data over a distance by any electrical or electromagnetic medium.

Teleconference Simultaneous conference to two or more sites distributed via telephone, satellite video-conferences, and video-conferences using compressed video. It is helpful to prefix "teleconference" with either "audio" or "video."

Telecourses Any course delivered via telecommunication technology (e.g., radio, television, or computer networks) but most commonly applied to courses delivered by video.

Threaded Discussion Forums Commonly used on bulletin boards or listservs, these are indexed collections that allow a user to follow one particular subject in a series of messages. When messages are threaded, all messages are grouped together by topic making it easier to follow a single line of discussion.

URLs (Uniform Resource Locators) The address system used by the Internet to locate resources such as Web sites. A URL includes: the type of resource being accessed, the address of the server, and the location of the file. For example, the complete URL for *The American Journal of Distance Education* Web site is: http://www.ajde.com /index.htm.

Video-conference A meeting, instructional session, or conversation between people at different locations relying on video technology as the primary communication link. Communication is often by video in one direction, and feedback to the video-studio is by audio. The term videoconference is sometimes used to refer to conferences via compressed video, conferences via land lines, and broadcasts via satellite. To avoid confusion, using the term which describes the type of technology employed is recommended.

Web Conference A teleconference involving both audio and online activities (usually slide presentations or whiteboards). All participants can interact with each via voice or shared online tools. Audio may be delivered by telephone or computer (Voice Over IP).

Web Site Related collection of Web documents. The address for a Web site (see URL) takes you to the initial page, or home page. From the home page you can go to all the other pages on the Web site.

World Wide Web (WWW) A hypertext-based, distributed information system originally created by researchers at CERN, the European Laboratory for Particle Physics, to facilitate sharing research information. The Web presents the user with documents, called Web pages, full of links to other documents or information systems. Selecting one of these links, the user can access more information about a particular topic. Web pages include text as well as multimedia (images, video, animation, sound). Servers are connected to the Internet to allow users to traverse (or "surf") the Web.

REFERENCES

Achtemeier, S. D., Morris, L. V., & Finnegan, C. L. (2003, Feb.). Considerations for developing evaluations of online courses. *Journal of Asynchronous Learning Networks, 7*(1). Available at: http://www.aln.org/publications/jaln/v7n1/v7n1_achtemeier.asp

ACRL. (1998). ACRL guidelines for distance learning library services. *College & Research Libraries, 59*(9), 689–694.

Adelman, C. (1997). *Leading, Concurrent, or Lagging? The Knowledge Content of Computer Science in Higher Education and the Labor Market.* Washington, DC: U.S. Department of Education and the National Institute for Science Education.

Ahlm, M. (1972). Telephone instruction in distance education. *Epistolodidactica, 2*, 49–64.

Aiken, M. P. (2000). *Commercialism in Public Schools: Focusing on Channel One.* Available at: http://www.edrs.com/Webstore/Download.cfm?ID = 721086

Alsunbul, A. (2002). Issues relating to distance education in the Arab world. *Convergence, 35*(1), 59–81.

Al-Rawaf, H., & Simmons, C. (1992). Distance higher education for women in Saudi Arabia: Present and proposed. *Distance Education, 13*(1), 65–81.

Altbach, P. G. (1998). *Comparative Higher Education: Knowledge, the University and Development.* Greenwich, CT: Ablex Publishing Corporation.

Altbach, P. G. (Ed.) (2001). *The American Academic Model in Comparative Perspective.* Baltimore and London: The Johns Hopkins University Press.

American Council on Education. (2000). *Developing a distance education policy for 21st century learning.* Washington, DC: American Council on Education.

Anderson, J. S. (1987). A historical overview of telecommunications in the health care industry. *The American Journal of Distance Education, 1*(2), 53–60.

Anderson, T. D., & Garrison, D. R. (1995). Transactional issues in distance education: The impact of design in audioteleconferencing. *The American Journal of Distance Education, 9*(2), 27–45.

Anderson, T., & Kanuka, H. (1997). On-line forums: New platforms for professional development and group collaboration. *Journal of Computer Mediated Communication, 3*(3). Available at: http://www.ascusc.org/jcmc/vol3/issue3/anderson.html

Anderson, T., Rourke, L., Garrison, D. R., & Archer, W. (2001, Sept.). Assessing teacher presence in a computer conferencing context. *Journal of Asynchronous Learning Networks, 5*(2). Available at: http://www.sloan-c.org/publications/jaln/v5n2/index.asp

Armstrong, M., Toebe, D., & Watson, M. (1985). Strengthening the instructional role in self-directed learning activities. *Journal of Continuing Education in Nursing, 16*(3), 75–84.

Baker, D. R. (2002). Teacher perceptions of the educational outcomes for direct instruction compressed video classroom environment within remote classrooms at the secondary school level. *Dissertation Abstracts International, 63*(06), 2105A. (UMI No. 3056384)

Banathy, B. (1993). *A Systems View of Education.* Englewood Cliffs, NJ: Educational Technology Publications.

Barker, B. O. (1987). The effects of learning by satellite on rural schools. Paper presented at Learning by Satellite Conference, Tulsa, OK. (ERIC # ED284693)

Barron, T. (2000, Jan.). Online learning goes synchronous. *ASTD Learning Circuits, 1*(1). Available at

http://www.learningcircuits.org/jan2000/trends
.html

Barron, T. (2003, May). LoD survey: Quality and effectiveness of E-learning. *ASTD Learning Circuits, 4*(5). Available at: http://www.learningcircuits.org /2003/may2003/qualitysurvey.htm

Bates, A. W. (2000). *Managing Technological Change. Strategies for College and University Leaders.* San Francisco: Jossey-Bass.

Bates, A. W. (2003). *Technology, Distributed Learning and Distance Education.* London: Routledge.

Baynton, M. (1992). Dimensions of "control" in distance education: A factor analysis. *The American Journal of Distance Education, 6*(2), 17–31.

Beijer, E. (1972). A study of students' preferences with regard to different models of two-way communications. *Epistolodidactica, 2,* 83–90.

Batey, A., & Cowell, R. N. (1986). *Distance Education: An Overview.* Portland, OR: Northwest Regional Educational Lab. (ERIC # ED 278519)

Beer, V. (2000). *The Web Learning Fieldbook: Using the World Wide Web to Build Workplace Learning Environments.* San Francisco: Jossey-Bass.

Berge, Z. L. (2003). Managing and planning distance training and education in the corporate sector. In M. G. Moore & Anderson, W. G. (Eds.), *Handbook of Distance Education.* Mahwah, NJ: Lawrence Erlbaum Associates.

Berge, Z., & Kearsley, G. (2003, Nov.–Dec.). The sustainability of distance training: Follow-up to case studies. *The Technology Source.* Available at: http://ts.mivu.org/default.asp?show = article&id = 2027

Berge, Z. L., & Mrozowski, S. (2001). Review of research in distance education, 1990 to 1999. *The American Journal of Distance Education, 15*(3), 5–19.

Berk, E., & Devlin, J. (1991). *Hypertext/Hypermedia Handbook.* New York: McGraw-Hill.

Betts, K. (1998). An institutional overview: Factors influencing faculty participation in distance education in postsecondary education in the United States: An institutional study. *Online Journal of Distance Learning Administration, 1*(3). Available at: http:// www.westga.edu/ ~ distance/betts13.html

Bi, J. (2000). Instructional design attributes of web-based courses. *World Conference on the WWW and Internet, Vol. 2000*(1), 38–43. (ERIC # ED 448746)

Billings, D. M. (1988). A conceptual model of correspondence course completion. *The American Journal of Distance Education, 2*(2), 23–35.

Biner, P. M., Bink, M. L., Huffman, M. L., & Dean, R. S. (1995). Personality characteristics differentiating and predicting the achievement of televised-course students and traditional-course students. *The American Journal of Distance Education, 9*(2), 46–60.

Bischoff, W. R., Bisconer, S. W., Kooker, B. M., & Woods, L. C. (1996). Transactional distance and interactive television in the distance education of health professionals. *The American Journal of Distance Education, 10*(3), 4–19.

Bittner, W. S., & Mallory, H. F. (1933). *University Teaching by Mail.* New York: Macmillan.

Blanch, G. (1994). Don't all faculty want their own TV show? Barriers to faculty participation in distance education. *DEOSNEWS, 4*(1). Available at: http://www.ed.psu.edu/acsde/deos/deosnews /deosnews4_1.asp

Bloom, Benjamin S. (1956). *Taxonomy of Educational Objectives: The Classification of Educational Goals.* New York: David McKay Co.

Blum, K. D. (1999). Asynchronous, computer-mediated communication (CMC)-based higher education at a distance: Gender differences in preferred learning styles, participation barriers, and communication patterns (Doctoral dissertation, Walden University). *Dissertation Abstracts International, 60*(11), 3923A. (UMI No. 9949329)

Blumenstyk, G. (1999). California Virtual University will end most of its operations. *The Chronicle of Higher Education, 45*(30), A30.

Bof, A. (2002). Proformação Evaluation Report. Unpublished paper, Brasilia, Ministry of Education.

Bond, C., Poker, F., & Pugh, J. (1998). *The National Guard Distributed Training Technology Project: Training Soldiers and Serving Communities.* Proceedings of the 14th Annual Conference on Distance Teaching and Learning, 79–82. Madison: The University of Wisconsin System.

Bond, C., Poker, F., & Pugh, J. (1999). *The National Guard Distributed Learning Initiative: A Systems Approach.* Proceedings of the 15th Annual Conference on Distance Teaching and Learning, 45–49. Madison: The University of Wisconsin System.

Bond, C., & Pugh, J. (2000). *Aviation Skills Training in the Army National Guard.* Proceedings of the 16th Annual Conference on Distance Teaching and Learning, 57–62. Madison: The University of Wisconsin System.

Bonk, C. J. (2002). *Online training in an online world.* Bloomington, IN: CourseShare.com. Available at http://www.courseshare.com/reports.php

Bonk C. J., & Dennen, V. (2003). Frameworks for research, design, benchmarks, training and pedagogy in Web-based distance education. In M. G. Moore & Anderson, W.G. (Eds.), *Handbook of Distance Education*. Mahwah, NJ: Lawrence Erlbaum Associates.

Book, E. (2001). Plugfests help standardize online learning technology. *National Defense, 86*(577), 22–23.

Boston, R. L. (1992). Remote delivery of instruction via the PC and modem: What have we learned? *The American Journal of Distance Education, 6*(3), 45–57.

Bothel, R. (2001). Bringing it all together. *Online Journal of Distance Learning Administration, 4*(1), 9.

Boyd, R., & Apps, J. (1980). *Redefining the Discipline of Adult Education*. San Francisco: Jossey-Bass.

Brennan, C., & Maltese, J. (2000). Bridging the digital divide: A tale of two cities. *Nation's Cities Weekly, 23*(13), 3.

Briggs, L. J., Gustafson, K. L., & Tillman, M. H. (1991). *Instructional Design: Principles & Applications* (2nd ed.). Englewood Cliffs, NJ: Educational Technology Publications.

Brigham, D. (2001). Converting student support services to online delivery. *International Review of Research in Open and Distance Learning, 1*(2), 11.

Bringelson, L. S., & Carey, T. (2000). Different (key) strokes for different folks: Designing online venues for professional communities. *Educational Technology & Society, 3*(3). Available at: http://ifets.ieee.org/periodical/vol_3_2000/a01.html

Brookfield, S. (Ed.). (1985). Self-directed learning: From theory to practice. *New Directions for Continuing Education, No. 25*. San Francisco: Jossey-Bass.

Brothers, W. L. (1971). The world wide campus. In O. Mackenzie & Christensen, E. L. (Eds.), *The Changing World of Correspondence Study*. University Park: Pennsylvania State University Press.

Brown, R. E. (2001). The process of community-building in distance learning classes. *Journal of Asynchronous Learning Networks, 5*(2), 18–35.

Bunker, E. L. (1998a). An historical analysis of a distance education forum: The International Council for Distance Education world conference proceedings, 1938 to 1995 (Doctoral Dissertation. The Pennsylvania State University, 1998). *Dissertation Abstracts International, 59*(06), 1864A. (UMI No. 9836630)

Bunker, E. L. (1998b). Gaining perspective for the future of distance education from early leaders. *The American Journal of Distance Education, 12*(2), 46–53.

Bunker, E. (2003). The history of distance education through the eyes of the International Council for Distance Education. In M. G. Moore & Anderson, W. G. (Eds.), *Handbook of Distance Education*. Mahwah, NJ: Lawrence Erlbaum Associates.

Bunker, E., Gayol, Y., Nti, N., & Reidell, P. (1996). *A Study of Transactional Distance in an International Audio-Conferencing Course*. Proceedings of Seventh International Conference, 40–44. Phoenix, AZ: The Society for Information Technology and Teacher Education.

Burge, E. (1988). Beyond andragogy: Some explorations for distance learning design. *Journal of Distance Education, 3*(1), 5–23.

Burge, E. J. (1994). Learning in computer conferenced contexts: The learners' perspective. *Journal of Distance Education, 9*(1), 19–43.

Burge, E. J. (2001). *People Development: Reflective Practice for Educators*. Keynote speech for the Networking 2001 conference, Brisbane, Australia, October 16, 2001.

Candy, P. C. (1991). *Self-direction for lifelong learning*. San Francisco: Jossey-Bass.

Canning, R. (2002). Distance or Distancing Education? A case study in technology-based learning. *Journal of Further and Higher Education, 26*(1), 29–42. Available at: http://taylorandfrancis.metapress.com/app/home/contribution.asp?wasp = 159 wymqrvp72jryxvcby&referrer = parent&backto = issue,3,9;journal,9,15;linkingpublicationresults,id:104618,1

Cannings, T. R., & Finkel, L. (1993). *The Technology Age Classroom*. Wilsonville, OR: Franklin, Beedle & Associates.

Cantor, A. (2001). Accommodating people with disabilities in web-based training programs. In B. Khan (Ed.), *Web-Based Training*. Englewood Cliffs, NJ: Educational Technology Publications.

Carabajal, K., LaPointe, D., & Gunawardena, C. N. (2003). Group development in online learning communities. In M. G. Moore & Anderson, W. G. (Eds.), *Handbook of Distance Education*. Mahwah, NJ: Lawrence Erlbaum Associates.

Carnwell, R. (2000). Approaches to study and their impact on the need for support and guidance in distance learning. *Open Learning, 15*(2), 5.

Carnwell, R., & Harrington, C. (2001). Diagnosing student support needs for distance learning. *Education Resource Information Clearinghouse, 23*.

Carr, S. (2000, Mar.). Online psychology instruction is effective, but not satisfying, study finds. *The Chronicle of Higher Education.* March 10, A48.

Carr, S. (2000, Nov.). Navy picks institutions for online learning effort. *Chronicle of Higher Education,* Nov. 17, A60.

Cavanaugh, C. (2001). The effectiveness of interactive distance education technologies in K–12 learning: A meta-analysis. *International Journal of Educational Telecommunications, 7*(1), 73–88.

Chang, S. L. (2003). What types of online facilitation do students need? ERIC accession. (ERIC # ED 470183) Available at: http://www.ericfacility.net /teams/Search.do?action = 102

Chen, Y. J. (2001). Dimensions of transactional distance in world wide web learning environment: A factor analysis. *British Journal of Educational Technology, 32*(4), 459–470.

Chen, Y. J., & Willits, F. K. (1999). Dimensions of educational transactions in a videoconferencing learning environment. *The American Journal of Distance Education, 13*(1), 45–59.

Cheng, H. C., Lehman, J., & Armstrong, P. (1991). Comparison of performance and attitude in traditional and computer conferencing classes. *The American Journal of Distance Education, 5*(3), 51–59.

Chisholm, P. (2003, Dec.). Learning from a distance. *Military Training Technology, Online Edition, 8*(4). Available at: http://www.mt2-kmi.com/archive _article.cfm?DocID = 269

Christensen, E., Anakwe, U., & Kessler, E. (2001, Spring). Receptivity to distance learning: The effect of technology, reputation, constraints, and learning preferences. *Journal of Research on Computing in Education, 33*(3).

Chute, A. (2003). The Corporate learning environment: From teletraining to knowledge management and e-Learning. In M. G. Moore & Anderson, W. G. (Eds.), *Handbook of Distance Education.* Mahwah, NJ: Lawrence Erlbaum Associates.

Chute, A. G., Hulik, M., & Palmer, C. (1987). Teletraining Productivity at AT&T. Paper presented at the International Teleconferencing Association Annual Convention, Washington, DC.

Chute, J. (1996). *Virtual Teaching in Higher Education.* Available at: http://www.csun.edu /sociology/virexp.htm.

Clark, T. (2001). *Virtual High Schools: State of the States.* Macomb, IL: Center for the Application of Information Technologies, Western Illinois University.

Clark, T. (2003). Virtual Schools: Trends and Issues. Available at: http://www.dlrn.org/k12/virtualstudy .pdf.

Coggins, C. (1989). Preferred learning styles and their impact on completion of external degree programs. In M. G. Moore & Clark, G. C. (Eds.), *Readings in Distance Learning and Instruction,* Number 2. University Park, PA: American Center for the Study of Distance Education.

Cole, S., Coats, M., & Lentell, H. (1986). Towards good teaching by correspondence. *Open Learning, 1*(1): 16–22.

Collins, J. E. (2002). A true experiment comparing learning outcomes of a two-way interactive telecourse and a traditional face-to-face course. *Dissertation Abstracts International, 63*(04), 1308A. (UMI No: 3050786)

Collison, G., Elbaum, B., Haavind, S., & Tinker, R. (2000). *Facilitating Online Learning: Effective Strategies for Moderators.* Madison: Atwood.

Compora, D. P. (2003). Current trends in distance education: An administrative model. *Online Journal of Distance Learning Administration, 6*(2). Available at: http://www.westga.edu/%7Edistance /ojdla/summer62/compora62.html

Conour, D. (2000). Crossing the digital divide. *Sunset, 204*(4), 204.

Conrad, D. (2002a). Inhibition, integrity and etiquette among online learners: The art of niceness. *Distance Education, 23*(2): 197–212.

Conrad, D. (2002b). Engagement, excitement, anxiety, and fear: Learners' experiences of starting an online course. *The American Journal of Distance Education, 16*(4), 205–226.

Cookson, P. S. (1990). Persistence in distance education. In M. G. Moore (Ed.), *Contemporary Issues in American Distance Education.* Oxford: Pergamon.

Cookson, P. S., Quigley, B. A., & Borland, K. W. (1994). *Audioconferencing in Major Research Universities: A National Survey.* Proceedings of International Distance Education Conference. State College: ACSDE, Penn State University.

Cooper, R., Dempsey, P. R., Menon, V., & Millson-Martula, C. (1998). Remote library users: Needs and expectations. *Library Trends 47*(1), 42–64.

Cornell University (2001). From domesticity to modernity: What was home economics? Division of Rare and Manuscript Collections, Cornell University.

Available at: http://rmc.library.cornell.edu/homeEc /default.html.

Crow, S. (1999). Virtual universities can meet high standards. *The Chronicle of Higher Education, 46*(10), B5–B6.

Crump, R. E. (1928). Correspondence and class-extension work in Oklahoma. Doctoral dissertation, Columbia University. *Dissertation Abstracts International,* L1928, (Not Available from UMI)

Cukier, J. (1997). Cost-benefit analysis of telelearning: Developing a methodology framework. *Distance Education, 18*(1), 137–152.

Curry, R. F. (1997). Academic advising in distance education. (Doctoral dissertation, College of William and Mary, 1997). Dissertation Abstracts International, 58(02A), 396. (UMI No: 9722676)

Curtis, D., & Lawson, M. (2001, May). Exploring online collaborative learning. *Journal of Asynchronous Learning Networks, 5*(1), 18–35.

Curtis, J. A., & Biedenbach, J. M. (1979). *Educational Telecommunications Delivery Systems.* Washington, DC: American Society for Engineering Education.

Cyrs, T. (1998). Evaluating distance learning programs and courses. Available at: http://www .zianet.com/edacyrs/tips/evaluate_dl.htm

Cyrs, T., & Smith, F. (1990). *Teleclass Teaching: A Resource Guide* (2nd ed.). Las Cruces: New Mexico State University.

Daft, R. L., & Lengel, R. H. (1986). Organizational information requirements, media richness and structural design. *Management Science, 32*(5), 554–571.

Damarin, S. K. (2000). The "digital divide" versus digital differences: Principles for equitable use of technology in education. *Educational Technology, 40*(4), 17–22.

Daniel, J. S. (1996). *Mega-universities and knowledge media: Technology strategies for higher education.* London: Kogan Page.

Davis, D. J. (2003). Developing text for Web-based instruction. In M. G. Moore & Anderson, W. G. (Eds.), *Handbook of Distance Education.* Mahwah, NJ: Lawrence Erlbaum Associates.

Department of Education Training and Youth Affairs, Australia (2000). The business of borderless education. Available at: http://www.detya.gov.au/archive /highered/eippubs/eip00_3/bbe.pdf.

Deubel, P. (2003). Learning from reflections: Issues in building quality online courses. *Online Journal of Distance Learning Administration, 6*(3). Available

at: http://www.westga.edu/~distance/ojdla/fall63 /deubel63.htm

Diaz, D. P., & Cartnal, R. B. (1999). Students' learning styles in two classes: Online distance learning and equivalent on-campus. *College Teaching 47*(4), 130–135.

Dick, W., & Carey, L. (1990). *The Systematic Design of Instruction* (3rd Ed.). Glenview, IL: Scott, Foresman, and Company.

Dillon, A., & Gabbard, R. (1998). Hypermedia as an educational technology: A review of the quantitative research literature on learner comprehension, control, and style. *Review of Educational Research, 68,* 322–349.

Dirr, P. J. (1991). Understanding television-based distance education: Identifying barriers to university attendance. *Research in Distance Education, 3*(1), 2–4.

Dirr, P. J. (2003). Distance education policy issues: Towards 2010. In M. G. Moore & Anderson, W. G. (Eds.), *Handbook of Distance Education.* Mahwah, NJ: Lawrence Erlbaum Associates.

DiBiase, D. (2000). Is distance teaching more work or less work? *The American Journal of Distance Education, 14*(3), 6–20.

Dick, W., & Carey, L. (1985). *The Systematic Design of Instruction.* Glenview, IL: Scott, Foresman & Co.

Dillon, C. L., & Walsh, S. J. (1992). Faculty: The neglected resource in distance education. *The American Journal of Distance Education, 6*(3), 5–21.

DiPaolo, A. (1992). The Stanford Instructional Television Network: A partnership with Industry. *Ed, 6*(7), 4.

Distance Education and Training Council. (1998). *Survey of member institutions.* Washington DC: Author.

Dodge, B. (1995). Webquests: A technique for internet-based learning. *Distance Educator, 1*(2), 10–13.

Donlevy, J. G. (2000). College success in a technological society: Increasing access and services for economically disadvantaged students. *International Journal of Instructional Media, 27*(3), 225–230.

Donovan, D. P. (2000). *Distributed Training Technology Project: Promoting Distributed Learning "Anytime, Anywhere."* Proceedings of the 16th Annual Conference on Distance Teaching and Learning, 123–126. Madison: The University of Wisconsin System.

Driscoll, J. (2001). Designing and delivering live online training. *ACM E-Learn.* V2001(10). Available

at: http://elearnmag.org/subpage/sub_page.cfm?
section=3&list_item=3&page=1

Driscoll, M., & Alexander, L. (1998). *Web-Based Training: Using Technology to Design Adult Learning Experiences.* San Francisco: Jossey-Bass.

Duchastel, P. (1988). Toward the ideal study guide: An exploration of the functions and components of study guides. *British Journal of Educational Technology, 14*(3), 216–231.

Duckworth, C. (2001, July). An instructor's guide to live e-learning. *ASTD Training Circuits, 2*(7). Available at: http://www.learningcircuits.org/2001/jul2001/duckworth.html

Dunham, R. S. (1999, Aug. 2). Across America, a troubling "digital divide." *Business Week, Industrial/Technology Edition, 3640,* 40.

Dutton, W., & Lievrouw, L. (1982). Teleconferencing as an educational medium. In L. Parker & Olgren, C. (Eds.), *Teleconferencing and Electronic Communications.* Madison, WI: University of Wisconsin-Extension, Center for Interactive Programs.

Eastman, A. B. (2003). A study of distance education policy at metropolitan universities. *Dissertation Abstracts International, 64*(02), 348A. (UMI No. 3081520)

Eastman, M. A. (2002). The comparative effectiveness of using distance education methods with and without a supplemental gaming simulation. Dissertation Abstracts International, *2A*(63), 479. (UMI No. 3042010)

Eastmond, D. V. (1998). Adult learners and Internet-based distance education. *New Directions for Adult and Continuing Education, 78,* 33–41.

Edwards, R. (1994). From a distance? Globalisation, space-time compression and distance education. *Open Learning, 9*(3), 9–17.

Ellertson, E. K., Wydra, D., & Jolley, H. (1987). *Report on Distance Learning: A National Effectiveness Survey.* Mansfield, PA: Mansfield University.

Evans, T., & Nation, D. (2003). Globalization and the reinvention of distance education. In M. G. Moore & Anderson, W. G. (Eds.), *Handbook of Distance Education.* Mahwah, NJ: Lawrence Erlbaum Associates.

Falk, R. (1998, March). Web lectures: Increasing student interest and involvement. *UC, Davis Information Times.* Available at: http://ittimes.ucdavis.edu/v6n6mar98/falk.html.

Feasley, C. E. (2003). Evolution of Distance Education Organizations. In M. G. Moore &

Anderson, W. G. (Eds.), *Handbook of Distance Education.* Mahwah, NJ: Lawrence Erlbaum Associates.

Fjortoft, N. F. (1996). Persistence in a distance learning program: A case in pharmaceutical education. *The American Journal of Distance Education, 10*(3), 49–59.

Flagg, B. (1990). *Formative Evaluation for Educational Technologies.* Hillsdale, NJ: Erlbaum.

Foley, M. (2003). The Global Development Learning Network: A World Bank initiative in distance learning for development. In M. G. Moore & Anderson, W. G. (Eds.), *Handbook of Distance Education.* Mahwah, NJ: Lawrence Erlbaum Associates.

Franks, K. (1996). Attitudes of Alaskan distance education students toward media and instruction. *The American Journal of Distance Education, 10*(3), 60–74.

Fredericksen, E., Pickett, A., Shea, P., Pelz, W., & Swan, K. (2000, Sept.). Student satisfaction and perceived learning with online courses: Principles and examples from the SUNY Learning Network. *Journal of Asynchronous Learning Networks, 4*(2). Available at: http://www.aln.org/publications/jaln/v4n2/index.asp.

Fredrickson, S. (1990). Audiographics for Distance Education: An Alternative Technology. Paper presented at the Annual Conference of the Alaska Association for Computers in Education. (ERIC # ED 345711)

Freeman, M. W. (2003). Distance learning in the U.S. Army: Meeting the readiness needs of the 21st century armed forces. In M. G. Moore & Anderson, W. G. (Eds.), *Handbook of Distance Education.* Mahwah, NJ: Lawrence Erlbaum Associates.

Freeman, M. W., Grimes, L. W., & Holliday, J. R. (2000). Increasing access to learning with audio-data collaboration. *Educational Technology & Society, 3*(3). Available at: http://ifets.ieee.org/periodical/vol_3_2000/a07.html

Fusco, M., & Ketcham, S. E. (2002). *Distance Learning for Higher Education: An Annotated Bibliography.* Greenwood Village, CO: Libraries Unlimited.

Gagne, R. M., Briggs, L. J., & Wagner, W. W. (1992). *Principles of Instructional Design.* Fort Worth, TX: Holt, Rinehart & Winston.

Gardner, M. K., Rudolph, S., & Della-Piana, G. (1987). Learning over the lines: Audio-graphic teleconferencing comes of age. *Educational Technology, 27*(4), 39–42.

Garrison, D. R. (1989). *Understanding Distance Education: A Framework for the Future.* Boston: Routledge & Kegan Paul.

Garrison, D. R. (1990). An analysis and evaluation of audioteleconferencing to facilitate education at a distance. *The American Journal of Distance Education, 4*(3), 13–24.

Garrison, D. R. (2000). Theoretical challenges for distance education in the 21st Century: A shift from structural to transactional issues. *International Review of Research in Open and Distance Learning, 1*(1). Available at: http://www.irrodl.org/content /v1.1/randy.html

Garrison, D. R., Anderson, T., & Archer, W. (2001). Critical thinking, cognitive presence, and computer conferencing in distance education. *The American Journal of Distance Education, 15*(1), 7–23.

Garrison, D. R., & Baynton, M. (1987). Beyond independence in distance education: The concept of control. *The American Journal of Distance Education, 1*(3), 3–15.

Garrison, D. R., & Shale, D. (1987). Mapping the boundaries of distance education: Problems in defining the field. *The American Journal of Distance Education, 1*(1), 7–13.

Gayol, Y. (1995). The use of computer networks in distance education: Analysis of the patterns of electronic interactions in a multinational course. In C. Gibson (Ed.), *Learners and Learning: Research Monograph No 13.* University Park, PA: ACSDE.

Gery, G. (1991). *Electronic Performance Support Systems.* Boston: Weingarten Publications.

Gibson, C. C. (1990). Learners and learning: A discussion of selected research. In M. G. Moore (Ed.), *Contemporary Issues in American Distance Education.* Oxford: Pergamon.

Gibson, C. C. (1998). *Distance learners in higher education: Institutional responses for quality outcomes.* Madison, WI: Atwood Publishers.

Gilbert, S. (2000). *How To Be A Successful Online Student.* Columbus, OH: McGraw-Hill.

Gilcher, K. W., & Johnstone, S. M. (1989). *A Critical Review of the Use of Audiographic Conferencing Systems by Selected Educational Institutions.* College Park, MD: International University Consortium.

Gormly, E. K. (1999). Commercials on campus: A qualitative study of educators' reactions to the advertisements on Channel One. *New Jersey Journal of Communication, 7*(1), 106–135.

Granger, D., & Benke, M. (1998). Supporting learners at a distance from inquiry through completion.

In C. C. Gibson (Ed.), *Distance Learners in Higher Education.* Madison, WI: Atwood.

Gray, B. A. (1996). Student achievement and temperament types in traditional and distance learning environments. *Dissertation Abstracts International 57*(04), 1549A. (UMI No. AAT 9628894)

Green, K. C. (1999). *The 1999 National Survey of Information Technology in American Higher Education.* Encino, CA: The Campus Computing Project.

Green, K. C. (2001). *The 2001 National Survey of Information Technology in US Higher Education.* Encino, CA: Campus Computing Project.

Greenspan, R. (2002). Two-thirds hit the net. *Cyberatlas.* Available at: http://cyberatlas.internet .com/big_picture/geographics/article/0,,5911 _1011491,00.html#table

Guernsey, L. (1998). College librarians plan for floods of digital users. *The Chronicle of Higher Education, 45*(12), A28.

Gunawardena, C. N. (1992). Changing faculty roles for audiographics and online teaching. *The American Journal of Distance Education, 6*(3), 58–71.

Gunawardena, C. N. (1995). Social presence theory and implications for interaction and collaborative learning in computer conferences. *International Journal of Educational Telecommunications, 1*(2/3), 147–166.

Gunawardena, C., & Zittle, F. (1997). Social presence as a predictor of satisfaction within a computer-mediated conferencing environment. *The American Journal of Distance Education, 11*(3), 8–26.

Gunawardena, C. Wilson, P. and Nolla A. (2003). Culture and online education. In M. G. Moore & Anderson, W. G. (Eds.), *Handbook of Distance Education.* Mahwah, NJ: Lawrence Erlbaum Associates.

Hall, B. (1997). *Web-Based Training Cookbook.* New York: John Wiley & Sons.

Hall, R. H., Watkins, S. E., & Eller, V. M. (2003). A model of Web-based design for learning. In M. G. Moore & Anderson, W. G. (Eds.), *Handbook of Distance Education.* Mahwah, NJ: Lawrence Erlbaum Associates.

Halsne, A., & Gatta, L. (2002, Spring). Online versus traditionally-delivered instruction: A descriptive study of learner characteristics in a community college setting. *Online Journal of Distance Learning Administration, 5*(1). Available at: http://www

.westga.edu/%7Edistance/ojdla/spring51/halsne51.html

Hanna, D. E., Glowacki-Dudka, M., & Conceicao-Runlee, S. (2000). *147 Practical Tips for Teaching Online Groups: Essentials of Web-Based Education.* Madison, WI: Atwood Publishing.

Hara, N., & Kling, R. (1999, Dec.). Students' frustrations with a web-based distance education course, *First Monday, 4*(12). Available at: http://www.firstmonday.dk/issues/issue4_12/hara/index.html

Harkness, W., Lane, J. L., & Harwood, J. (2003, July). A cost-effective model for teaching elementary statistics with improved performance. *Journal of Asynchronous Learning Networks, 7*(2). Available at: http://www.aln.org/publications/jaln/v7n2/v7n2_harkness.asp

Harrison, P. J., Seeman, B. J., Behm, R., Saba, F., Molise, G., & Williams, M. D. (1991). Development of a distance education assessment instrument. *Educational Technology Research & Development, 39*(4), 65–77.

Hartigan, P., & St. John, R. K. (1989). AIDS training in third-world countries: An evaluation of telecommunications technology. *Educational Technology, 29*(10), 20–23.

Hashim, Y. (1999). Are instructional design elements being used in module writing? *British Journal of Educational Technology, 30*(4), 341–358.

Heinich, R. M., Molenda, M., & Russell, J. R. (1985). *Instructional Media and the New Technologies.* New York: Macmillan.

Heinzen, T. E., & Alberico, S. M. (1990). Using a creativity paradigm to evaluate teleconferencing. *The American Journal of Distance Education, 4*(3), 3–12.

Hill, L. (1999). Racial digital divide. *Nation, 268*(15), 10.

Hillman, D. C., Willis, D., & Gunawardena, C. N. (1994). Learner-interface interaction in distance education: an extension of contemporary models and strategies for practitioners. *The American Journal of Distance Education, 8*(2), 30–42.

Hiltz, S. R., Coppola, N., Rotter, N., Turoff, M., & Benbunan-Fich, R. (2000). Measuring the importance of collaborative learning for the effectiveness of ALN: A multi-measure, multi-method approach. *Journal of Asynchronous Learning Networks 4*(2). Available at: http://www.aln.org/publications/jaln/v4n2/v4n2_hiltz.asp

Hislop, G. (2000, Sept.). Working professionals as part-time online learners. *Journal of Asynchronous Learning Networks, 4*(2). Available at: http://www.aln.org/publications/jaln/v4n2/v4n2_hislop.asp

Hmieleski, K. M., & Champagne, M. V. (2000). Plugging in to course evaluation. *Technology Source.* Available at: http://ts.mivu.org/default.asp?show=article&id=795

Hodgins, W., & Conner, M. (2000, Fall). Everything you ever wanted to know about learning standards but were afraid to ask. *LineZine.* 2(1). Available at: http://www.linezine.com/2.1/features/wheyewtkls.htm

Hofmann, J. (2000, Jan.). Making synchronous training a success. *ASTD Learning Circuits, 1*(1). Available at: http://www.learningcircuits.org/2000/jan2000/Hofmann.htm

Holmberg, B. (1981). *Status and Trends of Distance Education.* London: Kogan Page.

Holmberg, B. (1986). *The Growth and Structure of Distance Education.* London: Croom Helm.

Holmberg, B. (1987). The development of distance education research. *The American Journal of Distance Education, 24*(1), 11–46.

Holmberg, B. (1989). *Theory and Practice of Distance Education.* Boston: Routledge & Kegan Paul.

Holmberg, R. G., & Bakshi, T. S. (1992). Postmortem on a distance education course: Successes and failures. *The American Journal of Distance Education, 6*(1), 27–39.

Holmes, G. A., & Branch, R. C. (1994). *Cable Television in the Classroom.* (ERIC # ED 371727)

Holstein, J. A. (1992). Making the written word "speak": Reflections on the teaching of correspondence courses. *The American Journal of Distance Education, 6*(3), 22–34.

Hong, K-S. (2002). Relationships between students' and instructional variables with satisfaction and learning from a Web-based course. *The Internet and Higher Education, 5*(3), 267–281.

Hopper, D. A. (2000). Learner characteristics, life circumstances, and transactional distance in a distance education setting. *Dissertation Abstracts International, 61*(10), 3962A. (UMI No. 9992211)

Horton, W. (2000). *Designing Web-Based Training: How to Teach Anyone Anything Anywhere Anytime.* New York: John Wiley & Sons.

Horton, W. (2001). *Evaluating E-Learning.* Alexandria, VA: American Society for Training and Development.

Hosley, D. L., & Randolph, S. L. (1993). Distance Learning as a Training and Education Tool. Lockheed Space Operations Co., Kennedy Space Center, FL. (ERIC # ED 355936)

Howell, S. L., Williams, P. B., & Lindsay, N. K. (2003, Fall). Thirty-two trends affecting distance education: An informed foundation from strategic planning. *Online Journal of Distance Learning Administration, 6*(3). Available at: http://www.westga.edu/~distance/ojdla/fall63/howell63.html

Hughes, S. E., Wickersham, L. E., Ryan-Jones, D. L., & Smith, S. A. (2002). Overcoming social and psychological barriers to effective on-line collaboration. *Educational Technology and Society, 5*(1), 86–92.

Idrus, R. M. (1992). Enhancing teletutorials via collaborative learning: The Malaysian experience. *DEOSNEWS, 2*(14). Available at: http://www.ed.psu.edu/acsde/deos/deosnews/deosnews2_14.asp

Inglis, A. (2003). A comparison of online delivery costs with some alternative distance delivery methods. In M. G. Moore & Anderson, W. G. (Eds.), *Handbook of Distance Education.* Mahwah, NJ: Lawrence Erlbaum Associates.

Inglis, A., Ling, P., & Joosten, V. (1999). *Delivering Digitally: Managing the Transition to the Knowledge Media.* London: Kogan Page.

Irele M. (2002). Institutional mainstreaming of distance education: Guiding policies. Doctoral dissertation, The Pennsylvania State University. *Doctoral dissertation International, 64*(01), 46A. (UMI No. 3076962)

Irons, L., Jung, D., & Keel, R. (2002). Interactivity in distance learning: The digital divide and student satisfaction. *Educational Technology & Society, 5*(3). Available at: http://ifets.ieee.org/periodical/vol_3_2002/jung.html

Jensen, M. 1999. Sub-Saharan Africa. In *World Communication and Information Report, 1999–2000.* Paris: UNESCO.

Johnston, J., & Brzezinski, E. (1992). Taking the measure of Channel One: The first year. *ED, 6*(6), 4–9.

Jonassen, D. H. (1989). *Hypertext/Hypermedia.* Englewood Cliffs, NJ: Educational Technology Publications.

Jonassen, D., & Mandl, H. (1990). *Designing Hypermedia for Learning.* New York: Springer Verlag.

Jones, S., Blevins, L. A., Mally, W., & Monroe, J. E. (2003). The U. S. Marine Corps distance learning program. In M. G. Moore & Anderson, W. G. (Eds.), *Handbook of Distance Education.* Mahwah, NJ: Lawrence Erlbaum Associates.

Juliussen, K. P., & Juliussen, E. J. (1993). The 6th Annual Computer Industry Almanac. Arlington Heights, IL: Computer Industry Almanac Inc.

Jung, I. (2001). Building a theoretical framework of web-based instruction in the context of distance education. *British Journal of Educational Technology, 32*(5), 525–534.

Jung, I. (2003). Cost effectiveness of online education. In M. G. Moore & Anderson, W. G. (Eds.), *Handbook of Distance Education.* Mahwah, NJ: Lawrence Erlbaum Associates.

Jung, I., Choi, S., Lim, C., & Leem, J. (2002). Effects of different types of interaction on learning achievement, satisfaction and participation in Web-based instruction. *Innovations in education and teaching international, 39*(2), 153–162.

Kaufman, R., & Watkins, R. (2003). Strategic planning for distance education. In M. G. Moore & Anderson, W. G. (Eds.), *Handbook of Distance Education.* Mahwah, NJ: Lawrence Erlbaum Associates.

Kearsley, G. (1983). *Computer Based Training.* Reading, MA: Addison-Wesley.

Kearsley, G. (2000). *Online Education: Learning and Teaching in Cyberspace.* New York: Wadsworth.

Kearsley, G., Hunter, B., & Furlong, M. (1992). *We Teach with Technology.* Wilsonville, OR: Franklin, Beedle & Associates.

Keegan D. (1980). On defining distance education. *Distance Education, 1*(1), 13–35.

Keegan D. (1986). *The Foundations of Distance Education.* London: Croom Helm.

Keister, L. W. (1997, June). Training: Impact of technology: On-the-go learning. *Mobility Magazine of the Employee Relocation Council.* Available at: http://www.erc.org/MOBILITY_Online/index.shtml

Kelsey, K. D. (2000). Participant interaction in a course delivered by interactive compressed video technology. *The American Journal of Distance Education, 14*(1), 63–74.

Kember, D. (1989). An illustration, with case studies, of a linear process model of drop-out from distance education. *Distance Education, 10*(2), 196–211.

Kember, D. (1995). *Open learning for adults: A model of student progress.* Englewood Cliffs. NJ: Educational Technology Publications.

Kenyon, H. S. (2002, Feb.). Learning online from the front line. *Signal, 56*(6), 49–51.

Kerzner, H. (2001). *Project Management: A Systems Approach to Planning, Scheduling, and Controlling* (7th ed.). New York: John Wiley & Sons.

Khan, B. (1997). *Web Based Instruction.* Educational Technology Publications.

Khan, B. (2001). *Web Based Training*. Educational Technology Publications.

Kim, J. W. (1999). Present problems and future challenges of the Korea National Open University. Hagen Germany, Fernuniversitat.

Kim-Rupnow, W. S., Dowrick, P. W., & Burke, L. S. (2001). Implications for improving access and outcomes for individuals with disabilities in postsecondary distance education. *The American Journal of Distance Education, 15*(1), 25–40.

Kirk, E. E., & Bartelstein, A. M. (1999). Libraries close in on distance education. *Library Journal, 124*(6), 40–42.

Knapczyk, D. R. (1990). Use of audiographic technology in distance education of practicing teachers. *Educational Technology, 30*(6), 24–27.

Knowles, M. (1978). *The Adult Learner*. Houston, TX: Gulf Publishing.

Ko, S., & Rossen, S. (2001). *Teaching Online: A Practical Guide*. Boston: Houghton Mifflin Co.

Koory, M. (2003, July). Differences in learning outcomes for the online and F2F versions of "An introduction to Shakespeare". *J. Asynchronous Learning Networks, 4(2)*. Available at http://www.aln.org /publications/jaln/v7n2/v7n2_koory.asp

Krieger, T. J. (2001). *A Virtual Revolution: Trends in Expansion of Distance Education*. American Federation of Teachers. Available at: http://www .aft.org/higher_ed/downloadable/VirtualRevolution .pdf

Kruse, K., & Keil, J. (2000). *Technology-Based Training: The Art and Science of Design, Development and Delivery*. San Francisco: Jossey-Bass.

Kuramoto, A. (1984). Teleconferencing for nurses: Evaluating its effectiveness. In L. Parker & Olgren, C. (Eds.), *Teleconferencing and Electronic Communications*, III. Madison, WI: University of Wisconsin-Extension, Center for Interactive Programs.

Kutner, J. A. (2000, Aug.). Army to offer soldiers online education in $600m program. *National Defense, 85*(561), 13.

Laidlaw, B., & Layard, R. (1974). Traditional versus Open University teaching methods: A cost comparison. *Higher Education, 3*, 439–468.

Lane, C. (1989). A selection model and pre-adoption evaluation instrument for video programs. *The American Journal of Distance Education, 3*(3), 46–57.

Lauzon, A. C. (1992). Integrating computer-based instruction with computer conferencing: An evaluation of a model for designing online education. *The American Journal of Distance Education, 6*(2), 32–46.

Lazarus, B. D. (2003, Sept.). Teaching courses online: How much time does it take? *Journal of Asynchronous Networks, 7*(3). Available at: http://www.aln.org/publications/jaln/v7n3/v7n3 _lazarus.asp

Lee, L. (2002). Faculty and administrator perceptions of instructional support for distance education. *International Journal of Instructional Media, 29*(1), 27–46.

Lee, W., & Owens, D. (2000). *Multimedia-Based Instructional Design: Computer-Based Training, Web-Based Training, and Distance Learning*. San Francisco: Jossey-Bass.

Leshin, C. B., Pollock, J., & Reigeluth, C. M. (1992). *Instructional Design Strategies and Tactics*. Englewood Cliffs, NJ: Educational Technology Publications.

Levenson, W. B. (1945). *Teaching through Radio*. New York: Farrar & Rinehart.

Levine, T. K. (1988). *Teaching telecourses: Opportunities and Options*. Washington, DC: Annenberg/CPB.

Levine, T. K. (1992). *Going the Distance: A Handbook for Developing Distance Degree Programs*. Washington, DC: Annenberg/CPB.

Levy, S. P., & Beaulieu, R. (2003). Online distance learning among the California community colleges: Looking at the planning and implementation. *The American Journal of Distance Education, 17*(4), 207–220.

Lezberg, A. (2003). Accreditation: Quality control in higher distance education. In M. G. Moore & Anderson, W. G. (Eds.), *Handbook of Distance Education*. Mahwah, NJ: Lawrence Erlbaum Associates.

Li, Y., & Chen, J. (1999). Comparative Research into Chinese Conventional and Television-based Higher Education. *Open Learning, 14*(2), 3–13.

Li, Y., & Li, L. (2003). Construct learning support system for distance education in China. In A. Tait & Gaskell, A. (Eds.). *Proceedings of Conference on Learner Support*. Cambridge, UK: The Open University.

Lipinski, T. A. (2003). Legal issues in the development and use of copyrighted material in Web-based distance education. In M. G. Moore & Anderson, W. G. (Eds.), *Handbook of Distance Education*. Mahwah, NJ: Lawrence Erlbaum Associates.

Long, H. B., & Associates. (1989). *Self-directed Learning: Emerging Theory and Practice*. Norman,

Oklahoma: Oklahoma Research Center for Continuing Professional and Higher Education, University of Oklahoma.

Longmire, W. (2000). A primer on learning objects. *ASTD Learning Circuits, 1*(3).

Lynch, M. (2002). *The Online Educator: A Guide to Creating the Virtual Classroom.* London: Routledge Falmer.

Lynch, P. J., & Horton, S. (2002). *The Web Style Guide: Basic Design Principles for Creating Web Sites.* New Haven, CT: Yale University Press.

MacDonald, P. J. (2001). Integrating multimedia technology into continuing nursing education: Examining the effectiveness. *Masters Abstracts International, 39*(04), 965.

Machtmes, K., & Asher, J. W. (2000). A meta-analysis of the effectiveness of telecourses in distance education. *The American Journal of Distance Education, 14*(1), 27–46.

MacGregor, C. J. (2001). A comparison of student perceptions in traditional and online classes. *Academic Exchange Quarterly, 5*(4), 143–149.

MacKenzie, O., & Christensen, E. L. (1971). *The Changing World of Correspondence Study.* University Park: Penn State University Press.

MacKenzie, O., Christensen, E. L., & Rigby, P. H. (1968). *Correspondence Instruction in the United States.* New York: McGraw-Hill.

Maddux, C. D. (2001). *Educational computing: Learning with tomorrow's technologies.* Needham Heights, MA: Allyn & Bacon.

Major, M. B., & Shane, D. L. (1992). Use of interactive television for outreach nursing education. In M. G. Moore (Ed.), *Readings in Distance Education, Number 3.* University Park, PA: American Center for the Study of Distance Education.

Maki, R. H., Maki, W. S., Patterson, M., & Whittaker, P. D. (2000) Evaluation of a Web-based introductory psychology course. *Behavior Research Methods, Instruments, & Computers, 32,* 230-239.

Marchese, T. (1998, May). Not-so-distant competitors: How new providers are remaking the postsecondary marketplace. *AAHE Bulletin.* Available at: http://aahebulletin.com/public/archive/Not-So-Distant%20Competitors.asp

Martin, C. M. (1993). Oklahoma's Star Schools: Equipment use and benefits two years after grant's end. *The American Journal of Distance Education, 7*(3), 51–60.

Mason, R. (1998). *Globalising Education: Trends and Applications.* London: Routledge.

Mason, R. (2003). Global education: Out of the ivory tower. In M. G. Moore & Anderson, W. G. (Eds.), *Handbook of Distance Education.* Mahwah, NJ: Lawrence Erlbaum Associates.

McCollum, K. (1999). Accreditation of on-line university draws fire. *The Chronicle of Higher Education, 45*(30), A33.

McCormick, C., & Jones, D. (1997). *Building a Web-Based Education System.* New York: John Wiley & Sons, Inc.

McDonald, J., & Gibson, C. C. (1998). Interpersonal dynamics and group development in computer conferencing. *The American Journal of Distance Education, 12*(1), 7–25.

McGowan, J. (1992). Distance education as a medium for promoting the college preparation of attendance of minority students. *DEOSNEWS, 2*(8). Available at: http://www.ed.psu.edu/acsde/deos/deosnews/deosnews2_8.asp

McGreal, R. (1993). Exemplary programs of secondary distance education in Canada. *DEOSNEWS, 3*(6). Available at: http://www.ed.psu.edu/acsde/deos/deosnews/deosnews3_6.asp

McIsaac, M. S., Blocher, J. M., Mahes, V., & Vrasidas, C. (1999). Student and teacher perceptions of interaction in online computer-mediated communication. *Educational Media International, 36*(2), 121–131.

McKnight, S. (2003). Distance education and the role of academic libraries. In M. G. Moore & Anderson, W. G. (Eds.), *Handbook of Distance Education.* Mahwah, NJ: Lawrence Erlbaum Associates.

McLuhan, M. & McLuhan, E. (1988). *Laws of the Media: The New Science.* Toronto, ON: University of Toronto Press.

McMahill, J. M. (1993). Videotape distance learning courses: Administrative implications for colleges and universities. *ED Journal, 7*(6), 16–20.

McNeil, D. R. (1980). UMA: Progress of an experiment. In M. N. Chanberlain (Ed.), *Providing Continuing Education By Media and Technology.* San Francisco: Jossey-Bass.

Meister, M. (2000). Testimony before Web-Based Education Commission. Available at: www.hpcnet.org/cgi-bin/global/a_bus_card.cgi?SiteID=179527

Michel, D. P. (1999). Leadership development in a distributed learning environment: The influence of learning preferences on satisfaction (Doctoral dissertation, Regents University). *Dissertation Abstracts International, 61*(03), 860A. (UMI No. 9964402)

Moore, D. M., Burton, J. K., & Dodl, N. R. (1991). The role of facilitators in Virginia's Electronic Classroom project. *The American Journal of Distance Education, 5*(3), 29–39.

Moore, M. G. (1972). Learner autonomy: The second dimension of independent learning. *Convergence, 5*(2), 76–88. Available at: http://www.ajde.com /Documents/learner_autonomy.pdf

Moore, M. G. (1973). Towards a theory of independent learning and teaching. *Journal of Higher Education, 44,* 661–679.

Moore, M. G. (1976). Investigation of the interaction between the cognitive style of field independence and attitudes to independent study. (Doctoral dissertation, University of Wisconsin-Madison). 37(06), 3344A. (UMI No. 7620127)

Moore, M. G. (1980). Independent study. In R. Boyd & Apps, J. (Eds.), *Redefining the Discipline of Adult Education.* San Francisco: Jossey-Bass. Available at: http://www.ajde.com/Documents/independent _study.pdf

Moore, M. G. (1986). Self-directed learning and distance education. *Journal of Distance Education, 1*(1). Available at: http://cade.athabascau.ca/vol1.1 /moore.html

Moore, M. G. (1989). Three types of interaction. *The American Journal of Distance Education, 3*(2), 1–6.

Moore, M. G. (Ed.), (1990). *Contemporary Issues in American Distance Education.* London: Pergamon Press.

Moore, M. G. (1993). Theory of transactional distance. In D. Keegan (Ed.), *Theoretical Principles of Distance Education.* London and New York: Routledge. Available at: http://www.uniolden berg.de/zef/ede/support/readings/moore93.pdf

Moore, M. G., & Anderson, W. G. (2003). *Handbook of Distance Education.* Mahwah, NJ: Lawrence Erlbaum Associates.

Moore, M. G., & Savrock, J. T. (Eds.), (2001). *Distance Education in the Health Sciences,* Readings in Distance Education, No. 8. University Park, PA: The American Center for the Study of Distance Education.

Morgan, B. M. (2000). *Is Distance Learning Worth It? Helping to Determine the Costs of Online Learning.* Huntington, WV: Marshall University. Available at http://webpages.marshall.edu/~morgan16 /onlinecosts

Morse, K. (2003, Feb.). Does one size fit all? Exploring asynchronous learning in a multicultural environment. *Journal of Asynchronous Learning Networks, 7*(1). Available at: http://www.aln.org /publications/jaln/v7n1/v7n1_morse.asp

Munro, J. (1991). *Presence at a distance: The educator-learner relationship in distance education and dropout.* Ed.D. dissertation, The University of British Columbia, 53(09), 3083A. (UMI No. NN69709)

Munro, J. S. (1998). *Presence at a distance: The educator-learner relationship in distance education* (ACSDE Research Monograph No. 16). University Park, PA: The American Center for the Study of Distance Education.

Murphy, K. L., Mahoney, S. E., & Harvel, T. J. (2000). Role of contracts in enhancing community building in web course. *Educational Technology & Society, 3*(3). Available at: http://ifets.ieee.org/peri odical/vol_3_2000/e03.html

Naidu, S. (2003). Designing instruction for e-learning environments. In M. G. Moore & Anderson, W. G. (Eds.), *Handbook of Distance Education.* Mahwah, NJ: Lawrence Erlbaum Associates.

Nasseh, B. (1997). *A Brief History of Distance Education.* SeniorNet. Available at: http://www .seniornet.org/edu/art/history.html

Nelson, D. M. (2000). A case study of distance education policies in the University of Wisconsin system. *Dissertation Abstracts International, 61*(02), 525A. (UMI No. 9956187)

Nelson, R. N. (1985). Two-way microwave transmission consolidates, improves education. *NASSP Bulletin, 69*(4), 38–42.

Nielsen, J. (1999). Designing Web Usability. Berkeley, CA: New Riders Press. *See also* http://www.useit.com.

Nevada State Department of Human Resources. (1990). *Project NETWORC Final Report.* (ERIC # ED 329073)

Neuhauser, C. (2002). Learning style and effectiveness of online and face-to-face instruction. *The American Journal of Distance Education, 16*(2), 99–113.

Neumann, Y., & Shachar, M. (2003, Oct.). Differences between traditional and distance education academic performances: A meta-analytic approach. *International Review of Research in Open and Distance Learning, 4*(2). Available at: http://www.irrodl.org/content/v4.2/shachar- neumann.html

Noffsinger, J. S. (1926). *Correspondence Schools, Lyceums, Chautauquas.* New York: Macmillan.

Noffsinger, J. S. (1938). The Story of the Benton Harbour Plan. *Report of the First International*

Conference on Correspondence Education, Victoria, BC, Canada: The Department of Education.

Norenberg, C. D., & Lundblad, L. (1987). *Distance Delivery of Vocational Education: Technologies and Planning Matrixes.* St. Paul, MN: Minnesota R&D Center for Vocational Education.

Nova Southeastern University. (2003). *Institutional Description.* Available at: http://www.nova.edu /cwis/urp/description.html

Nyirenda, J. E., Indabawa, S. A., & Avoseh, M. B. M. (1999). *Developing Professional Adult Education Programmes in Namibia.* Windhoek: University of Namibia.

Oblinger, D. and Rush, S. (2003). The involvement of corporations in distance education. In M. G. Moore & Anderson, W. G. (Eds.), *Handbook of Distance Education.* Mahwah, NJ: Lawrence Erlbaum Associates.

Olson, J. S., Olson, G. M., & Meader, D. K. (1995). What mix of video and audio is useful for small groups doing remote real-time design work? Paper presented at the 1995 Conference on Human Factors in Computing Systems. Available at: http://www .acm.org/sigchi/chi95/Electronic/documnts/papers /jso_bdy.htm

Olson, M. T., & Wisher, A. R. (2002). The effectiveness of web-based instruction: An initial inquiry. *International Review of Research in Open and Distance Learning.* Available at: http://www .irrodl.org/content/v3.2/olsen.html

Ory, J. C. (1997). Gender similarity in the use of and attitudes about ALN in a university setting. *Journal of Asynchronous Learning Networks, 1*(1). Available at: http://www.aln.org/publications/jaln/v1n1 /v1n1_ory.asp

Osborn, V. (2001). Identifying at-risk students in videoconferencing and web-based distance education. *The American Journal of Distance Education, 15*(1), 41–54.

Pacey, L., & Keough, E. (2003). Public policy, institutional structures and strategy implementation. In M. G. Moore & Anderson, W. G. (Eds.), *Handbook of Distance Education.* Mahwah, NJ: Lawrence Erlbaum Associates.

Palloff, R., & Pratt, K. (1999). *Building Learning Communities in Cyberspace: Effective Strategies for the Online Classroom.* San Francisco: Jossey-Bass.

Palloff, R., & Pratt, K. (2001). *Lessons from the Cyberspace Classroom: The Realities of Online Teaching.* San Francisco: Jossey-Bass.

Parker, L. A. (1984). *Teleconferencing Resource Book.* New York: Elsevier.

Paulsen, M. F., & Pinder, P. W. (1990). Research in distance education. Setting a goal for the nineties. *The American Journal of Distance Education, 4*(3), 83–84.

Payne, H. (1999). *A Review of the Literature: Interactive Video Teletraining in Distance Learning Courses* (2nd ed.). Atlanta, GA: Spacenet, Inc. and the USDLA.

Peirce, N. (2000). Digital divide? *Nation's Cities Weekly, 23*(10), 13.

Perdue, K., & Valentine, T. (2000). Deterrents to participation in web-based continuing professional education. *The American Journal of Distance Education, 14*(1), 6–26.

Perley, J., & Tanguay, D. M. (1999). Accrediting online institutions diminishes higher education. *The Chronicle of Higher Education, 46*(10), B4–B5.

Perraton, H. (2000). Rethinking the research agenda. *International Review of Research in Open and Distance Learning, 1*(1). Available at: http://www .irrodl.org/content/v1.1/hilary.html

Peters, B. B. (1999). Use of the Internet to deliver continuing education in social work practice skills: An evaluative study. *Dissertation Abstracts International, 61*(02), 770A. (UMI No.AAT9962580)

Peters, O. (1965). Der Fernunterricct. Materialien zur Diskussion einer neuen Unterrichtsform, Weinheim, Berlin: Boltz.

Peters, O. (1983). Distance teaching and industrial production: A comparative interpretation in outline. In D. Sewart, Keegan, D., & Holmberg, B. (Eds.), *Distance Education: International Perspectives.* London: Croom Helm.

Phelps, R. H., Wells, R. A., Ashworth, R. L., & Hahn, H. A. (1991). Effectiveness and costs of distance education using computer-mediated communication. *The American Journal of Distance Education, 5*(3), 7–19.

Picciano, A. (2002). Beyond student perceptions: Issues of interaction, presence, and performance in an online course. *Journal of Asynchronous Learning Networks, 6*(1). Available at: http://www.aln.org /publications/jaln/v6n1/v6n1_picciano.asp

Pittman, V. V. (1986). Station WSUI and the early days of instructional radio. *The Palimpset, 67*(2), 38–52.

Pittman, V. V. (2003). Correspondence study in the American university: A second historiographic perspective. In M. G. Moore & Anderson, W. G. (Eds.), *Handbook of Distance Education.* Mahwah, NJ: Lawrence Erlbaum Associates.

Porter, L. (1997). *Creating the Virtual Classroom: Distance Learning with the Internet.* New York: John Wiley & Sons.

Postman, N. (1992). *Technopoly: The Surrender of Culture to Technology.* New York: Knopf.

Pratt, D. D. (1988). Andragogy as a relational construct. *Adult Education Quarterly, 38*(3), 160–172.

Radcliff, J. (1990). Television and distance education in Europe: Current roles and future challenges. In A. W. Bates (Ed.), *Media and Technology in European Distance Education.* Milton Keynes, UK: Open University for the European Association of Distance Teaching Universities.

Reigeluth, C., & Garfinkle, R. (1994). *Systematic Change in Education.* Englewood Cliffs, NJ: Educational Technology Publications.

Reiser, R. A., & Gagne, R. M. (1983). *Selecting Media for Instruction.* Englewood Cliffs, NJ: Educational Technology Publications.

Resmer, M. (1998). Media Review: The Educom/Nlii Instructional Management Systems Project. *The American Journal of Distance Education, 12*(1), 78–80.

Rice, R. E. (1992). Task analyzability, use of new media, and effectiveness: A multisite exploration of media richness. *Organization Science, 3*(4), 475–500.

Richey, R. (1986). *The Theoretical and Conceptual Basis of Instructional Design.* New York: Nichols.

Rifkind, L. J. (1992). Immediacy as a predictor of teacher effectiveness in the instructional television classroom. *Journal of Interactive Television, 1*(1), 31–40.

Roberts, T. (2003). *Online Collaborative Learning: Theory and Practice.* Hershey, PA: The Idea Group.

Robertson, J. S. (2002). Making online information accessible to students with disabilities. *The Technology Source.* Available at: http://ts.mivu.org /default.asp?show = article&id = 948

Roblyer, M. D., & Wiencke, W. (2003). Design and use of a rubric to assess and encourage interactive qualities in distance courses. *The American Journal of Distance Education, 17*(2), 77–98.

Rockwell, K., Furgason, J., & Marx, M. B. (2000, Winter). Research and evaluation needs for distance education: A Delphi study. *Online Journal of Distance Learning Administration, 3*(3). Available at: http://www.westga.edu/ ~ distance/ojdla/fall33 /rockwell33.html

Rockwell, K., Scheuer, J., Fritz, S. J., & Marx, D. B. (1999, Winter). Incentives and obstacles influencing higher education faculty and administrators to teach via distance. *Online Journal of Distance Learning Administration, 2*(4). Available at: http://www .westga.edu/ ~ distance/rockwell24.html

Rockwell, K., Schauer, J., Fritz, S. M., & Marx, D. B. (2000, Spring). Faculty education, assistance and support needed to deliver education via distance. *Online Journal of Distance Learning Administration, 3*(2). Available at: http://www.westga.edu/ ~ distance/rockwell32.html

Rogers, E. (1983). *Diffusion of Innovations* (3rd ed.). New York: Free Press.

Romiszowski, A. J. (1974). *The Selection and Use of Instructional Media.* New York: John Wiley & Sons.

Rosenberg, M. (2000). *E-Learning: Strategies for Delivering Knowledge in the Digital Age.* New York: McGraw-Hill.

Rourke, L., Anderson, T., Garrison, D. R., & Archer, W. (1999). Assessing social presence in asynchronous text-based computer conferencing. *Journal of Distance Education, 14*(2), 51–70.

Rowntree, D. (1986). *Teaching Through Self-Instruction: A Practical Handbook for Course Developers.* London: Kogan Page.

Rudestam, K. E., & Shoenholtz-Read, J. (2002). *Handbook of Online Learning: Innovations in Higher Education and Corporate Training.* Thousand Oaks, CA: Sage.

Rule, S. M., DeWulf, M. J., & Stowitschek, J. J. (1988). An economic analysis of inservice teacher training. *The American Journal of Distance Education, 2*(2), 12–22.

Rumble, G. (1986). *The Planning and Management of Distance Education.* London: Croom Helm.

Rumble, G. (2000). Student support in distance education in the 21st century: Learning from service management. *Distance Education, 21*(2), 216–235.

Rumble, G. (2003). Modeling the costs and economics of distance education. In M. G. Moore & Anderson, W. G. (Eds.), *Handbook of Distance Education.* Mahwah, NJ: Lawrence Erlbaum Associates.

Russell, F. K., Jr. (1991). *Receive-Site Facilitator Practices and Student Performance in Satellite-Delivered Instruction.* Proceedings of Selected Research Presentations at the Annual Convention of the Association for Educational Communications and Technology. Anaheim, CA. (ERIC # ED 335011)

Russell, T. L. (1999). *The No Significant Difference Phenomenon.* Available at: http://teleeducation .nb.ca/nosignificantdifference

Russell, T. L. (1999). *The No Significant Difference Phenomenon as Reported in 355 Research Reports,*

Summaries and Papers. A Comparative Research Annotated Bibliography on Technology for Distance Education. Raleigh, North Carolina: Office of Instructional Telecommunications, North Carolina State University. Available at: http://ifets.ieee.org /periodical/vol_3_99/book_review_russell.html

Saba, F. (1988). Integrated telecommunications systems and instructional transaction. *The American Journal of Distance Education, 2*(3), 17–24.

Saba, F. (1998). Corporate learning and training: Changing the context of higher education. *Distance-Educator.com, 2*(8). Available at: http://www .distance_educator.com/Arcieve/v2n8/1dercor porate.281.htm

Saba, F. (2003). Distance education theory, methodology and epistemology: A pragmatic paradigm. In M. G. Moore & Anderson, W. G. (Eds.), *Handbook of Distance Education.* Mahwah, NJ: Lawrence Erlbaum Associates.

Saba, F., & Shearer, R. L. (1994). Verifying key theoretical concepts in a dynamic model of distance education. *The American Journal of Distance Education, 8*(1), 36–57.

Saba, F., & Twitchell, D. (1988). Research in distance education. A system modeling approach. *The American Journal of Distance Education, 2*(1), 9–24.

Saettler, P. (1990). *The Evolution of American Educational Technology.* Littleton, CO: Libraries Unlimited.

Salmon, G. (2000). *E-moderating: The Key to Teaching and Learning Online.* London: Kogan Page.

Schaffer, J. M. (1990). Preparing faculty and designing courses for delivery via audio teleconferencing. *Journal of Adult Education, 18*(2), 11–18.

Schank, R. (1997). *Virtual Learning: A Revolutionary Approach to Building a Highly Skilled Workforce.* New York: McGraw-Hill.

Schauer, J. A. (2002). Role of the department chair in implementing distance education in colleges of agriculture in land-grant institutions. *Dissertation Abstracts International, 63*(03), 840A. (UMI No. 3045534)

Schrum, L., & Benson, A. (2000). Online professional education: A case study of an MBA program through its transition to an online model. *Journal of Asynchronous Learning Networks, 4*(1). Available at: http://www.aln.org/publications/jaln/v4n1/v4n1 _schrum.asp

Schrum, L., & Ohler, J. (2003). *Distance education at one Alaskan University: A case study.* Unpublished paper, University of Alaska.

Scott, J. C. (1999). The Chautauqua Movement: Revolution in popular higher education. *The Journal of Higher Education, 70*(4), 389–412.

Seay, R., Rudolph, H., & Chamberlain, D. (2001). Faculty perceptions of interactive television instruction. *Journal of Education for Business, 77*(2), 99–106.

Sener, J., & Stover, M. (2000, Sept.). Integrating ALN into an independent study program: NVCC case studies. *Journal of Asynchronous Learning Networks, 4*(2). Available at: http://www.aln.org /publications/jaln/v4n2/v4n2_sener.asp

Sewart, D., Keegan, D., & Holmberg, B. (1983). *Distance Education: International Perspectives.* London: Croom Helm.

Shaeffer, J. M., & Farr, C. W. (1993). Evaluation: A key piece in the distance education puzzle. *THE Journal, 20*(9), 79–82.

Shapley, P. (2000). Online education to develop complex reasoning skills in organic chemistry. *Journal of Asynchronous Learning Networks, 4*(2). Available at: http://www.aln.org/publications/jaln /v4n2/v4n2_shapley.asp

Sherry, A. C. (2003). Quality and its measurement in distance education. In M. G. Moore & Anderson, W. G. (Eds.), *Handbook of Distance Education.* Mahwah, NJ: Lawrence Erlbaum Associates.

Shin, N. (2002). Beyond interaction: The relational construct of "transactional presence." *Open Learning, 17*(2), 121–137.

Short, J., Williams, E. & Christie, B. (1976). *The Social Psychology of Telecommunications.* London: John Wiley & Sons.

Showalter, R. G. (1983). *Speaker Telephone Continuing Education for School Personnel Serving Handicapped Children: Final Project Report.* Indianapolis, IN: Indiana State Dept. of Public Instruction. (ERIC # ED 231150)

Simonson, M., & Bauck, T. (2003). Distance education policy issues: Statewide perspectives. In M. G. Moore & Anderson, W. G. (Eds.), *Handbook of Distance Education.* Mahwah, NJ: Lawrence Erlbaum Associates.

Simpson, O. (2002). *Supporting Students in Online, Open and Distance Learning.* London: Kogan Page.

Smith, K. D., Eddy, J. P., Richards, T. C., & Dixon, P. N. (2000). Distance education copyright, intellectual property, and antitrust concerns. *The American Journal of Distance Education, 14*(2), 5–13.

Smith, T. W. (1992). The evolution of audiographics teleconferencing for continuing engineering education at the University of Wisconsin-Madison.

International Journal of Continuing Engineering Education, 2(4).

Snyder, C. A., Logue, S., & Preece, B. G. (1996). *The Role of the Libraries in Distance Education: A SPEC Kit #216.* Washington, DC: Association of Research Libraries.

Sparks, R. K. (1997). The effect of personality types on two-way video instruction *Dissertation Abstracts International, 58*(02), 430A. (UMI No. AAT9723651)

Spitzer, D. R., Bauwens, J., & Quast, S. (1989). Extending education using video: Lessons learned. *Educational Technology, 29*(5), 28–30.

Sponder, B. M. (1990). *Distance Education in Rural Alaska. Monograph Series in Distance Education.* Fairbanks, AK: University of Alaska.

Staffo, M. J. (2002). The influence of government instructional technology policy on decision-making in rural Alabama school districts. *Dissertation Abstracts International, 63*(01), 153A. (UMI No. 3038885)

Steinfield, C. W. (1986). Computer-mediated communication in an organizational setting: Explaining task-related and socio-emotional uses. In M. McLaughlin (ed.) *Communication Yearbook,* Vol. 9. (pp. 777-804). Beverly Hills, CA: Sage

St. Pierre, S., & Olson, L. K. (1991). Student perspectives on the effectiveness of correspondence instruction. *The American Journal of Distance Education, 5*(3), 65–71.

Stevens, G. & Stevens, E. (1995). Designing Electronic Performance Support Tools. Englewood Cliffs, NJ: Educational Technology Publications.

Stevenson, N. (2000). *Distance Learning for Dummies.* New York: John Wiley & Sons.

Stone, H. (1988). Variations in the characteristics and performance between on campus and video-based off-campus engineering graduate students. *Journal of Continuing Higher Education, 36*(1), 18–23.

Swan, K. (2001). Virtual interaction: Design factors affecting student satisfaction and perceived learning in asynchronous online courses. *Distance Education, 22*(2), 306–331.

Swan, K., Shea, P., Fredericksen, E. E., Pickett, A. M., & Pelz, W. E. (2000). *Course Design Factors Influencing the Success of Online Learning.* Available at: www.ericit.org/fulltext/IR020523.pdf

Tait, A. (2000). Planning student support for open and distance learning. *Open Learning, 15*(3), 287–299.

Tait, J. (2002). From competence to excellence: A systems view of staff development for part-time tutors at-a-distance. *Open Learning, 17*(2), 153–166.

Taplin, M., & Jegede, O. (2001). Gender differences in factors influencing achievement of distance education students. *Open Learning, 16*(2), 133–154.

Tapscott, D. (1998). The private sector and the digital divide. *Computerworld, 32*(10), 109.

Taylor, R. G., & Reid, W. M. (1993). Distance education course sequencing: An application of probabilistic PERT with cycles. *The American Journal of Distance Education, 7*(2), 49–58.

Taylor, R. W. (2002). Pros and cons of online learning—a faculty perspective. *Journal of European Industrial Training, 26*(1), 24–48.

Thomson, Inc. (2002). *Job Impact Study: The Next Generation of Corporate Learning.* Available at: http://www.netg.com/DemosAndDownloads/Downloads/JobImpact.pdf

Thompson, G. (1984). The cognitive style of field dependence as an explanatory construct in distance education drop-out. *Distance Education, 5*(2), 286–293.

Thompson, M. M., & Irele, M. (2003). Evaluating distance education programs. In M. G. Moore & Anderson, W. G. (Eds.), *Handbook of Distance Education.* Mahwah, NJ: Lawrence Erlbaum Associates.

Thorpe, M. (1988). *Evaluating Open and Distance Learning.* London: Longmans.

Thorpe, M. (2002). Rethinking learner support: The challenge of collaborative online learning. *Open Learning, 17*(2), 105–119.

Tiene, D. (1993). Exploring the effectiveness of the Channel One school telecasts. *Educational Technology, 33*(5), 36–42.

Tiwana, A. (2000). *The Knowledge Management Toolkit.* Upper Saddle River, NJ: Prentice Hall.

Tough, A. M. (1971). *The Adult's Learning Projects.* Toronto: Ontario Institute for Studies in Education.

Turoff, M. (1997, Mar.). Costs for the development of a virtual university. *Journal of Asynchronous Learning Networks, 4*(2). Available at: http://www.aln.org/publications/jaln/v1n1/v1n1_turoff.asp

UNESCO. (1999). *World Communication and Information Report 1999–2000.* Paris: UNESCO.

UNESCO. (2000). *World Education Report 2000.* Paris: UNESCO.

UNESCO. (2002a). *Open and distance learning: trends, policy and strategy considerations.* M. G. Moore & A. Tait (Eds.). Paris: UNESCO.

UNESCO. (2002b). *Institute for Information Technologies in Education (IITE) Specialized Training Course "ICTs in Distance Education."* Moscow: IITE.

UNESCO Institute for Information Technologies in Education. (2000). *Analytical Survey. Distance Education for the Information Society: Policies, Pedagogy and Professional Development.* Moscow: IITE.

United States General Accounting Office, National Security and International Affairs Division. (1997). *Distance learning: Opportunities Exist for DoD to Capitalize on Services' Efforts.* Washington, DC: United States General Accounting Office. (ERIC # ED 415409)

Unwin, D., & McAleese, R. (1988). *The Encyclopedia of Educational Media Communications and Technology.* New York: Greenwood Press.

Usher, R., Bryant, I., & Johnston, R. (1997). *Adult Education and the Post Modern Challenge: Learning beyond the Limits.* London: Routledge.

Valentine, D. (2002, Fall). Distance learning: Promises, problems, and possibilities. *Journal of Distance Learning Administration, 5*(3). Available at: http://www.westga.edu/%7Edistance/ojdla/fall53/valentine53.html

Valore, L., & Diehl, G. E. (1987). *The Effectiveness and Acceptance of Home Study.* Washington, DC: National Home Study Council.

Vandergrift, K. E. (2002, July). The anatomy of a distance education course: A case study analysis. *Journal of Asynchronous Learning Networks, 6*(1), 76–90.

Venkatraman, N., & Henderson, J.C. (1998). Real strategies for virtual organizing. *Sloan Management Review, 40*(1), 33–48.

Visser, J. A. (2000). Faculty work in developing and teaching web-based distance courses: A case study of time and effort. *The American Journal of Distance Education, 14*(3), 21–32.

Visser, J. (2003). Distance education in the perspective of global issues and concerns. In M. G. Moore & Anderson, W. G. (Eds.), *Handbook of Distance Education.* Mahwah, NJ: Lawrence Erlbaum Associates.

Von Euler, M., & Berg, D. (1998). *The Use of Electronic Media in Open and Distance Education.* Paris: UNESCO.

Vrasidas, C., & McIsaac, M. S. (1999). Factors influencing interaction in an online course. *The American Journal of Distance Education, 13*(3), 22–36.

Vygotsky, L. (1978). *Mind in Society.* Cambridge, MA: Harvard University Press.

Wagner E., & Reddy N. (1987). Design considerations in selecting teleconferencing for instruction. *The American Journal of Distance Education, 1*(3), 49–56.

Wagner, L. (1977). The economics of the Open University revisited. *Higher Education, 6,* 359–381.

Watkins, B. L. (1991). A quite radical idea: The invention and elaboration of collegiate correspondence study. In B. L. Watkins & Wright, S. J. (Eds.), *The Foundations of American Distance Education: A Century of Collegiate Correspondence Study.* Dubuque, IA: Kendall/Hunt.

Watkins, B. L., & Wright, S. J. (Eds.), (1991). *The Foundations of American Distance Education: A Century of Collegiate Correspondence Study.* Dubuque, IA: Kendall/Hunt.

Wedemeyer, C. A. (1963). *Brandenburg Memorial Essays on Correspondence Study,* Volume I. Madison, WI: University of Wisconsin-Extension.

Wedemeyer, C. A. (1966). *Brandenburg Memorial Essays on Correspondence Study,* Volume II. Madison: University of Wisconsin-Extension.

Wedemeyer, C. A. (1971). Independent study. In L.C. Deighton (Ed.), *The Encyclopedia of Education,* Vol. 4. New York: Macmillan.

Wedemeyer, C. A. (1982). The birth of the Open University, a postscript. *Teaching at a Distance, 21,* 21–27.

Wedemeyer, C. A., & Najem, C. (1969). *AIM: From Concept to Reality. The Articulated Instructional Media Program at Wisconsin.* Syracuse, NY: Center for the Study of Liberal Education for Adults, Syracuse University.

Wegerif, R. (1998). The social dimension of asynchronous learning networks. *Journal of Asynchronous Learning Networks, 2*(1). Available at: http://www.aln.org/publications/jaln/v2n1/v2n1_wegerif.asp

Wei, R. (1991). China's network of radio and television universities. *The American Journal of Distance Education, 5*(2), 59–64.

Wei, R. and Tong, Y. (1994): *Radio and TV Universities: The Mainstream of China's Adult and Distance Higher Education.* Nanjmg, China: Yilin Press.

Western Cooperative for Educational Telecommunications (WICHE). (1998). *The Distance Learner's Guide.* Prentice-Hall.

Westfall, P. (2003). Distance education in the U.S. Air Force. In M. G. Moore & Anderson, W. G. (Eds.), *Handbook of Distance Education*. Mahwah, NJ: Lawrence Erlbaum Associates.

White, K., & Weight, K. (1999). *The Online Teaching Guide: A Handbook of Attitudes, Strategies, and Techniques for the Virtual Classroom*. Boston: Allyn & Bacon.

Winiecki, D. J. (2003). Instructional discussions in online education: Practical and research-oriented perspectives In M. G. Moore & Anderson, W. G. (Eds.), *Handbook of Distance Education*. Mahwah, NJ: Lawrence Erlbaum Associates.

Wisher, R. A., & Curnow, C. K. (2003). Video-based instruction in distance learning: From motion pictures to the Internet. In M. G. Moore & Anderson, W. G. (Eds.), *Handbook of Distance Education*. Mahwah, NJ: Lawrence Erlbaum Associates.

Wisher, R. A., Curnow, C. K., & Seidel, R. J. (2001). Knowledge retention as a latent outcome measure in distance learning. *The American Journal of Distance Education, 15*(3), 20–35.

Wolcott, L. L. (2003). Dynamics of faculty participation in distance education: Motivations, incentives and rewards. In M. G. Moore & Anderson, W. G. (Eds.), *Handbook of Distance Education*. Mahwah, NJ: Lawrence Erlbaum Associates.

The World Bank. (1999). *Knowledge for Development: The World Development Report 1998/99*. New York: Oxford University Press.

Worley, L. K. (1993). Educational television and professional development: The Kentucky model. *THE Journal, 20*(11), 70–73.

Woudstra, A., & Adria, M. (2003). Issues in organizing for the new network and virtual forms of distance education. In M. G. Moore & Anderson, W. G. (Eds.), *Handbook of Distance Education*. Mahwah, NJ: Lawrence Erlbaum Associates.

Wright, S. J. (1991). Opportunity lost, opportunity regained: University independent study in the Modern Era. In B. L. Watkins & Wright, S. J. (Eds.), *The Foundations of American Distance Education: A Century of Collegiate Correspondence Study*. Dubuque, IA: Kendall/Hunt.

Youngblood, P., Trede, F., & DeCorpo, S. (2001). Facilitating online learning: A descriptive study. *Distance Education, 22*(2), 264–284.

Zhang, J., et al. (2001). Review of web-based assessment tools. In B. Khan (Ed.), *Web Based Training*. Englewood Cliffs, NJ: Educational Technology Publications.

Zigerell, J. (1991). *The Uses of Television in American Higher Education*. New York: Praeger.

Zucker, A., & Kozma, R., with Yarnall, L., & Marder, C. (2003). *The Virtual High School: Teaching Generation V*. New York: Teachers College Press.

NAME INDEX

Achtemeier, S. D., 124
Adelman, C., 64
Adria, M., 299
Ahlm, M., 246
Aiken, M. P., 52
Alberico, S. M., 124
Alexander, L., 117
Al-Rawaf, H., 277
Alsunbul, A., 277
Altbach, P. G., 26
Anakwe, U., 178
Anderson, J., 86
Anderson, T., 153, 229, 230
Anderson, W., 99
Apps, J., 223
Archer, W., 153, 230
Armstrong, M., 169
Armstrong, P., 231
Asher, J. W., 241
Ashworth, R. L., 240, 250
Avoseh, M. B. M., 282
Baker, D. R., 248
Bakshi, T. S., 108
Banathy, B., 23
Barker, B. O., 176
Barron, T., 64, 88
Bartelstein, A. M., 194
Bates, A. W., 54, 55, 76, 94, 99
Batey, A., 249
Bauck, T., 209
Bauwens, J., 77
Baynton, M., 229
Beer, V., 88
Behm, R., 124
Beijer, E., 246
Benbuanan-Finch, R., 247
Benke, M., 178
Benson, A., 239
Berg, D., 259

Berge, Z. L., 65, 157, 190, 237
Betts, K., 157
Bi, J., 244
Billings, D. M., 169
Biner, P. M., 242
Bink, M. L., 242
Bischoff, W. R., 231
Bisconer, S. W., 231
Bittner, W. S., 25, 26, 27, 220
Blanch, G., 156
Blevins, L. A., 67, 68
Blocher, J. M., 247
Bloom, B. S., 101
Blum, K. D., 184
Blumenstyk, G., 61
Bond, C., 67
Bonk, C. J., 88, 118
Book, E., 67
Borland, K. W., 83
Boston, R. L., 247
Bothel, R., 186
Boyd, R., 223
Branch, R. C., 81
Brennan, C., 214
Briggs, L. J., 101, 103
Brigham, D., 182, 186
Bringelson, L. S., 153
Brookfield, S., 228
Brothers, W. L., 30
Brown, R. E., 153
Brzezinski, E., 52
Bunker, E. L., 44, 232, 238
Burge, E., 230, 294
Burke, L. S., 119
Candy, P. C., 228
Canning, R., 239
Cannings, T. R., 86
Cantor, A., 119
Carabajal, K., 153, 154

Carey, L., 101
Carey, T., 153
Carnwell, R., 186
Cartnal, R. B., 171
Cavanaugh, C., 241
Chamberlain, D. 157
Champagne, M. V., 124
Chang, S. L., 248
Chen, J., 260
Chen, Y.-J., 232
Cheng, H. C., 231
Chisholm, P., 250
Choi, S., 243
Christensen, E., 27, 178, 220
Christie, B., 94
Chute, A., 85, 86, 91, 118, 250
Chute, J., 240
Clark, T., 62, 208, 209
Coats, M., 138
Coggins, C., 171
Cole, S., 138
Collins, J. E., 241
Collison, G., 151
Compora, D. P., 202
Conceicao-Runlee, S., 152
Conner, M., 97
Conour, D., 214
Conrad, D., 153, 163, 164
Cookson, P. S., 83, 166
Cooper, R., 194
Coppola, N., 247
Costa, M., 94
Cowell, R. N., 249
Crow, S., 60
Crump, R. E., 240
Cukier, J., 249
Curnow, C. K., 86, 146, 241
Curry, R. F., 186
Curtis, D., 153
Cyrs, T., 124, 146
Daft, R. L., 94
Damarin, S. K., 212, 213
Daniel, J. S., 35, 36, 56
Davis, D. J., 118
Dean, R. S., 242
DeCorpo, S., 247
Della-Piana, G., 83
Dempsey, P. R., 194
Dennen, V., 118
Deubel, P., 239, 246
DeWulf, M. J., 250
Diaz, D. P., 171
DiBiase, D., 251
Dick, W., 101
Diehl, G. E., 241
Dillon, A., 245

Dillon, C., 155
DiPaolo, A., 32
Dirr, P. J., 166, 205, 237
Dixon, P. N., 252
Dodge, B., 86
Donlevy, J. G., 186
Donovan, D. P., 67
Dowrick, P. W., 119
Driscoll, J., 148
Driscoll, M., 117
Duchastel, P., 109
Duckworth, C., 148
Dunham, R. S., 212
Dutton, W., 245
Eastman, A. B., 253
Eastman, M. A., 246
Eastmond, D. V., 181
Eddy, J. P., 252
Edwards, R., 300
Elbaum, B., 151
Eller, V. M., 118
Ellertson, E. K., 250
Evans, T., 286
Falk, R., 239
Farr, C. W., 124
Feasley, C. E., 44, 251
Felker, P., 109
Finkel, L., 86
Finnegan, C. L., 124
Fjortoft, N. F., 242
Flagg, B., 124
Foley, M., 285
Franks, K., 174
Fredericksen, E. E., 239, 244
Fredrickson, S., 250
Freeman, M. W., 67, 68, 240
Furgason, J., 253
Furlong, M., 86
Fusco, M., 59
Gabbard, R., 245
Gagne, R. M., 93, 101
Gardner, M. K., 83
Garfinkle, R., 23
Garrison, D. R., 83, 153, 229, 230
Gatta, L., 171
Gayol, Y., 232
Gery, G., 89
Geyer, D., 94
Gibson, C. C., 166, 186, 230
Gilbert, S., 175
Gilcher, K. W., 83
Glowacki-Dudka, M., 152
Gormly, E. K., 52
Granger, D., 178
Gray, B. A., 240
Green, K. C., 44

Greenspan, R., 43
Grimes, L. W., 240
Guernsey, L., 194
Gunawardena, C. N., 83, 153, 154, 230, 246, 286
Gustafson, K. L., 103
Haavind, S., 151
Hahn, H. A., 240, 250
Hall, B., 117
Hall, R. H., 118
Halsne, A., 171
Hanna, D. E., 151
Hara, N., 176
Harkness, W., 250
Harrington, C., 186
Harrison, P. J., 124
Hartigan, P., 86
Harvel, T. J., 244
Harwood, J., 250
Hashim, Y., 244
Heinich, R. M., 93
Heinzen, T. E., 124
Hill, L., 213
Hillman, D. C., 230
Hiltz, S. R., 247
Hislop, G., 240
Hmieleski, K. M., 124
Hodgins, W., 97
Hofmann, J., 88, 148
Holliday, J. R., 240
Holmberg, B., 101, 108, 221, 222, 225
Holmes, G. A., 81
Holstein, J. A., 139
Hong, K-S., 248
Hopper, D. A., 232
Horton, W., 117, 124
Hosley, D. L., 250
Howell, S. L., 253
Huffman, M. L., 242
Hughes, S. E., 153
Hulik, M., 250
Hunter, B., 86
Idrus, R. M., 83
Indabawa, S. A., 282
Inglis, A., 42, 43, 248
Irele, M., 204, 252
Irons, L., 178
Irwin, S., 58
Jegede, O., 184, 186
Jensen, M., 280
Johnston, J., 52
Johnstone, S. M., 83
Jolley, H., 250
Jones, D., 88
Jones, S., 67, 68
Joosten, V., 42, 43
Jung, D., 178

Jung, I., 232, 243, 248, 249
Kanuka, H., 153
Kaufman, R., 190
Kearsley, G., 86, 88, 190
Keegan, D., 222, 229
Keel, R., 178
Keil, J., 99
Keister, L. W., 57
Kelsey, K. D., 248
Kember, D., 169, 170
Kenyon, H. S., 67
Keough, E., 205
Kerzner, H., 23
Kessler, E., 178
Ketcham, S. E., 59
Khan, B., 88
Kim-Rupnow, W. S., 119
Kirk, E. E., 194
Kling, R., 176
Knapczyk, D. R., 83
Knowles, M., 161
Ko, S., 152
Kooker, B. M., 231
Koory, M., 244
Kosma, R., 62
Krieger, T. J., 55, 60
Kruse, K., 99
Kuramoto, A., 86
Kutner, J. A., 67
Laidlaw, B., 251
Lane, C., 93
Lane, J. L., 250
LaPointe, D., 153, 154
Lauzon, A. C., 246
Lawson, M., 153
Layard, R., 251
Lazarus, B. D., 251
Lee, W., 117, 157
Leem, J., 243
Lehman, J., 231
Lengel, R. H., 94
Lentell, H., 138
Leshin, C. B., 103
Levenson, W. B., 31
Levine, T. K., 77, 146
Levy, S. P., 253
Lezberg, A., 204
Li, L., 260, 261
Li, Y., 260, 261
Lievrouw, L., 245
Lim, C., 243
Lindsay, N. K., 253
Ling, P., 42, 43
Lipinski, T., 124
Logue, S., 194
Long, H. B., 228

Longmire, W., 97
Lundblad, L., 245
Lynch, M., 117, 186
MacDonald, P. J., 240
MacGregor, C. J., 240
Machtmes, K., 241
MacKenzie, O., 27, 220
Maddux, C. D., 43
Mahes, V., 247
Mahoney, S. E., 244
Major, M. B., 86
Maki, R. S., 176
Maki, W. S., 176
Mallory, H. F., 25, 26, 27, 220
Mally, W., 67, 68
Maltese, J., 214
Marchese, T., 64
Marder, C., 62
Martin, C. M., 41
Marx, M. B., 157, 253
Mason, R., 286, 301
McAleese, R., 31
McCormick, C., 88
McGowan, J., 168
McGreal, R., 83
McIsaac, M. S., 232, 244, 247
McKnight, S., 195
McLuhan, E., 294
McLuhan, M., 294
McMahill, J. M., 77
McNeil, D. R., 37
Meader, D. K., 245
Meister, J. C., 291
Menon, V., 194
Michel, D. P., 243
Millson-Martula, C., 194
Molenda, M., 93
Molise, G., 124
Moore, M. G., 86, 99, 171, 221, 224, 228, 230
Morgan, B. M., 249
Morris, L. V., 124
Morse, K., 239
Mrozowski, S., 237
Munro, J., 228, 230
Munroe, J. E., 67, 68
Murphy, K. L., 244
Naidu, S., 118
Najem, C., 33, 34
Nasseh, B., 26
Nation, D., 286
Nelson, D. M., 252
Nelson, R. N., 176
Neuhauser, C., 241
Neumann, Y., 241
Nielsen, J., 117
Noffsinger, J. S., 28, 30, 220

Norenburg, C. D., 245
Nti, N., 232
Nyirenda, J. E., 282
Oblinger, D., 65
Ohler, J., 174
Olsen, L. K., 176
Olson, G. M., 245
Olson, J. S., 245
Olson, M. T., 241
Ory, J. C., 184
Osborn, V., 242
Owens, D., 117
Pacey, L., 205
Palloff, R., 86, 152, 153
Palmer, C., 250
Parker, L. A., 83
Paulsen, M. F., 221
Payne, H., 115
Peirce, N., 213
Pelz, W. E., 244
Perdue, K., 119, 178
Perraton, H., 237
Peters, O., 222, 242
Phelps, R. H., 240, 250
Picciano, A., 243
Pickett, A. M., 244
Pinder, P. W., 221
Pittman, V. V., 32, 44
Poker, F., 67
Pollock, J., 103
Porter, L., 88
Postman, N., 304
Pratt, D. D., 228
Pratt, K., 86, 152, 153
Preece, B. G., 194
Pugh, J., 67
Quast, S., 77
Quigley, B. A., 83
Radcliff, J., 79
Randolph, S. L., 250
Reddy, N., 245
Reid, W. M., 198
Reidell, P., 232
Reigeluth, C., 23, 103
Reiser, R. A., 93
Resmer, M., 296
Rice, R. E., 94
Richards, T. C., 252
Richey, R., 101
Rifkind, L. J., 85
Rigby, P. H., 27, 220
Roberts, T., 153
Robertson, J. S., 119
Roblyer, M. D., 141, 144
Rockwell, K., 157, 253
Rogers, E., 297

Romiszowski, A. J., 93
Rosenberg, M., 88
Rossen, S., 152
Rotter, N., 247
Rourke, L., 153, 230
Rowntree, D., 109
Rudestam, K. E., 61
Rudolph, H., 157
Rudolph, S., 83
Rule, S. M., 250
Rumble, G., 186, 224, 248, 251
Rush, S., 65
Russell, F. K., 242
Russell, J. R., 93
Ryan-Jones, D. L., 153
Saba, F., 64, 124, 231, 237, 238
Saettler, P., 31
Salmon, G., 151
Savrock, J. T., 86
Schaffer, J. M., 83
Schank, R., 86
Schauer, J. A., 252
Schoenholtz-Read, J., 61
Schrum, L., 174, 239
Scott, J. C., 25
Seay, R., 157
Seeman, B. J., 124
Seidel, R. J., 241
Sener, J., 239
Sewart, D., 222
Shachar, M., 241
Shaeffer, J. M., 124
Shale, D., 229
Shane, D. L., 86
Shapley, P., 239
Shea, P., 244
Shearer, R. L., 231
Sherry, A. C., 204
Shin, N., 243
Short, J., 94
Showalter, R. G., 250
Simmons, C., 277
Simonson, M., 209
Simpson, O., 186
Smith, F., 146
Smith, K. D., 252
Smith, S. A., 153
Smith, T. W., 83
Snyder, C. A., 194
Sparks, R. K., 243
Spitzer, D. R., 77
Sponder, B. M., 83, 174
Staffo, M. J., 253
Stern, 60
Stevens, E., 89
Stevens, G., 89

Stevenson, N., 175
St. John, R. K., 86
Stone, H., 77
Stover, M., 239
Stowitschek, J. J., 250
St. Pierre, S., 176
Swan, K., 244
Tait, A., 186
Tait, J., 272
Taplin, M., 184, 186
Tapscott, D., 213
Taylor, R. G., 198
Taylor, R. W., 157
Thompson, G., 171
Thompson, M., 204
Thorpe, M., 124, 184, 186
Tiene, D., 52
Tillman, M. H., 103
Tinker, R., 151
Tiwana, A., 88
Toebe, D., 169
Tong, Y., 258
Tough, A., 223
Trede, F., 247
Turoff, M., 247, 251
Twitchell, D., 231
Unwin, D., 31
Usher, R., 301
Valentine, D., 246
Valentine, T., 119, 178
Valore, L., 241
Vandergrift, K. E., 247
Visser, J., 251, 286
Von Euler, M., 259
Vrasidas, C., 232, 244, 247
Vygotsky, L., 225
Wagner, E., 245
Wagner, L., 251
Wagner, W. W., 101
Walsh, S. J., 155
Watkins, B. L., 30, 221
Watkins, R., 190
Watkins, S. E., 118
Watson, M., 169
Wedemeyer, C., 33, 34, 35, 220, 222
Wegerif, R., 153, 232
Wei, R., 258, 260
Weight, K., 152
Wells, R. A., 240, 250
Westfall, P., 68
White, K., 152
Wickersham, L. E., 153
Wiencke, W., 141, 144
Williams, E., 94
Williams, M. D., 124
Williams, P. B., 253

Willis, D., 230
Willits, F. K., 232
Winiecki, D. J., 152
Wisher, R. A., 86, 146, 241
Wolcott, L. L., 157
Woods, L. C., 231
Worley, L. K., 41
Woudstra, A., 299

Wright, S. A., 30, 32, 37, 220, 221
Wydra, D., 250
Yarnall, L., 62
Youngblood, P., 247
Zhang, J., 155
Zigerell, J., 37
Zittle, F., 153, 230
Zucker, A., 62

SUBJECT INDEX

AACIS. *See* American Association for Collegiate Independent Study (AACIS)

Accessibility for disabled students, 118–119

Accreditation, 204–205

Achievement, student, 199–200, 240–243

ACRL Distance Learning Sections Guideline Committee, 194

Administration, 187. *See also* Policy
  administering a program, 191
  assessment activities, 193
  barriers to adoption of distance education, 206–207
  budgeting tasks, 195–199
  decision for distance education, 188–190
  duties of, 18
  full-time vs. part-time staffing, 192
  of learning support centers, 193–194
  library services, 193–195
  quality assessment function, 198–204
  scheduling responsibilities, 197–198
  staffing decisions, 191–193
  strategic planning, 187–190
  students, administrative assistance for, 182
  technology tracking by, 190
  of teleconference learning sites, 193, 195
  training in distance education, 192–193

Adult Learning Service (ALS), 33, 50, 146

Adult students. *See* Students

Advanced Distributed Learning Initiative, 296

Advanced Research Projects Agency (ARPA), 42

AFL-CIO, 40

Africa, 279–282

African Virtual University, 285–286

Agassiz, Elizabeth Carey, 27

AG*SAT, 58

AIM project, 33–35, 38

Air and Correspondence High School, 261

Air Force Institute for Advance Distributed Learning (AFIADL), 47, 68

Air Force Institute of Technology, 66

Air Technology Network (ATN), 66

Alaska, 41, 174

Algeria, 276, 277

Allama Iqbal Open University, 273–274

Al Quds Open University, 36, 276

American Association for Collegiate Independent Study (AACIS), 27, 49

American Association of Community and Junior Colleges, 59

American Bar Association, 40

American Center for the Study of Distance Education (ACSDE), 220

American Council on Education (ACE), 124

American Distance Education Consortium, 58

American Express, 56

American Hospital Association, 40

American Journal of Distance Education, 12–13, 220, 237

American Law Institute, 40

American Rehabilitation Education Network (AREN), 40

American School, The, 28–29, 46

American Symposium on Research in Distance Education, 220

Americans with Disabilities Act (ADA), 253

Anadolu University, 36, 272–273

Andragogy theory, 161

Andra Pradesh Open University, 36

Annenberg/CPB Project, 33, 49–50, 146

Appalachian Community Service Network, 32

Arab Open University, 277

Arab states, 276–277

Arizona State University, 48

Armed forces. *See* Military

Army Continuing Education System (ACES), 67

Army Logistics Management College, 66

Army University Access Online (e-ArmyU), 5, 67

Articulated Instructional Media project. *See* AIM project

Arts and Sciences Teleconferencing Service (ASTS), 41
Assessment activities of administration, 193, 198–204
Assignments, 138
Association of College and Research Libraries (ACRL), 194
Asynchronous learning, 149–150, 157, 239, 246
Asynchronous Transfer Mode (ATM) networks, 84
AT&T, 65
Athabasca University, 4, 36, 108, 275
Audioconferencing, 82, 111–113
Audiographics, 83, 148–149, 246
Audio media, 76–77, 92
Australia, 266–268
Author-editor model, 103–106
Authoring tools, Web-based courses, 116
Automotive Satellite Television Network (ASTN), 57
Automotive Virtual University, 5
Autonomy of learner. See Learner autonomy

Bahrain, 277
Bahrain University, 277
Baptist Union Theological Seminary, 26
Barnes & Noble University, 61
Barriers to adoption of distance education, 206–207
BBSs. See Bulletin board systems
Beaudoin, Michael, 216
Benton Harbor, 28–30
Berge, Zane L., 97
Billings's Model of Course Completion, 169, 171–172
Black College Satellite Network (BCSN), 59
Blind students, 47
Boeing, NTU programs, 58
Bonk, Curtis, 255
Botswana, 281
Boyd, Robert, 223
Brandenburg Memorial Essays, 220
Brazil, 262–263
Brevard Community College, 180, 201
Bridges for Learning, 63
Brigham Young University, 48, 208
British Aerospace Virtual University, 5
British Open University, 34–39, 51–54, 76
　BBC, courses in association with, 54
　birth of, 34–35
　cost-effectiveness in, 251
　course design, 272
　courses at, 271
　course team model, 105–106
　economies of scale at, 251
　Institute of Educational Technology, 272
　Knowledge Media Institute, 272
　learner support, 272
　and technology, 272
　training in distance education, 192–193

Broadcasting, 78–79. *See also* Radio; Television
　in China, 258–259
　history of, in distance education, 25, 31–33
Broady, K. O., 28
Budgeting tasks, 195–199
Buffalo State College, 59
Buhler, Charlotte, 223
Bulletin board systems, 165
Business television (BTV), 56–58

Cable television (CATV), 32–33, 56–59, 81
California Digital Library, 194
California State University, Chico, 32
California State University, Dominguez Hills, 166, 168
California State University system, 69
California Virtual School, 209
California Virtual University, 5, 61
Canadian Virtual University, 61
Capella University, 60
Cardean University, 61
Carnegie Commission on Educational Television, 31
Carnegie Corporation, 33
CatGlobal, 66
Catholic Distance University, 189
CATV. *See* Cable television (CATV)
CBS. *See* Columbia Broadcasting System (CBS)
Center for Applied Research in Interactive Technologies (CARIT), 59
Centra, 65
Central Michigan University, 194
Central Texas College, 67
Centre for Flexible and Distance Learning, 268
Centre National d'Enseignement Generalise, 277
CERP. *See* Correspondence Education Research Project (CERP)
Certification companies, 66
Change and distance education, 20–22, 209–210, 288
Channel One, 52
Chat room, 152
Chautauqua Institute, 25–26
Chicago TV College, 31
China, 36, 258–260
China Central Radio and TV University (CCRTVU), 258, 261
China, issues in, 258–260
China TV University System, 36
Chute, A. G., 21
Cisco, 61, 64
City University, Renton, Washington, 68
Classroom vs. distance learning, 175–176
Class roster, 112
CNET Electronic Schoolhouse Network, 66
Coast Learning Systems, 50
Coastline Community College, 33, 50, 68

Collaborative learning, 230–231
College Board, The, 213
Colliery Engineer School of Mines, 25
Colorado Community Colleges Online, 61
Columbia Broadcasting System (CBS), 31
Commercialization, 300
Communication technology. *See* Technology
Community College Satellite Network (CCSN), 59
Completeness of materials, 125
Completion time, 104
Compressed digital video (CDV), 58
CompTV, 57
CompUSA, 57
Computer conferencing, 87–88
  instructor's role in, 145–149
  learner-learner interaction in, 141
Computer, education by, 42–45
Computer-mediated communication (CMC), 232
  in military, 240
Computer networks, 42–43
Connect Ed, 43
Consortia, 5
  international consortia, 277–279
Consortium of Distance Education (CODE), 50
Consorzio Per L'Universita a Distanza (CUD), 278
Content-content interaction, 230
Content of distance courses, 14
Continental Classroom, 31
Control, teacher/learner, 231
COOLSchool, 63
Copyright, in course design, 124
Cornell University, 26
  eCornell, 61
Corporate training, 56–58, 64–65
Corporation for Public Broadcasting (CPB), 31–33, 49
Correspondence Education Research Project (CERP), 27
Correspondence Instruction in the U.S., 220
Correspondence study, 3, 46–47, 70
  in the armed forces, 30
  completion model for, 171–172
  history of, 24–30
  learner-instructor interaction in, 141
  in New Zealand, 267
  print media and, 73
Correspondence Study Division, 27
Correspondence Teacher, reflections of, 139
Corvallis Online, 63
Costa Rica, 36, 276
Cost-effectiveness, 248–252
Council for Higher Education Accreditation (CHEA), 204
Council on Postsecondary Accreditation (COPA), 204
Counseling and counselors, 179

Course design, 100
  benchmarks for development and structure, 201, 202
  at the British Open University, 271
  and copyright, 124
  development team for, 103–108, 118, 128–134
  dialog and, 226–227
  effectiveness of, 243–244
  evaluation of, 104, 121–124
  general principles for, 124–126
  Instructional Systems Design (ISD), 100–103
  monitoring, 121–124
  participation in, 120
  PROFORMACAO (in Brazil), 262
  study guide, 108–111
  systematic approach to, 14–15
  teams for, 244–245
  in transactional distance theory, 226–227
  Web-based courses, 115–118
Courses. *See also* Correspondence study; Course design
  effective course design, 243–246
  examples of studies of, 244
  media and technology selection for, 245–246
  and programs, 6
Course sharing initiatives, 69–70
Course team approach, 103–108
  strengths and weaknesses of, 106
Critical Path Method, 198
CRM Portal, 90–91
Cultural considerations for distance learning, 174

Dallas County Community College District, 68
Dallas Telelearning, 50
Daniel, Sir John, 184
DANTES. *See* Defense and Non Traditional Education Services (DANTES)
DBS. *See* Direct broadcast satellites (DBS)
DeAnza College, 181
Defense Acquisition University, 250
Defense and Non Traditional Education Services (DANTES), 30
Delling, M., 222
Dell University
Delta Airlines, 213
Demand-driven model, 299–300
Department of Education Training and Youth Affairs, 300
Designing courses. *See* Course design
Desktop video conferencing, 84–85
DETC. *See* Distance Education and Training Council (DETC)
Developing countries, distance education in, 282–286
Development teams, for course development, 103–108, 118, 128–134

Dewey, John, 223
Dialog
  course structure and, 227, 231–232
  as guided didactic conversation, 225
  in transactional distance theory, 224–226,
    229–230, 231–234, 238
Digital divide and policy, 210–214
Digital Millennium Copyright Act, 124, 206
Digital Think, 66
Direct broadcast satellites (DBS), 39, 82
Disabled students, 118–119
Distance Education, 220, 229, 237
Distance education defined, 2–3
Distance Education and Training Council (DETC),
    27, 46, 55, 104, 163
  Accrediting Commission, 204
Distance Education Clearinghouse, 62, 189
Distance Education Student Programs (DESP)
    questionnaire, 170
Distributive Training Project, 67
Dohmen, Gunther, 222, 229
Domino's Pizza, 40
Dreamweaver, 116
Drexel University, 65
Dropout rates, 169
Dual-mode institutions, 4–6, 60, 107, 179–180, 251

Early Bird satellite, 38
e-ArmyU. *See* Army University Access Online
    (e-ArmyU)
Eastman Kodak Corporation, 40
  NTU programs, 58
eCollege, 65
Economic development, and changes in distance
    education, 290–291
Ed, 81
Educational Television Facilities Act of 1962, 31
Education Direct, 25, 47
Education Service Provider (ESP), 84
Education Telephone Network (ETN), 38, 83
Effectiveness. *See also* Cost-effectiveness
  of course design, 243–246
  as dependent on technologies, 238–239
  of instructors, 200
  quality assessment and, 198–204
  of teaching strategies, 246–248
  variables determining, 248–249
Egypt, 277
Electronic Connections Online, 194
Electronic publishing, 74–75
Electronic University Network (EUN), 32, 43
ElementK, 66
Embry-Riddle Aeronautical University, 67, 68
Empire State College, 36, 55
Empire State University, 68
Epistolodidaktica, 220
Ethiopia, 277

European Commission, 283
European Home Study Council, 220
Evaluation
  benchmarks, 203
  of course design, 104, 121–124, 126
Examinations, 155
Executive Leadership Foundation Transfer
    Technology Project, 213
ExecuTrain, 66
Expectations of students, 138–140
Extracurricular concerns of students, 172–173

Faculty. *See* Instructors
Fathom, 61
FCC. *See* Federal Communications Commission
    (FCC)
Federal Communications Commission (FCC), 32
Federal Department of Education, 40–41
Federal Express, 40
Federal Radio Commission, 32
Federal Star Schools Program Assistance Act of
    1987, 40–41
Feedback
  in course design, 126
  expectations of students, 138–140
  in teleconferencing, 146
FernUniversität, 36, 274
Field independent students, 171
Fielding Graduate Institute, 61
Finland, 264–265
Finnish Virtual Polytechnic, 265
Finnish Virtual University, 265
Fisher, Dorothy Canfield, 26
Florida Community College, 68
Florida Distance Learning Reference and Referral
    Center, 194
Florida State University, 68
Foley, Michael, 286
Ford Cretid Inc., 57
Ford Foundation, 31
Ford Motor Company, 56, 213
FORDSTAR, 57
Fort Hays State University, 68
Foundations of American Distance Education, 221
France, consortium in, 277–278
Franklin, Benjamin, 297
FrontPage, 116
Full-time vs. part-time staffing, 192
Funding of K–12 programs, state policy, 208–209

GALILEO online library, 68
Gantt Chart, 198
Garrison, Randy, 126, 229–230
Gates Foundation, 213
General Agreement on Trade in Services (GATS), 300
General Electric, 56
  NTU programs, 58

George Washington University, 68, 157
Georgia Statewide Academic and Medical System
     (GSAMS), 86
Georgia Virtual Technical College, 61
Germany, 36, 274
Gibson, Chere Campbell, 69
Global Development Learning Network, 284
Global Distance Education Network, 89
Globalization, 300
Global Knowledge, 66
Global Virtual University (New Zealand), 6
Goddard College, 37
Government Education and Training Network, 66
Grading of courses, 155
Graff, K., 222
Grantham, J. O., 39
Great Plains National, 50
Guidance for students, 179–181
Gunawardena, Lani, 156

Hadley School for the Blind, 47
Handicapped students. See Disabled students
Harper, William R., 26
Hawaii Community College, 158
Hawaii, instructional television in, 80–81
Hawaii Interactive Television System (HITS), 80
Health Education Network, 40
Hermods Correspondence School, 222
Hewlett-Packard, California State University, Chico,
     courses to, 32
High school, 28–30
     "High School Instruction by Mail," 28
     independent study courses, 48
History of distance education, 24
History of term distance education, 222
Holmberg, Börge, 221, 222, 225, 229
Home study, 46–47, 70, 104
Howard University, 59

IBM, 61, 65
     Interactive Satellite Education Network (ISEN), 40
     and K–12 schools, 62
     NTU programs, 58
ICS. See International Correspondence Schools (ICS)
ILLINET, 194
Illinois Online Network, 158, 181
Illinois Virtual Campus, 61
Illinois Virtual School, 209
Independent study, 3, 47–49, 70
Independent Study Division (ISD), 27, 30, 221
India, 36, 273
Indiana Higher Education Telecommunications
     System (IHETS), 59
Indiana University
     high school courses, 48
     libraries, 194
     School of Continuing Studies, 159

Indira Gandhi National Open University, 36, 273
Indonesia, 36
Information, changes in, 288–290
Inputs and outputs of system, 19–20
Institute of Educational Technology, 272
Institute for Higher Education and Policy (IHEP),
     201–203
Institute for Information Technologies in Education
     (IITE), 284
Institute for Women and Technology, 213
Instructional Systems Design (ISD), 100–103, 126
Instructional Television Fixed Service (ITFS), 32,
     39, 49, 79–81
Instructors, 5, 135. See also Interaction
     administration staffing decisions, 191–193
     assessment of faculty satisfaction, 200
     audiographics, role in, 148–149
     benchmarks, 201
     compensation of, 190
     computer conferencing, role in, 145–149
     differences in distance teaching, 135–136
     full-time vs. part-time staffing, 192
     functions of, 136–140
     interaction vs. presentation by, 145
     online teaching, 149–154
     perspective of faculty, 155–157
     presentations by, 145
     social aspects, 153–154
     support for, 202
     teleconferencing, role in, 145–149
     tips for online teaching, 150–152
     training instructors, 155–159
     workload, 190
Integrated Services Digital Network (ISDN), 292
Integrated learning systems, 88, 116, 231
Integrity, 155
Intel, 42
INTELECOM, 50
Intellectual property, 125, 208
Interaction
     chat room, 182–183
     content-content, 230
     hierarchy of, 141–145
     instructor-content, 230
     instructor-instructor, 230
     learner-content, 140, 230
     learner-instructor, 140–141, 227, 229–230, 237,
       248
     learner-learner, 141, 230, 237
     vs. presentation, 145
     and the role of instructors, 15–17
     social, as student support, 182–183
     via technologies, 15
     in teleconference, 115
Interactive Satellite Education Network (ISEN), 40
Interactive television (ITV), 56–59, 70, 84

Interactive video, 58–59
International Conference on Correspondence
    Education, First, 28
International Correspondence Schools (ICS), 25, 29,
    46–47
International Council for Correspondence
    Education (ICCE), 221, 257
International Council for Distance Education
    (ICDE), 238, 257
International issues, 257
  Australia, issues in, 266–268
  Brazil, issues in, 262–263
  China, issues in, 258–260
  consortia, 277–279
  developing countries, distance education in,
    282–286
  Finland, issues in, 264–265
  globalization and commercialization, 300–302
  national distance education institutions, 273–276
  New Zealand, issues in, 266–268
  Norway, issues in, 264–266
  Republic of South Africa (RSA), 268–271
  United Kingdom, 271–272
  virtual systems, 277–279
International School of Information Management,
    43
International Telecommunications Satellite
    Organization (INTELSAT), 38
International Telecommunications Union (ITU), 84
International University Consortium (IUC), 32
Internet, 25, 43–44, 59, 70–71, 84–85
Internet Protocol (IP), 87
Internet2, 89
Inter-Regional Accrediting Committee (IRAC), 54
Iran, 36
Irish National Distance Education Centre (OSCAIL),
    278
ISD. *See* Independent Study Division (ISD)
ISDN. *See* Integrated Services Digital Network
    (ISDN)
Israel, 36
Italy, consortium in, 278
ITFS. *See* Instructional Television Fixed Service
    (ITFS)

James, Walter, 35
Japan, 36
Johns Hopkins University, 31
Johnstone, S., 22
Jones, Glenn, 60
Jones International University, 60, 61
Jordan, 36, 277
Journal of Distance Education, 237
Jung, I., 232–233

Keegan, Desmond, 222, 229
Kember's Open Learning Model, 169–171

Kentucky Educational Television (KET), 41
Kentucky Virtual University, 61
Keystone National High School, 62
Knowledge management systems, 88–89
Knowledge Media Institute, 272
Knowledge Net, 90–91
Knowledge, sources of, 12–13
Knowles, Malcolm, 161, 223
Kodak. *See* Eastman Kodak Corporation
Korea, 36, 261–262, 282
  Air and Correspondence High School, 261
  Korea Multimedia Education Center, 261
  Korean Air and Correspondence University, 261
  Korean Educational Broadcasting System, 261
  Korean Multimedia Education Center, 261
  Korean National Open University, 36, 261–262
  Korean Research and Information Center, 261
  Virtual University Trial Project, 261–262
K-12 programs, 62–63
  in Australia, 266
  funding of, state, 208–209
  interactive video, 40–41
Kuwait, 277

Land Grant universities, 26, 252
Langenscheidt, Gustav, 25
Latter Day Saints' University, 31
LearnAlaska network, 41
Learner autonomy, 227–228, 234, 238, 299
  Garrison on, 229–230
  Moore, M. G., on, 221–222, 227–228
  Saba, F., on, 231
  in transactional distance theory, 227–228
Learner-content interaction, 140, 230
Learner-instructor interaction, 140–141, 227, 229,
    230, 237, 248
Learner-learner interaction, 141, 230, 237
Learning benchmarks, 201
Learning environments, 17–18
Learning support centers, 193–194
Lebanon, 277
Levels of distance education, 4–7
Library services, 194–195
LibrarySpot, 194
Libya, 276
Lotus Notes, 42
Lucent Technologies, 90–91

Macromedia, Dreamweaver, 116
Macromedia University, 61
Malawi, 281
Malaysia, 274
Management. *See* Administration
Management Vision, 40
Maricopa College, 158
Maricopy Learning Exchange, 69
Maryland Faculty Online, 158

Maslow, Abraham, 223
Massachusetts Institute of Technology (MIT),
    OpenCourseWare initiative, 22, 69–70
Massey University, 267
McNeil, D., 37
Mechanical Universe, The, 33, 50
Media, 6–7, 49. *See also* Print media
    comparative use of, in developing and industrial
        countries, 259
    comparison of types of, 49
    electronic, 49
    integration of, 95–98
    matrices for, 245
    print media, 49, 73–76
    selection of, 245–246
    standards, 96–97
    and technology, 72–99, 246
    technology distinguished, 6–7
Medical education, teleconferencing for, 86
Mega-universities, list of, 36
Memphis City Schools, 158
MERLOT. *See* Multimedia Educational Resource for
    Learning and Online Teaching (MERLOT)
MetLife, 65
Mexico, 278–279
Michigan Virtual High School, 209
Michigan Virtual University, 61
Microsoft Corporation, 61, 64–65
    FrontPage, 116
Middle States Commission on Higher Education,
    205
Midlands Consortium, 41
Midwest Program on Airborne Television
    Instruction, 31
Military, 66–68
    correspondence study by, 30
    cost-effectiveness of programs, 250
    economies of scale at, 250–251
    enrollment in distance courses, 37
    research on distance education in, 246
Mind Extension University (MEU), 32, 60, 166, 167
MindLeaders, 66
Minorities using two-way television, 168
Mission statements, 188–189
Mississippi State University, 59
MIT. *See* Massachusetts Institute of Technology
    (MIT)
Mitchell, S. C., 28, 30
Monitoring
    course design, 121–124
    staff, 193
Montgomery College, 180
Moore, M. G., 42–43, 221–223, 227–229
Morrill Act, 26
Mosaic Web browser, 43
Motorola, NTU programs, 58

Motorola University, 64
Moulton, Richard, 25–26
Multimedia Educational Resource for Learning and
    Online Teaching (MERLOT), 69

Namibia, 282
National Broadcasting Company (NBC), 31
National Cancer Institute, 117
National Center for Educational Statistics (NCES),
    50–51, 303
National Centre for Distance Learning (CNED),
    France, 277–278
National Education Association (NEA), 40, 153–154
National Governors' Association Report for 1989,
    41
National Home Study Council (NHSC), 27, 37, 220
National Institutes of Health (NIH), 65
National Open University, Taiwan, 36
National Sciences Foundation (NSF), 42
National Security and International Affairs
    Division, 67
National Technological University (NTU), 5, 39–40,
    58
National Telecommunications Information
    Administration (NTIA), 212
National University Continuing Education
    Association (NUCEA), 27, 30, 37, 39, 221
National University Extension Association (NUEA),
    27, 220
National University Teleconference Network
    (NUTN), 39–40, 58
NBC. *See* National Broadcasting Company (NBC)
NCES. *See* National Center for Educational
    Statistics (NCES)
NETg, 65–66
Netherlands, The, 36, 274–275
Netscape, 65
Networks. *See* Computer networks
Nevada State Department of Human Resources, 250
New England Association of Schools and Colleges,
    205
New Horizons, 66
New School for Social Research, 43
Newspapers/newsletters, 74
New York Institute of Technology, 43
New York University, 61
New Zealand
    Global Virtual University, 6
    issues in, 266–268
    Open Polytechnic, 36
NHSC. *See* National Home Study Council (NHSC)
Ninthhouse, 66
Noffsinger, J. S., 28–30, 220
Nokia, 265
Nordland College, 266
Norsk Korrespondanseskole (NKS), 265, 266

North Central Association of Colleges and Schools, 60, 205
Northern Ontario Education Access Network, 278
North Norwegian Conservatory of Music, 266
Northwest Association of Schools and of Colleges and Universities, 205
Norway, issues in, 264–266
Norwegian Association for Distance Education (NADE), 266
Norwegian Center for Distance Education (SEFU), 266
Norwegian College of Public Administration and Social Work, 266
Norwegian Executive Board for Distance Education at University and College Level (SOFF), 266
Norwegian State Institution for Distance Education (NFU), 265–266
Nova Southeastern University, 36, 55
Nova University, 37
Novell, 61, 64
NPS. *See* U.S. National Park Service (NPS)
NSF. *See* National Sciences Foundation (NSF)
NSFNet, 42
NTU. *See* National Technological University (NTU)
NUCEA. *See* National University Continuing Education Association (NUCEA)
NUEA. *See* National University Extension Association (NUEA)
NUTN. *See* National University Teleconference Network (NUTN)
NW WebSchool, 63
NYU Online, 61

Objectives of course, 125
Office of Educational Research and Improvement, 40
Ohio University, high school courses, 48
Oklahoma State Department of Education, 41
Oklahoma State University, 39, 41
Oklahoma Telecommunications Network, 59
Old Dominion University, 39, 68
Oman, 277
OneNet, 59
Online Campus, 43
Online Computer Library Center (OCLC), 194
OpenCourseWare initiative. *See* Massachusetts Institute of Technology (MIT)
Open-ended course design, 125
Open Learning, 108, 237
Open Polytechnic, New Zealand, 36, 268
Open Universiteit Heerlen, 36
Open Universiteit of the Netherlands, 274–275
Open universities, 33–35, 51–56, 70–71, 103. *See also* British Open University
  full-time vs. part-time staffing, 192
  ISD approach, 103, 105
  list of, 36

Open University of Israel, 36
Open University of Tanzania, 280–281
Opplan College, 266
Opportunity Colleges, 67
Oracle, 64, 65
Oregon Network for Education, 63–64
Oregon State University, OSU K-12 Online, 63
Organizational change, 297–300
Organization for Economic Cooperation and Development (OECD), 282
Organizations, systems view, 12–13
OSU K-12 Online, 63
Outputs and inputs of system, 19–20
Oxford University, 33

Pakistan, 273–274
Palestine, 276
Pan-Pacific Education and Communications Experiments by Satellite (PEACESAT), 38
Participation, student, in course design, 120, 125
Payame Noor University, 36
PBS. *See* Public Broadcasting System (PBS)
Pedagogical theory, 222–223
Pennarama Network, 32
Pennsylvania Academic Library Connection Initiative (PALCI), 194
Pennsylvania State University, 5, 32, 42–43, 48, 150, 159, 221
  cost-effectiveness in distance course, 250
  library cooperatives, 194
  Pennarama Network, 32
  policy, 211
  and universities in Finland, 265
  World Campus, 5, 43, 61, 118, 128–134, 158, 180, 211
PERT techniques for scheduling, 198
Peters, Otto, 222, 228, 229
Pitman, Isaac, 25
Pittman, V. V., 31–32, 44
Placeware, 65
Plagiarism, 155
Plainedge School System, 32
Planning by administration, 187–190
  deciding to proceed, 188–190
  defining the mission, 188–189
  tracking technology, 190
PLATO project. *See* Programmed Logic for Automatic Teaching (PLATO) project
Policy, 204
  barriers to distance learning, 206–207
  change by institutions, 209–210
  community, 214
  and the digital divide, 210–214
  federal, 206, 212
  institutional, 207–208, 209–211
  national, 210–212, 214–216

nonprofit sector, 213
private sector, 213
regional, 206
research, 252–254
state, 206–207, 208–209
Portland State University, 63
Portugal, 36, 275
Postman, Neil, 304
Presidential Commission on Education Reform, 261
PriceWaterhouse Coopers, 68
Primedia, Inc., 52
Print media, 49, 91–92
electronic publishing, 74–75
limitations of, 75–76
study guides, 73
Program, defined, 6
Program design, changes in, 295–297
Program for Training of In-Service Teachers (PRO-FORMACAO), 262–263, 299
Programmed Logic for Automatic Teaching (PLATO) project, 42
Progressive Policy Institute, 212
Project NETWORC, 250
Prometric, 66
Provincial Radio and TV Universities (PRTVUs), China, 260
Public Broadcasting Act of 1967, 31
Public Broadcasting System (PBS), 49–50, 146
Public Service Satellite Consortium (PSSC), 40

Quality assessment function of administration, 198–204

Radio, 25, 31–32, 78–79, 92
Rand Afrikaans University, 270
Rebel, K. H., 222
Regents College, 37, 201
Regional Accrediting Commissions, 204–206
RE/MAX, 56–57
Republic of South Africa (RSA), 268–271
Research
on policy, 252–254
and studies of effectiveness, 236
theory and, 232
Rio Salado College, 67, 157, 181
Rogers, Carl, 223
Rogers State University, 68

Saba, Farhad, 231, 233
Sagene College, 266
Saint Leo University, 67
Salem-Keizer School District, 64
Santa Barbara City College, 181
Satellite Communications for Learning (SCOLA), 59
Satellite Educational Resources Consortium (SERC), 59

Satellite Education Network, 66
Satellite technology
designing a satellite videoconference, 113–115
and higher education, 58–59
television networks, 56–59
Saturn Corporation, 65
Saudi Arabia, 276, 277
SCORM. *See* Sharable Content Object Reference Model (SCORM)
Self-directed learning, 120–121
Self-esteem of students, 168
SERC, 41
Shank, Steve, 60
Shattuck, Kay, 152
Sharable Content Object Reference Model (SCORM), 97, 296
Share Application, 85
Single-mode institutions, 4, 105, 107, 179
Site coordinator
communication by, 146–147
competence of, 147
continuity of, 147–148
control of, 148
learning sites, 195
for satellite videoconference, 113
SITN. *See* Stanford Instructional Television Network (SITN)
SkillSoft, 66
SK Online, 64
Sloan Center for Asynchronous Learning Environments, 157
SmartForce, 65
SmartPlanet, 66
Smarthinking, 68
Smith, L. D., 29
Smithsonian Institute, 39
Social construct of knowledge, 230–231
Society to Encourage Studies at Home, 26
Somalia, 277
South Africa, Republic of, 214, 268–271
Southeastern University of the Health Sciences, 37
Southern Association, 29
Southern Association of Colleges and Schools (SACS), 205
Southern California Consortium, 33, 50
Southern Oregon Online School, 64
Spain, 36, 275
Staffing decisions, 191–193
full-time vs. part-time, 192
monitoring and assessment, 193
training and orientation, 192–193
Stanford Instructional Television Network (SITN), 32
Star Schools program, 40–41, 59, 212
State University of Iowa, 31–32

State University of New York, 55
  SUNY Learning Network, 61, 244
State University of West Georgia, 159
Stavanger College, 266
Stord College, 266
St. Petersburg College, 158
Strategic planning by administration, 187–190
Streaming video, 82
Structure of course design, 125
Students, 161
  access for, 118, 166, 167
  administrative assistance for, 182
  adult students, nature of, 161–164
  andragogy theory, 161
  anxieties of adult students, 163–164
  attitudes, 175–176
  blind, 47, 119
  classroom vs. distance learning, 175–176
  comments on distance education, 165, 174,
    176–178, 180
  course concerns of, 173
  disabled, 118–119
  in distance education system, 21
  educational background and success, 171
  extracurricular concerns of, 172–173
  guidance and counseling, 179
  orientation for, 181–182
  participation, 120
  personality characteristics, success and, 171–172
  predictors of course completion, 169
  quality assessment and administration, 199
  reasons for enrolling, 162–163
  resistance to distance education, 176–179
  responses of, 165, 174, 176–178, 180
  satisfaction of, 176, 180, 200
  scheduling for, 198
  social interaction, 182–183
  success, factors affecting, 166–169
  support for, 179–184, 203
Study guide, 73
  for audioconference, 111–112
  creating lessons or units, 109–110
  design of, 108–111
  layout of, 111
  principles for text design, 109
  writing style for, 110–111
Success in Internet-based education, benchmarks
    for, 201–203
Sudan, 277
Sudan Open Learning Organisation, 277
Sukhothai Thammathirat Open University (STOU),
    36, 274
Sultan Qaboos University, 277
Sun, 61, 65
Sunrise Semester, 31
SUNY Learning Network, 61

Supervised Correspondence Study, conference, 28
Supply model, 298–299
Support, institutional
  benchmarks, 201, 202
  for teaching online, 158
Support services for students, 104
Synchronous learning, 149, 152, 246
Syracuse University, 37, 48
Systems dynamics model, 231
Systems view (Systems approach), 1
  AIM and the invention of, 33–34
  inputs and outputs of system, 19–20
  model for, 8, 10, 14
  spread of, 35–36

Taiwan, 36
Tandem Computers, 40
Tanzania, 280–281
Teachers. *See* Instructors
Teachers' College Columbia University, 29
Teaching at a Distance, 108
Teaching strategies, effectiveness of, 246–248
Teaching Telecourses: Opportunities and Options,
    146
Technikon SA, South Africa, 214, 215, 269–270
Technology. *See also* Satellite technology
  administration tracking, 190
  at the British Open University, 272
  changes in, 292–295
  comparative use of, in developing and industrial
    countries, 259
  developments in, 292–294
  and effectiveness of learning, 238–239
  integration of, 95–98
  and media, 72–99, 246
  media distinguished, 6–7
  policies, 204
Technology & Learning magazine, 74
Technology, Education and Copyright
    Harmonization (TEACH) Act, 124, 206
Technology Literacy Challenge Fund, 212
Telecommunication Education for Advances in
    Math and Science (TEAMS), 59
Teleconferencing, 25, 38–42, 82–86, 92
  audioconferencing, 82
  audiographics, 83, 148–149
  components of teleconference, 113–115
  costs of, 250
  instructor's role in, 145–149
  interaction in, 115
  interactive video in K–12, 40–41
  learning sites, 195
  postconference activity, 115
  presenter and moderator, selection of, 114
  rehearsal for, 114
  by satellite, 38–40

satellite teleconference, preparation for, 113–115
site coordinators for, 113, 146–148
television (business), 40
test period for, 115
videoconferencing, 38–40, 84–85
Telecourses, 32–33, 49–50
sources for, 50
Telesecundaria Project, 279
Television, 25, 31, 78–82, 92
business television, 40
cable television (CATV), 32–33, 56–59, 81
Instructional Television Fixed Service (ITFS), 32
instructors on, 135
interactive, 56–59, 70
minorities using two-way television, 168
Temple University, Virtual Temple, 61
Terminology, 302–304
Testing companies, 66
Tests, 155
Texas A&M, 159
Text design for study guides, 109
Thailand, 36, 274
Thomas A. Edison State College, 37, 43, 55, 67, 68
Thomson Publishing, 25, 46–47
Ticknor, Anna Eliot, 26–27
TI-In network, 41, 167, 175
Time to complete, 104
Tips for online instructors, 150–152
Toussaint, Charles, 25
Training
instructors, 159
programs, 192–193
vendors. See Vendors, training
Transactional distance theory, 223–227, 231–232, 238
course structure in, 226–227
dialog in, 224–225, 227, 231–232
importance of, 219
Saba, F., on, 231
Troy State University, 67, 68
Tübingen group, 222
Turkey, 36, 272–273
12 hour rule, 206
Two-way television, 168
Two-way videoconferencing, 41–42

UCEA. See University Continuing Education Association (UCEA)
UCLA. See University of California, Los Angeles (UCLA)
UKOU. See British Open University
Uncompletion rates, 169
UNESCO. See United Nations Educational, Science and Cultural Organization (UNESCO)
United Arab Emirates, 276, 277

United Kingdom, 271–272
British Aerospace Virtual University, 5
Open University. See British Open University
University for Industry, 5–6
United Nations Educational, Science and Cultural Organization (UNESCO), 279, 283–284
Universidade Aberta, Portugal, 36, 275
Universidad Estatal a Distancia (UNED), Costa Rica, 36, 276
Universidad Nacional Abierta (UNA), Venezuela, 36, 276
Universidad National de Educaciûn a Distancia, Spain, 36, 275
Universidad Virtual de Systema Tecnologico de Monterrey, 278
Universitas Terbuka, 36
University of the Air, 34, 54
in Japan, 36
University of Alaska, 38, 174
high school courses, 48
University of Alaska, Southeast (UAS), 174
University of Auckland, 268
University of California, 194
University of California Berkeley, 288–289
University of California, Davis, 251–252
University of California, Los Angeles (UCLA), 31
Extension, 48
University of Cambridge, 25
University of Chicago, 194
University of Colorado, eCollege, 65
University of Connecticut, School of Education, 74
University Continuing Education Association (UCEA), 27
standards for quality assessment, 200
University of Hawaii, 38, 80–81, 231
University of Helsinki, 265
University of Idaho, high school courses, 62
University of Illinois, 42
Online, 61
University of Illinois at Urbana-Champaign, 201
University of Indiana, Bloomington, 55
University for Industry (UK), 5–6
University of Iowa, high school courses, 48
University of Kansas, high school courses, 48
University of Kentucky, 32
University of Little Rock, mission statement, 189
University of Maryland University College, 61, 68, 159, 201
University of Michigan, high school courses, 48
University of Mid-America (UMA), 37
University of Minnesota, high school courses, 48
University of Missouri, high school courses, 48
University of Nebraska, 157
high school courses, 28, 30, 48, 62
University of North Dakota, high school courses, 48

University of Phoenix Online, 60, 61
University of Port Elizabeth, 270
University of Pretoria, 270
University of Queensland, 266
University Sains Malaysia, 274
University of South Africa (UNISA), 51, 214–215,
    268–271
University of South Carolina, high school courses,
    48
University System of Georgia, 68
University of Tampere, 265
University Teaching by Mail, 220
University of Tennessee, 65
University of Texas
    high school courses, 48
    Telecampus, 61
    World Lecture Hall, 69
University of Tübingen, 222
University of Turku, 265
University of Washington, 159
University of Wisconsin, 181
    Extension, 48
    high school courses, 48
University of Wisconsin-Madison, 30, 33, 38, 159,
    221
University of Wisconsin System, 252
University of Wyoming, 83
University of Yvaskylla, 265
University of Zimbabwe, 281
USAFI. *See* U.S. Armed Forces Institute (USAFI)
U.S. Armed Forces Institute (USAFI), 30
U.S. Army Institute, 30
U.S. Bureau of the Census, 42
U.S. Chamber of Commerce, 40
U.S. Department of Commerce, 212
U.S. Department of Defense, 30, 42, 67, 296. *See
    also* Military
    cost-effectiveness of programs, 250
    ISD approach, 103
U.S. Department of Education, 204, 206
    Community Technical Centers program, 212
U.S. General Accounting Office, 250
    National Security and International Affairs
        Division, 67
U.S. National Park Service (NPS), 4
U.S. Rehabilitation Act, 118
Utah State University, 201

Van Rensselaer, Martha, 26
VCampus Corporation, 65

Vendors, training, 65
Venezuela, 36, 221, 276
Videoconferencing, 38–40, 84–85
    satellite, design of, 113–115
    and transactional distance, 232
    two-way, 41–42, 241
    at University of South Africa, 269
Video media, 76–77, 92
Video Teletraining (VTT), 67
Vincennes University, 68
Vincent, John H., 25
Virtual Electronic Library (VEL), 194
Virtual High School, Inc., 62
Virtual institutions, 5–6, 59–69, 209
Virtual systems, international, 277–279
Virtual University of the Asia Pacific, 6
Virtual University Trial Project, Korea, 261–262
VISTA University, 269–270

Walden University, 55
Washington County, Maryland, 31
WCET. *See* Western Cooperative for Educational
    Telecommunications (WCET)
Web Accessibility in Mind (WebAIM), 119
Web-based courses
    authoring tools, 116
    design and development of, 115–119
Web-based instruction (WBI), 232–233
Web-based learning systems, 88, 92
Web documents, 116
Weber State University, 201
WebEx, 65
Wedemeyer, C. A., 30, 33–35, 220–223
Western Association of Schools and Colleges, 205
Western Cooperative for Educational
    Telecommunications (WCET), 22
Western Governors University, 5, 54–55, 65
World Bank, 89, 282–285
World Campus, 5, 43, 61, 118, 128–134, 158, 211
WorldCAT, 194
World Lecture Hall, 69
World Trade Organization, 300

Xerox, NTU programs, 58

Young, William, 30

Zaid University, 277
Zimbabwe, 281

TO THE OWNER OF THIS BOOK:

I hope that you have found *Distance Education: A Systems View*, Second Edition useful. So that this book can be improved in a future edition, would you take the time to complete this sheet and return it? Thank you.

School and address:_____

Department:_____

Instructor's name:_____

1. What I like most about this book is:_____

_____

_____

2. What I like least about this book is:

_____

_____

3. My general reaction to this book is:

_____

_____

4. The name of the course in which I used this book is:

_____

5. Were all of the chapters of the book assigned for you to read?_____

   If not, which ones weren't?_____

6. In the space below, or on a separate sheet of paper, please write specific suggestions for improving this book and anything else you'd care to share about your experience in using this book.

_____

_____

_____

BUSINESS REPLY MAIL
FIRST-CLASS MAIL   PERMIT NO. 34   BELMONT CA

POSTAGE WILL BE PAID BY ADDRESSEE

Attn: Dan Alpert, Education Editor

Cengage Learning

10 Davis Drive

Belmont, CA 94002-9801

OPTIONAL:

Your name: _____ Date: _____

May we quote you, either in promotion for *Distance Education: A Systems View*, Second Edition, or in future publishing ventures?

Yes: _____   No:_____

Sincerely yours,

Michael G. Moore and Greg Kearsley